Y0-BEB-224

AUTHORS DIGEST

VOLUME XX

A DICTIONARY OF
FAMOUS NAMES IN FICTION, DRAMA,
POETRY, HISTORY AND ART.

Issued under the auspices of the
AUTHORS PRESS

FAMOUS NAMES IN FICTION

Compiled—with a staff of experts—by E. M. O'Connor, author of the only analytical index to the works of Shakespeare.

Abbot, Eliakim, a young preacher wandering under supposed divine guidance for the practise of his calling, in Hawthorne's tale, *The Fellow-Traveler*.

Abdael, in Dryden's *Absalom and Achitophel*, stands for General Monk, Duke of Albemarle.

Abdalazis, Moorish governor of Spain in Southey's *Roderick, the Last of the Goths*.

Abdaldar, a magician in Southey's *Thalaba, the Destroyer*, who is stricken by the angel of death as he is about to stab Thalaba.

Abdallah, in Byron's *Bride of Abydos*, has been murdered by his brother and successor, Giaffir, pasha of Abydos.

Abd-el-Kadr, the Emir of Mascara who led the resistance to the French in Algeria. Browning's poem, *Through the Metidja to Abd-el-Kadr*, is the expression of an Arab patriot galloping over the plain of Metidja, to join the forces of the Emir.

Abderites, The, the subject of a satirical romance by Christoph Martin Wieland.

Abderus, a beautiful youth, a favorite of Hercules, who instituted games in his honor after he fell in the contest at Abdera over the horses of Diomedes.

Abdiel, a seraph in Milton's *Paradise Lost*, "faithful found among the faithless."

Abélard, the celebrated priest whose story is often alluded to in literature; it is the foundation of Pope's poem, *Eloisa to Abélard*. He was engaged to instruct Eloisa, but took his opportunity to lead her astray. Her relatives took dire vengeance upon him, after which he returned to a monastery and Eloisa to a convent.

Abellino, a beggar and bandit in *The Bravo of Venice*, by Matthew Gregory Lewis; he marries a niece of the Doge.

Aben Ezra, Raphael, a friend of the Prefect of Alexandria in Kingsley's *Hypatia.*

Abercrombie, General Ralph, is introduced in Hawthorne's tales, *Old Ticonderoga* and *Edward Randolph's Portrait.*

Abessa, a damsel in Spenser's *The Faerie Queene,* an impersonation of abbeys and convents. She shuts herself into the cottage of Superstition when Una and the Lion (Truth and England) appear.

Abigail, as a name for a lady's maid, is traced to Abigail, a handmaid of King David, as she calls herself in the *Book of Samuel.*

Abou Hassan, the hero of the story *The Sleeper Awakened,* in the *Arabian Nights.* He is made to believe that he is the caliph.

Abraham Cupid, used in Shakespeare's *Romeo and Juliet,* has been variously explained. The most plausible supposition is that it is a corruption of Auburn, since Cupid is represented as having auburn hair.

Abrane, Captain, a character in George Meredith's *The Amazing Marriage.*

Absalom, in Dryden's poem, *Absalom and Achitophel,* stands for the Duke of Monmouth, whose conspiracy against his uncle, afterward James II, is likened to that of Absalom.

Absolute, name of two characters in Sheridan's *The Rivals,* Sir Anthony and his son, Captain Absolute. The father is irritable and wrong-headed, but at heart kind and generous. Captain Absolute and Bob Acres are rivals for the hand of Lydia Languish.

Abudah, in Ridley's *Tales of the Genii,* is a merchant of Bagdad who is haunted at night by a fury, a little old hag, and discovers finally that the only way to set himself free is to "fear God and keep his commandments."

Achates, a friend of Æneas, whose name has become a synonym for a faithful friend, *fidus Achates.*

Achitophel, in Dryden's poem, *Absalom and Achitophel,* is the Earl of Shaftesbury, the counselor of Monmouth in his rebellion, as the Bible character of that name was of Absalom.

Ackermann aus Bohmen, in an old German dialogue by Johannes Ackermann, holds a conversation with death, "which attains a most dramatic ending in the final appeal of both to God for his judgment on the matter." It was written on the occasion of the death of the author's wife, 1399.

Acrasia, in Spenser's *The Faerie Queene,* is the personification of intemperance, a witch who had the power of changing her lovers into grotesque shapes. She lives in the Bower of Bliss on a floating island.

Acrates, in *The Faerie Queene,* is the personification of lawlessness.

Acres, Bob, in Sheridan's *The Rivals,* the rival of Beverly (Captain Absolute) for the hand of Lydia Languish; he is a swaggering and amusing coward.

Adah, wife of Cain, in Byron's *Cain.*

Adam, the faithful old servant who follows Orlando in Shakespeare's *As You Like It.* There is a tradition to the effect that this character was played by Shakespeare himself.

Adam, a college tutor, "white-tied, clerical, silent," in *Bothie of Tober-na-Vuolich,* a poem by Arthur Hugh Clough.

Adam and Eve, the New, an imaginary pair created and placed in the world just after the present human race has been swept away, in Hawthorne's sketch of that name.

Adamastor, spirit of the Cape of Good Hope, described by Camoëns in *The Lusiad* as a phantom, wrecking ships that dare trespass on his territory.

Adams, Abraham, known as Parson Adams, a famous character in Fielding's *Joseph Andrews.* "He is one of the simplest and at the same time manliest of men; has 'every virtue under heaven' except that of superiority to the common failings of humanity."—*Leigh Hunt.*

"The type which shows best the force and the limits of Fielding's genius is Parson Adams. He is a collateral descendant of Don Quixote."—*Leslie Stephen.*

Adderwood, Lord, a character in George Meredith's novel *Lord Ormont and His Aminta.*

Adeline, Lady Amundeville, a character in Byron's *Don Juan.*

Adicia, a character in Spenser's *The Faerie Queene,* wife of the Soldan, who maltreats the ambassador Samient sent by Mercilla to treat with the Soldan. Samient is protected and avenged by Sir Artegal, and Adicia is transformed into a tigress. The Soldan is explained to be Philip II of Spain; Mercilla is Queen Elizabeth; Samient, the Dutch ambassadors who were imprisoned by Philip, and Adicia, represents either Injustice or Religious Bigotry.

Admirable Crichton. See CRICHTON.

Adonaïs, a name applied to John Keats by Shelley in the elegy *Adonaïs.*

"As an utterance of abstract pity and indignation, *Adonaïs* is unsurpassed in literature; with its hurrying train of beautiful spectral images and the irresistible current and thrilling modulation of its verse, it is perhaps the most perfect and sympathetic effort of Shelley's art; while its strain of transcendental consolation for mortal loss contains the most lucid exposition of his philosophy. But of Keats as he actually lived the elegy presents no feature, while the general impression it conveys of his character and fate is erroneous."—*Sidney Colvin.*

Adriana, the jealous wife of Antipholus of Ephesus in Shakespeare's *A Comedy of Errors.*

Adriano de Armado, Don, a grandiloquent Spaniard in Shakespeare's *Love's Labor's Lost,* chosen by the King to amuse him and his companions in their seclusion. The original is said to be John Florio, surnamed "The Resolute," a philologist.

Ægeus, King of Athens and father of Theseus. The Ægean Sea received its name from him. When Theseus was returning from a journey to Crete to deliver Athens from paying tribute, he forgot to show the white sail, the signal of success which had been agreed upon; and Ægeon, watching for it and seeing a black sail, thought his son had perished and threw himself into the sea.

Aella, the hero of Chatterton's tragedy of that name.

Æneas, a Trojan prince, hero of Virgil's *Æneid.* He is also a character in Shakespeare's *Troilus and Cressida.*

Aennchen, a character in George Meredith's novel, *The Adventures of Harry Richmond.*

Æsacus, a son of Priam, lover of the nymph Hesperia. Upon her death he threw himself into the sea, and was changed by Thetis into a cormorant. Dryden translated the story of the incident from Ovid.

Æsop. The name of the ancient fabulist is applied to writers of fables of later times—as, Æsop of France, La Fontaine; of England, John Gay; of Germany, Lessing and Hagedorn. *Æsop at the Court* is a French comedy in verse by Boursault (1701).

Ætion, a character in Spenser's *Colin Clout's Come Home Again,* supposed to be intended for Shakespeare, though Drayton also has been suggested as its original.

Agamemnon, King of Mycenæ, brother of Menelaus and commander-in-chief of the Grecian forces at the siege of Troy —the subject of a drama by Æschylus, a character in the *Ajax* of Sophocles, the subject of a tragedy attributed to Seneca, and a character in Shakespeare's *Troilus and Cressida.*

Agape, a fay in Spenser's *The Faerie Queene,* to whom the fates granted that when the life-thread of the first of her three sons to die was severed, his remaining portion should pass to the next, and when he died both their lives should likewise be annexed unto the third.

Agapida, Fray Antonio, the imaginary chronicler of Washington Irving's *The Conquest of Granada.*

Agatha, the heroine and title of a story in blank verse of rural life in Germany by George Eliot.

Agathocles, a tyrant of Sicily, subject of a tragedy by Voltaire and a German novel by Caroline Pichler; also of a play by Richard Perrinchief, printed in 1676 and intended to represent the career of Oliver Cromwell. Agathocles had been a potter and always had an earthen vessel at his table to remind him of his origin.

Agdistes, in Spenser's *The Faerie Queene* the evil keeper of the Bower of Bliss.

Agelastes, a professed philosopher in Scott's *Count Robert of Paris.*

Agesilaus, King of Sparta, the title of a tragedy by Corneille.

Aglaura, the heroine of Sir John Suckling's drama of the name.

Aglavaine, the chief character in Maeterlinck's drama, *Aglavaine and Sêlysette.*

Aglionby, Bernard, the hero of Jessie Fothergill's novel, *Kith and Kin.*

Agnes, the second wife of David Copperfield in Dickens's novel of that name.

Agnés, in Molière's *École des Femmes*, is a young girl brought up in complete ignorance of the world, saying and doing most *risqué* things in all innocence. There is a proverbial expression in French, "to play the Agnes."

Agnes of Sorrento, the heroine of a novel by Harriet Beecher Stowe.

Agnes, Saint, who was martyred at Rome during the persecution of Diocletian, is the subject of a poem by Prudentius, a Latin poet of the fourth century. There is a tradition that she escaped from the Roman prison to Cornwall, pursued by devils whom she turned into stones by her indignant glances, the large stones remaining between St. Piran and St. Agnes.

Agramante, king of the Moors in the two Italian poems, *Orlando Innamorato* by Boiardo and *Orlando Furioso* by Ariosto.

Agravain or **Agriwain,** one of the Knights of the Round Table, slain with twelve others by Sir Launcelot for spying upon him. He was surnamed "The Desirous" and "The Proud."

A-Green, George, the subject of an old prose romance, *The History of George A-Green, Pindar* [pen- or pound-keeper] *of the Town of Wakefield.*

Agricane, in Boiardo's *Orlando Innamorato,* is a king of Tartary who besieges Angelica in the Castle of Albracca and is killed by Orlando.

Ague-cheek, Sir Andrew, a character in Shakespeare's *Twelfth Night*, a simpleton and coward of a most original and engaging type.

Ahasuerus, the name of the Wandering Jew (*q.v.*). *Ahasuerus at Rome* is the title of an epic in six cantos by Robert Hamerling (1866), and Edgar Quinet (France, 1803–75) has a novel, *Ahasuerus,* described by the author as "the history of the world, of God in the world, and of the doubt in the world."

Ahmed, a prince in the *Arabian Nights,* to whom a fairy gave a tent that could be made to cover an army, and yet could be folded so small as to be carried in his pocket.

Aholibamah, in Byron's unfinished lyrical drama, *Heaven and Earth,* is a granddaughter of Cain, beloved by Irad and by the seraph Samiasa, who carries her away from the earth when the Deluge comes. Her pride and arrogance are contrasted with the humility and piety of her sister Anah, whom the seraph Azaziel takes to heaven.

Aiglon, L'. See REICHSTADT, DUKE OF.

Aimwell, Thomas, a viscount, one of the beaux in Farquhar's comedy, *The Beaux' Stratagem.*

Ajax, son of Telamon, King of Salamis, one of the leaders of the Greeks in the Trojan war, ranking next to Achilles in strength and valor. A character in Homer's *Iliad,* the *Ajax* of Sophocles, and Shakespeare's *Troilus and Cressida.*

Ajax, son of Oïleus, King of the Locrians, one of the Greek heroes in the Trojan war, but inferior to Ajax Telamon, whence he is called "the lesser Ajax."

Ajut, the maiden in the story "Anningait and Ajut" in Johnson's *The Rambler.* The scene of the story is Greenland.

Aklis, The Sons of, appear in George Meredith's *The Shaving of Shagpat.*

Aladdin, a character in the *Arabian Nights,* who obtains a magic lamp and a magic ring by rubbing which he can command two genii, the slave of the lamp and the slave of the ring, able to bring him anything he requires.

Aladine, in Tasso's *Jerusalem Delivered,* is the King of Jerusalem.

Alaric Cotin, or **Cottin,** a name given to Frederick the Great by Voltaire, because as a warrior he was great like Alaric, but as a poet on a plane with Abbé Cotin, poet and preacher, satirized by Boileau and by Molière, who drew him in *Les Femmes Savantes* as Trissotin (Threefold fool). Macaulay alludes to Frederick as "half Mithridates and half Trissotin."

Alasco, or **Dr. Doboobius,** an astrologer in Scott's *Kenilworth.*

Alasnam, the hero of a story in the *Arabian Nights,* who has eight golden statues, and has to seek a ninth for a vacant pedestal, finding it at last as the best and most beautiful woman in the world, whom he marries.

Albany, the Duke of, the husband of Goneril in Shakespeare's *King Lear.*

Albert, the husband of Lotte in Goethe's romance, *The Sorrows of Young Werther.* The original was his friend Kestner, who married Charlotte Buff.

Albert of Geierstein, in Scott's *Anne of Geierstein,* is president of the Secret Tribunal.

Albert, Lord Wilfrid, assumes the character of the blind beggar in Sheridan Knowles's play, *The Blind Beggar of Bethnal Green.*

Albertazzo, a character in Ariosto's *Orlando Furioso,* represented as an ancestor of the royal family of England.

Albina, in a legend accounting for Albion as a name of England, was the eldest of fifty daughters of a fabulous King Dioclesian of Syria. All but one of them murdered their husbands and were put to sea by their surviving brother-in-law in an unmanned ship, which was driven upon the English coast, where they mated with wild men of the island.

Albion, in another fable concerning the origin of the name, was a giant son of Neptune, who conquered the island and reigned there forty-four years.

Al-Borak (the lightning), the milk-white beast with a human face and voice, the cheeks of a horse and the wings of an eagle, which Gabriel brought to convey Mahomet to Jerusalem and then to the seventh heaven. It had a mane of fine pearls, its eyes were two large emeralds, bright as stars, and its wings were enameled with pearls and precious stones and were bordered with light. It had a human soul and understood what was said, but could not speak, except once, when speech was given to it to ask Mahomet that it might have a place in paradise, which the prophet promised.

Albovine, King of Lombardy, or Alboin, hero of a tragedy of the name by Sir William Davenant, played in 1629. The story on which this play is founded is told by Caxton in his *Golden Legend,* and may be read in Belleforest's *Histoires Tragiques.*

Albret, Charles d', Constable of France, a character in Shakespeare's *Henry V,* who fell at Agincourt, the finest character among the French nobles in the play.

Albumazar, a Persian astronomer, hero of a play of the name by Tomkis, acted before James I in Trinity College Hall,

1614. It was revived after the Restoration, when Dryden wrote a prologue for it, in which he says it was the model for Ben Jonson's *The Alchemist*, and that Albumazar was the prototype of Subtle.

Albyon Knight, the hero of an old play of which only a part remains. The hero is a personification of England, and other characters were Temporalty, Spiritualty, Principalty, Commonalty, Sovereignty, Peace and Plenty. It is described as having for its object "to enforce the right rules of government for a state"; and the supposition is that it was the play acted before Queen Elizabeth at Christmas, 1558–'59, of "such matter that the players were commanded to leave off."

Alceste, the hero of Molière's comedy, *The Misanthrope*, "an upright, manly character, but rude, and impatient even of the ordinary civilities of life," from having seen so much deceit and treachery disguised under the forms of politeness. The name is used to designate a cynic of merciless frankness.

Alcibiades, the Athenian general, is a character in Shakespeare's *Timon of Athens*. He is the subject of a tragedy by Otway and also of one by the French poet Campistron.

Alcides, Hercules.

Alcina, in Boiardo's *Orlando Innamorato* a fairy, and in Ariosto's *Orlando Furioso* an enchantress, who transforms her lovers into trees, stones, wild beasts, etc.

Alciphron, the hero of *The Epicurean*, by Thomas Moore.

Aldabella, in Dean Milman's tragedy, *Fazio*. Bianca, Fazio's wife, being jealous of her, accused him to the duke of being privy to Bartoldo's death, for which he is executed. Bianca dies of grief, and Aldabella is condemned to a nunnery.

Alden, John, a cooper, one of the mechanics brought over by the Pilgrims in the *Mayflower*, a character in Longfellow's *The Courtship of Miles Standish*.

Aldibo-ronte-phosco-phornio, a character in Henry Cary's farce, *Chronon-hoton-thologos*. The name was applied by Sir Walter Scott to James Ballantyne on account of his solemn and pompous manner.

Aldingar, Sir, in an old ballad given in Percy's *Rêliques*, is a steward in the service of Eleanor, Queen of Henry II. He impeached the Queen's honor, and agreed to substantiate his charge in combat; but an angel in the guise of a child appeared as her champion and established her innocence.

Aldovrand, Father, a chaplain in Scott's *The Betrothed.*

Aldrick, in Scott's *Peveril of the Peak* the Jesuit confessor of the Countess of Derby.

Alençon, Duke of, character in Shakespeare's *Henry VI*, first part, called by York "a notorious Machiavel."

Aleshine, Mrs., one of the heroines of Frank Stockton's story, *The Casting Away of Mrs. Lecks and Mrs. Aleshine.*

Alexander the Great, hero of John Lyly's drama, *Alexander and Campaspe*, the subject also of a tragedy by Nathaniel Lee (1678), a French romance of the twelfth century by Lambert-li-cors, and of a tragedy by Racine; and Dryden has the well-known poem, *Alexander's Feast.* He is one of the Nine Worthies represented in *Love's Labor's Lost.*

Alexander, the Albanian. See SCANDERBEG.

Alexandra, in Ariosto's *Orlando Furioso,* Queen of the Amazons and one of the ten wives of Elbanio.

Alfonso, in Horace Walpole's *The Castle of Otranto,* appears in the moonlight as a gigantic apparition.

Alfred, King, is the subject of a long poem by Sir Richard Blackmore. In the *Masque of Alfred,* by James Thomson and David Mallet, occurs the song, "Rule, Britannia."

Alhadra, a character in Coleridge's tragedy, *Remorse.*

Ali, the eyes of, a proverbial expression in Persia, referring to the beautiful eyes of Ali, the cousin and son-in-law of Mahomet.

Ali Baba, the hero of the story of *The Forty Thieves* in the *Arabian Nights,* a poor Persian wood-carrier, who, accidentally learning the magic words "Open, Sesamé," and "Shut, Sesamé," gains entrance to the den of the thieves, takes possession of their plunder, and finally exterminates them.

Ali Mahbub, in Rudyard Kipling's *Kim,* a man in the Indian secret service.

Alice, a lady attending the Princess Katharine in Shakespeare's *Henry V,* who teaches the Princess English in an amusing scene.

Alice, the heroine of Bulwer Lytton's *Alice: or, The Mysteries,* a sequel to *Ernest Maltravers.*

Alice, the heroine of Lewis Carroll's (Charles Leftwich Dodgson) *Alice in Wonderland* and *Through the Looking-Glass.*

Alice, name of the heroines of Tennyson's poems *The May Queen* and *The Miller's Daughter.*

Alice, the White Lady of Avenel in Scott's *The Monastery.*

Alice du Clos, the heroine of a ballad by Coleridge.

Alice Fell, the heroine of a ballad by Wordsworth.

Alice, Mistress, the heroine of the story told to Gog by Magog in Dickens's *Master Humphrey's Clock.*

Alicia, a character in Rowe's drama, *Jane Shore,* whose jealousy leads to the death of Lord Hastings and the persecution of Jane Shore for witchcraft.

Alinda, in Thomas Lodge's *Rosalynde,* is the original of Celia in *As You Like It.*

Alison Noble, the chief character in Dr. John Brown's *Rab and His Friends.*

All-All, Sir Positive, in Thomas Shadwell's *The Sullen Lover,* a pretentious braggart, said by Pepys and Evelyn to be intended for Sir Robert Howard, brother-in-law of Dryden.

Allan of Ravenswood, the hero of Scott's *The Bride of Lammermoor.*

Allen, Barbara, the subject of a ballad by Allan Ramsay.

Allen-a-Dale, one of Robin Hood's archers.

Alleyn of Winstead, the hero of A. Conan Doyle's romance, *The White Company.*

All-Fair, a princess in the Comtesse D'Aulnoy's *Fairy Tales.*

Allmers, Alfred, in Ibsen's drama *Little Eyolf,* the father of the child who follows the Rat-wife to his death.

Allworth, Lady, and **Tom,** characters in Massinger's play, *A New Way to Pay Old Debts.*

Allworthy, Mr., a character in Fielding's *Tom Jones,* the original of which, Ralph Allen of Bristol, is celebrated in Pope's lines:

> " Let humble Allen, with an awkward shame,
> Do good by stealth and blush to find it fame."

Alma, in Spenser's *Faerie Queene,* the Queen of Body Castle—the human soul.

Alma, the subject of a poem by Matthew Prior, *The Progress of the Mind.*

Almanzor, the hero of an old romance attributed to Sir Philip Sidney, *Almanzor and Almanzaida*.

Almeria, heroine of Congreve's play, *The Mourning Bride*.

Almeyda, the heroine of a tragedy of the name by Sophia Lee, a character taken by Mrs. Siddons.

Almighty Dollar, The, an expression first used by Washington Irving in *The Creole Village*—"that great object of universal devotion throughout our land."

Alnaschar, in the *Arabian Nights*, the dreamer, who invested his money in a basket of glassware, and while dreaming of the riches he would make from it, enabling him to marry the vizier's daughter, gave it a kick in a moment of anger against his supposed wife, and broke every piece.

Alonzo the Brave and **the Fair Imogene,** the hero and heroine of a ballad by Matthew Gregory Lewis.

Alp, the hero of Byron's *The Siege of Corinth*.

Alphonsus, King of Aragon, the hero of a play by Robert Greene.

Alquife, an enchanter in the stories of Amadis de Gaul.

Altamont, in Rowe's *The Fair Penitent*, the husband of Calista, who kills Lothario after discovering that he has betrayed Calista.

Althea, in Lovelace's poem, was Lucy Sacheverell, to whom he wrote it when imprisoned in the Gatehouse, Westminster, for presenting to the House of Commons a petition in favor of King Charles.

Alzire, the chief character in Voltaire's tragedy of that name.

Amadis de Gaul, the hero of a famous romance of chivalry. The first four books were by Vasco de Lobeira of Oporto, who is thought to have died about 1403. The original Portuguese is no longer extant; but it was translated into Spanish about a century later by Montalvo, who added another book. The French translator, Herberay, increased the number of books to twenty-four. It is believed that Gaula in the original means Wales, though the French version makes it France. Amadis was called the Lion Knight from the device on his shield, also the Knight of the Burning Sword and Beltenebros from his dark beauty. The French version of the romance was translated into English by Thomas Paynel, 1567, and later by Anthony

Munday and others. Robert Southey wrote an abridgment of the story, which is praised, as is also the translation by William Stewart Rose, published in 1803. An addition to the romance under the title *Amadis of Greece* was written by Feliciano de Silva; and the name appears again in the titles *Amadis of Colchis, Amadis of Trebizond, Amadis of Cathay.*

Amaimon, one of the four demon kings of the principalities into which the realm of devils was supposed to be divided. They could be restrained from doing harm from nine o'clock till noon and from three till night.

Amalthea, the name of the Cumæan sibyl who offered the prophetic books to Tarquin.

Amaranth, Lady, a character in John O'Keefe's play, *Wild Oats,* made famous by the actress, Mrs. Pope.

Amaryllis, in the *Idylls* of Theocritus and the *Eclogues* of Virgil, the name of a rustic beauty, commonly used as the name of a sweetheart.

Amasis, Ring of. See POLYCRATES.

Amaurots, in the *Pantagruel* of Rabelais a people whom Pantagruel defended against the Dipsodes.

Amazons, the warrior-women of Asia.

Ambree, Mary, the heroine of an old ballad, sometimes called the English Joan of Arc.

Ambrosio, the hero of Matthew Gregory Lewis's *The Monk.* He is called the Man of Holiness for his reputed saintliness, but he falls into temptation and goes from bad to worse till he is condemned by the Inquisition, sells his soul to Satan, and is released from prison only to be dashed to pieces on a rock. From this book the author received the sobriquet, "Monk Lewis."

Amelia, the heroine of Fielding's novel of that name, said to have been modeled from the character of his wife. Dr. Johnson says: "*Amelia* is perhaps the only book of which, printed off betimes one morning, a new edition was called for before night," but "that vile broken nose, never cured, ruined the sale of it."

Amelia, a beautiful young woman in "Summer" of Thomson's *The Seasons,* killed by lightning when walking with her lover, Celadon.

Amiens, one of the lords attending the banished Duke in Shakespeare's *As You Like It.*

Amine, the beautiful wife of Sidi Nouman in the *Arabian Nights,* who picked up the grains of her rice with a bodkin. When her husband watched her to find out what she really fed upon, he discovered that she was a ghoul, stealing away at night to the cemetery to feed upon the dead.

Aminta, the heroine of George Meredith's *Lord Ormont and His Aminta.*

Amintas, in Spenser's *Faerie Queene,* supposed to be an allusion to Sir Philip Sidney:

> "To whom sweet poet's verse hath given endlesse date."

Amis the Priest, the hero of a German comic epic of the thirteenth century, an Englishman, ignorant, but witty. By his wit he turns the laugh against his superiors who are trying to degrade him by exposing his ignorance. The author is supposed to be one Stricker, an Austrian.

Ammiani, Carlo. See VITTORIA.

Amoret, a faithful shepherdess in Fletcher's *The Faithful Shepherd.*

Amory, Blanche, one of the hero's numerous loves in Thackeray's *Pendennis.*

Amoury, Sir Giles, in Scott's *The Talisman,* the Grand Master of the Knights Templars. As he is raising a cup of wine to his lips his head is cut off by Saladin.

Amundeville, Lady Adeline, a character in Byron's *Don Juan.*

Amys and **Amylion,** heroes of an ancient metrical romance in English, supposed to be translated from the French. They were inseparable friends and knights of Charlemagne.

Anacharsis Clootz (Clōtz), a name assumed by Baron Jean Baptiste Clootz, of Cleves (1755–1794), who called himself "The Orator of the Human Race." He was one of the originators of the Worship of Reason. The name was assumed in allusion to Anarcharsis the Scythian, who traveled in foreign countries to gain knowledge for improving his ignorant countrymen, so that "Anarcharsis among Scythians" became a proverbial expression for a wise man among the ignorant.

Anael, the heroine of Browning's tragedy, *The Return of the Druses*, who dies of grief when she finds that Djabal is not the prophet of the Druses returned to life, but an impostor.

Anak, a giant of Palestine. John Murray was called by Lord Byron the "Anak of Publishers."

Ananias, a character in Ben Jonson's *The Alchemist.*

Anastasius, the hero of a novel, *Memoirs of Anastasius*, by omas Hope (1770–1831), one of the merchant princes of gland.

Ancæus, an Arcadian, to whom a slave foretold that he would not live to drink of the wine of his vineyard. As he was about to taste the first goblet of it, he called in the slave to show him his mistake, when he was called away to the hunt of the Calydonian boar, where he met his death. This is said to be the origin of the proverb "There's many a slip 'twixt cup and lip."

Ancient Mariner, The, hero of Coleridge's famous poem of the name, who after suffering punishment for shooting an albatross, the bird of good omen to sailors, was pardoned, but was compelled to tell the story at times as a warning against cruelty toward God's innocent creatures. De Quincey thought the suggestion of the poem came from an incident told by the navigator Shelvocke of an officer on his ship who was of a saturnine mood and shot an albatross, believing that it was responsible for continued bad weather.

Andermatt, Christiane, the heroine of De Maupassant's novel, *Mount Oriol.*

Anderson, Anthony, an important character in George Bernard Shaw's play, *The Devil's Disciple.*

Anderson, John, hero of a famous Scottish song.

André, hero of a novel of the name by George Sand.

Andrea del Sarto, the "faultless painter," is the subject of a poem by Robert Browning.

Andrews, Joseph, a model young man, in Fielding's story of the name, said to have been written to ridicule Richardson's *Pamela.* Fielding makes him a brother of Pamela.

Andrews, Mistress, the heroine of the play called *The New World,* by Villiers de L'Isle Adam, written for a dramatic competition in Paris to commemorate the hundredth anni-

versary of the proclamation of the independence of th
States.

Androclus, a runaway Roman slave who drew a thor
the paw of a lion that came into the cave where he was hid
he was afterward caught and sent into the arena to fight a li
which proved to be the same one; for when it saw him it fawned upon him with demonstrations of joy. When the story was made known, the slave was set free.

Andromeda, a princess of Ethiopia, who was chained to a rock and exposed to a sea-monster, in revenge for her mother having boasted that her beauty exceeded that of the Nereids. She was saved by Perseus and married to him. Corneille has a tragedy-opera on the subject, and Charles Kingsley made it the theme of a poem.

Andronica, in Ariosto's *Orlando Furioso*, the beautiful maid of Logistilla.

Andronicus, Titus, hero of a play attributed to Shakespeare. He was a Roman general, and Marcus Andronicus, his brother, was a tribune. An anonymous tragedy with the title *Andronicus* was published in London in 1661, with the subtitle *Impieties' Long Increase; or, Heaven's Late Revenge.* It was a violent attack on the Puritans and a celebration of the Restoration.

Androvsky, the hero of Robert Hichens's novel, *The Garden of Allah.*

Andy, the hero of *Handy Andy*, an Irish story by Samuel Lover (1797–1868).

Anemolians, a nation in Sir Thomas More's *Utopia.*

Angelica, a beautiful infidel princess in Boiardo's *Orlando Innamorato* and Ariosto's *Orlando Furioso*, whose mission it is to cause dissension among the Christian leaders. Orlando is one of her lovers and goes mad when she falls in love with Medoro, an obscure soldier, after being in love with Rinaldo.

Angelica, the heroine of Farquhar's plays, *The Constant Couple* and *Sir Harry Wildairs.*

Angélique, name of the heroines of two of Molière's comedies, *Le Malade Imaginaire* and *Georges Dandin.*

Angelo, the hypocritical villain of Shakespeare's *Measure for Measure.*

Angelo, the tyrant of Padua, subject of a historical drama by Victor Hugo.

Angennes, Julie d', the heroine of *La Guirlande,* written by the poets of the Hôtel Rambouillet.

Angot, Madame, a name standing for the typical parvenu, "retaining the language, tastes, and habits of her first estate, together with the pretentiousness inspired by the second." Lecoq wrote an opera-bouffe entitled *La Fille de Madame Angot.*

Anjou, The Fair Maid of. See PLANTAGENET, EDITH.

Anna Comnena, Princess, a character in Scott's *Count Robert of Paris.*

Anne, a character in Arthurian romance, daughter of King Uther and sister of Arthur, married to Lot, King of Norway. In the *History of Prince Arthur* she is called Margawse, and Tennyson calls her Bellicent in *Gareth and Lynette.*

Anne, Princess of Wales, widow of Henry VI's son, a character in Shakespeare's *Richard III,* married to Richard, her husband's murderer.

Anne, Queen of Jutland, a combination of Lady Macbeth, Messalina, and Phædra, in Maeterlinck's drama, *Princess Maleine.*

Anne Boleyn, wife of Henry VIII and mother of Queen Elizabeth, a character in Shakespeare's *Henry VIII.*

Anne of Austria, a character in *The Three Musketeers,* by Dumas.

Anne of Geierstein, the heroine of Scott's novel of that name.

Anne, Sister, in the story of *Bluebeard* is the sister of Fatima, his seventh wife, who watches from the tower for the approach of the brothers to rescue Fatima.

Annesley, in Mackenzie's *The Man of the World,* a man whose adventures among Indians are narrated.

Annesley, the hero of Charles Reade's *The Wandering Heir.*

Annette, the heroine of a story by Marmontel, *Annette and Lubin,* a pastoral after the manner of *Daphnis and Chloe.*

Annie, Fair, the heroine of an old ballad, who was married to a noble lord, and was forced to receive a new bride of his; this turns out to be her own sister, who has brought with her seven loaded ships.

Annie of Lochroyan, Fair, the heroine of an old Scottish ballad, *Lord Gregory*. She sailed to the castle of Lord Gregory, her lover, was refused admittance by his mother, and was drowned on her way home.

Annus Mirabilis, in Dryden's poem of the name, the year 1666, a year of war and of the great fire in London.

Anselmo. See LOTHARIO.

Antar, the hero of *The Romance of Antar*, Arabian, of the sixth century.

Antenor, in Shakespeare's *Troilus and Cressida*, a Trojan commander, exchanged for Cressida. In the Æneid he is the founder of Padua.

Antheman, Jeanne, a religious fanatic, the subject of Daudet's novel, *The Evangelist*.

Anthia, a character in the Greek romance, *The Loves of Anthia and Abrocomas*, by Xenophon of Ephesus.

Antigone, the daughter of Œdipus and Jocasta, famous for filial and sisterly devotion. She is the subject of two tragedies by Sophocles, and of one by Alfieri; also of a symbolic poem by Ballanche (Lyons, 1776–1847).

Antigone, The Modern. See FILIA DOLOROSA.

Antigonus, in Shakespeare's *A Winter's Tale*, a lord sent by Leontes to dispose of Perdita.

Antinoüs, the beautiful page of the Emperor Hadrian, enrolled among the gods after his death.

Antiochus, in Shakespeare's *Pericles, Prince of Tyre*, King of Antioch, who sought the life of Pericles.

Antiope, the Queen of the Amazons.

Antipholus, the name of twin brothers in Shakespeare's *The Comedy of Errors*.

Antisthenes, a Greek philosopher who affected to despise worldly pleasure and advantages; to whom Socrates said, "O Antisthenes, I see thy pride through the holes in thy cloak."

Antomasio, in *Don Quixote*, a princess changed by enchantment into a brass monkey.

Antonio, the hero of John Marston's dramas, *Antonio and Mellida* and *Antonio's Revenge*.

Antonio, the usurping Duke of Milan, Prospero's brother, in Shakespeare's *The Tempest*.

Archer, Isabel, the chief character of Henry James's novel, *The Portrait of a Lady.*

Archimage, in Thomson's *The Castle of Indolence,* is the personification of Indolence.

Archimago, in Spenser's *The Faerie Queene,* personifies Hypocrisy.

Archy M'Sarcasm, Sir, a character in Macklin's comedy, *Love à-la-Mode* (1779), a Scotchman absurdly boastful of his ancestors and family connections.

Arcite, a character in Chaucer's *The Knight's Tale.* Palamon and Arcite were two Thebans who contended in single combat for the hand of Emilia. Dryden's version of *The Knight's Tale* is entitled *Palamon and Arcite,* the title also of a drama by Richard Edwards (1566). Arcite is a character in Fletcher's *Two Noble Kinsmen,* founded on the same story. The tale was taken originally from Boccaccio.

Arden, Enoch, the hero of Tennyson's poem of the name, a sailor who has been shipwrecked and returning after a long absence, and finding his wife married to his dearest friend, goes away without letting them know of his return.

Arden of Feversham, the hero of a drama of the name, attributed to George Lillo, and said to be founded upon an incident of 1551. It was translated into German by Tieck as a drama of Shakespeare. Arden is a fine and honorable character whose murder is instigated by his wife and her paramour.

Aresby, Captain, an affected militia captain in Fanny Burney's *Cecilia.*

Argalia, a brother of Angelica in Boiardo's *Orlando Innamorato,* the owner of an enchanted lance.

Argalus, the lover of Parthenia in Sidney's *Arcadia,* and the hero of *Argalus and Parthenia,* by Francis Quarles (1592–1644).

Argan, the leading character in Molière's comedy, *Le Malade Imaginaire,* a miserly invalid who tries various devices to avoid paying the expenses of his imaginary illness.

Argante, a sensual giantess in Spenser's *The Faerie Queene.*

Argante, a character in Molière's *Les Fourberies de Scapin.*

Argantes, in Tasso's *Jerusalem Delivered,* the bravest hero of the infidel army. He is slain by Rinaldo.

Argenis, the heroine of a political allegorical romance, *Argenis: or, The Loves of Poliarchus and Argenis*, written in Latin by John Barclay (1582–1621).

Argillan, in Tasso's *Jerusalem Delivered*, a disloyal knight, who heads a revolt against Godfrey.

Argyle, Duke of, a character in Scott's *The Legend of Montrose*.

Ariel, in Shakespeare's *The Tempest*, an airy spirit in the service of Prospero, by whom he was released from the pine-rift where he had been imprisoned by the enchantment of Sycorax.

Ariel, in Milton's *Paradise Lost*, one of the fallen angels.

Ariel, a sylph in Pope's *The Rape of the Lock*.

Arimanes, the god of evil, introduced into Byron's *Manfred*, seated on his throne surrounded by attendant spirits.

Ariodante, a character in Ariosto's *Orlando Furioso*, the lover of Ginevra. A play founded upon the incident, entitled *Ariodante and Ginevra*, was performed by children before Queen Elizabeth on the nights of Shrove Tuesday, 1582–'83.

Aristeas, in Grecian fable a character like the Wandering Jew.

Aristippus, a Greek philosopher, founder of the Cyrenaic school, which makes pleasure and quiet engagement the basis of its ethical system. C. M. Wieland, the German poet, set forth his doctrines in a historic novel, *Aristipp*.

Aristocles, the real name of Plato.

Armadale, the name of a family in a novel of the name by Wilkie Collins.

Armado. See Adriano de Armado.

Armande, a learned woman in Molière's *Les Femmes Savantes*.

Armgart, a singer, the subject of a poem in dramatic form by George Eliot.

Armida, a beautiful sorceress employed to tempt the leading Crusaders in Tasso's *Jerusalem Delivered*. She has an enchanted girdle with the power of attracting love to its wearer. Rinaldo and others are taken by her to an island where she has a beautiful palace and gardens, and where they forget their duties and the cause they are to serve, until they are rescued by a powerful talisman sent from the Christian camp.

Armine, Ferdinand, the hero of Disraeli's love story, *Henrietta Temple.*

Armstrong, Johnny, a freebooter of the time of James V of Scotland, subject of a ballad existing in various versions. The story is that he and his men met the King and he demanded a pardon, which was refused, whereupon a fight ensued in which the freebooters were all slain. Their graves are shown in a deserted churchyard at Carlenrig, near Hawick.

Armstrong, Robert, a character in George Meredith's *Rhoda Fleming.*

Arnheim, Baron von, in Scott's *Anne of Geierstein,* Anne's father, called "The Black Monk."

Arnold, in Byron's poem, *The Deformed Transformed,* is the hunchback hero, whom an evil spirit changes into the likeness of Achilles.

Arnolphe, an old cynic in Molière's comedy, *L'École des Femmes.* See AGNES.

Arpington, Lady, a character in George Meredith's novel, *The Amazing Marriage.*

Arronax, Prof. Pierre, the supposed narrator of the story in Jules Verne's *Twenty Thousand Leagues Under the Sea.*

Artaban, a character in a romance by La Calprenède (1610–1663), sometimes regarded as the source of the proverbial phrase, "proud as Artaban"; but other authority derives it from one of the four kings of the Parthians of that name.

Artagnan, d', a Gascon gentleman (1611–1673) rendered famous in the romances of Alexandre Dumas, *père.*

Artamenes, the hero of a romance (1650) by Mademoiselle de Scudéry, *Artamène, ou le Grand Cyrus.*

Artegal, Arthgallo, or **Arthegal,** a mythical king of Britain, who was deposed in favor of his brother Elidure. The incident in Geoffrey of Monmouth's *Chronicle* is the basis of Wordsworth's poem, *Artegal and Elidure.*

Artegal, Sir, personification of Justice in Spenser's *The Faerie Queene,* supposed to have been drawn from his friend, Lord Grey. One of Sir Artegal's deeds was the deliverance of Irena (Ireland) from Grantorto (Rebellion). The son of Sir

Artegal and Britomart was Aurelius Conan, from whom the Tudor dynasty was descended. Reference is to the Earl of Desmond's rebellion (1580).

Artevelde, Van, the name of a family prominent in Flemish history, characters in Sir Henry Taylor's play, *Philip Van Artevelde.*

Artful Dodger, The, sobriquet of John Dawkins, a young thief in Dickens's *Oliver Twist.*

Arthur, King, a king of Britain, supposed to have died in 542 from wounds received at the battle of Camlan, identified with Camelford in Cornwall. So many miracles and other fables have been gathered about his name that he is often regarded as a purely mythical character. According to story he was the son of King Uther and Ygerna, the beautiful wife of the Duke of Tintagel, who was deceived by Uther's visiting her in the guise of her husband, Gorlois, which he was enabled to assume by the enchantment of the wizard Merlin. Arthur's sister was the fairy Morgana. He lived at Caerleon on the Usk in Wales, in magnificent state with a brilliant court. The famous Round Table (*q.v.*), at which his knights had their seats, came to him as a gift to his wife Guinevere from her father, King Leodegrance. Many poems and romances have been written upon the story of Arthur. Sir Thomas Malory collected the old romances for his *History of Prince Arthur.*

Arthur, Duke of Brittany, son of Richard I and nephew of King John, is a character in Shakespeare's *King John.* He is supposed to have been put to death by John's orders.

Arundel. See ASCAPART.

Arviragus, in Shakespeare's *Cymbeline,* is a son of Cymbeline, kidnapped in infancy, and disguised under the name Cadwal.

Asaph, in the second part of *Absalom and Achitophel,* mainly written by Nahum Tate, Dryden is praised under this name. Asaph was a musician in the time of David.

Ascapart, a giant of romance, thirty feet high, who carried Sir Bevis of Southampton, his wife Josian, and his horse Arundel under one arm, but was vanquished by Sir Bevis. His effigy is said to be on the gates of Southampton. He figures in Drayton's *Polyolbion.*

Ashburton, Mary, the girl loved by Paul Flemming in Longfellow's *Hyperion.*

Ashe, William, the hero of a novel by Mrs. Humphry Ward, *The Marriage of William Ashe.*

Ashfield, the name of a family, characters in *Speed the Plough,* by Thomas Morton (1764–1838). The proverbial "Mrs. Grundy" received her name from a neighbor who, in Dame Ashfield's opinion, was a social autocrat.

Ashton, Lucy, the heroine of Scott's *The Bride of Lammermoor,* betrothed to Ravenswood. *Lucia di Lammermoor* is the title of Donizetti's opera, founded on the plot of the novel.

Asmodai, or **Asmodeus,** an evil angel, a character in the story of Tobit, in the Apocrypha, and one of the rebellious angels in Milton's *Paradise Lost.* In the Talmud he is the demon of dress, and is called "King of the devils."

Asmodeus, the chief character in *Le Diable Boîteux,* The Lame Devil, or *The Devil on Two Sticks,* by Le Sage. *The Flight of Asmodeus* is a nocturnal excursion in which Don Cleofas Leandro Perez Zambullo takes hold of the demon's cloak and is carried through the air to the spire of San Salvador. Then the demon unroofs all the houses of Madrid by a movement of his arm and shows his companion what is going on in each habitation.

Aspasia, the friend of Pericles, a character in one of Walter Savage Landor's *Imaginary Conversations.*

Aspatia, character in Beaumont and Fletcher's *The Maid's Tragedy.* She is forsaken by Amintor for Evadne.

Asper, in Ben Jonson's *Every Man Out of His Humor,* is supposed to be intended as a portrait of the author.

Asper, Constance, a character in George Meredith's *Diana of the Crossways.*

Aspramonte, Brenhilda of, the heroine of Scott's *Count Robert of Paris.*

Astarte, in Phenician mythology, the moon-goddess.

Astarte, the lady loved by the hero of Byron's play, *Manfred.*

Astery, a nymph in Spenser's *Muiopotmos,* who, having aroused the jealousy of others by her greater success in gathering flowers for Venus, was accused to the goddess of having had the help of Cupid; whereupon Venus, remembering Cupid's secret love for Psyche, became suddenly enraged and turned the nymph into a butterfly, placing in her wings all the flowers she had gathered, "for memorie of her pretended crime."

Astolat, in the Arthurian romances, is Guildford, in Surrey.

Astolpho, an English prince, one of the paladins in the Charlemagne romances. A fairy gave him a magic horn, in comparison with the sound of which "the fury of the winds, the rolling of thunder, the dull rumblings of an earthquake were like the strains of a flageolet." In Ariosto's *Orlando Furioso,* he ascends upon a hippogriff to the terrestrial paradise, learns from St. John the Evangelist of the madness of Orlandol, and goes with him to the moon, where he obtains the phial containing Orlando's mind, which he brings to earth.

Astragon, a physician and philosopher in Davenant's *Gondibert* (1668), who is there said to have discovered the use of the lodestone.

Astrée, the subject of a famous pastoral romance by Honoré d'Urfé (1610), translated into English in 1657, said to be imitated from the Portuguese of Montemayor's *Diana,* remarkable for its length and as bringing in the vogue for the pastoral romance that raged not only on the Continent, but in England. Its popularity was extraordinary. See CELADON.

Astrophel, meaning star-lover, a name applied to himself by Sir Philip Sidney in his poems, *Astrophel and Stella,* Stella being Penelope Devereux, to whom he was betrothed.

Atala, the heroine of a novel by Chateaubriand (1801), the daughter of a white man and a Christian Indian, who commits suicide in fear of being tempted to break her vow of virginity.

Ataliba, an inca of Peru, in Sheridan's *Pizarro* (from Kotzebue) (1799).

Athaliah, a wicked queen of Judah, the subject of Racine's tragedy in verse, *Athalie,* produced at Versailles in 1671. It is his masterpiece, and was called by Voltaire "the *chef-d'œuvre* of human genius."

Athelstane, "the Unready," Thane of Coningsburgh, in Scott's *Ivanhoe.*

Atkins, Tommy, a slang name applied generally to the British soldier.

Atlantis, a great island, supposed by the ancients to have been in the Atlantic Ocean. Plato wrote an imaginary description and history of the island, representing that an Egyptian priest described it to Solon. He says that it sank into the ocean nine thousand years before his time. It has been supposed that some ancient merchant-ship may have been driven to the coast of America, giving rise to the story of the island. Some have identified it with the Canaries, others with Scandinavia.

Atlantis, The New, an imaginary island, also in the Atlantic, the subject of an unfinished work by Bacon, intended to present a model of a perfect commonwealth.

Atlantis or **Atalantis,** a supposed island in the Mediterranean, the scene of a work of the name by Mrs. De La Rivière Manley (1736), satirizing the leaders of the revolution of 1688, "full of court and party scandals and in a loose effeminacy of style and sentiment," but having a great vogue at the time.

Atli, in the Norse epic, the *Volsunga Saga,* the King of Hunland, who marries Gudrun and kills her brothers in order to seize the "sunlight," the golden treasure they had received from Sigurd, which they had buried in the Rhine. He is identified with Attila, who figures largely in medieval epic story.

Atossa, the mother of Xerxes, an important character in *The Persians,* a tragedy of Æschylus. Mentioned by Herodotus as a friend of Sappho.

Attila, King of the Huns, the "scourge of God." In the Nibelungenlied he is called Etzel. See also ATLI. His name is often used as synonymous with destroyer. Attila is the subject of a tragedy by Corneille (1667).

Atys, Attis or **Attin,** a beautiful Phrygian shepherd, beloved by Cybele, who exacted from him a vow of perpetual chastity. She appeared among the guests at his marriage to the daughter of the King of Pessinus, striking Atys with terror. He escaped to the mountains, maimed himself, and was changed into a pine-tree, while from his blood violets sprang around the roots of the tree.

Aubrey, Augusta, the heroine of Cumberland's *The Fashionable Lover.*

Aubrey, Mr., a character, afterward called Lord Drelincourt, in Warren's novel, *Ten Thousand a Year.*

Audley, John, an imaginary character whose name was used in theater parlance as a verb, meaning to cut short a play —to "John Audley" it. In 1749 one Bartholomew Shuter had an entertainment constantly repeated to successive audiences. When a large enough audience was gathered outside, the attendant looked in and called for John Audley, a signal for the entertainment to be cut and the audience changed. Sometimes given as Orderley.

Audley, Lady, the leading character in Miss Braddon's novel, *Lady Audley's Secret.*

Audouin, Clotilde, the heroine of Edouard Rod's novel, *The Sacrificed.*

Audrey, an awkward country girl, married to Touchstone, in Shakespeare's *As You Like It.*

Aufidius, Tullus, general of the Volscians, a character in Shakespeare's *Coriolanus,* whose ambition is to bring about the fall of the Roman General, which he attains by trickery.

Augustan Age, the golden age of a nation's literature, so called from the fact that the greatest Roman writers lived in the reign of Augustus. That of Portugal is the time of Camoëns, in the reign of Don Alphonse Henrique; of England, the age of Elizabeth; of France, the age of Louis XIV; of Germany, the time of Goethe and Schiller.

Augustin, King, the chief character of Anthony Hope's novel, *The King's Mirror.*

Auld Robin Forbes, the subject of a lyric by Susanna Blamire, in Cumberland dialect.

Auld Robin Gray, the subject of a famous ballad by Lady Anne Barnard, which she wrote to an old Scottish tune. The name Robin Gray was that of an old herdsman in the service of Lord Balcarras, Lady Anne's father. Charles Gibbon has elaborated the plot into a prose story, *Robin Gray.*

Aulularia (aulula, a little jar), the subject of a comedy of Plautus, so called from the money-pot of the miser, its hero.

Aurelio, the hero of a romance, *Aurelio and Isabell, Daughter of the King of Schotlande* (1586), by Jean de Flores, translated into several languages from the Italian.

Aurelius, in Thomas Frognall Dibdin's *Bibliomania,* is said to be intended for the antiquary, George Chalmers.

Aurispa, Giorgio, the hero of D'Annunzio's novel, *The Triumph of Death.*

Aurora Leigh, the heroine and title of Mrs. Browning's longest poem.

Aurora Raby, in Byron's *Don Juan,* an English orphan, "a rose with all its sweetest leaves yet folded."

Ausonia, a name for Italy, from Auson, son of Ulysses.

Austin, Seymour, a character in George Meredith's novel, *Beauchamp's Career.*

Austria, Leopold, Archduke of, a character in Shakespeare's *King John.*

Autolycus, a pedler in Shakespeare's *A Winter's Tale,* a merry and witty thief, the "snapper-up of unconsidered trifles."

Automathes, the hero of John Kirkby's philosophical romance, *The Capacity and Extent of the Human Understanding Exemplified in the Extraordinary Case of Automathes, a Young Nobleman, Who Was Accidentally Left in His Infancy upon a Desolate Island, and Continued Nineteen Years in That Solitary State, Separate from All Human Society.* The object is to show how a youth, wholly untaught, might discover many philosophical, scientific, and religious principles.

Auvergne, The Countess of, a character in Shakespeare's *King Henry VI.*

Avalon, Avallon, or **Avillion,** in medieval romance, an enchanted island, the home of Arthur and Morgan la Faye. It is sometimes said to have been in the ocean, but it is usually identified with Glastonbury in England, which is nearly surrounded by the river.

Avenel, Dick, a Yankee in Bulwer-Lytton's *My Novel.*

Avenel, The White Lady of, in Scott's *The Monastery,* the tutelar spirit of the Avenel family.

Avernus, a small, deep, and gloomy lake in Campania, shut in by steep hills and called by the Roman poets the entrance to the underworld.

Avery, Captain, the hero of DeFoe's story, *The King of Pirates.*

Aveugle, in Spenser's *The Faerie Queene,* the son of Erebus and Nox.

Aveugle, L' (the blind man), in André Chenier's famous idyl of the name, is Homer.

Axel, the subject of a narrative poem by the Swedish author, Esaias Tegnér.

Aylmer, the name of the husband in Hawthorne's story, *The Birthmark.*

Aylmer, Colonel, a character in Blackmore's *Alice Lorraine.*

Aylmer, Rose, the subject of a famous short poem by Walter Savage Landor.

Aylmer, Sir Aylmer, the father of Edith in Tennyson's poem, *Aylmer's Field.*

Aymon, Duke of Dordogne, a character in the Charlemagne romances, the father of four knights, whose adventures are the subject of a French romance, *History of the Four Sons of Aymon,* by Huon de Villeneuve.

Azaria, in Samuel Pordage's *Azaria and Hushai,* is intended for the Duke of Monmouth.

Azarian, Constantine, the chief character of Mrs. Spofford's novel, *Azarian.*

Azazel, in Milton's *Paradise Lost,* the standard-bearer of Satan, "a cherub tall." He was one of the djinns, disobedient spirits created before Adam.

Azaziel, a seraph, lover of Cain's granddaughter Anah, in Byron's *Heaven and Earth.*

Azo, the Marquis d'Este, who marries the heroine of Byron's *Parisina.* The poem is founded on an actual incident, and the Marquis was Nicholas III of Ferrara.

Azor, the bear in Marmontel's tale, *Beauty and the Beast.*

Azrafil, in the Koran, the archangel who is to blow the trumpet of resurrection.

Baba, Ali, the narrator of The Forty Thieves in the *Arabian Nights.*

Baba, Cassim, the brother of the preceding, who forgot the password "Sesamé."

Babbie, the heroine of James M. Barrie's novel, *The Little Minister.* She pretends to be a gipsy and wins the young minister's heart.

Babe Christabel, subject of an elegy by Gerald Massey on his own child.

Baby Bell, subject of a poem by Thomas Bailey Aldrich.

Baby's Début, The, a parody on Wordsworth in Smith's *Rejected Addresses.*

Bacchantes, priestesses of Bacchus, subject of a tragedy of Euripides.

Bachelor of Salamanca, Don Cherubim, The (*q.v.*).

Backbite, Sir Benjamin, a scandal-monger in Sheridan's play, *The School for Scandal.*

Badebec, in the *Pantagruel* of Rabelais, the mother of Pantagruel, who died at his birth; for he brought into the world with him nine dromedaries, seven camels, all loaded, besides eighty-one sellers of salt each leading a mule, and twenty-five wagons loaded with vegetables.

Badoura, in the *Arabian Nights,* daughter of Gaiour, King of China, "the loveliest woman that ever lived," married to Camaralzaman.

Badroul'boudour, the daughter of the Sultan of China and wife of Aladdin in the *Arabian Nights.*

Bagarag, Shibli, a youth of many adventures in George Meredith's *The Shaving of Shagpat.*

Bagot, William, the artist known as "Little Billee" in George du Maurier's novel, *Trilby.*

Bagstock, Joe, an egotistical major in Dickens's *Dombey and Son,* who always spoke of himself as "old Joey Bagstock, sir —sly, devilish sly."

Bahman, son of the Sultan of Persia in the *Arabian Nights.* When he started on his adventures, he gave his sister a knife which would remain bright and clean as long as he was alive and well; but a drop of blood upon it would show that he was no longer living.

Bailey, Tom, the title character of Thomas Bailey Aldrich's classic juvenile tale, *The Story of a Bad Boy.*

Bajazet, a sultan of Turkey (1347–1403), surnamed the Thunderbolt, a character in N. Rowe's tragedy, *Tamerlane.* Racine also has a tragedy entitled *Bajazet,* produced in 1672.

Balaam, a character in a religious novel by Johannes Damascenus, *Balaam and Josaphat* (eighth century).

Balafré, Le. See Lesly, Ludovic.

Baland of Spain, in medieval romance, a Saracen of great strength who called himself Fierabras.

Balaustion, a Greek girl of Rhodes in Robert Browning's *Balaustion's Adventure* and *Aristophanes' Apology.* She recites from memory the plays of Euripides.

Baldassare, Calvo, foster-father of Tito, the hero, in George Eliot's novel, *Romola.*

Balder, the hero of a poem of the name by Sidney Dobell.

Balderstone, Caleb, the faithful servant of Edgar in Scott's novel, *The Bride of Lammermoor.*

Baldinucci, Filippo, author of a history of art, the supposed narrator of the story in Browning's poem, *Filippo Baldinucci on the Privilege of Burial.*

Baldrick, in Scott's *The Betrothed,* an ancestor of Eveline Berenger, who believes she sees his ghost.

Baldwin, one of the leaders of the Crusaders in Tasso's *Jerusalem Delivered*—introduced also in Scott's *Count Robert of Paris.*

Baldwin, the ass in the story of *Reynard the Fox.*

Balfour, David, the title and hero's name of a novel by Robert Louis Stevenson.

Balfour of Burley, John, in Scott's *Old Mortality,* a leader in the Covenanters' army.

Balin, Sir, a brave knight, in Malory's *History of Prince Arthur,* called "The Savage."

Baliol, Edward, usurper of Scotland, introduced in Scott's *Redgauntlet.*

Baliol, Mrs., appears in the introductory chapter of Scott's *The Fair Maid of Perth,* and in that to *The Highland Widow.* She lived in the Canongate and bequeathed *The Chronicles of Canongate* to Mr. Croftangry.

Balisarda, the enchanted sword of Ruggiero, made to kill Orlando with—in Ariosto's *Orlando Furioso.*

Baliverso, in Ariosto's *Orlando Furioso,* the basest knight in the infidel army.

Balkis, the Queen of Sheba, called also Aaziz.

Ballendino, Don Antonio, in Ben Jonson's *The Case Is Altered,* said to be intended for Anthony Munday, the dramatist.

Balmawhapple, an obstinate and stupid laird in Scott's *Waverley.*

Balmung, in the *Nibelungenlied,* the sword of Siegfried, so fine that when Amilias was cut through the waist with it, he did not know until he fell apart upon moving that he had been hurt.

Balsam of Fierabras (Fe-ā-ra-brah), the balsam with which Christ's body was embalmed, brought from Rome by Fierabras, the hero of some of the Charlemagne romances. One drop swallowed would heal any wound, even—as Don Quixote says—if one were cut in two.

Balsamo, Joseph, Count Cagliostro, hero of a romance of the name by Dumas.

Balue, Cardinal, introduced in Scott's *Quentin Durward.*

Balwery, The Great Witch of, was Margaret Aiken, who confessed to witchcraft, but, to save her life, pretended that she could detect a witch by a secret mark in the eyes; she was taken about the country to hunt out all such malefactors.

Balwhidder, Rev. Micah, in John Galt's *Annals of the Parish,* a prejudiced but sincere and kindly Presbyterian minister.

Bampfylde, name of a family in R. D. Blackmore's *The Maid of Sker.* The Maid is Bertha, or Bardie, Bampfylde.

Ban, King, of Benwick, a knight of the Round Table and father of Sir Launcelot.

Banastar, Humfrey, a character in *The Mirror for Magistrates,* by many writers, published in 1559. It is a collection of narratives in verse of the illustrious but unfortunate characters in English history from the Conquest to the year 1400. The life of Henry Stafford, Duke of Buckingham, who was betrayed to his death by his adopted son, Banaster, was written by Thomas Sackville, Earl of Dorset (1527–1608), who planned the series.

Banquo, in Shakespeare's *Macbeth,* a Scottish thane murdered by Macbeth's order. The witches prophesy that he shall be the father of a line of kings. He is tempted to take measures to realize the prophecy, but, unlike Macbeth, he thrusts aside the temptation. His son Fleance escapes and becomes the ancestor of the Scottish and English Stuart kings. Banquo's ghost appears to Macbeth at a banquet.

Banshee, or **Benshie,** an imaginary spirit attached to a family and giving warning of an approaching death by shrieks and wailings. Every important family in Ireland was supposed to have its banshee, and the idea figures in many Irish tales.

Bap, or **Baphomet,** which the Templars were accused of employing in their mysterious worship, was a small female figure of stone with two heads, one male and one female. Specimens are preserved in some of the museums of Europe. The word Baphomet is supposed to be a corruption of Mahomet; the Templars were accused of secretly believing in the Prophet.

Barabas, the Jew in Marlowe's *The Jew of Malta.*

Baradas, Count, the King's favorite, but a conspirator against him in Bulwer-Lytton's drama, *Richelieu.*

Barataria, the island over which Sancho Panza was made governor, in Cervantes's *Don Quixote.*

Barbara, Major, a Salvation Army officer, heroine of George Bernard Shaw's play, *Major Barbara.*

Barbarossa (Red-beard), surname of Frederick I, Emperor of Germany (1121–1190).

Barbary, Roan, the favorite horse of Richard II, ridden by Bolingbroke on the day of his coronation—described in Shakespeare's *King Richard II.*

Barbe Bleu, a character in a libretto by Maeterlinck, *Ardiane and Barbe Bleu.*

Bardell, Mrs. Martha, Mr. Pickwick's landlady, in Dickens's *Pickwick Papers,* who brings a suit against him for breach of promise of marriage.

Bardo di Bardi, Romola's father, a rich scholar of Florence, in George Eliot's novel, *Romola.*

Bardolph, a follower of Falstaff in Shakespeare's *Merry Wives of Windsor, Henry IV,* and *Henry V,* witty and disreputable. Falstaff calls him the "Knight of the Burning Lamp," in allusion to his red nose, the inspiration of frequent jests.

Barebones' Parliament, a nickname of the Parliament of 1653, called also "The Little Parliament" and "The Assembly of Nominees." It was convened by Cromwell, who with his officers chose the members from lists of "God-fearing" men furnished by the churches, and took its name from one Praise-

God Barbon or Barebones, a leather-seller of Fleet Street, who took a prominent part in the proceedings.

Barguest, a terrible goblin, according to the fairy superstitions of the North of England, armed with teeth and claws, which sometimes makes night hideous with its cries and shrieks. One who had the peculiar faculty of seeing it could impart the faculty to another by touching him at the time of its appearance.

Barker, Peter, the title character of Marmion W. Savage's novel, *The Bachelor of the Albany.*

Barkis, a carrier in *David Copperfield,* whose declaration, "Barkis is willin'," sent to Nurse Peggotty by little David, to signify his desire to marry her, has become proverbial.

Barlaham, a hermit by whom an Indian prince, Josaphat, was converted, in a popular medieval romance, *Barlaham and Josaphat,* by Rudolph of Ems, a minnesinger of the thirteenth century.

Barlasch, an old soldier of Napoleon, the hero of Merriman's novel, *Barlasch of the Guard.*

Barlass, Kate, in Dante Gabriel Rossetti's *The King's Tragedy,* thrusts her arm through the staple of a door to save the life of James I of Scotland, and thence received the name, which, it is said, remains to her descendants, whose crest is a broken arm.

Barleycorn, Sir John, the personification of malt liquors, the subject of a famous old song which Burns altered in parts; it is generally attributed to him. There was also an ancient tract, *The Arraigning and Indicting of Sir John Barleycorn, Knt.* The jury consisted of Benjamin Bumper, John Six-go-downs, and others with like names.

Barmby, Reverend Septimus, a character in George Meredith's novel, *One of Our Conquerors.*

Barmecide, The, a prince of the family of that name, who in the *Arabian Nights*—The Barber's Sixth Brother—gives the beggar Schacabac a pretended feast, ordering dishes which are not brought, and pretending to serve and eat of them. The beggar humors the joke and does the same, praising every dish; but begs to be excused from wine, as he is not used to it and it may make him fail of respect to his lordship; but as the prince insists, he pretends to drink and then gives his host such a blow as to knock him down, explaining that he had given warning that he could not be trusted to drink wine. The Barmecide, instead of being offended, was so pleased with the spirit in which the joke had been taken, that he gave Schacabac a real feast and appointed him to the care of his household. "Barmecide feast" is a proverbial expression for an illusory pleasure. La Harpe, the celebrated French critic, wrote a tragedy, entitled *Les Barmecides.*

Barnes, Mr., the title character of Archibald Clavering Gunter's novel, *Mr. Barnes of New York.*

Barnwell, George, the hero of Lillo's tragedy of the name, in love with a girl who incites him to crime, ending in an ignominious death through her treachery. It is founded upon an old ballad.

Barons, The, in Drayton's historical poem, *The Barons' Wars,* are the Barons of Edward II.

Barraclough, Amos, a Methodist minister in Kipling's *Life's Handicap.*

Barrel-Mirabeau (Mirabeau Tonneau), a nickname given on account of his size and drinking habit to a brother of the great Mirabeau.

Barrington, Lady Ursula, the heroine of Anthony Hope's comedy, *The Adventure of Lady Ursula.*

Bartholo, a tutor, jealous and suspicious, who is an important character in *The Marriage of Figaro* and *The Barber of Seville,* comedies by Beaumarchais.

Barton, Rev. Amos, subject of *The Sad Fortunes of the Rev. Amos Barton,* by George Eliot.

Barton, Mary, heroine of Mrs. Gaskell's novel of the same name, a Lancashire factory-girl.

Bas Bleu, The, is a poem by Hannah More.

Basil, Count, the hero of Joanna Baillie's drama of the name.

Basilisco, a braggart knight in an old play, *Soliman and Perseda* (1592), who insists on being addressed by his title. Shakespeare makes Philip in *King John* refer to him when his mother calls him a knave, and he answers, "Knight, knight, good mother, Basilisco-like."

Baskelette, Captain Cecil, a character in George Meredith's novel, *Beauchamp's Career.*

Bassanio, the lover of Portia in Shakespeare's *The Merchant of Venice;* it is in order to furnish him with money to go as a suitor that Antonio mortgaged a pound of his own flesh to Shylock the Jew.

Bastard of Orleans, The, Jean, Count Dunois, natural son of Louis, Duke of Orleans, a brilliant soldier. He is a character in Schiller's *The Maid of Orleans.*

Bateman, or **Beichan, Lord,** the hero of an old ballad, thought to be Gilbert Becket, father of St. Thomas of Canterbury.

Bath, Major, a poor, proud, and noble-minded gentleman in Fielding's novel, *Amelia,* who tries to conceal his poverty.

Bath, The King of, Richard, or Beau Nash (1674–1761), who was master of the ceremonies there for fifteen years.

Bath, The Wife of, one of the pilgrims in Chaucer's *The Canterbury Tales.*

Bat Parliament, that of 1426 was so called because the partizans of the Duke of Gloucester and their opponents, the adherents of Cardinal Beaufort, carried "bats," that is, clubs.

Battle, Ben, the hero of Hood's poem, *Faithless Nellie Gray.*

Battle, Mrs. Sarah, a woman famous as a whist player in Charles Lamb's *Essays of Elia—Mrs. Battle's Opinions on Whist,* whose celebrated wish was "a clear fire, a clean hearth, and the rigor of the game."

Battles. Many battles have received names other than their historical names, either descriptive or from some incident connected with them. Among them are: *Battle of the Three Emperors*—Austerlitz (1805), where Napoleon commanded on the one side and the Austrian and Russian Emperors on the other; *The Tearless Battle,* so called because not one Spartan fell in the fight against the Arcadians and Argives, B.C. 367; *Battle of the Giants,* Marignano, 1515, where Francis I of France led his troops against the Swiss under the Duke of Milan. Francis lost 8,000 men but gained renown as a general; *Battle of Spurs,* Courtray, 1302, between nobles and burghers, where the nobles were completely vanquished; among the spoils were 4,000 golden spurs; the same name is given to an engagement between the French and the English under Henry VIII at Guinegate near Calais in 1513, but for a different reason: the speed with which the defeated French forces left the field; *Battle of the Barriers*, which led to the abdication of Napoleon, where he fought against the allies just outside the walls of Paris, March 30, 1814; *Battle of the Herrings*, an engagement in 1429, where Sir John Fastolf gained a victory over 6,000 French troops near Rouvrai and brought to the English camp a quantity of stores, a large part of which consisted of herrings; the *Battle of the Standard* was fought in 1137 near Northallerton in Yorkshire; King David of Scotland having invaded England, the bishops of the North of England collected an army, and, to inspire it with courage, brought out the consecrated banners of St. Peter of York, St. Wilfred of Ripon, St. John of Beverly, and St. Cuthbert of Durham; these were suspended from one pole which was surmounted by a cross in the center of which was fixed a silver casket containing the consecrated wafer; and the pole was fixed into a car on which Raoul, Bishop of Durham, was standing; the Scots were routed with great disorder. The Battle of Leipsic, 1813, is sometimes called the *Battle of the Nations* from the several nationalities represented there; the *Battle of the Thirty* was an engagement where, by agreement, there were but thirty combatants on each side; the English and Bretons engaged at Ploermel in Brittany, 1350, and the English were defeated.

Bavieca, the Cid's horse, which survived him two years and a half, and was buried in front of the monastery-gate at Valencia, with an elm at his head and another at his feet.

Bavius, a general name for a stupid poet.

Bawdin, Sir Charles, the hero of a ballad by Chatterton, *The Bristowe Tragedie*.

Bayard, the famous horse of the four sons of Aymon. It could stretch its body to a length sufficient for all the four to ride at once; but when only one was to go it was of normal size. One of its footprints is said to be still visible in the Forest of Soignes and another on a rock near Dinant.

Bayard, the charger of FitzJames, in Scott's *The Lady of the Lake*.

Bayardo, Rinaldo's famous steed, which once belonged to Amadis de Gaul. In Tasso's *Rinaldo* it is said:

> "His color bay and hence his name he drew,
> Bayardo called. A star of silver hue
> Emblazed his front."

Bayes, the chief character in *The Rehearsal* (1671), a farce by George Villiers, Duke of Buckingham, intended as a caricature of the poet Dryden. He is represented as vain, obsequious to those that can benefit him, greedy for applause, and, in regard to the drama, of opinion that the plot "does not signify except to bring in fine things." The farce is a satire on the plays in vogue at the time.

Bayou State, The, a name sometimes applied to Mississippi.

Bayruffle, The Honorable Mrs., a character in George Meredith's novel, *Sandra Belloni.*

Beamish, Beau, a society leader in George Meredith's *A Tale of Chloe.*

Bear, the Bloody, in Dryden's *The Hind and the Panther* is meant for the Independents.

Bear, the Brave, a name applied to the Earl of Warwick, whose cognizance was a bear and a ragged staff; the staff is from a legend of Earl Morvid, who overcame a giant with a tree stripped of its branches.

Béarnais, The, Henri IV of France, who was a native of the ancient province Béarn.

Beast, The Blatant, a name by which Spenser in *The Faerie Queene* characterizes Slander or Popular Rumor.

Beata, Countess von Kellinghausen, a woman that "thinks and feels over much" in Sudermann's drama, *The Joy of Living.*

Beatrice, the witty heroine of Shakespeare's *Much Ado about Nothing.*

Beatrice, the heroine of Hawthorne's story, *Rappaccini's Daughter.*

Beatrice, Sister, the chief character in a libretto of the name by Maeterlinck, from an old Dutch legend of a nun who left her convent for love of a man, and returned years after, wrecked in body and mind. But she had not been missed, for the Virgin had stepped down from her niche and filled the nun's place.

Beatrice Cenci, a beautiful Roman girl falsely accused and executed in 1599 for complicity in the murder of her father. She is the subject of a romance in Italian by Francesco Guerrazzi (1804–'73) and of Shelley's dramatic poem. Browning's poem, *Cenciaja,* refers to incidents not directly concerned with the tragedy, but having an influence upon it.

Beatrice Portinari, of Florence, the object of Dante's adoration, who is his guide through Paradise.

Beatrix de Casteran, the heroine of Balzac's *Beatrix.*

Beatrix Esmond, the beautiful heroine of Thackeray's *Henry Esmond;* she coquets with her cousin Henry, intrigues with the Scottish Pretender, and finally makes a marriage beneath her station.

Beau Brummel, George Bryan Brummel, a real personage, a fop in the days of George IV, hero of the play of that name by Richard Mansfield and Clyde Fitch.

Beaucaire, Monsieur, the name assumed by Prince Louis Philippe de Valois, Duke of Orléans, the subject of Booth Tarkington's novel, *Monsieur Beaucaire.*

Beauchamp. See WARWICK.

Beauchamp, Nevil, a young naval officer, the hero of *Beauchamp's Career,* by George Meredith.

Beauclerc (fine scholar), the surname of Henry I of England, who was well educated—for a king.

Beaufort. See EXETER, SOMERSET, and WINCHESTER.

Beaumains, an ironical name given to Gareth by Sir Kay (two of King Arthur's knights), on account of his large hands.

Beaumanoir, Sir Lucas, Grand Master of the Templars in Scott's *Ivanhoe.*

Beauté, La dame de, Agnes Sorel, so called from the Château de Beauté, given to her by Charles VII.

Beau Tibbs, a character in Goldsmith's *A Citizen of the World,* who liked to fancy that he was rich and distinguished, and, though poor and shabby, put on the airs of a man of fashion familiar with all fashionable people.

Beautiful Ropemaker, The, a sobriquet of Louise Labé (1526–'66), a poetess and wife of a rope manufacturer, distinguished for her bravery at the siege of Perpignan.

Beauty and the Beast, the hero and heroine of a famous fairy tale by Madame Villeneuve, of which a version is given in Miss Thackeray's *Seven Old Friends.*

Beck, Madame, proprietor of a school in Brussels, in Charlotte Brontë's *Villette.*

Bede, Adam and **Seth,** his brother, characters in George Eliot's novel, *Adam Bede,* said to be drawn from the father and uncle of the author.

Bedford, The Duke of, third son of Henry IV, a character in Shakespeare's *Henry V* and the First Part of *Henry VI;* also as Prince John of Lancaster in the Second Part of *Henry IV.* He is held responsible for the burning of Joan of Arc as a witch.

Bedivere, Sir, the last of Arthur's knights, sent by the dying King to throw his sword Excalibur into the mere, as told in Malory's and Tennyson's *Morte d'Arthur.*

Bedott, Priscilla Pool, heroine of *The Widow Bedott Papers,* by Frances M. Whitcher (1867).

Bedreddin Hassan, a character in the *Arabian Nights,* the story of Noureddin and his Son, who was discovered by his "cheese-cakes," as no one but himself knew the secret of them except his mother.

Beef-eaters, yeomen of the guard, a corruption of "buffetiers," so called because their place was near the buffet.

Beefington, Milor, an exiled English nobleman in Canning's burlesque, *The Rovers.*

Befana, La, a fairy in Italian romance who goes about with gifts for children on Twelfth Night. The legend says that La Befana was too busy to look after the Magi when they went to offer their gifts and said she would see them on their return. But they went another way; and she watches for them every Twelfth Night.

Beggar Maid, The, was named Penelophon. The story of King Cophetua and the Beggar Maid is told in a ballad in Richard Johnson's *Crowne Garland of Goulden Roses* (1612), is referred to several times by Shakespeare and in one of Ben Jonson's plays, and is the subject of a lyric by Tennyson, *The Beggar Maid.*

Beggar of Bethnal Green, The Blind, said to have been Henry, son of Sir Simon de Montfort, who assumed the guise of a beggar to escape detection by King Henry's officers. The story is in Percy's *Rêliques*, and is the subject of a play by Chettle and Day, and one by Sheridan Knowles.

Belch, Sir Toby, in Shakespeare's *Twelfth Night*, the uncle of Olivia, a dissipated, amusing old carouser.

Belge, in Spenser's *The Faerie Queene*, the mother of seventeen sons, who asks Mercilla to help her against Geryoneo, who had taken all her sons but five. Belge is explained to be Holland and Geryoneo, Spain, who had taken her provinces; and Mercilla is intended for Queen Elizabeth.

Belial, an evil spirit, the lowest in hell, according to Milton's *Paradise Lost*, "than whom a spirit more lewd fell not from heaven," though "his tongue dropt manna and could make the worse appear the better reason."

Belinda, the heroine of Maria Edgeworth's novel of that name.

Belinda, the name of the heroine in Pope's *Rape of the Lock*. The poem was founded on a real incident. Lord Petre cut off a lock of Arabella Fermor's hair in a playful spirit; but the lady's family felt so much resentment as to cause a breach with Lord Petre's; and Pope's poem was designed to effect a reconciliation.

Belisarius, the ablest of Justinian's generals. The tradition that he was disgraced, deprived of his sight, and reduced to beggary is now discredited. The name is often used to designate a poor blind man with something of distinction in his manner. Marmontel wrote a romance (1767) with Belisarius for the subject, and Donizetti an opera (1836).

Bell, Adam, a noted outlaw and skilful archer, subject of an old ballad.

Bell, Bessie, character in the ballad *Bessie Bell and Mary Gray* by Allan Ramsay, said to be founded on fact.

Bell, Peter, the subject of Wordsworth's poem of the name. Shelley wrote, in ridicule of it, *Peter Bell the Third*.

Bellair, a character in Etherege's play, *The Man of Mode*, supposed to be the author's portrait of himself.

Bellairs, Lady Kitty, chief character in *The Bath Comedy*, by Agnes and Egerton Castle.

Bellenden, Lady Margaret, her brother the Major, and Edith, characters in Scott's *Old Mortality*.

Belloni, Sandra. See VITTORIA.

Bell-the-Cat, a name given to Archibald Douglas, Earl of Angus, who died in 1514. The Scottish nobles were in consultation at Lander when certain abuses of James III's administration came up for consideration. These were attributed to the influence of an architect, Cochran, a favorite of the King, whom he had made Earl of Mar. The question was how to act against him. And Lord Grey told the story of the council of mice who agreed on the policy of hanging a bell on the cat to give notice of her approach, when the question arose, "Who will bell the cat?" Douglas started up at the conclusion of the story and said: "I will bell the cat," and he did.

Belphegor, the subject of a novel by Machiavelli. See ONESTA.

Belphœbe, in Spenser's *The Faerie Queene,* "cold as an icicle, passionless, immovable," supposed to be meant for Queen Elizabeth. See TIMIAS.

Belshazzar, the last king of Babylon, subject of a drama by Dean Milman, and two poems by Brou—*To Belshazzar* and *The Vision of Belshazzar.*

Beltane, a Druid festival in honor of the sun, observed in the beginning of May, when a great fire was kindled on some height. The name is still occasionally used for Whitsunday.

Beltham, Squire, a rich and hot-tempered country gentleman in George Meredith's novel, *The Adventures of Harry Richmond.*

Belvidera, the unfortunate heroine of Otway's tragedy, *Venice Preserved.*

Ben, Big, the great bell of Westminster, named for Sir Benjamin Hall, commissioner when it was cast (1856).

Ben Hur, a young Jew, the leading character in General Lewis Wallace's novel of that name, the scene of which is laid in the time of Jesus. A popular drama has been made from the story.

Benassis, Dr., a character in Balzac's *The Country Doctor,* who, after an irregular life in his youth, wavered between suicide and a monastery; but stopping by chance at a miserable cretin village devoted himself to transforming it into a prosperous town, the chief place of the canton.

Benedick, the witty hero of Shakespeare's *Much Ado about Nothing.*

Benengeli, Cid Hamet (thed ā-mat banenhālee). The Moorish chronicler from whom Cervantes professed to have obtained his story of Don Quixote. It is an Arabian form of Cervantes's own name.

Bennet, Elizabeth, the heroine of Jane Austen's *Pride and Prejudice,* a witty and high-spirited girl whose prejudice clashes with the pride of Fitzwilliam D'Arcey. Other members of the Bennet family are characters in the story—her father, cynical and bitter over the mortifications he has brought upon himself by a foolish marriage; her silly mother—Jane, refined and gentle—Mary, the pedant—and two wild and coarse younger sisters.

Benvolio, the cousin and friend of the Montagues in Shakespeare's *Romeo and Juliet,* who, Mercutio says, has "quarreled with a man for waking his dog by coughing in the street."

Beowulf, the hero of the Anglo-Saxon epic poem of the same name, who slew Grendel, a half-human monster. The poem dates from the sixth century and is the earliest known of English origin.

Beppo, the hero of Byron's poem of the name.

Berault, Gil de, the hero of Weyman's novel, *Under the Red Robe.*

Berengaria, the Queen of Richard I, Cœur de Lion, introduced in Scott's *The Talisman.*

Berenger, Lady Eveline, the heroine of Scott's novel, *The Betrothed.*

Berenice, wife of Ptolemy III, whose hair, which she sacrificed as a thank-offering to the war-god, was said to have been taken to the sky and to form the seven stars near the tail of Leo, still called Berenice's Hair. Pope makes use of the fable in *The Rape of the Lock.* Catullus has a poem on the hair of Berenice.

Berenice, a Jewish Princess whom Titus took to Rome and wished to marry, but the Romans forced him to send her back to Judea; the heroine of Otway's tragedy, *Titus and Berenice,* and of Racine's *Berenice.*

Bergerac, Cyrano de (1620–1655), a famous duelist, and a burlesque writer, author of *Comic Histories of the States and*

Empires of the Sun and of the Moon, which are said to have given Swift suggestions for *Gulliver's Travels*. He is noted for the size and ugliness of his nose and his sensitiveness in regard to it, a characteristic that is freely exploited in Edmond Rostand's drama, *Cyrano de Bergerac*, though it represents him as an unselfish and noble character with a pathetic fate, as he seems to have been in reality. "While I stood below in the black shadow, others mounted to cull the kiss of glory. That is my life."

Bergius, Prince. See GROUCH.

Berkely, Lady Augusta, in Scott's *Castle Dangerous*, disguises herself as a minstrel, Augustine.

Bernardo del Carpio, a hero of old Spanish romance, who distinguished himself in the victory over the French at Roncesvalles (778), where Orlando, or Roland, was slain. *The March of Bernardo del Carpio* is among the Spanish ballads translated by J. G. Lockhart, and Mrs. Hemans wrote a once popular poem, *Bernardo del Carpio*.

Bernick, Consul, the chief character in Ibsen's play, *The Pillars of Society*. In early years he had imposed upon his younger brother Johan the guilt of his own embezzlement and his own intrigue with a French actress, which had made Johan a fugitive. In the play Johan returns from America and finds his brother a pillar of society who is making religion and patriotism profitable.

Berowne, or **Biron,** a witty lord in Shakespeare's *Love's Labor's Lost*.

Berry, Nathaniel, "Uncle Nat," in James A. Herne's drama, *Shore Acres*.

Bertha, or **Agatha,** betrothed of Hereward in Scott's *Count Robert of Paris*.

Bertha, Joseph, the title character of *The Conscript*, by Erckmann-Chatrian.

Bertha Broadfoot, the mother of Charlemagne, so called because one foot was larger than the other. She is mentioned in Villon's famous poem, *Ballade of Dead Ladies*.

Bertha the Spinner, the wife of Rudolph II, King of Burgundy beyond Jura, called by Longfellow "Queen of Helvetia," who even had a distaff fixed to her saddle that she might spin as she rode.

Berthier, name of a Parisian notary and his wife, characters in Balzac's *Cousin Bette* and also in *Cousin Pons.*

Bertram, Count of Rousillon, a contemptible character in Shakespeare's *All's Well that Ends Well.*

Bertram, Edmund, in Jane Austen's *Mansfield Park,* is a young clergyman, very good, but a little of a prig.

Bertram, Harry, an important character in Scott's *Guy Mannering,* son of the Laird of Ellangowan.

Bertrand, the monkey in La Fontaine's fable, *The Monkey and the Cat.* Bertrand is used metaphorically for one who puts another (Raton) forward to take the risk, while he himself takes the profit. Scribe has a comedy, *Bertrand et Raton,* a satire on the French administration of the time (1833).

Bertrand du Guesclin, Constable of France (d. 1380), whose adventures are related in a romance of chivalry bearing his name.

Bess, Good Queen, a title of Elizabeth, as it was the fashion to attribute to her the prosperity of England during her reign.

Bette, Cousin, pet name of heroine of Balzac's *Cousin Bette.*

Bettina, to whom Goethe's *Letters to a Child* were addressed, was Elizabeth Brentano (b. 1785), afterward wife of Ludwig Achim von Arnim.

Beulah, The Land of, in Bunyan's *Pilgrim's Progress,* a land of rest this side the river of Death, where pilgrims await the summons to cross the stream and enter the Heavenly City.

Beverley, Ensign. See ABSOLUTE.

Bevis, Marmion's horse in Scott's poem, *Marmion* (1808).

Bevis, Sir, of Southampton or **Hampton,** a famous knight of romance. His mother, not unlike Hamlet's, was "reproved" by him for murdering his father, so that she tried to have him killed; and when he afterward struck at her second husband, he was sent to Armenia. Here he attained to great honors and married the King's daughter. Among his exploits were the enslaving of the giant Ascapart and the killing of the great dragon Colein. He returned to England and was restored to his lands and title. In French story he figures as Beuves de Hautone and in Italian as Buovo d'Antona. His story is told in Drayton's *Polyolbion* (1612). His sword was named Morglay, and his horse Arundel.

Bianca, in Shakespeare's *Othello,* is bribed by Iago to steal Desdemona's handkerchief.

Bianchon, Horace, a physician in Paris, celebrated during the reigns of Charles X and Louis Philippe. He appears in his professional capacity in many of Balzac's novels. He was a brilliant talker; and "gave to society the adventures known by the following titles: *A Study of Woman; Another Study of Woman; La Grande Bretêche.*"

Bible Butler, sobriquet of Stephen Butler in Scott's *Heart of Midlothian.*

Bickerstaff, Isaac, a pseudonym used by Swift in a satirical pamphlet against one Partridge, an almanac-maker. A second, in answer to Partridge's reply, kept up the fun; and Steele, in starting *The Tatler,* took advantage of the popularity of the name, announcing "Isaac Bickerstaff, Esq., Astrologer," as the editor.

Biederman, Arnold (d. 1482), and his four sons, Rudiger, Ernest, Sigismund, and Ulrich, characters in Scott's *Anne of Geierstein.* He was chief magistrate of Unterwalden, Switzerland.

Big-Endians. See LITTLE-ENDIANS.

Biglow, Hosea, the name under which James Russell Lowell published *The Biglow Papers,* "edited by Homer Wilbur, A.M.," satirical poems in Yankee dialect, directed against slavery and the War with Mexico (1846–'48); a second series appeared at the time of the Civil War (1861–'65).

Bigot, in Lamb's *Essays,* is John Fenwick, editor of a newspaper, *The Albion.*

Bigot, Robert, Earl of Norfolk, one of the twenty-five barons opposed to the King, a character in Shakespeare's *King John.*

Bilboquet, a character in *Les Saltimbanques* (The Mountebanks), by Dumersan and Varin (1838). His name is proverbial for one who knows how to turn everything to his own profit by means not always legitimate.

Billee, Little, the one of three Bristol sailors whom the others resolved to eat, in Thackeray's comic poem, *Little Billee.*

Billee, Little. See BAGOT. WILLIAM.

Billevich, Pana Aleksandra, the heroine of Sienkiewicz's novel, *The Deluge.*

Bilton, Stephen, a character in Meredith's novel, *Rhoda Fleming.*

Bimini, an island where the fabulous fountain of perpetual youth was supposed to be—the fountain sought by the famous navigator, Ponce de Leon. The name is now applied to a group of islets east of Cape Florida.

Bingen, The Bishop of. See HATTO.

Bingham, Major Christopher, the chief character in Robert Marshall's comedy, *The Second in Command.*

Bingley, Mr., the lover of Jane Bennet in Jane Austen's *Pride and Prejudice.*

Binks, Sir Bingo and **Lady,** a fox-hunting baronet and his wife in Scott's *St. Ronan's Well.*

Binnie, James, an old Anglo-Indian in Thackeray's *The Newcomes.*

Binnorie, the sisters of, subjects of a ballad, *The Twa Sisters o' Binnorie.* One sister drowned the other out of jealousy. A harper found the drowned one and strung his harp with three locks of her yellow hair; and when the harp was played it said plainly, "There sits my sister wha drowned me."

Birch, Harvey, a celebrated character in Cooper's novel, *The Spy.*

Bird, The Little Green, in the *Fairy Tales* of the Comtesse d'Aulnoy, could reveal all secrets and foretell the future. Fairstar found it and by its help freed the princess.

Biron, a character in *Love's Labor's Lost.* See BEROWNE.

Biron, or **Byron, Charles de Gontant, Duke of,** a favorite of Henry IV of France, who entered into treasonable negotiations with Spain, for which he was executed in 1602. He is the subject of two tragedies by George Chapman (1557–1634), *Byron's Conspiracy,* and *Byron's Tragedy.*

Biron, Harriet, a character in Richardson's novel, *Sir Charles Grandison,* with whom Sir Charles is in love.

Birotteau, César, a perfumer, the subject of one of Balzac's novels; he appears also in *A Bachelor's Establishment.*

Birotteau, François, older brother of César, is a character in *César Birotteau,* and also in *The Lily of the Valley.*

Birtha, in Davenant's *Gondibert*, the daughter of Astragon, in love with Gondibert.

Bixion, Jean Jacques, a celebrated cartoonist, and a practical joker, is a character in several novels of Balzac's—*A Bachelor's Establishment* and others.

Blachington, Sir Rodwell and **Lady,** characters in George Meredith's novel, *One of Our Conquerors*.

Black Act, The, an act passed in England in 1722, so called because aimed at the wanton destruction of game by persons with blackened faces, calling themselves Blacks.

Black Acts, the acts of the Scottish Parliament previous to 1586; so called because printed in black or Saxon characters.

Black Agnes, a favorite palfrey of Mary Queen of Scots.

Black Bartholomew, name given to the day when two thousand Presbyterian ministers were ejected for refusing to subscribe to the Articles of Uniformity.

Blackbeard, an American pirate, Edward Teach, killed about 1720.

Black Brunswickers, The, a name applied to a corps of seven hundred volunteer hussars commanded by the Duke of Brunswick, whom Napoleon had forbidden to succeed his father. The name was given them because they were wearing mourning for the late duke. Millais has a noted picture, The Black Brunswicker.

Black Colin, General Campbell, a character in Scott's *Redgauntlet*.

Black Dick, a nickname applied by his sailors to Admiral Howe, afterward Earl and Baron Howe of Laugar, who was sent with his brother to America in 1776, to restore peace with the colonies. He commanded a fleet sent against the French who were aiding the Americans in 1778, and was later, 1793, victorious over the French off Ushant.

Black Douglas, William Douglas, Lord of Nithsdale (d. 1390).

Black-eyed Susan, the subject of a ballad by John Gay (1688–1732) and of a play by Douglas Jerrold (1803–1857).

Black Lord Clifford, John, ninth Lord (d. 1461), called also "the Butcher."

Black Monday, Easter Monday, 1360, so called from a

violent storm to which Edward III and his army were exposed near Chartres, France, so that many men and horses died. After that, Easter Monday of any year was sometimes called Black Monday.

Black Prince, The, Edward Prince of Wales, son of Edward III of England, so called "for terror of his arms."

Blacks, The (Neri), one of the factions of the Guelph party in Florence. Dante belonged to the Whites, and was sent into exile in 1302 by the Blacks, who were in control.

Black Saturday, August 4, 1621, so called in Scotland because of a violent storm at the time the Parliament was taking action to enforce conformity to Episcopal worship.

Blacksmith, The Flemish, Quentin Matsys, the painter (1460–1529).

Blacksmith, The Learnèd, a name given to Elihu Burritt (1811–1879), a self-educated American and writer in favor of reforms.

Black Snake, a name given by the Indians to General Anthony Wayne.

Blackstone, Rev. William (d. 1675), a clergyman of the Church of England, and the first settler in what is now Boston, afterward in Blackstone, R. I. Is berated by Endicott in Hawthorne's *The Maypole of Merry Mount* as countenancing ungodly pastimes. In *The Scarlet Letter* he is mentioned as "that half-mythological personage who rides through our early annals seated on the back of a bull." In his later years, having no horse, he rode a bull when he went to preach in Providence.

Black Watch, The, companies dressed in very dark plaid, whose office was to watch the Scottish Highlands (1725) and who afterward formed the Forty-second Regiment. Their tartan is still called "Black Watch Tartan."

Bladud, Prince, the mythical founder of Bath, said to have been a king of England and father of King Lear, and to have been cured of leprosy by the water of the springs. He is the hero of the "True Legend," discovered by Mr. Pickwick.

Blair, Adam, a Scottish minister in Lockhart's novel of that name.

Blair, Father Clement, a Carthusian monk in Scott's *The Fair Maid of Perth.*

Blaize, Giles and **Tom,** characters in George Meredith's novel, *The Ordeal of Richard Feverel.*

Blaize, Madame, subject of a humorous elegy by Goldsmith.

Blamont-Chauvry, Princesse de, a character in Balzac's *The Thirteen* and also in *The Lily of the Valley.* "Her drawing-room set the fashion in the Faubourg Saint-Germain, and the sayings of this feminine Talleyrand were listened to as oracles."

Blanca. See GANDULF.

Blanche and **Rose,** the heroines of Eugène Sue's *The Wandering Jew.* Their prototypes are said to have been the daughters of Dr. Nathaniel Niles, at one time American minister to Sardinia.

Blanche of Spain, daughter of King Alfonso of Castile, and niece of King John, appears in Shakespeare's *King John.*

Blanchefleur, the heroine of an old English romance, *Flores and Blanchefleur,* taken from the French, which was founded on an older tale, made use of by Boccaccio and by Chaucer.

Blancove, Algernon Edward, Squire, and Sir William, characters in George Meredith's *Rhoda Fleming.*

Blandamour, Sir, a false knight in Spenser's *The Faerie Queene,* wounded in a fight with Britomart.

Blarney, Lady, a character in Goldsmith's *The Vicar of Wakefield.*

Blas, Gil. See GIL BLAS.

Blasphemous Balfour, a name applied to Judge Balfour of Scotland (d. 1583).

Blatant Beast, The. See BEAST.

Blattergrowl, Rev. Mr., the minister of Trotcosey in Scott's *The Antiquary.*

Bleeding Heart of Lady Hatton, The, according to a popular tradition, after being torn out by the devil, was thrown into what was therefore called Bleeding Heart Yard, in London.

Blefuscu, an island inhabited by pygmies, in *Gulliver's Travels,* supposed to be intended to represent France.

Blenheim, Bavaria, scene of Marlborough's victory, the subject of a poem by Addison and one by Southey.

Blenheim Spaniels, a nickname given to the electors of Oxford because of their subserviency in electing the candidates of the Duke of Marlborough.

Blimber, Dr., in Dickens's *Dombey and Son,* the proprietor of a school at Brighton, "a great hothouse, in which there was a forcing-apparatus incessantly at work." Mrs. Blimber said "that, if she could have known Cicero, she thought she could have died contented." Cornelia, the daughter, "was dry and sandy with working in the graves of deceased languages."

Blind Girl of Castel-Cuillé, The, subject of a poem translated by Longfellow from the Gascon of Jasmin.

Blind Harry, a Scottish minstrel at the court of James IV, author of an epic, *Sir William Wallace.*

Blind Poet, The, a name applied to an Italian, Luigi Groto (1541–1585), to Homer, and to Milton.

Blinkins, Mr., the Latin master in Dickens's short sketch, *Our School,* who seemed "as having had the best part of his life ground out of him in a mill of boys."

Blonde of Oxford, one of the subjects of a metrical romance (about 1190) by Philip de Rames, *Blonde of Oxford and Jehan of Dammartin.*

Blondel de Nesle, the favorite minstrel of Richard I, who discovered his master's prison by singing under the windows of every keep in Germany a romance that they had composed together, until the strain was taken up from within by Richard. The incident is the text of a French opera, *Richard Cœur de Lion,* by Sedaine and Gretry. Blondel is a character in Scott's *The Talisman.*

Blood, Col. Thomas, a historic scoundrel, emissary of the Duke of Buckingham, introduced in Scott's *Peveril of the Peak.*

Blood-Bath, The, a name given to a massacre of Swedish nobles and leaders in 1520, under pretext of religious zeal.

Bloody Assizes, The, a name given to the assizes in western England in 1685, presided over by Chief Justice George Jeffreys, when about three hundred persons were executed, nearly one thousand sent as slaves to the American colonies, and many were whipped, imprisoned, and fined.

Bloody Bill, The, a name given to a statute of the reign of Henry VIII, imposing the death penalty for denial of the doctrine of transubstantiation.

Bloody Butcher, the Duke of Cumberland, son of George II, so called for his barbarous treatment of the Highlanders who had risen in favor of the "Young Pretender," Charles Edward Stuart, after their defeat at Culloden, 1746.

Bloody Hand, The, Cathal, ancestor of the O'Connors.

Bloody Mary, a sobriquet of Mary Tudor, Queen of England, from her persecution of Protestants, of whom two hundred are said to have been burned during her reign, 1553–'58.

Bloody Wedding, that of Henri of Navarre and Margaret, sister of Charles IX. The leading Protestant nobles were invited to the wedding; and on St. Bartholomew's Eve, 1572, a general slaughter of Protestants was begun in Paris, and carried on in the provinces afterward. The number killed has been estimated at from thirty thousand to seventy thousand.

Blotton, Mr., a member of the Club in Dickens's *The Pickwick Papers,* whose quarrel with Mr. Pickwick is made up by mutual apologies, each explaining that the offensive words were used, not in their common, but in a parliamentary, or merely technical or constructive sense. The incident was intended to ridicule a somewhat similar one that took place in Parliament about the time the *Pickwick Papers* were written.

Blougram, Bishop, in Robert Browning's poem, *Bishop Blougram's Apology,* answers a newspaper man, Gigadibs, who does not see how one not a believer in all the Church teaches can hold an office that implies such belief. The Bishop's reply is to the effect that "belief diversified by doubt" is at least as good as "doubt diversified by belief," since no one can be perfectly sure; and that it has, moreover, the advantage of being positive and definite and adapted to the state of society in which he lives; and to the objection that he ought at least to prune away what he concedes to be the superstitions from his creed, he gives the usual answer, that when such a process is once begun, there is no logical place to stop short of "slashing at God Himself."

Blowselinda, a shepherdess in Gay's pastoral, *The Shepherd's Week,* written as a satire on the pastorals where "shepherdesses piped on oaten reeds" and shepherds slept under myrtle shades. His shepherdesses milked the kine and his shepherds drove stray hogs to their styes.

Blubb, Mr., a member in Dickens's sketch, *The Mudfog Association,* who lectures on a cranium which turns out to be a carved cocoanut-shell.

Bluebeard, the hero of a French story by Charles Perrault. It is said to have been founded upon the real history of Giles de Laval, Marshal of France in 1429. He was Lord of Raiz and immensely wealthy, but a monster of cruelty, using the blood of his victims in incantations to discover hidden treasures. By another account, the original of Bluebeard was Count Conomar, the husband of St. Triphyna. Ludwig Tieck founded a drama on the story, and Offenbach an opera-bouffe (1866).

Blue-Coat School, a popular name for Christ's Hospital, London, an institution for the education of orphans.

Blue Knight, The. See PERIMONES.

Blue Laws, The, a nickname given to the strict regulations of the early days of the Connecticut colony. After the Restoration, "blue" was applied to those who disapproved of the immorality of the times—the dissenters generally, and especially to the Presbyterians. It is said that some of the preachers used to throw a blue apron over the tub on which they stood to preach.

Blue-Noses, a nickname of Nova Scotians.

Blue-Stockings, a nickname applied to literary women from 1780, when "Mrs. Montagu exhibited the badge of the Bas-Bleu Club of Paris at her evening assemblies." Some of the habitual guests actually wore blue stockings. Byron wrote a satire on them in dramatic form—*The Blues: a Literary Eclogue*, which he said was "a mere buffoonery, never meant for publication."

Bluestring, Robin, a nickname given to Sir Robert Walpole in allusion to the blue ribbon of the Knights of the Garter.

Bluff Harry, or **Hal,** sobriquet of King Henry VIII of England.

Blumine, in Carlyle's *Sartor Resartus,* a beautiful and high-born maiden with whom Teufelsdröckh falls in love.

Blunderbore, a giant in the story of *Jack the Giant-Killer.*

Blunt, Sir Walter, a character in *King Henry IV*. In the battle of Shrewsbury he wears one of the King's coats, and is killed by Douglas, who mistakes him for the King.

Bluntschli, Captain, the hero of Shaw's play, *Arms and the Man,* who thinks he has spoiled his chances in life by his romantic disposition.

Blushington, Edward, a shy youth in Moncrieff's play, *The Bashful Man.*

Bluphocks, an adventurer and spy in Browning's *Pippa Passes.*

Boabdelin, so Boabdil (Abu-Abdillah), the last Moorish king of Granada, is called in Dryden's play, *The Conquest of Granada.*

Boadicea, Queen of the Iceni, in Britain, who led resistance to the Romans A.D. 61, is the subject of Fletcher's play, *Bonduca.*

Boanerges, a loud sectarian parson in Mrs. Oliphant's novel, *Salem Chapel.*

Boar, The, Richard III, whose device was a boar. See CALLINGBOURNE.

Boar, The Bristled Baptist, a name applied in Dryden's *The Hind and the Panther* to the sect of Anabaptists.

Boar, The Wild, of Ardennes, William Count of La Marck, introduced in Scott's *Quentin Durward.*

Bobadil, Captain, a cowardly braggart in Jonson's comedy, *Every Man in His Humor,* regarded as his best invention.

Bodach Glas, or the Gray Specter, a family spirit in Scotland, like the Irish banshee.

Bodard de St. James, a character in Balzac's *Catherine de' Medici.*

Boel, Eli, the heroine of Björnson's novel, *Arne.*

Boemondo, or Bohemond, a crusader, the Christian King of Antioch, a character in Tasso's *Jerusalem Delivered,* also in Scott's *Count Robert of Paris.*

Bœuf, Sir Reginald Front de, in Scott's *Ivanhoe,* a fierce partizan of Prince John.

Boffin, Nicodemus, or **Noddy,** "the golden dustman," in Dickens's *Our Mutual Friend,* and Mrs. Boffin become rich through the will of their master, but turn over the fortune to his disinherited son when he is found, reserving only the house of their master, Mr. Harmon, called "Harmony Jail" because Harmon lived alone and never agreed with anyone, but renamed by Mrs. Boffin "Boffin's Bower." See WEGG.

Bois-Guilbert, Sir Brian de, a preceptor of the Knights Templars in Scott's *Ivanhoe.* When Rebecca is charged with sorcery, Sir Brian appears in the lists against her, while Ivanhoe is her champion. Sir Brian is killed, and Rebecca's innocence is established.

Boisterer, in the Countess d'Aunoy's *Fortunio* (1682), could overturn a windmill with his breath, and "perhaps the hill, too."

Bokhara, the King of, the subject of Matthew Arnold's poem, *The Sick King in Bokhara.*

Boldheart, Captain, hero of Robin Redforth's story in Dickens's juvenile novel, *A Holiday Romance.* In his schooner, *Beauty,* he captures the *Scorpion,* commanded by his old enemy, the Latin Grammar Master, whom he sets adrift in an open boat.

Boleyn, or **Bullen, Anne,** second wife of King Henry VIII and mother of Queen Elizabeth, a character in Shakespeare's *Henry VIII;* the subject of Henry Hart Milman's dramatic poem, *Anne Boleyn* (1826).

Bolingbroke, a character in Shakespeare's *Richard II,* and as Henry IV in the play of that name—the first of the Lancastrian kings.

Bolster, a gigantic wraith in Cornish tradition, associated with Wraith's Hole in Cornwall.

Bolton, Billy, the hero of George Ade's comedy, *The College Widow.*

Bomba, King, a nickname of Ferdinand II of Naples and Sicily (1830–1859). Several explanations have been given—one that he ordered his soldiers to "bombard" some insurrectionists, which is denied; another that the word was used in Italy to signify that the King's word was not to be believed, or was worthless.

Bombastes Furioso, the hero of a burlesque opera of the name, by W. B. Rhodes.

Bombastus, the family name of Paracelsus (*q.v.*).

Bompas, Teddy, and his wife, **Aurora,** characters in George Bernard Shaw's play, *How He Lied to Her Husband.*

Bonaparte, Napoleon, appears in several of Balzac's novels. Napoleon appears also in Victor Hugo's *Les Misérables,* in Lever's *Maurice Tierney* and in *Tom Burke of Ours,* in some of the Erckmann-Chatrian novels, in Tolstoi's *War and Peace,* and in Dichrichstein's play, *The Song of the Sword.* He is the subject of the play, *The Man of Destiny,* by George Bernard

Shaw, and a character in Conan Doyle's *Brigadier Gérard,* also in Lepelletier's novel, *Madame Sans-Gêne.*

Bonaventure, Father, a name and disguise assumed by Charles Edward, the "Young Pretender," in Scott's *Redgauntlet.*

Bonduca. See BOADICEA.

Bonfons, Cruchot de, in Balzac's *Eugénie Grandet,* married Eugénie for her wealth. He looked like "a big rusty nail."

Bonhomme, Jacques, meaning James Goodman, a nickname applied to the French peasant by the nobles in the fourteenth century. When the peasants of the Île-de-France rose against the nobles, May 21, 1358, the insurrection was called the Jacquerie, a word that has come to be employed for a rising accompanied by arbitrary executions, and for industrial movements attended with violence.

Boniface, a general name for a landlord, from the Lichfield landlord in Farquhar's play, *The Beaux' Stratagem.* His catchword, "as the saying is," he introduces into nearly every sentence.

Boniface, the Abbot, a character in Scott's *The Monastery.*

Boniface, Father, ex-Abbot in Scott's *The Abbot.*

Bonnet, Abbé, an old curé of Montegnac, where by a lifetime of toil he brought about an entire regeneration of a wretched country, in Balzac's *The Country Parson.*

Bonnie Lesley, in Burns's song, was Leslie Baillie, of Ayrshire.

Bonnie Lesley, a character in William Black's *Kilmeny.*

Bonnivard. See CHILLON.

Bontemps, Roger, one living contentedly and free from care, or a personification of that kind of life; subject of a song of Béranger, translated under the title *Light-hearted Dick.*

Booby, Lady, in Fielding's *Joseph Andrews,* a caricature of Richardson's novel, *Pamela.*

Booth, Captain, the husband of the heroine of Fielding's novel, *Amelia,* said to have been drawn from the author himself.

Borachio, the villain that invents the plot against Hero in Shakespeare's *Much Ado about Nothing.*

Border Minstrel, The, Sir Walter Scott, who collected The Minstrelsy of the Scottish Border. He was descended from a Border family; his home, Abbotsford, is on the Tweed; the scene of his poem, *The Lay of the Last Minstrel*, is Melrose, near the English line.

Border-Thief School of Fiction, The, is a name sometimes given to the kind of fiction inaugurated by Scott.

Borgia, Cæsar, a character in *Ettore Fieramosca*, a novel by D'Azeglio.

Borgia, Francesco, Duke of Gandia, the subject of Swinburne's poetic drama, *The Tragedy of the Duke of Gandia*, in which his brother Cæsar also is a character.

Borgia, Lucretia, Duchess of Ferrara, a well-known personage of history and tradition, is the subject of a drama by Victor Hugo (1833), and of an opera by Donizetti (1834).

Borkman, John Gabriel, a character of Ibsen's drama of the name. Though in love with Ella Rentheim, he married her sister, because an influential man who could advance his interests wished to marry Ella. He failed as a speculator and was in prison for swindling. The action of the drama takes place thirteen years after his failure, when he is living on Ella's charity, never leaving the house, and alluded to, when he paces the long gallery, as "the sick wolf up there." His son, Erhart, is a gay, selfish young man who leaves the suffering family and goes out into the world to enjoy himself.

Borrioboula-Gha, on the Niger, the place where the philanthropic Mrs. Jellyby, in Dickens's *Bleak House*, proposes to settle some of the superfluous population of England.

Bors, or **Bohort, Sir,** Launcelot's nephew, a knight of the Round Table.

Boston Tea-Party, a name given to the affair at Boston, December 16, 1773, when a party of men disguised as Indians destroyed several hundred chests of tea which they took from three English ships in the harbor, in order to carry out the non-importation policy of the colony.

Boswal, the hero of a Scottish romance of the sixteenth century, *Boswal and Lillian*.

Boswell, Rhona, the heroine of a poem, *The Coming of Love*, by Theodore Watts-Dunton.

Bothwell, Earl of, husband of Mary Queen of Scots, is the hero of a tale in verse by W. E. Aytoun (1856), a novel by James

Grant (1851), and a drama by Swinburne (1874). He is a character in Maurice Hewlett's novel, *The Queen's Quair.*

Bottle Riot or **Conspiracy, The,** a disturbance at a Dublin theater December 14, 1822, when a bottle was thrown into the box of the Lord Lieutenant, the unpopular Marquess Wellesley.

Bottom, Nick, a weaver, the most important character in the play performed before the Duke in Shakespeare's *A Midsummer Night's Dream,* and the most individual and amusing in the drama.

Bouchard, Sir, a knight of Flanders in Knowles's play, *The Provost of Bruges,* where all the leading characters are killed, or die in consequence of a law of 1127, that once a serf always a serf till manumitted, and that marriage to a serf made one a serf. Bertulphe, the Provost, became a serf under the law.

Bouchier, Thomas, Archbishop of Canterbury and Cardinal, character in Shakespeare's *Richard III.* He was a Yorkist, and crowned Edward IV, Richard III, and Henry VII.

Bouillon, Godfrey of, a leader in the First Crusade, a character in Tasso's *Jerusalem Delivered* and in Scott's *Count Robert of Paris.*

Bounderby, Josiah, a rich Coketown manufacturer in Dickens's *Hard Times,* who marries Louisa Gradgrind—"a big, loud man with a stare and a metallic laugh."

Bountiful, Lady, a benevolent old lady in Farquhar's play, *The Beaux' Stratagem.*

Bourbonne, De, in Balzac's *Madame Firmiani* and *The Vicar of Tours,* a man of wealth and sagacity, who gives wise but unregarded advice which would have saved Francis Birotteau's inheritance.

Bourgh, Lady Catherine de, a stupid and vulgar woman of rank in Jane Austen's *Pride and Prejudice,* the patroness of the Rev. Mr. Collins.

Boustrapa, a sobriquet given to Napoleon III, made from syllables of Boulogne, Strasburg, and Paris, where he made attempts at *coups d'état* in 1840, 1836, and 1851 respectively, the last successfully.

Bovary, Madame, heroine of a romance of the realistic school bearing her name, by Gustave Flaubert (1857).

Bower of Bliss, The, in Tasso's *Jerusalem Delivered*, the garden of the enchantress Armida, who holds Rinaldo under her spell.

Bowre of Blisse, The, in Spenser's *The Faerie Queene*, the dwelling of the witch Acrasia, on a floating island, destroyed by Guyon.

Bowley, Sir Joseph, M.P., in Dickens's short story, *The Chimes*, endeavors to educate the poor man in his district with the "one great moral lesson" he needs—"entire dependence on myself."

Bowling, Tom, a heroic naval lieutenant in Smollett's novel, *Roderick Random.*

Bowling, Tom, the hero of a famous song by Charles Dibdin.

Box, one of the characters in J. M. Morton's "dramatic romance of real life," *Box and Cox.*

Boy Bishop, The, a name applied to St. Nicholas (fourth century) for his early piety.

Boy Preacher, The, an appellation given to Crammond Kennedy (b. 1842), who made religious addresses as early as 1857; and to Joshua Soule (Methodist Episcopal bishop, 1781–1867), who was preaching when he was seventeen.

Boyet, a lord attending on the Princess of France in Shakespeare's *Love's Labor's Lost.*

Boythorn, Lawrence, in Dickens's *Bleak House*, a loud, impetuous, warm-hearted, handsome old gentleman, said to be intended as a portrait of Walter Savage Landor.

Boz, the pseudonym used by Charles Dickens in the *Sketches by Boz*, which were his first attempts at authorship. He says it was the pet name of his younger brother Augustus, whom he called Moses in honor of the Vicar of Wakefield, "which, being facetiously pronounced through the nose, became Boses, and, being shortened, became Bōz.

Bozzarris, Marco, subject of a poem by Fitz-Greene Halleck.

Brabantio, a Venetian senator in Shakespeare's *Othello*, father of Desdemona.

Braccio, a character in Robert Browning's drama, *Luria*, employed by the Florentine government to find out something to the discredit of Luria, in which he fails.

Bridge of Gold, a traditionary bridge across the Rhine at Bingen, on which Charlemagne's spirit crosses to bless the fields and vineyards.

Bridgenorth, Major Ralph, and **Alice,** his daughter, who is the heroine, characters in Scott's *Peveril of the Peak.*

Briennius, Nicephorus, a Byzantine nobleman, who married the celebrated Anna Comnena, character in Scott's *Count Robert of Paris.*

Brisetout, Héloïse, a literary young woman, elegant and gracious, at one time a *danseuse* in a theater—a character in Balzac's *Cousin Bette, Cousin Pons,* and *The Middle Classes.*

Brisk, Fastidious (1599), "a neat, spruce, affecting courtier, who swears tersely and with variety," in Jonson's *Every Man Out of His Humor.*

Britain, Benjamin, called Little Britain in Dickens's short story, *The Battle of Life;* a small man, who summarized his condition as follows: "I don't know anything; I don't care for anything; I don't make out anything; I don't believe anything; and I don't want anything."

Britannicus, the son of Claudius and Messalina, poisoned by Nero, A.D. 55. He is the subject of a tragedy by Racine (1669).

Britannus, Cæsar's British secretary in George B. Shaw's play, *Cæsar and Cleopatra.*

British Aristides, The, Andrew Marvell (1620–1678), poet and patriot.

Britomartis, or **Britomart,** in Spenser's *The Faerie Queene,* represents chastity. Having fallen in love with the image of Sir Artegal in her magic mirror, and having been told by Merlin that she was to be the mother of a line of kings, and that after eight hundred years a royal virgin of her line would shake the power of Spain, she set out in quest of Sir Artegal in the armor of Angela and armed with her magic spear.

Brittany, The Eagle of, Bertrand du Guesclin (d. 1380).

Broadbent, a civil engineer in George Bernard Shaw's play, *John Bull's Other Island.*

Brobdingnag, the country of the giants in Swift's *Gulliver's Travels.*

Broceliande, a great forest in Brittany where the wizard Merlin lived, now the forest of Paimpont.

Brocken, The Specter of the, a magnified reflection from the mists about the highest mountain of the Hartz range, which looks like a gigantic figure.

Brocklehurst, Rev. Mr., the pompous director of Lowood school in Charlotte Brontë's novel, *Jane Eyre.*

Bronckhorst, Paul, the hero and title of a novel by Levin Schücking.

Bronckhorst, Teddy, the brutal husband in Kipling's story, *The Bronckhorst Divorce Case.*

Brook Farm, Roxbury, Mass., the site of the communistic experiment where the scene of Hawthorne's *Blithedale Romance* is laid.

Brooke, Dorothea, the heroine of George Eliot's novel, *Middlemarch;* **Celia,** her sister.

Brother Jonathan, a name applied to the American nation. It is said to have originated with Washington, who, when greatly in want of army supplies after he was appointed commander-in-chief, said, "We must consult Brother Jonathan," meaning Jonathan Trumbull, Governor of Connecticut. As Trumbull found a way out of some of the difficulties, "We must consult Brother Jonathan" was a common saying when difficulties arose in the army, and became a general byword, losing its original signification in the course of time and being applied to the whole people. Brother Jonathan is represented with striped trousers, a swallow-tailed coat, and an old-fashioned "stovepipe" hat. Another derivation suggested for the name is from Jonathan Carver (d. 1780), who received large grants of lands from the Indians, in the deeds for which he was called "our dear Brother Jonathan." His account of his American travels was published in London; so that it is quite possible that the name might have been taken up in England and applied to Americans in general. Again, there is some evidence to show that the title was applied to the Roundheads or Puritans in the seventeenth century, an old pamphlet (1643) speaking of Brother Jonathan "before he abjured the University or had a thought of New England."

Brother Sam, a brother of Lord Dundreary, in Tom Taylor's comedy, *Our American Cousin,* and title of an older play adapted from a German drama. See SAM.

Brown, one of three conceited, snobbish English travelers, Brown, Jones, and Robinson, whose adventures, by Richard Doyle, were published in *Punch.*

Brown, Adam, the hero of a ballad in Scott's *Border Minstrelsy.*

Brown, Sally, the heroine of Hood's poem, *Faithless Sally Brown.*

Brown, Tom, the hero of Thomas Hughes's *Tom Brown at Rugby* and *Tom Brown at Oxford.*

Brown, Valentine, the chief character of Barrie's play, *Quality Street.*

Brownie, in Scottish folk-lore, a family spirit and helper, like Robin Goodfellow.

Brownie of Blednoch, The, subject of a ballad by W. Nicholson (d. 1849), *The Galloway Poet.*

Brownlow, Mr., an old gentleman who rescues Oliver from his life among thieves in Dickens's *Oliver Twist.*

Bruce, Robert, King Robert I of Scotland, hero of a historical poem of about fourteen thousand lines, *The Bruce,* by John Barbour (1316–1396). Robert Bruce is one of the heroes of Jane Porter's story, *The Scottish Chiefs* (1810).

Bruel, the name of a family in Balzac's novels, *A Bachelor's Establishment, A Start in Life, The Middle Classes, A Distinguished Provincial at Paris,* and others. Du Bruel was chief of division to the Ministers of the Interior under the Empire. His wife was the mother of the dramatic author, Jean-François du Bruel, and though a "*bourgeoise* of strict ideas," welcomed a dancer of doubtful character, Claudine Chaffaroux, called Tullia, as her son's wife. Jean-François rose, through the influence of his wife, to be chief of bureau, director, councillor of state, deputy, peer of France, and commander of the Legion of Honor. He wrote vaudeville sketches over the name Cursy, and collaborated with Nathan, the poet, taking his ideas and "condensing them into small, sprightly skits that always scored successes for the actors.

Bruin, Bridget, a character in William Butler Yeats's poetic drama, *The Land of Heart's Desire.* Marie Bruin, her son's wife, is lured away by dreams of fairies.

Brummel, Beau. See BEAU BRUMMEL.

Brunehild, Brunhild, or **Brynhilda,** in *The Nibelungenlied*, a warrior woman who promised to marry the man that could surpass her in hurling the lance, throwing a stone, and leaping after the stone. Siegfried by his invisible cloak was able to help his friend Guenther, himself unseen, so that she was beaten. When she discovered the deception she revenged herself upon Siegfried and his wife Chriemhild. There are varying versions of the story.

Brunellus, an ass, the hero of an old Latin satire, *Speculum Stultorum*, by Nigelus Wireker (about 1190). Brunellus is intended to represent the monks; he is discontented with his condition and goes forth to seek a better one and a longer tail. Deciding to become a monk, he examines one monastic order after another, but is not suited with any. At length he is discovered by his owner and compelled to return to his condition of servitude with a still shorter tail.

Brunhilde, a singer in the novel (1891) of her name, by Pedro Antonio de Alarcon.

Bruno, Bishop of Herbipolitanum, the hero of Southey's ballad, *Bishop Bruns*, founded on an old tradition, was traveling with the Emperor Henry III of Germany, when he heard a spirit voice: "Ho! ho! Bishop Bruno, whither art thou traveling? But go thy ways, Bishop Bruno, for thou shalt travel with me to-night." And when he was feasting with the Emperor that night, a rafter fell upon his head and killed him. Southey's version varies somewhat.

Brut, Brute, or **Brutus,** a mythical king of Britain, whose story is told by Geoffrey of Monmouth, Drayton, and Spenser. He was the great-great-grandson of Æneas of Troy, and, having to fly from Alba Longa in consequence of having killed his father accidentally, he reached England with his followers and founded London, which he called Troynovant—New Troy.

Brutus, Junius, name given to James Lynch Fitz Stephen because he condemned his son to death for murder and, in order to prevent a rescue, had him executed from a window of his own house in Galway.

Brutus, Lucius Junius, first Consul of Rome, who condemned his two sons to death for having joined in a conspiracy to restore Tarquin to the throne. He himself had been one of the leaders in the expulsion of the Tarquins. He is the subject of a tragedy entitled *Lucius Junius Brutus*, by Nathaniel Lee (1679) and one with the same title by H. Duncombe (1784); also *Brutus : or, The Fall of Tarquin*, by John Howard Payne (1820); *Junius Brutus*, by Alfieri (1783); and *Junius Brutus*, by Andrieux (1828).

Brutus, Marcus, one of the slayers of Cæsar, and the most important character in Shakespeare's tragedy, *Julius Cæsar.* His character, as Shakespeare intended it, has been a puzzle to critics; but Dowden's view of it seems most reasonable. He says Brutus "acts as an idealist and theorizer might, with no eye for the actual bearing of facts, and no sense of the true importance of persons. Intellectual doctrines and moral ideas rule the life of Brutus; and his life is most noble, high, and stainless; but his public action is a series of practical mistakes. . . . He fails to see how full of power Antony is, because Antony loves pleasure, and is not a Stoic like himself; he addresses calm arguments to the excited Roman mob; he spares the life of Antony and allows him to address the people; he advises ill in military matters." He is the subject of a tragedy by Alfieri, *Marcus Brutus* (1783), one by Chénier, *Brutus and Cassius*, and of *The Conspiracy of Brutus* by Antoni (1691).

Brutus, The Spanish, an appellation of Alfonso Perez de Guzman, Governor of Tarifa in 1293, who sacrificed his son rather than surrender to the besiegers.

Bubble Act, the popular name of an act passed by the English Parliament in 1819 and repealed in 1825, designed to punish the promoters of fraudulent speculative schemes, popularly called bubbles.

Bubenburg, Sir Adrian de, a veteran knight of Berne, in Scott's *Anne of Geierstein.*

Bucentaur, a monster half ox and half human. The name of the galley of the doges of Venice in which they went to wed the Adriatic.

Bucephalus, the famous horse of Alexander the Great, who built the city Bucephala in its honor.

Bucket, Mr. Inspector, a sagacious detective in Dickens's *Bleak House.* "Time and place cannot bind Mr. Bucket. Like man in the abstract, he is here to-day and gone to-morrow; but, very unlike man indeed, he is here again the next day." Mrs. Bucket had the makings of a detective in her, but her genius had not been cultivated. He is supposed to have been drawn from Inspector Field, a friend of Dickens and subject of one of his sketches.

Buckingham, Edward Stafford, Duke of, character in Shakespeare's *Henry VIII*. He calls himself Edward Bohun, being descended from the Bohuns. He was executed for treason in 1521.

Buckingham, George Villiers, Duke of, a favorite of James I of England, assassinated in 1628, a character in Scott's *The Fortunes of Nigel*. His son, George Villiers, a favorite of Charles II, is a character in Scott's *Peveril of the Peak*. He figures as Zimri in Dryden's *Absalom and Achitophel*.

Buckingham, Henry Stafford, Duke of, father of the preceding—a character in Shakespeare's *Richard III*. He was a friend of Richard, but became disaffected, headed a revolt, and was executed in 1483.

Buckler, Maurice, the hero of A. E. W. Mason's novel, *The Courtship of Maurice Buckler*.

Buddha, the founder of Buddhism, the Hindu sage Gautama, an incarnation of Vishnu, used also as a name for his prototypes and successors, of whom there are many. Gautama is called also Siddartha (*q.v.*).

Bull, John, a nickname for the English nation. John Bull is pictured as a sturdy, corpulent old fellow, with a three-cornered hat, red waistcoat, leather breeches, and stout oaken cudgel. The name was first used in a political satire (1713) by Dr. John Arbuthnot (*The History of John Bull*), intended to ridicule the Duke of Marlborough, who is called Humphrey Hocus, the lawyer in a suit between John Bull and Mr. Frog (Holland) on one side, and Lord Strutt (Philip, Duke of Anjou) on the other. France is referred to as Lewis Baboon. Lord Lytton wrote *Letters to John Bull, Esq., on the Management of His Landed Estates* (1851).

Bull, John, the hero and name of a comedy by George Colman the Younger.

Bullamy, in Dickens's *Martin Chuzzlewit*, is the porter of the "Anglo Bengalee Disinterested Loan and Life Company."

His red waistcoat inspired clients with confidence in the company. "Respectability, competence, property in Bengal or anywhere else; responsibility to any amount on the part of the company that employed him, were all expressed in that one garment."

Bullivant, Dr., the subject of a sketch by Nathaniel Hawthorne.

Bultitude, Paul and **Dick,** father and son in Anstey's novel, *Vice Versa.*

Bumble, Mr., an overbearing beadle in Dickens's *Oliver Twist.*

Bumppo, Natty, the name of Hawkeye the woodsman, in Cooper's novel, *The Deerslayer.*

Bunduca, a warrior-woman of Britain in Spenser's *The Faerie Queene.*

Bungay, Friar, one of the heroes of Richard Greene's Comedy, *Friar Bacon and Friar Bungay.*

Bungen, the street in Hamelin down which the Pied Piper of Browning's poem led the children to the mountain. No music is permitted to be played in that street, it is said.

Bunthorne, an esthetic youth in Gilbert's comic opera, *Patience,* said to be a caricature of Oscar Wilde in the early days of his "preciosity."

Bunting, the name of the piper in *The Pied Piper of Hamelin,* a poem by Robert Browning.

Burchell, Mr. See THORNHILL.

Burd, Helen, the heroine of an old Scotch song.

Burgh, Hubert de. See HUBERT.

Burgundy, Duke of, in Shakespeare's *King Lear,* a suitor for Cordelia, who withdraws when she is disinherited—called "waterish Burgundy."

Burgundy, Charles the Bold, Duke of, is introduced in Scott's *Quentin Durward* and also in *Anne of Geierstein.*

Burgundy, Philip the Good, Duke of, a character in Shakespeare's *Henry V* and *Henry VI,* where he is represented as won to the cause of the Dauphin by Joan of Arc.

Buridan, is referred to in Villon's *Ballad of Dead Ladies*—

> "Who willed that Buridan should steer
> Sewed in a sack's mouth down the Seine."

Buridan's Ass is used for a man of indecision, in reference to the problem of Buridan, the scholastic, who said that if a hungry donkey were placed between two bundles of hay of the same size and equal in every respect and equally distant from him, he would starve, not being able to decide between them.

Burleigh, Lord, in Sheridan's farce, *The Critic;* a character of Mr. Puff's tragedy, *The Spanish Armada,* "who could cram a whole complicated sentence into an expressive shake of his head."

Burleigh, William Cecil, Lord, Lord Treasurer to Queen Elizabeth, a character in Scott's *Kenilworth* and in Henry Jones's tragedy, *The Earl of Essex.*

Burley, a character in Bulwer's story, *My Novel,* "never sober, never solvent, but always genial and witty."

Burnbill, a name given to Henry de Londres, Archbishop of Dublin and Lord Justice of Ireland in the reign of Henry III, who was accused of burning all the bills by which the tenants of the archepiscopal lands held their estates, which he had fraudulently obtained.

Burnet, Governor, of Massachusetts, appears in Hawthorne's stories, *Howe's Masquerade* and also *The Prophetic Pictures.*

Burning Pestle, Knight of the, hero of Beaumont's burlesque comedy of the name.

Burns, Helen, a pupil at Lowood in Charlotte Brontë's novel, *Jane Eyre,* a portrait of Maria Brontë, the author's sister, who died of consumption at an early age.

Burton, Arthur, in *The Gadfly,* by Ethel Lillian Voynich, returns to Europe from South America under the name of Felice Rivarez, and is called "the Gadfly" on account of his stinging sarcasms in political writings and speeches.

Busiris, the mythical king that sacrificed all strangers coming into his kingdom; he is the subject of a tragedy by Edward Young, *Busiris, King of Egypt* (1719). Milton gives the name to the Pharaoh that was drowned in the Red Sea.

Busqueue, Lord, plaintiff in a lawsuit in the *Pantagruel* (1533) of Rabelais. His learned plea and that of the defendant were both unintelligible to the judge, who, however, rendered a verdict that satisfied them both, as each felt that he had won his case.

Butcher, The, name applied to Achmet Pacha, who struck off the heads of seven of his wives at once. The name is applied also to John, ninth Lord Clifford (d. 1461), also called the Black Clifford. Oliver de Clisson, Constable of France (1320–1407), earned the name by his cruelties.

Butcher of England, The, John Tiptoft, Earl of Worcester (d. 1470), noted for his learning and as a patron of learning. He impaled forty Lancastrian prisoners and put to death the infant children of the Irish chief, Desmond.

Butler, the name of a family in Scott's *The Heart of Midlothian*, one of whom, Reuben, a Presbyterian minister, is married to Jeanie Deans.

Buttercup, Little, a character in Gilbert and Sullivan's comic opera, *H. M. S. Pinafore.*

Butterfly, Madame, heroine of a story of the name by John Luther Long, dramatized by the author and David Belasco. An opera founded upon it has music by Giacomo Puccini.

Buzfuz, Serjeant, in Dickens's *The Pickwick Papers,* is the counsel for Mrs. Bardell in her action for breach of promise against Mr. Pickwick. He is said to be intended for a caricature of Serjeant Bumpus, a lawyer in London at the time *The Pickwick Papers* appeared.

Buzzard, The, in Dryden's *The Hind and the Panther,* is said to have been intended for Dr. Gilbert Burnet.

Bycorne, a fabulous monster that fed on good and enduring husbands; in the old ballad where it is described there is another beast, Chichevache, that fed on good and patient wives. Bycorne was fat to bursting; Chichevache was lean and hungry. It is alluded to in Chaucer's *The Clerke's Tale.*

Byron, Cashel, a prize-fighter, hero of George Bernard Shaw's novel, *Cashel Byron's Profession,* which has been dramatized by Stanislaus Stange. The author published with the novel a dramatic version in blank verse.

Byron, Harriet, a beautiful woman, the heroine of Richardson's novel, *Sir Charles Grandison.*

Caàba, the shrine of Mecca on the spot to which, in Arabian tradition, the Tabernacle was let down from heaven at the prayer of Adam, when he was pardoned after two hundred years of wandering. The stone, once white, was turned black by the kisses of penitents. The shrine was built by Ishmael, and the stone was given by Gabriel to Abraham, who built it into the wall.

Cade, Jack, the leader of a rebellion in England, in 1450, a character in Shakespeare's *Henry VI* (Part II), where he takes possession of London by striking his staff on London stone.

Cadenus, an anagram of *decanus* (dean), applied to himself by Dean Swift in the poem, *Cadenus and Vanessa* (*q.v.*).

Cadet Roussel, a typical simpleton, popularized by a French song.

Cadignan, Prince de, a powerful lord of the old régime, introduced in Balzac's novel, *Modeste Mignon.*

Cadine, Jenny, a frolicsome actress in Balzac's *Cousin Bette, Beatrix,* and *The Member for Arcis.*

Cadwallader, Mr., the rector in George Eliot's novel, *Middlemarch,* who was so good-tempered that he "even spoke well of his bishop."

Cadwalton, a bard in Scott's novel, *The Betrothed,* also known as Renault Vidal.

Cæsar, Don, de Bazan, a character in Hugo's play, *Ruy Blas,* and the hero of the play bearing his name by Dumanoir and D'Ennery, and of two adaptations of the latter in English, *Don Cæsar's Return,* by Victor Mapes, and *A Royal Rival,* by Gerald du Maurier. An opera based upon his adventures is entitled *Maritana.*

Cæsar, Julius, is the subject of Shakespeare's play of the name (see BRUTUS, CASSIUS, ANTONY) and of George Bernard Shaw's *Cæsar and Cleopatra,* giving a quaint and original conception of his character—unpretending, far-seeing, and consenting to cruelty only when no other means will serve the common good.

Cæsar, Octavius, is a character in Shakespeare's *Julius Cæsar* and *Antony and Cleopatra.*

Cagliostro, Count de, the assumed name of Joseph Balsamo, the subject of the novel of the name by Dumas, who introduces him in other of his novels.

Cain, the subject of Byron's dramatic poem, *Cain: a Mystery,* and of Coleridge's prose-poem, *The Wanderings of Cain.*

Calchas, a Trojan priest, Cressida's father, and a character in Shakespeare's *Troilus and Cressida,* also in Chaucer's *Troylus and Cryseyde.*

Calderon, the hero of Bulwer's historical romance, *Calderon the Courtier.*

Calenders, The Three, are princes in the *Arabian Nights,* who disguised themselves as "calenders," that is, wandering and begging devotees.

Caliban, a deformed monster, the slave of Prospero in Shakespeare's *The Tempest,* and subject of Browning's poem, *Caliban upon Setebos.*

Calidore, the hero of a fragmentary poem by Keats.

Calidore, Sir, the hero of the sixth book of Spenser's *The Faerie Queene,* said to have been modeled after Sir Philip Sydney.

Caligorant, a gigantic Egyptian cannibal in Ariosto's *Orlando Furioso.*

Calino, a French vaudeville character, whose name has become proverbial for a simpleton.

Calipolis, a character in Peele's play, *The Battle of Alcazar,* referred to in *Henry IV,* Part II.

Calista, a character in Rowe's *The Fair Penitent,* whose intrigue with Lothario causes a duel between him and Altamont, her fiancé.

Callaghan O'Brallaghan. See O'BRALLAGHAN.

Callirrhoë, the heroine of *The Loves of Chæreas and Callirrhoë,* a Greek romance of the eighth century by Chariton.

Calmody, Sir Richard, the subject of a novel by Lucas Malet (Mrs. Harrison), pen-name of a daughter of Charles Kingsley. Sir Richard is a cripple, who succeeds, despite grotesque deformity, in winning the love of women.

Calverley, a gamester in *The Yorkshire Tragedy,* which was at one time attributed to Shakespeare.

Calvo, Baldassare, a character in George Eliot's novel, *Romola.*

Calydon, in Ætolia, where Meleager and Atalanta slew the Calydonian boar.

Calydon, a forest in the northern part of Great Britain, celebrated in the Arthurian romances.

Calypso, in mythology the queen of the island Ogygia, supposed to be Gozo, near Malta. Calypso, in Fénelon's *Télémaque,* is said to be intended for Madame de Montespan.

Camacho, in Cervantes's *Don Quixote,* the richest of men, who is cheated of his bride Quiteria, fairest of women, by Basilius.

Camaralzaman, a prince, hero of many love adventures, in the *Arabian Nights.*

Cambuscan, or **Cambyuscan,** King of Sarra, in Tartary, a character in Chaucer's *The Squire's Tale,* to whom the King of Araby and Ind sent a brazen horse, a glass mirror, a sword, and a ring, all with magic properties.

Cambyses, the hero of a play by Thomas Preston, *A Lamentable Tragedy conteyning the Life of Cambyses, King of Persia.* King Cambyses Vein is alluded to in Shakespeare's *Henry IV,* Part I.

Cameliard, in Arthurian legend, the realm of Guinevere's father.

Camelot, in Arthurian romance, has been supposed to be the town of Winchester by some; others make it Queen's Camel in Somersetshire. Camelot, referred to in *King Lear,* may be the latter, or Camelford, in Cornwall.

Cameristus, a celebrated physician, a character in Balzac's *The Magic Skin.*

Camilla, a maiden queen of the Volscians, famous for her swiftness and lightness in running.

Camilla, the heroine of a novel of the name by Fanny Burney.

Camille, sister of the Horatii, a character in Corneille's tragedy, *Les Horaces;* she is killed by her brother for weeping for her lover, one of the Curiatii. She is a character also in Whitehead's drama, *The Roman Father.*

Camille. See GAULTIER, MARGUERITE.

Camillo, a lord of Sicilia in Shakespeare's *A Winter's Tale,* the protector of Perdita, the lost child of Queen Hermione.

Camors, an aristocrat and free-thinker, in Feuillet's novel of the time of the Second Empire, *Monsieur de Camors.*

Campaspe, the heroine of Lyly's drama, *Cupid and Campaspe.*

Campbell, Sir Duncan, Sir Duncan of Auchembreek and Murdoch (Marquis of Argyle), character in Scott's *The Legend of Montrose.*

Campeador. See CID.

Camper, Lady Angela, and **Sir Scrope,** characters in George Meredith's story, *The Case of General Ople and Lady Camper.*

Campsius (Lawrence Campeggio), a cardinal and legate in Shakespeare's *Henry VIII.*

Campo-Basso, The Count of, an officer in Scott's *Quentin Durward,* also in *Anne of Geierstein.*

Camwell, Augustus, a character in George Meredith's *The Tale of Chloe.*

Canacë, in Chaucer's *The Squire's Tale,* the daughter of King Cambuscan, had a ring enabling her to talk with birds and understand the medicinal properties of all roots.

She appears also in Spenser's *The Faerie Queene,* where her suitors had to meet her brother Cambalo in single combat; he was at length defeated by Triamond.

Canalis, Baron, a poet, chief of "the angelic school" in several of the novels of Balzac's *Comédie Humaine.*

Candida. See MORELL, CANDIDA.

Candide, hero of Voltaire's novel of the name, where he "exposes to eternal ridicule the famous maxim of Leibnitz: 'All is for the best in the best of all possible worlds.'"

Candiola, Maraquilla, the heroine of *Saragossa,* by Galdos.

Candour, Mrs., a character in Sheridan's comedy, *The School for Scandal,* whose name has become a synonym for an ill-natured gossip.

Cantwell, Dr., a canting swindler, the hero of Bickerstaff's comedy, *The Hypocrite,* after Molière's *Tartuffe.*

Canty, Tom, one of the characters of Mark Twain's *The Prince and the Pauper.* He changes clothes with the boyish King Edward VI, and reigns for a few weeks.

Canynge, Sir William, a rich and liberal merchant in Chatterton's story, *The Rowley Romance.*

Capability Brown, a name applied to Lancelot Brown, an English landscape gardener, not only for his professional genius, but also on account of his continual use of the word.

Capechi, Cavalieri, the wicked brother of Lauretta in Shorthouse's story, *John Inglesant.*

Capella, Bianca, the wife of Cosmo de' Medici, a character in Lady Lytton's novel of the name.

Capitan, a personage of Italian comedy, type of the swaggerer.

Caponsacchi, Giuseppe, the noble young priest in Robert Browning's poem, *The Ring and the Book.*

Capperston, Sir Walter, a character in George Meredith's *Diana of the Crossways.*

Captain Rock, a name under which orders were sent to Irish insurgents about 1822, standing for all of the leaders. *Captain Right* was previously used in a similar way.

Capucius, Eustachius, an ambassador from Charles V in Shakespeare's *Henry VIII.*

Capulet, name of the family of Juliet, at feud with the Montagues in Shakespeare's *Romeo and Juliet.* The Capelletti and the Monticoli were rival families of Verona in centuries XIII–XIV.

Capys, a blind prophet, who foretells the glories of Rome to Romulus, in Macaulay's *Lays of Ancient Rome.*

Carabas, Marquis of, a name occurring in Perrault's *Puss in Boots,* but introduced into a song by Béranger as the title of a bragging aristocrat.

Caractacus, a British king carried captive to Rome in 51 A.D. He is introduced in a play by Beaumont and Fletcher, afterward converted into a pantomimic spectacle; and William Mason was author of a tragedy bearing his name, of which Caratach is one form.

Caradoc, or **Cradock, Sir,** a knight of the Round Table, celebrated in the ballad, *The Boy and the Mantle* in Percy's *Reliques.*

Carathis, in Beckford's *Vathek,* the wicked mother of the Caliph.

Carbonek, a castle containing the Grail, described by Lancelot in Tennyson's idyl, *The Holy Grail.* See GRAALBURG.

Carew, Lydia, the heroine of Shaw's novel, *Cashel Byron's Profession,* a great heiress, cultivated and clever.

Carewe, Betty, the heroine of Tarkington's *The Two Van Revels.*

Carlisle, Lady, one of the chief characters of Browning's *Strafford.*

Carlisle, Lady Mary, the heroine of Tarkington's *Monsieur Beaucaire.*

Carlo Khan, a nickname given to Charles James Fox, on account of a bill he introduced in Parliament that gave rise to a suspicion that he aimed at being a dictator in Eastern affairs.

Carlos, Don, the deformed son of Philip II of Portugal, who joined the Netherlanders against his father in revenge for his exclusion from the succession. His career is the subject of tragedies by Otway, by Campistron, and Chenier in French, Schiller in German, and Alfieri in Italian.

Carlyle, Archibald, and his wife, **Lady Isabel,** the chief characters of Mrs. Henry Wood's novel, *East Lynne,* and the play founded upon it.

Carmen, a Spanish gipsy, the heroine of the opera of the name by Georges Bizet, the book by Meilhac and Halévy. It is taken from Prosper Mérimée's novel, *Carmen.*

Carmen Sylva, the pseudonym of Queen Elizabeth of Rumania.

Carmichael, Allan, the hero of Fiona Macleod's *Green Fire,* first known as De Kerival.

Carmilhan, a phantom ship which appears to doomed vessels with a kobold, Klabotermann, sitting on the bowsprit.

Carnaby, Isabel, the heroine of a novel by Ellen Thorneycroft Fowler.

Caroline, queen consort of George II, introduced in Scott's novel, *The Heart of Midlothian.*

Carrillo, Fray, referred to in Longfellow's poem, *The Spanish Student.* The only place where he never was to be found was his own cell.

Carrington, Louisa, character in George Meredith's novel, *Evan Harrington.*

Carstone, Richard, a lovable character in Dickens's *Bleak House,* who is ruined by the delays of a suit in Chancery.

Cartaphilus, the name, according to some accounts, of the Wandering Jew.

Carter, Mr., the recounter in Anthony Hope's *The Dolly Dialogues,* an adept in all the arts, humors, and possible rascalities of a rake of the eighteenth century, living a happy and harmless life in the moral atmosphere of the Victorian era.

Carthew, Mrs., a character in George Meredith's *The Amazing Marriage.*

Carton, Sydney, a noble character in Dickens's *Tale of Two Cities,* who died for his friend, Charles Darnay, and in the drama, *The Only Way,* by Freeman Wills.

Cartwright, Philip, a clergyman in Ellen Thorneycroft Fowler's novel, *A Double Thread.*

Carvel, Richard, the subject of a novel of the time of the American Revolution, by Winston Churchill.

Carvel, Virginia, the heroine of *The Crisis,* a novel by Winston Churchill, and of a drama with the same name.

Caryl, Edward, a young lawyer and writer in Hawthorne's story, *The Antique Ring.*

Casabianca, a French naval officer who with his son perished at the battle of Aboukir, 1798. The son is the subject of a well-known poem by Felicia Hemans.

Casa Guidi, a house in Florence occupied by Elizabeth Barrett Browning, which gave the name to her poems on events in Italian history, under the general title of *Casa Guidi Windows.*

Casamassiana, Princess, the subject of a novel by Henry James.

Casaubon, Rev. Edward, the pedantic and selfish husband of Dorothea Brooke in George Eliot's *Middlemarch,* who married her in order to have an interested secretary in his futile literary endeavors.

Casca, "the envious," one of the conspirators against Cæsar, a character in Shakespeare's *Julius Cæsar.*

Caschcasch, a horned hunchback in the *Arabian Nights,* who was asked to be a judge of beauty.

Casella, a musician and friend of Dante, who met him in Purgatory and asked him to sing; and he complied, singing Dante's own second *canzone.*

Caspar, the tempter of Max in Weber's opera, *Der Freischütz,* who has sold himself to Samiel (or Zamiel), the Black Huntsman.

Cass, Godfrey, a character in George Eliot's *Silas Marner.*

Cassandra, a daughter of Priam, a prophetess doomed to be never believed, introduced in Shakespeare's *Troilus and Cressida.*

Cassibelan, or **Cassivelaun,** King of Britain at the time of Cæsar's invasion, mentioned in Shakespeare's *Cymbeline.*

Cassio, Michael, lieutenant in Shakespeare's *Othello,* against whom Iago arouses Othello's jealousy regarding Desdemona.

Cassius, Caius, friend and brother-in-law of Brutus and instigator of the conspiracy against Cæsar. In Shakespeare's *Julius Cæsar* he is represented as influenced partly by patriotism and partly by envy.

Castaly, The Fount of, a spring at the foot of Mount Parnassus, whose waters gave poetic inspiration. Castalia was the nymph of the spring.

Castara, a name given to Lucy Herbert in her husband's, William Habington's, collection of poems, entitled *Castara.*

Castine, Baron, the French noble who married the daughter of a Penobscot chief, is the subject of a poem in Longfellow's *Tales of a Wayside Inn.*

Castle Perilous, the prison of Lady Lionês or Lyonors, in the Arthurian stories; a version is given in Tennyson's *Gareth and Lynette.*

Castlewood, Beatrix, the daughter of Colonel Francis Esmond; **Lord Castlewood,** and **Lady Rachel.** Her mother is the heroine of Thackeray's *Henry Esmond.*

Castracani, Castruccio: the giving of his sword to Victor Emmanuel is the subject of Mrs. Browning's poem, *The Sword of Castruccio Castracani.*

Catesby, Sir William, a partizan of York in Shakespeare's *Richard III,* executed after Bosworth by order of Henry VII. See COLLINGBOURNE.

Catgut, Dr., in Samuel Foote's *The Commissary,* is said to be a caricature of Dr. Arne.

Cathcart, Barton, the hero of Henry Ward Beecher's only novel, *Norwood.*

Catherick, Anne, the heroine of Wilkie Collins's novel, *The Woman in White.*

Catherine, the queen of Charles II, introduced in Scott's *Peveril of the Peak.*

Catherine, a murderess whose story was written by Thackeray to protest against the sentimental sympathy felt for criminals, by showing them without any false glamour.

Catherine de' Medici is a character in Dumas's *Marguerite de Valois*, *Chicot the Jester*, and some of his other novels, and in Balzac's novel of that name and Swinburne's tragedy, *The Queen-Mother*. See CECROPIA.

Catiline, the chief of a revolutionary conspiracy in Rome discovered by Cicero, the subject of Ben Jonson's tragedy, *Catiline*, and a character in Voltaire's *Rome Sauvée;* Crébillon also wrote a tragedy, *Catiline*, and Stephen Gosson a play, *Catiline's Conspiracies*.

Catius, the name under which Charles Dartineuf, said to be a "celebrated glutton," is alluded to in Pope's *Moral Essays*, as preferring "a rogue with venison to a rogue without."

Cato, of Utica, the subject of Addison's tragedy, *Cato*. He appears in the fifth act of Shakespeare's *Julius Cæsar*.

Caudle, Margaret, in Douglas Jerrold's *The Caudle Papers*, in *Punch*, gave her meek husband, Job, a curtain lecture every night for thirty years.

Cauline, Sir, hero of a ballad in Percy's *Reliques*.

Caustic, Christopher, a pseudonym of T. G. Fessenden, author of a Hudibrastic poem, *Terrible Tractoration*.

Cavalier, an imaginary character whose "history" was written by De Foe with an extraordinary air of verisimilitude.

Cavall, spoken of in Tennyson's *Enid* as "Arthur's hound of deepest mouth."

Cawdor, Thane of, a rebel who is executed and his title given to Macbeth by Duncan, in Shakespeare's tragedy, *Macbeth*.

Caxton, Pisistratus, the hero of Bulwer's novel, *The Caxtons*, and the name under which Bulwer wrote *My Novel* and the papers called *Caxtoniana*.

Cayenne, Mr., a Virginian gentleman who leaves his home on account of his loyalist principles, in John Galt's *Annals of the Parish*.

Cecil, the hero of Catherine Gore's novel of London club-life, *Cecil: or, The Adventures of a Coxcomb*.

Cecil, Bertie, the hero of Ouida's novel, *Under Two Flags*, who serves under the French flag in Africa, after leaving England under suspicion of crime.

Cecil's Fast, an act of Parliament introduced by Cecil, Lord Burleigh, to promote the fish-trade by enjoining the eating of fish on certain days because the Reformation had reduced the consumption of fish.

Cecilia, the heroine of Fanny Burney's novel of the name.

Cecilia, St.: her story is told by the Second Nun in Chaucer's *Canterbury Tales*. Odes for her festival were written by Dryden, Addison, and Pope, with music by Handel, Purcell, and Maurice Greene, respectively.

Cecropia, in Sir Philip Sidney's *Arcadia*, cruel, deceitful, and bloody, is supposed to be intended for Catherine de' Medici.

Cedric, thane of Rotherwood, in Scott's *Ivanhoe*, called "the Saxon."

Celadon, in an episode in Thomson's *Seasons*, the lover of Amelia, who is killed in his arms by a stroke of lightning.

Celadon, a character in D'Urfé's romance, *Astrée*. The name is a synonym for a constant but timid lover.

Celia, the cousin and friend of Rosalind in Shakespeare's *As You Like It*.

Celimène, a coquette in Molière's *The Misanthrope*, remarkable for her caustic tongue.

Cenci, Beatrice. See BEATRICE.

Censor of the Age, The, a title applied to Thomas Carlyle.

Century White, a sobriquet of John White, whose chief work was *The First Century of Scandalous Malignant Priests* (1590–1645).

Cerdon, a leader of the rabble in Butler's *Hudibras;* the original of the character was said to be a cobbler preacher named Hewson, who was a colonel in the Parliamentary army.

Cerimon, in Shakespeare's *Pericles, Prince of Tyre*, is a lord of Ephesus, "master of the secrets of nature," who restored Thaisa, supposed to be dead.

Certainpersonio, Prince, the bridegroom of Alicia in Alice Rainbird's story in Dickens's juvenile novel, *A Holiday Romance*.

Cesario, a name assumed by Viola in Shakespeare's *Twelfth Night.*

Chabót, Philippe de, Admiral of France, falsely accused of dishonesty, the subject of a tragedy by Chapman and Shirley.

Chadband, Rev. Mr., an unctuous hypocrite in Dickens's *Bleak House.*

Chaffington, Percy, M.P., a stock-broker in J. M. Morton's *If I Had a Thousand a Year.*

Chalkstone, Lord, a character played by David Garrick in his own drama, *Lethe* (1743).

Challoner, Lady Joan, the principal character in Ouida's novel, *Friendship,* a strong, passionate, clever, vile woman, said to be intended for an intimate friend of the author, who wrote the story in revenge for having her lover stolen from her.

Cham, a pseudonym of Count Amédée de Noé, a caricaturist of *Charivari.* He was the second son of the Count de Noé (Noah) as Cham (Ham) was of Noah.

Cham of Literature, the Great, a name given by Smollett to Dr. Johnson.

Champion of the Virgin, a title given to St. Cyril of Alexandria on account of his work on the Incarnation or doctrine of the hypostatic union in the argument with Nestorius, Bishop of Constantinople.

Champneys, the name of a family of broken-down aristocrats in Henry J. Byron's comedy, *Our Boys* (1875).

Chanticleer, the cock in *Reynard the Fox* (1498) and in Chaucer's *The Nonne Preste's Tale* (1388).

Chantry, Rose, a character of Mrs. Humphry Ward's novel, *Lady Rose's Daughter.*

Chaonian Bird, the dove, because doves delivered the oracles of Chaonia or Dodona.

Chapel Perilous, where Launcelot saw the Holy Grail.

Chapman, Sir Remnant, and his son, characters in W. D. Blackmore's novel, *Alice Lorraine.*

Charalois, in Massinger's tragedy, *The Fatal Dowry* (1632), undergoes imprisonment to redeem his father's dead body.

Chardon, Lucien, a character in Balzac's *A Provincial at Paris.*

Chargebœuf, Marquis de, the head of an ancient house in the time of the Consulate and the Empire. He and others of the family are characters in Balzac's *The Member from Arcis* and other stories.

Charicleia, the heroine of a Greek romance of the fourth century by Heliodorus, Bishop of Trikka, *The Loves of Theagenes and Charicleia.* The Bishop was ordered to burn his book or give up his bishopric; he chose the latter.

Charlemagne is the hero of many legends, and the subject, with his paladins, of many medieval French romances, among them *Ogier the Dane*, *Huon of Bordeaux*, and *Maugis the Enchanter.*

Charles I, of England, appears as Prince of Wales in Scott's *The Fortunes of Nigel;* he is the subject of plays by Havard (1750), by E. C. Brewer (1828), Miss Mitford (1830), Gurney (1853), and Wills (1872), and is a character in Browning's poetic drama, *Strafford.*

Charles II, of England, is a character in Scott's *Peveril of the Peak* and in *Woodstock;* in Dumas's *Le Vicomte de Bragelonne;* in Anthony Hope's *Simon Dale;* in Clyde Fitch's play, *His Grace de Grammont;* in Paul Kester's play, *Sweet Nell of Old Drury;* in a play that bears his name, and in George C. Hazelton's play, *Mistress Nell.* In Dryden's *Absalom and Achitophel* he figures as King David, and his son, the Duke of Monmouth, as Absalom.

Charles VI, of France, is the subject of an opera by Halévy (1841), the libretto by Germain and Casimir Delavigne, in which occurs the famous song, *Guerre aux Tyrans* ("War to Tyrants"). He is a character in Shakespeare's *Henry V.*

Charles VII, of France, is the subject of a drama by Dumas *père* (1831), and is a character in Schiller's *Maid of Orleans*, and in Shakespeare's *Henry VI*, Part I.

Charles IX, of France, is the subject of Chénier's drama, *Charles IX: or, The School of Kings* (1789). He is a character in Dumas's novel, *Marguerite de Valois.*

Charles XII, of Sweden, is the subject of a drama by Planché (1826), and of *Karl XII*, by Esaias Tegnèr (d. 1846).

Charles Albert, King of Sardinia, a character in George Meredith's *Vittoria.*

Charles Emmanuel, son of Victor Amadeus of Sardinia, a character in Browning's *King Victor and King Charles.*

Charles the Bold, of Burgundy, is a character in Scott's *Anne of Geierstein* and in *Quentin Durward.*

Charles the Good, Earl of Flanders, is introduced in Sheridan Knowles's tragedy, *The Provost of Bruges* (1836).

Charlotte, the lady beloved by Werther in Goethe's *The Sorrows of Young Werther.*

Charlotte, a girl who pretends to be dumb in order to escape a distasteful marriage in Fielding's farce, *The Mock Doctor,* made from Molière's *Le médecin malgré lui.*

Charlotte Lambert in Bickerstaff's comedy, *The Hypocrite* (1768), the original of which, *The Non-juror* (1706), by Cibber, was taken from Molière's *Tartuffe.*

Charmian, one of the Queen's attendants in Shakespeare's *Antony and Cleopatra.*

Charney, The Count de, the hero of Saintine's novel, *Picciola.*

Charnock, Luke, the hero of A. E. W. Mason's *Miranda of the Balcony.*

Charnot, Jeanne, the heroine of René Bazin's novel, *The Ink-Stain.*

Charteris, Leonard, the title character of Shaw's play, *The Philanderer*—a clever, imaginative, humorous, but unfeeling man, who declares positively that he can love any pretty woman.

Charteris, Winifred (or **Winsome**), the heroine of Stephen Crockett's novel, *The Lilac Sunbonnet* (1894).

Charyllis, in Spenser's *Colin Clout's Come Home Again,* is Anne Spenser, Lady Compton.

Chassagnol, a Bohemian and esthete in *Charles de Mailly,* by Edmond and Jules de Goncourt, who despises all talent save his own, and sneers at everyone's work, though he himself has accomplished nothing.

Chassediane, Jennie, a character in Meredith's *The Adventures of Harry Richmond.*

Chastelard, a grandson of the Chevalier Bayard, in love with Mary Stuart, the subject of a tragedy (1865) by Algernon Charles Swinburne.

Chat, Dame, a gossip in the second English comedy, *Gammer Gurton's Needle* (1551), attributed to Bishop Still.

Chatterton, Thomas, the young English poet, is the subject of a French drama by Alfred de Vigny (1835).

Chauvin, a veteran soldier and worshiper of Napoleon in Scribe's *Le Soldat Laboureur;* from this comes the word *chauvinism.*

Cheeryble Brothers, The, in Dickens's *Nicholas Nickleby,* two kind and generous merchants, who have been poor and homeless boys. Their nephew, Frank, marries Kate Nickleby.

Chemos, the same as Baal-peor, a god of the Moabites, whom Milton calls "the obscene dread of Moab's sons."

Cherubim, Don, the bachelor in Le Sage's *Bachelor of Salamanca* (1737).

Chery, in the Countess D'Aulnoy's *Fairy Tales* (1682), married Fairstar and obtained for her the dancing-water which imparted beauty, the singing-apple which gave wit, and the little green bird which could tell secrets.

Chester, Sir John, in Dickens's *Barnaby Rudge,* is an elegant but unprincipled and heartless gentleman, said to be drawn from the famous Lord Chesterfield. His son Edward marries a poor girl, Emma Haredale, in spite of Sir John's opposition.

Chesterfield, Charles, the title and hero's name of a novel by Mrs. Trollope.

Chesterton, Paul, a character in J. M. Morton's *If I Had a Thousand a Year.*

Chettam, Sir James, the good-natured baronet who marries Celia Brooke, sister of Dorothea, the heroine, in George Eliot's *Middlemarch.*

Chevalier d'Harmental, the subject of a romance by Dumas, *père* (1845).

Chevalier de Maison-Rouge, The, the subject of a historical romance by the elder Dumas (1846).

Chevalier de St. George, the subject of a romance by Roger de Beauvoir (1838).

Chevelere Assigne (Knight of the Swan), subject of an old English poem from a French original.

Cheveral, Sir David, the title character of *The Star Dreamer,* by Agnes and Egerton Castle.

Cheverel, Sir Christopher and **Lady,** leading characters in George Eliot's short tale, *Mr. Gilfil's Love-Story* (in *Scenes from Clerical Life*).

Cheveril, Hans, the leading character in Holcroft's comedy, *The Deserted Daughter,* altered into *The Steward.*

Chevy Chase, the famous old ballad, is the story of the fray between a Percy and a Douglas, and their followers, in which both the leaders fell and "representatives of every noble family on either side of the border lay on the bloody greensward at the ringing of the curfew-bell."

Cheyne, Harvey, the spoiled son of a millionaire in Kipling's story, *Captains Courageous,* who is reformed and made a man of by being accidentally thrown on his own resources.

Chibiabos, a musician, ruler in the land of spirits, in Longfellow's *Hiawatha.*

Chicaneau, a leading character in Racine's *Les Plaideurs,* a man whose only subjects of conversation are his lawsuits.

Chicard, the Harlequin of the French carnival.

Chichi-Vache. See BYCORNE.

Chick, Louisa and **John,** sister and brother-in-law of Mr. Dombey in Dickens's *Dombey and Son.* Mrs. Chick is famous for her faith in "making an effort."

Chicot, a Gascon at the court of Henri III, celebrated for his wit and fun, the subject of a novel by the elder Dumas.

Chiddingford, Sibylla, afterward Mrs. Grantley Mason, the heroine of Anthony Hope's novel, *In Double Harness.*

Chignon, a typical French valet in Burgoyne's play, *The Heiress.*

Childe Harold, the hero of Byron's poem, *Childe Harold's Pilgrimage.*

Childe of Elle, the subject of an old ballad given in Percy's *Reliques.*

Childe Rowland (Roland), the hero of an old Scottish ballad, now lost, from which a line is quoted in Shakespeare's *King Lear:* "Childe Roland to the dark tower came." From this line Robert Browning wrote a highly imaginative poem. This Roland is identified with Charlemagne's famous paladin of the name.

Childe Waters, the subject of an ancient ballad in Percy's *Reliques*.

Children in the Wood, the subject of the famous story told in an old ballad. They were left in Wayland Wood by the man their uncle had hired to murder them in order that their inheritance might fall to him. They died in the night of cold and terror, and Robin Redbreast covered them with leaves. Misfortune pursued the uncle, who died in jail; and the ruffian he hired was convicted of highway robbery after seven years; he then confessed the crime against the children.

Chillingly, Kenelm, the hero and title of a novel by Bulwer.

Chillingworth, Lady Charlotte, a character in Meredith's *Sandra Belloni*.

Chillingworth, Roger, the wronged and revengeful husband of Hester Prynne in Hawthorne's *The Scarlet Letter*.

Chillip, the meek little doctor in Dickens's *David Copperfield,* who assists in bringing the hero into the world.

Chillon, The Prisoner of, in Byron's poem of the name, was François de Bonnivard (1496–1571), who was imprisoned by the Duke-Bishop of Savoy for his efforts to preserve the independence of Geneva. His two brothers died in prison, but he was liberated after six years by the people of Berne. Chillon is on a rock on the shore of Lake Geneva, not far from Montreux.

Chingachcook, an Indian chief, called by the French "the great serpent," appears in Cooper's *The Pathfinder, The Pioneer, The Deerslayer,* and *The Last of the Mohicans*.

Chinn, John, a "slender little hookey-nosed boy" in Kipling's *The Tomb of His Ancestors*.

Chloe, a name given to shepherdesses in pastoral poetry.

Chloe, the assumed name of Catherine Martinsward in Meredith's *The Tale of Chloe*.

Cho-Cho, San. See BUTTERFLY, MADAME.

Choephores, the bearers of libations, subject of a tragedy by Æschylus, introductory to the *Eumenides*.

Chœreas, the hero of a Greek romance of the eighth century by Chariton, *The Loves of Chæreas and Callirrhoë*.

Chollop, Major Hannibal, one of the caricatures of Western Americans in Dickens's *Martin Chuzzlewit*.

Chrestien, Michel, a "great though unknown" Liberalist Republican statesman, in Balzac's *A Distinguished Provincial at Paris.*

Chriemhild, or **Kriemhild,** in the *Nibelungenlied,* the wife of Siegfried, and, after his death, of Etzel (Attila). After Siegfried's death, she changed from a gentle and amiable woman into a revengeful fury, and slew her brother Gunther, and Hagan, Siegfried's murderer, with her own hand.

Christabel, the heroine of an old romance, *Sir Eglamour of Artois.*

Christabel, the heroine of the ballad *Sir Cauline* in Percy's *Reliques,* whose lover was banished, and, returning in disguise, was killed in a tournament.

Christabel, the subject of an unfinished poem by Coleridge.

Christabel, Babe, the subject of an elegiac poem by Gerald Massey.

Christian, the pilgrim of Bunyan's *Pilgrim's Progrses.*

Christian, the banished King of Illyria in Daudet's *Kings in Exile.*

Christian, Edward and **William,** brothers, conspirators, and Edward's daughter, **Fenella,** or **Zarah,** characters in Scott's *Peveril of the Peak.*

Christian, Fletcher, mate of the *Bounty* and chief mutineer in Byron's poem, *The Island.*

Christian, the surname of several characters in Hall Caine's novel, *The Manxman.* Philip is the Deemster, and Iron, his grandfather, the Great Deemster.

Christian II, King of Norway, Sweden, and Denmark, is a character in Brooke's tragedy, *Gustavus Vasa* (1739).

Christian Virgil, The, Girolamo Vida (1490–1566) of Cremona, Bishop of Alba, author of a Latin epic, *Christias,* the material taken from the gospels and the form from Virgil. The name has been applied also to Jacopo Sannazzaro (1458–1530).

Christiana, Christian's wife in Bunyan's *Pilgrim's Progress.*

Christianson, Christian, the hero of Robert Buchanan's novel, *God and the Man.*

Christie of the Clint Hill, a character in Scott's *The Monastery.*

Christina, a daughter of Christian II, of Norway, appears in Brooke's tragedy, *Gustavus Vasa.*

Christopher, a head-waiter in Dickens's short story, *Somebody's Luggage,* the writer of an amusing essay on "waitering."

Christopher, the hero of William Morris's *Child Christopher and Goldilind the Fair.*

Chrononhotonthologos, King, the title and name of a pompous character in H. Carey's "half-act" burlesque. It was applied to General Burgoyne on account of his boastful and important manner, which also drew upon him the sobriquet, Sir Jack Brag.

Chrysanthème, Madame, the title-character of a novel by Pierre Loti.

Chrysaor, the golden sword of Sir 'Artegal, described in Spenser's *The Faerie Queene.*

Chrysosthemis, a character in Hugon von Hofmansthal's poetic drama, *Electra.*

Chrysostom (the golden-mouthed), a surname of the eloquent St. John, Bishop of Constantinople (347–407).

Chump, Mrs. Martha, a rich Irish woman in George Meredith's novel, *Sandra Belloni,* to whom the Pole family are unwillingly civil because their father is speculating with her money.

Churchill, Ethel, the title and heroine of a novel by Letitia E. Landon (long known to literature as "L. E. L."), in which appear Sir Robert Walpole and many of his contemporaries.

Churchill, Frank, the lover of Jane Fairfax in Jane Austen's novel, *Emma.*

Churchill, Mr., a schoolmaster in Longfellow's novel, *Kavanagh,* whom nature intended for a poet.

Chuzzlewit, Martin and **Anthony,** brothers; **George,** an elderly, but gay bachelor; **Jonas,** son of Anthony; and Martin's grandson, **Young Martin,** the hero, are characters in Dickens's *Martin Chuzzlewit.* Jonas is the villain of the story.

Cibber, Colley, the playwright, is a character in Reade's *Peg Woffington.*

Cibot, called the Great, a Chouan murdered by his cousin, Jean Cibot, both characters in Balzac's *The Chouans.*

Cicero, the great Roman orator, is a character in Shakespeare's *Julius Cæsar,* where also his death is reported.

Cicero, the **British,** George Canning, 1770–1827; and William Pitt, Earl of Chatham, 1708–1778; the **Christian,** Lucius Cœlius Lactantius (d. 330); the **French,** Jean Baptiste Massillon (1663–1742); the **German,** John, Elector of Brandenburg (1455–1499), and Johann Sturm (1507–1589).

Cicero's Mouth, applied to Philippe Pot (1428–1494), Prime Minister of Louis XI, on account of his eloquence.

Cid, The, also called **Cid Campeador** (Lord Champion), was Rodrique Diaz de Bivar of Castile (1030–1099), a general successful against the Moors. His horse was called Babieca; his swords Colada and Tizona. He is the subject of a tragedy by Corneille, founded upon one by the Spaniard Guilhem de Castro; and of one in English by Ross Neil. Southey wrote *The Chronicle of the Cid,* collecting the stories of his life; Sanchez a long poem on his career; and Massenet an opera (1885).

Cid Hamet. See BENENGELI.

Cidli, the name given in Klopstock's *Messiah* (1771) to the daughter of Jairus, restored to life by Jesus.

Cigarette, a brave little vivandière in the French army in Africa, one of the chief characters in Ouida's novel, *Under Two Flags.*

Cimmerians, a mythical people, placed by Homer in the farthest West in a land of perpetual gloom; by later writers in Italy near Lake Avernus, in Spain, or in the Crimea. The historical people of the name were driven from their home near the Sea of Azov into Asia Minor.

Cincinnatus, The American: George Washington, so called because he retired to private life after the success of his country's arms, like the Roman Cincinnatus, who resigned the dictatorship and retired to his farm.

Cinderella, the heroine of the well-known fairy-story, the English version of which is taken from the French of Perrault (1697). It is said that a similar tale is told by the geographer Strabo; and that the story of *Rhodopis and Psammiticus* in Ælian is much like it.

Cinna, Helvius, a Roman poet, friend of Catullus, who was killed by the populace, being mistaken for Cornelius Cinna. He appears in Shakespeare's *Julius Cæsar.*

Cinna, who conspired against Augustus Cæsar, is the subject of Corneille's drama, *Cinna: or, The Clemency of Augustus.*

Cinna, Lucius Cornelius, one of the conspirators against Cæsar, a character in Shakespeare's *Julius Cæsar.*

Cinq-Cygne, in Balzac's *The Gondreville Mystery, The Member for Arcis,* and others, is the name of an illustrious family of Champagne. The name, Cinq-Cygne (five swans), arose from the defense of a castle made by five beautiful daughters in the absence of their father. On the family blazon is the answer made by the eldest to the summons to surrender: "We die singing!"

Cinq-Mars, Marquis de, a favorite of Louis XIII, who, with his friend De Thou, was executed for conspiracy against Cardinal Richelieu. He is the subject of a novel by Alfred de Vigny (1826) and an opera by Gounod (1877).

Cipango, or **Zipango,** a wonderful island in the eastern seas, described by Marco Polo, and supposed by some to be Japan, but not clearly identified.

Circumlocution Office, The, is a term used by Dickens in his novel, *Little Dorrit,* to ridicule the "red-tape" of official transactions. He calls it the chief of "public departments in the art of perceiving how not to do it." Some of the indirect and needless routine he referred to has been done away with.

Cirongillo of Thrace, the hero of an old Spanish romance of chivalry by Bernardo de Vargas.

Cithæron, mountains separating Bœotia from Attica and Megaris, sacred to the Muses and the scene of many mythological incidents.

Citizen King, The, Louis Philippe, the first elected King of France, reigned 1830–'49.

City: Antique, Fustel de Coulanges gives an account of classic customs under this name; of Brotherly Love, Philadelphia; of Churches, Brooklyn; of David, Jerusalem; of Destruction, the worldly life; of Elms, New Haven, Conn.; of Enchantments, a magic city of the *Arabian Nights;* of God, used by St. Augustine in his famous work with that title to signify the whole body of Christian believers; of Lanterns, a cloud-city reached by way of the Zodiac, imagined by Lucian (see ISLAND OF LANTERNS); of Legions, Caerleon-on-Usk, where King Arthur held his court;

of Lilies, Florence; of Magnificent Distances, Washington; of Masts, London; of Monuments, Baltimore; of Notions, Boston; of Palaces, Rome, Calcutta, St. Petersburg; of Peace, Jerusalem; of Refuge, Medina, Arabia, where Mahomet took refuge when driven from Mecca; of Rocks, Nashville; of Spindles, Lowell, Mass.; of the Great King, Jerusalem; of the Prophet, Medina; of the Straits, Detroit; of the Sun, Balbec or Heliopolis; of the Sun, an imaginary city in Thomas Campanella's ideal republic; of the Tribes, Galway, Ireland; of the Violated Treaty, Limerick, on account of a broken treaty, guaranteeing religious toleration to Catholics; of the Violet Crown, Athens, the violet being the favorite flower for festal garlands; of Victory, Cairo; Cleveland, Savannah, and Portland, Me., are each called the Forest City; Rochester, N. Y., the Flour or Flower City, on account of its flour-mills and nurseries; New Orleans, at the bend of the Mississippi, the Crescent City; Buffalo, the Queen City of the Lakes; Cincinnati is called Porkopolis, and New York, Gotham; Pittsburg, the Iron City; Montreal, the Island City.

Clanconan, Lord, a character in Meredith's novel, *One of Our Conquerors*.

Clandon, Mrs. Lanfrey, in Shaw's play, *You Never Can Tell*, "belongs to the forefront of her own period" (say, 1860–'80). Her daughter Gloria is the heroine, haughty, high-minded, raging with the impatience of an impetuous, dominative character, paralyzed by the impotence of her youth.

Clara, the name given in Otway's English version of Molière's comedy, *The Cheats of Scapin*, to the heroine, Hyacinthe.

Clara d'Almanza, the heroine of Sheridan's comedy, *The Duenna*.

Clara Douglas, the heroine of Bulwer's comedy, *Money* (1840).

Clärchen, a fine character in Goethe's drama, *Egmont* (1788).

Clare, Ada, one of the wards in Chancery in Dickens's *Bleak House*.

Clarence, George, Duke of, a character in Shakespeare's *Henry VI*, Part III, and *Richard III*—"false, fleeting, perjured Clarence." He appears also in Scott's *Anne of Geierstein*.

Clarence, Thomas, Duke of, a character in Shakespeare's *Henry IV*, Part II.

Clarendon, The Earl of, Lord Chancelor to Charles II, is introduced in Scott's *Woodstock.*

Clarice, the wife of Rinaldo, introduced into the epics of chivalry of Boiardo, Ariosto, and others.

Claridiana, in the *Mirror of Knighthood,* marries the Knight of the Sun.

Clarinda, the name under which Mrs. Maclehose corresponded with Robert Burns, who signed himself Sylvander. An edition of the letters published in 1802 was suppressed; it was reprinted in 1845.

Clarion, in Spenser's *Mniopotmos: or, The Butterfly's Fate* (1590), was the fairest of the race of flies, killed by Aragnol, son of Arachnê (the spider).

Clark, Rev. Mr., the chief character in Hawthorne's short story, *The Minister's Black Veil.*

Claude, the hero of Arthur Hugh Clough's poem, *Amours de Voyage.*

Claude Melnotte, the hero of Bulwer's play, *The Lady of Lyons.*

Claudio, the brother of Isabella in Shakespeare's *Measure for Measure.*

Claudio, the lover of Hero in Shakespeare's *Much Ado about Nothing.*

Claudius, King of Denmark, the murderer of his brother, Hamlet's father, in Shakespeare's *Hamlet.* In the original history he is called Fengo.

Claudius, Doctor, the title and hero of a novel by F. Marion Crawford.

Claus, Santa: St. Nicholas.

Claverhouse, John Graham of, Viscount Dundee (1650–'89), noted for his cruel persecution of the Scottish Covenanters in the time of James II, is a character in Scott's *Old Mortality,* and is celebrated in his song, *Bonnie Dundee;* also in William E. Aytoun's *The Burial March of Dundee.*

Clavering, Harry, a character in Anthony Trollope's *The Claverings.* He is a well-meaning but easily influenced young man, wavering between his early love and his fiancée.

Clavering, Lawrence, the chief character of A. E. W. Mason's novel of the name (1897).

Clavigo, the title and hero of a tragedy by Goethe.

Clavileno, Aligero, a wooden horse constructed by Merlin and governed by a wooden pin in the forehead, used by Don Quixote to rescue the infanta Antonomasia and her husband.

Clay, Robert, the chief character of Richard Harding Davis's *Soldiers of Fortune,* and Augustus Thomas's play made from it.

Clayton, Sir Conrad, a leading character of Ellen Thornycroft Fowler's novel, *Place and Power.*

Cleanthes, son of Leonides, whom he saves from the operation of a law requiring all men over eighty to be put to death, a character in the comedy, *The Old Law,* by Massinger, Middleton, and Rowley (1620).

Cleaver, Fanny, called Jenny Wren, a doll's dressmaker, in Dickens's novel, *Our Mutual Friend.* Her father, a good workman, but never sober, was called Mr. Dolls.

Cleishbotham, Jedediah, and **Dorothea,** a schoolmaster and his shrewish wife in Scott's *Tales of My Landlord;* he is supposed to have collected the tales.

Clélie, the title and heroine of a romance by Madeleine de Scudéry. She is the Clœlia of whom it is related in early Roman history that she escaped from Porsena, to whom she had been given as a hostage, by swimming across the Tiber.

Clemanthe, the heroine of Talfourd's drama, *Ion* (1835).

Clennam, Arthur, the adopted son of the pious but dishonest Mrs. Clennam, is the hero of Dickens's story, *Little Dorrit* (1857).

Cleofas, or **Cleophas, Don,** the hero of Le Sage's novel, *Le Diable Boïteux* (translated *The Devil on Two Sticks*). See ASMODEUS.

Cleombrotus, of whom it is related that he was so charmed with Plato's *Phædo* that he leaped into the sea to reach the immortal life.

Cleon, the subject of a poem by Browning—a Greek philosopher who writes to King Protus on the subject of the soul's immortality, in which he does not believe.

Cleopatra, Queen of Egypt, wife of Ptolemy Dionysius, her brother, is the heroine of Shakespeare's *Antony and Cleopatra;* also of a tragedy by Samuel Daniel (1599); of Dryden's *All for Love, or the World Well Lost* (1682); and of tragedies in French by Jodelle (1552); De Mairet (1630); Benserade (1670); De Chapelle (1680); Marmontel (1750); Soumet (1824); and Madame de Girardin (1847); also of Shaw's drama, *Cæsar and Cleopatra.*

Cleveland, the subject of a French romance by the Abbé Prévost (1732).

Cleveland, Captain Clement, alias Vaughan, the hero of Scott's novel, *The Pirate.*

Clickett, an "orfling" girl, servant to the Micawber family in Dickens's *David Copperfield.*

Clicquot, a name given by *Punch* to Frederick William IV of Prussia on account of his love of Veuve Clicquot champagne.

Clifford, Jane, called the Fair Rosamond (*q.v.*).

Clifford, Lord John, son of Lord Thomas, character in Shakespeare's *Henry VI,* Parts II and III, called "the butcher" for his cruelty. His death is described in the play as having occurred at the battle of Towton, though he was in reality killed at Ferrybridge shortly before.

Clifford, Lord Thomas, a character in Shakespeare's *Henry VI,* Part II, a grandson of Hotspur.

Clifford, Paul, a highwayman, the hero and title of a novel by Bulwer.

Clim, or **Clym, of the Clough** (cliff), an outlaw in an old ballad, included in Percy's *Reliques.*

Clinker, Humphrey, the subject of a famous novel by Tobias Smollett.

Clio, a name often applied to Addison, formed from the initials of Chelsea, London, Islington, and Office, which he signed to his papers in *The Spectator.*

Clitandre, a character in Molière's *Les Femmes Savantes,* beloved by Henriette and by Armande, the learned ladies. He prefers Henriette.

Clive, Kitty, the actress, is a character in Charles Reade's *Peg Woffington* and in F. Frankfort Moore's play, *Kitty Clive,*

Actress (1895). She lived in the days of Colley Cibber and Peg Woffington.

Clive, Robert, the hero of India, is the subject of a poem by Browning, founded upon a singular incident of his youth.

Clorinda. See TANCRED.

Cloten, a "conceited, booby lord," son of the Queen and rejected lover of Imogen in Shakespeare's *Cymbeline.*

Clothaire, or **Clotharius,** a leader of the Franks in Tasso's epic poem, *Jerusalem Delivered.*

Cloud, Kate, the heroine of Haddon Chambers's play, *John-a-Dreams.*

Cloudesley, William of, an archer celebrated in an old English ballad in Percy's *Reliques.*

Clout, Colin, a shepherd's boy in Spenser's *The Shepheardes Calendar.* The name is applied to himself by Spenser there and in the poem, *Colin Clout's Come Home Again.* It is taken from a poem by Skelton, *Collyn Clout.*

Clutterbuck, Captain Cuthbert, the imaginary editor of some of Scott's novels—*The Monastery, The Fortunes of Nigel. The Abbot* is dedicated to him.

Clytemnestra. See AGAMEMNON, ORESTES.

Cobbler-Poet, The: Hans Sachs of Nuremberg.

Cocai, Merlin. See MACARONICS.

Cocheforêt, Renée, the heroine of Stanley J. Weyman's novel, *Under the Red Robe.*

Cockaigne, The Land of, an imaginary land of luxury and "paradise of do-nothings," where, according to a French poem of the thirteenth century, the houses were made of cakes and the streets paved with pastry. It is the subject of a very old poem given in Ellis's *Specimens of Early English Poets,* and of one by Hans Sachs in German. The name has been applied to Paris and to London, and is supposed to be the source of the word "cockney." It comes from a word in Provincial French, meaning cake.

Cock-Lane Ghost, The, the supposed cause of mysterious knockings and scratchings about the bed of a young girl in Cock Lane, West Smithfield, London, about 1762, which caused much excitement. An examination by the rector, Dr. Johnson, and others, convinced them that it was an imposture, that the noises were made on a piece of board the girl had concealed about her; and her parents were condemned to the pillory and imprisonment.

Cockney School, a name given by Lockhart to a literary coterie consisting of Leigh Hunt, Hazlitt, Keats, Shelley, and others. "Its chief Doctor and Professor is Mr. Leigh Hunt, a man certainly of some talents, of extraordinary pretensions both in poetry and politics, and withal of exquisitely bad taste and extremely vulgar modes of thinking and manners in all respects."

Cock of the North: The last Duke of Gordon is so described on a monument to him in Fochabers, Scotland.

Cockpen, The Laird of. See LAIRD.

Cockpit of Europe. Belgium, called so because many great battles have been fought on its soil.

Codlingsby, the hero of one of Thackeray's *Novels by Eminent Hands*—a burlesque on Disraeli's novel, *Coningsby.*

Cœlebs, the hero of Hannah More's famous story, *Cœlebs in Search of a Wife* (1809).

Coffin, Long Tom, a celebrated sailor in Cooper's novel, *The Pilot,* and W. E. Fitzball's drama founded upon that novel.

Colbrand, or **Coldbrand,** a Danish giant slain by Guy of Warwick.

Cole, or **Coil,** a legendary British king, whose name is familiar in a nursery rhyme, *Old King Cole.*

Colette, the heroine of a French novel, *Colette's Novena.*

Colin, a common name in literature for a shepherd.

Collet, Mary, the heroine of *John Inglesant,* by J. H. Shorthouse.

Colleville, a musician and government clerk, who, with his pretty and clever wife, figures in Balzac's stories, *The Middle Classes* and *Cousin Bette.*

Collin, Jacques, and his aunt, **Jacqueline,** are convicts and adventurers in Balzac's *Père Goriot, Lost Illusions,* and other novels of the *Comédie Humaine.*

Collingbourne, in Sackville's *The Mirror for Magistrates,* makes "complaynt" that he is to be executed for the rhyme he made on the King, Richard III, Catesby, Ratcliffe, and Lovel:

> "The cat, the rat, and Lovel the dog,
> Rule all England under the hog"——

saying that he only referred to the King's badge, a boar, and used the first syllables of the names of Ratcliffe and Catesby. The rhyme is used in Shakespeare's *Richard III*.

Collins, Rev. Mr., the heir of Mr. Bennet and rejected suitor of Elizabeth Bennet in Jane Austen's *Pride and Prejudice*—a vulgar toady.

Cologne, The Three Kings of, the Magi, who came to Bethlehem, usually called Gaspar, Melchior, and Balthazar. Their bones were said to have been brought to Constantinople by the Empress Helena, whence they were taken to Milan, and then to Cologne.

Colomba, the subject of a novel by Prosper Mérimée (1840). The heroine is a fiery Corsican, who pursues the traditional vendetta.

Colombe of Ravestein, Duchess of Juliers and Cleves, in Browning's drama, *Colombe's Birthday,* refuses to marry the kinsman whom the Salic law makes her father's heir, and marries Valence, an advocate who had been the bearer of the Prince's offer.

Colonna, Guido, the husband of Vanna and commander of the garrison of Pisa in Maeterlinck's drama, *Monna Vanna*.

Colonna, Vittoria, a celebrated Italian poetess, subject of sonnets by Michelangelo, is a character in Longfellow's dramatic poem, *Michelangelo,* and in *Ettore Fieramosca,* a novel by Massimo d' Azeglio.

Columbine, a character of Italian pantomime.

Comnenus, Isaac, the title and hero's name of a play (1827) by Sir Henry Taylor, founded on historical fact. Comnenus was the name of a Byzantine family of Italian origin, of which six were emperors at Constantinople (1057–1185). Anna Comnena appears in Scott's *Count Robert of Paris*.

Comparini, Pietro and **Violante,** the elderly couple in Browning's *The Ring and the Book,* who reared Francesca Pompilia as their own child, Pietro believing her to be so.

Comus, a god of mirth and revelry. In Milton's masque, *Comus,* he is an enchanter who offers a dangerous cup to the Lady Alice Egerton.

Conchubar, a son of the King of Ulster in the time of Cuchulain. In Irish legend he was the head of the Red Branch knights and waged the war against Maeve, Queen of Connaught, for the Brown Bull of Cuailgne.

Condé, Prince, appears in Balzac's *Catherine de' Medici*.

Coningsby, the chief character of a novel by Disraeli.

Coningsby, Arthur, the title character of a novel by John Sterling (1806–1844).

Conisbrough, Judith, the heroine of Jessie Fothergill's novel, *Kith and Kin*.

Conn, one of the children of Lir (*q.v.*).

Conn of the Hundred Battles, a hero of Irish legend.

Connell, Father, a priest whose name is the title of a novel by John Banim.

Connla, a son of Conn, who was carried away to many adventures in fairyland.

Conrad, a monk engaged in suppressing heresy, in Charles Kingsley's dramatic poem, *The Saint's Tragedy*.

Constance, the mother of Prince Arthur, pleads for his rights in Shakespeare's *King John*.

Constance of Beverley, in Scott's *Marmion*, a nun who broke her vows for love of Lord Marmion, and was walled up alive in the convent.

Constant, Benjamin, a French statesman (1767–1830) introduced in Balzac's *A Distinguished Provincial at Paris*, where he is noticed in a book-shop for his "splendid head and spiritual eyes."

Constantin, Abbé, the hero of a famous novel of the name by Ludovic Halévy.

Consuelo, the title and heroine's name of one of George Sand's most noted novels.

Conversation Kenge, a character in Dickens's *Bleak House*, in love with his own eloquence.

Cophetua, a mythical African king who married a beggar-girl—Penelophon, or Zenelophon, the subject of Tennyson's poem, *The Beggar Maid*.

Copper Captain, The, a famous character in Beaumont and Fletcher's comedy, *Rule a Wife and Have a Wife* (1610), whose name was Michael Perez. His wife, Estifania, whom he married supposing her to be an heiress, calls him "a man of copper"—meaning that everything about him is base and counterfeit.

Copperfield, David, title and hero's name of a novel by Charles Dickens, the author's own favorite among his works, and supposed to be largely autobiographical.

Copperheads, a nickname given in the United States to the Northern sympathizers with the Southern Confederates in the War of Secession, 1861–'65.

Coppernose, a sobriquet applied to Henry VIII, because his coins contained so much of the base metal that it soon showed on the parts in highest relief, as the nose.

Corah, in Dryden's *Absalom and Achitophel,* is intended for Titus Oates.

Corday, Charlotte, who was executed for the murder of Marat, is the subject of a drama by François Ponsard (1850).

Cordelia, the youngest daughter of Lear in Shakespeare's *King Lear,* disinherited because she does not make extravagant professions of love for her father, as her hypocritical sisters do. She is the subject of a poem by John Higgins (1574).

Cordière, La Belle. See LABÉ, LOUISE.

Corentin, a police-agent of great ability in Balzac's *The Chouans.*

Corineus, or **Corin,** a strong man in the following of Brute, the mythical British king, who overthrew the giant Goëmagot.

Corinna, a Greek poetess who gained a victory over Pindar at the public games about B.C. 490, mentioned in Tennyson's *The Princess.*

Corinne, the title and heroine's name of Madame de Staël's famous novel.

Corinthian Tom, a dissipated character in Pierce Egan's *Life in London,* a companion of Jerry Hawthorn—"Tom and Jerry."

Coriolanus, Caius Marcius, surnamed from his victory at Corioli, a Roman general, subject of a tragedy by Shakespeare, the material of which is taken from Plutarch. He is also the subject of a tragedy by James Thomson.

Cormac MacArt, a legendary king of Ireland.

Cormier, Phillis, the heroine of Hector Malot's psychological novel, *Conscience.*

Cornelia. See POMPEY THE GREAT, and MOTHER OF THE GRACCHI.

Corn-Law Poet, The, Ebenezer Elliott (1781–1849), author of *Corn-Law Rhymes*, which were influential in the agitation against those laws, resulting in their repeal in 1846.

Corporal, The Little, a title given to Napoleon after the battle of Lodi.

Corsair, The, in Byron's poem of the name, was Lord Conrad, afterward called Lara; he is said to have been drawn from Lafitte, a notorious buccaneer, pardoned by General Jackson for services to the American cause at the battle of New Orleans, in 1815.

Corsican Brothers, The. See FRANCHI.

Corydon, a common name for a shepherd, used by Theocritus, Virgil, Spenser, and others.

Coryphæus, the leader of the chorus in the Greek drama, hence a leader. Aristarchus was called the Coryphæus of grammarians; Goethe, the Coryphæus of German literature.

Cosette, a character in Hugo's novel, *Les Misérables.* She is a child of misfortune, adopted by the hero, Jean Valjean, and later the sweetheart of Marius, who wins her in the face of great suffering and mishap.

Costard, a clown in Shakespeare's *Love's Labor's Lost,* who imitates the pedantry and affectation of the courtiers, mistaking and misapplying their sounding words, but blundering into some shrewd remarks.

Costigan, Captain, an intemperate rascal, and his daughter **Emily,** an actress whose stage name is La Fotheringay, characters in Thackeray's *Pendennis.* The hero falls madly in love with Emily, only to fall out again with equal celerity.

Cote Mal-tailé, Sir (knight with the badly-cut coat), a nickname of Sir Brewnor le Noyre in Malory's *Prince Arthur,* because he wore his father's coat full of sword-cuts to remind him to avenge his father's death.

Cottar, George, the chief character of Kipling's short story, *The Brushwood Boy.*

Coulin, a British giant who leaped a chasm one hundred and thirty-two feet wide in escaping from Debon, but fell backward into it.

Country, The Father of his: Many besides Washington have been so called: Julius Cæsar, Cosmo de' Medici, Andrea Doria of Genoa, Andronicus Palæologus II.

Courtain, or **Courtana,** and **Sauvagine,** the swords of Ogier the Dane.

Courtly, Sir Harcourt, an elderly man of fashion in Dion Boucicault's play, *London Assurance.* Charles, his son, marries the heiress his father has been courting, Grace Harkaway.

Coverdale, Miles, a poet, narrator of the story in Hawthorne's novel, *The Blithedale Romance.* In this character the author is supposed to have portrayed himself in his part of the life at Brook Farm.

Coverley, Sir Roger de, the celebrated character in *The Spectator,* member of an imaginary club by whom it was edited. The character is said to have been originated by Richard Steele and "filled up" by Joseph Addison—a character made up of "modesty, generosity, hospitality, and eccentric whims."

Cradock, Sir, the only knight at Arthur's court whose wife could stand the magic tests of chastity, according to "The Boy and the Mantle" in Percy's *Reliques.*

Craig, Mr., the shipwrecked partner of the two heroines of Frank R. Stockton's story, *The Casting Away of Mrs. Lecks and Mrs. Aleshine.*

Crane, Ichabod, a schoolmaster in Irving's *Legend of Sleepy Hollow,* lank and awkward and full of superstitious terrors.

Cranmer, Thomas, a character in Louisa Mühlbach's *Henry the Eighth and His Court.*

Cranstoun, Henry, the lover of Margaret of Branksome in Scott's poem, *The Lay of the Last Minstrel.*

Crapaud, Johnny, a Frenchman, or, the French collectively. The device of the kings of France was formerly three toads, instead of the three fleur-de-lis as now. *Crapaud* is the French word for toad.

Cratchit, the name of a family in Dickens's short story, *A Christmas Carol.* Bob, the father, is clerk to Scrooge, the miser. Tiny Tim is his youngest son, a cripple.

Craven, Julia, a beautiful woman, emotional, ill-tempered, and sentimental, in Shaw's drama, *The Philanderer.*

Crawley, the name of several characters in Thackeray's novel, *Vanity Fair:* Sir Pitt Crawley, Mr. Pitt Crawley, Lady Crawley, and Captain Rawdon Crawley, who marries Becky Sharp. The Rev. Bute Crawley is a brother of Sir Pitt.

Creakle, Mr., the ignorant and brutal master of the school to which Dickens's hero, little David Copperfield, was sent by his stepfather, Mr. Murdstone.

Credhe, one of the Sidhe in Irish legend, who died of grief at the death of Cael, her husband. Her lament has appeared in many forms.

Cregeen, Cæsar, a Pharisaic scoundrel, and **Katherine,** his daughter, characters in Hall Caine's novel, *The Manxman.*

Crellin, Mona, a girl of humble birth in Hall Caine's novel, *The Manxman.*

Creseide, or **Cressida.** See TROILUS.

Cresswell, Madame, a woman of bad character introduced in Scott's *Peveril of the Peak.* She left ten pounds for a funeral sermon in which no ill should be spoken of her. The Duke of Buckingham wrote it, as follows: "She was born well, married well, lived well, and died well; for she was born at Shadwell, married Cresswell, lived at Clerkenwell, and died in Bridewell."

Creusa, the mother of Ion, a character in the *Ion* of Euripides and the subject of a tragedy (1754) by William Whitehead.

Crèvecœur, Count Philip de, in Scott's *Quentin Durward,* is an envoy sent to Louis XI with a defiance from Charles the Bold.

Crewe, Sarah, the subject of a story by Mrs. Burnett, which has been dramatized.

Crichton, The Admirable, James Crichton, a Scottish gentleman (1560–'83), so called from his extraordinary scholarship and many accomplishments.

Crichton, The Admirable, the subject of a play by James M. Barrie, the hero of which is a butler whose versatile ability is brought out by peculiar circumstances.

Crimsworth, Edward and **William,** characters in Charlotte Brontë's novel, *The Professor.* William is the hero.

Cringle, Tom, the hero of Michael Scott's (1789–1835) sea-story, *Tom Cringle's Log.*

Crispin, the hero of a comedy by Le Sage, *Crispin the Rival of His Master.*

Crispin-Catiline, a name fastened by Mirabeau upon D'Espréménil.

Crispinus, a bad poet, the hero of a play of the name by Jonson, aimed at his enemy, Marston.

Cristina, Queen of Sweden (abdicated 1654), is the subject of Browning's poem, *Cristina and Monaldeschi,* in which she orders the murder of her equerry and former favorite.

Critics, Prince of, applied to Aristarchus of Alexandria, a grammarian and Homeric critic who combated the critics, holding that *The Iliad* and *The Odyssey* were by different authors.

Critis, in Jonson's play, *Cynthia's Revels,* is supposed to be a portrait of the author.

Criton, a disciple of Socrates. One of Plato's dialogues is between him and his master and bears his name.

Croaker, a pessimist in Goldsmith's comedy, *The Good-Natured Man,* with an optimistic wife. The son, Leontine, marries Olivia Woodville.

Croasse, La, intended, it is said, for John Wilson Croker, in the novel, *Albert Lunel,* attributed to Lord Brougham, which was suppressed on the eve of its publication in 1844 and reprinted in 1872.

Crœsus, King of Lydia, whose dream is the subject of a tale in William Morris's *The Earthly Paradise.*

Croftangry, Mr. Chrystal, the imaginary editor of Scott's *Chronicles of the Canongate.* His history is given in *The Highland Widow* and the introduction to *The Fair Maid of Perth.* He is a portrait, according to Lockhart, of Sir Walter's father.

Croisnel, Renée de, a French girl in Meredith's novel, *Beauchamp's Career,* with whom Nevil Beauchamp falls in love.

Crombie, Hugh, landlord of an inn in Hawthorne's novel, *Fanshawe,* "something of a poet and musician, and a consummate liar."

Cromwell, Oliver, is the subject of Andrew Marvell's *Ode on Cromwell's Return from Ireland,* and of a sonnet by Milton. Dryden wrote laudatory stanzas on his death, and after the Restoration introduced him as Saul in his *Absalom and Achitophel.* Cromwell and his daughter Elizabeth are introduced in Scott's *Woodstock.* Matthew Arnold's poem, *Cromwell,* won the Newdigate prize of 1843. Victor Hugo wrote a drama, *Cromwell,* the preface to which is famous for its assault on the received theories of the drama. He is a character in James's novels of the civil war and in Whyte-Melville's; and figures in Macaulay's poem, *Naseby*, and Dumas's novel, *Twenty Years After*.

Cromwell, Thomas, chancellor and vicar-general under Henry VIII, a character in Shakespeare's *King Henry VIII*, in which Cardinal Wolsey's advice to him is one of the famous passages.

Croppies, a name given to the Irish insurgents of 1798, who wore their hair short, like the French revolutionists. John Banim's novel, *The Croppy*, was published in 1828.

Crothar, in Ossian's *Temora*, chief of bowmen in southern Ireland, who carried off the betrothed of Turloch, of the Cael, in the north; this led to a general feud which ended in Conar's becoming King of Ireland.

Crowdero, one of the leaders of a mob in Butler's *Hudibras*, said to be designed for Jackson, a milliner, who played a crowde, a stringed instrument, much like a violin.

Croye, Isabelle, Countess of, the heroine of Scott's *Quentin Durward*.

Croysado, The Great, in Butler's *Hudibras*, is General Lord Fairfax.

Crudor, Sir, a knight in Spenser's *The Faerie Queene*, who required Briana to bring him enough knights' and ladies' hair to purfle his cloak with before he would marry her.

Crummles, Vincent, in Dickens's *Nicholas Nickleby*, the manager of a traveling theatrical company joined by Nicholas and Smike. His daughter Ninetta was known as "The Infant Phenomenon." The original of the latter character is said to have become the wife of a distinguished American soldier, Gen. Frederick W. Lander.

Cruncher, Jerry, a resurrectionist (or body-snatcher) in Dickens's *A Tale of Two Cities*, who resents his pious wife's praying for his reformation—"being counterprayed and countermined and religiously circumvented into the worst of luck."

Crusca. See DELLA CRUSCA.

Crusoe, Robinson, the title and hero of De Foe's famous novel, said to be founded upon the story of Alexander Selkirk, a sailor whose captain left him in punishment for some offense on the desolate island of Juan Fernandez in 1704, where he remained four years. But it is more probable that it was suggested by a story in Garcilasso's *Royal Commentaries of Peru.*

Cruzado, Beltran, the count of the gipsies in Longfellow's poetic drama, *The Spanish Student.*

Cuchulain, a Red Branch knight, one of the great heroes of Irish legend. His name was Setanta until he killed with his stick and ball the fierce hound of Culain the smith and agreed to watch his goods for him thereafter; whence his name, the Hound of Culain. He performed many brave deeds in his boyhood. He married Emer after deserting Aoife, whose son he afterward killed unwittingly. In the war of the Brown Bull of Cuailgne, he was the only man of Ulster that did not suffer from Macha's curse. He fought four days with Ferdias, Maeve's champion, and killed him, thus defeating the Queen's army. Being finally engaged in the great battle of Muirthemne, to which Maeve aroused his enemies, he was killed there. Emer died upon his grave.

Cumberland, Duke of, son of George II and commander-in-chief of his forces, celebrated for his victory at Culloden (1746), called "the Butcher" from the severity of his measures against the Highlanders; introduced in Scott's *Waverley,* named in Campbell's poem, *Lochiel's Warning.*

Cumberland Poet, The, William Wordsworth.

Cumbrian Poet, The, Robert Anderson (1770–1833).

Cumnor Hall, scene of the death of Amy Robsart, the subject of a ballad by Mickle, and the original name given by Scott to his *Kenilworth,* which the publisher induced him to change for the present title.

Cunctator (the delayer), a name given to the Roman general, Quintus Fabius Maximus Verucosus (d. B.C. 203), for his policy of avoiding direct engagement with Hannibal and wearying him out by delay—whence the expressions "Fabian policy," "Fabian tactics."

Cunningham, Archie, an archer in Scott's *Quentin Durward.*

Cunningham, Bertie, a handsome lady-killer in W. E. Norris's novel, *A Bachelor's Blunder.*

Cunobeline, a legendary king of the Silures, father of Caractacus, whose capital was Colchester; he is supposed by some to be identical with Cymbeline.

Curate of Meudon, The, François Rabelais (1483–1553), who was parish priest at Meudon in his later years.

Curculio (the weevil), subject of a comedy of Plautus, where the patrimony of the rich man is lost by means of a parasite.

Curdle, Mr., in Dickens's *Nicholas Nickleby,* is the conceited author of a pamphlet of sixty-four pages, post octavo, on the character of the deceased husband of the Nurse in *Romeo and Juliet.*

Curiatii, The, three Albanian brothers conquered by the Horatii.

Curious Impertinent, The, an Italian gentleman in a story introduced by Cervantes in *Don Quixote.*

Current, Isabelle, a character in Meredith's *Evan Harrington.*

Curtmantle: Henry II of England was so called from the Anjou mantle he wore, shorter than those previously worn.

Curwen, Dorothy, the heroine of A. E. W. Mason's novel, *Lawrence Clavering.*

Cute, Alderman, in Dickens's short story, *The Chimes,* is a caricature of Sir Peter Laurie, a London alderman, and Lord Mayor in 1832, who was severe in his treatment of the poor, threatening to "put down" want, vagabondage, suicide, and everything of the kind.

Cutpurse, Moll, a nickname of a thief, Mary Frith, the heroine of Middleton's comedy, *The Roaring Girl* (1611), and a character in Field's drama, *Amends for Ladies* (1618).

Cuttle, Captain Edward, an ex-skipper in Dickens's *Dombey and Son,* with a hook in place of a right hand—a friend of Florence Dombey and of Walter Gay; on Walter's departure for Barbadoes, he gives him a great silver watch: "Put it back half an hour every morning and about a quarter toward the arternoon, and it's a watch that'll do you credit."

Cyclic Poets, so called because their works, sequels to *The Iliad* and *The Odyssey,* had to do with the cycle of the Trojan War. They were Agias, Arctenos, Eugamon, Lesches, Stasinos.

Cyclops, The Holy, applied by Dryden in *The Masque of Albion and Albanius* to Richard Rumbold, who had but one eye, and was executed for conspiracy in the Ryehouse Plot.

Cydalise, a beautiful woman in Balzac's *Cousin Bette.*

Cymbeline, a legendary king of Britain, the hero of Shakespeare's drama, *Cymbeline.*

Cynthia, a name given to Queen Elizabeth in Spenser's *Colin Clout's Come Home Again,* and in Phineas Fletcher's play, *The Purple Island.*

Cynthia, a name given to his lady-love in Sir Francis Kynaston's *Leoline and Sydanis.*

Cynthia (Diana) is the subject of poems by Richard Barnfield and Sir Walter Raleigh. Drayton wrote *The Quest of Cynthia,* and Jonson a satire, *Cynthia's Revels.*

Cypress, Mr., in Thomas Love Peacock's novel, *Nightmare Abbey,* is supposed to be intended for Lord Byron.

Cyrano de Bergerac. See BERGERAC.

Cyrene, a water-nymph who lived under the Peneus. The visit of her son Aristæus to her there is described in the fourth book of Virgil's *Georgics.*

Dabney, Colonel, a brutal old man in Hawthorne's incomplete story, *The Dolliver Romance,* who forces the elixir of life from the apothecary and dies of an over-draught.

Dacier, Percy, a young politician who breaks with Diana for giving to a newspaper a state secret he had confided to her, in Meredith's *Diana of the Crossways.*

Da Codra, Mila, the principal character in D'Annunzio's drama, *The Daughter of Jorio.*

Dactyle, Will, "smallest of pedants" in Steele's *Tatler.* Jorio is a magician and Mila is a girl of bad repute, loved by a father and son who quarrel over her; the son kills the father. She takes the blame on herself, and is sentenced to be burned alive as a witch.

D'Acuanha, Teresa, a Spanish waiting-woman in Scott's *The Antiquary,* "a fiend on earth."

Dacy, Sybil, the heroine of Hawthorne's story, *Septimius Felton.*

Dagonet, Sir, King Arthur's jester, knighted by the King.

Dale, Mr., an "old-fashioned" parson in Bulwer's story, *My Novel,* who is likened to Goldsmith's parson in *The Deserted Village.*

Dale, Mr. and **Lætitia,** characters in George Meredith's *The Egoist.* Mr. Dale is a tenant of Sir Willoughby Patterne, and Lætitia unwillingly becomes engaged to Sir Willoughby.

Dale, Simon, subject of a novel of the time of Charles II, by Anthony Hope.

Dalgarno, Lord Malcolm of, a profligate young Scot in Scott's *The Fortunes of Nigel.*

Dalgetty, Rittmaster Dugald, Laird of Drumthwacket, a celebrated character in Scott's *The Legend of Montrose;* he is a mercenary soldier of fortune, and an odd combination of pedant, braggart, and adventurer.

Dalrymple, Julie, the title character of *Lady Rose's Daughter* by Mrs. Humphry Ward. She assumes the name, Le Breton, and is a portraiture of Julie Lespinasse, a well-known woman in her day.

Dalton, Reginald, the hero of a novel of the same name, a tale of English University life, by John G. Lockhart.

Dame aux Camélias, La, the heroine of a famous romance (1848) and drama (1852) of Dumas, *fils.* See GAULTIER, MARGUERITE.

Dame blanche, La (the white lady), the subject of an opéra comique, *chef-d'œuvre* of Boieldieu, the libretto of which was written by Scribe (1825).

Damiano, the chief character of Giulio Carcano's novel of the name (1840).

Damiotti, Baptista, in Scott's *My Aunt Margaret's Mirror,* a Paduan doctor who professed to show his visitors in a mirror what their absent friends have been doing. He fled when about to be arrested as an agent for the Chevalier St. George.

Damocles, a courtier of the elder Dionysius, tyrant of Syracuse. He had praised the privileges of princes; and Dionysius, to give him an idea of the alloy in their happiness, had him seated at a sumptuous banquet, while over his head was a sword suspended by a single horse-hair.

Damon, the friend of Pythias, or Phintias. The latter was condemned to death by Dionysius, tyrant of Syracuse, and had permission to go home to take leave of his wife, Damon having promised to take his place and die in his stead if he did not return. Pythias was hindered by various obstacles, but returned just in time to save his friend. The tyrant was so affected by the faithfulness of the friends that he forgave Pythias, and asked to be made a third in their friendship. Schiller tells the story in a ballad, though giving Pythias the name Möros. It is the subject of a drama by Richard Edwards (1571), and another by John Banim (1825).

Damozel, The Blessed, the subject of a poem by Dante Gabriel Rossetti.

Damsel of Brittany, The, Eleonora, who was the heir to the throne of England after the death of her brother Arthur; she was kept in confinement in the castle of Bristol by her uncle, King John, until her death in 1241.

D'Amville, the atheist and murderer of his brother, in Cyril Tourneur's *The Atheist's Tragedy.*

Dana, the mother of the gods in Irish mythology; the subject of a poem by George Russell.

Dancing Chancellor, The, a name applied to Sir Christopher Hatton (1540–1591), a gay young cavalier who for his graceful dancing was made Chancellor and a Knight of the Garter by Queen Elizabeth, though he never had been called to the bar.

Dandin, Georges, the title and hero's name of a comedy (1668) by Molière; he is a wealthy *roturier* who marries a gentleman's daughter, and in addition to paying the family debts, maintaining the noble parents, and enduring the frivolities of his wife, is continually snubbed by them all. His reminder to himself on such an occasion is: *Vous l'avez voulu, Georges Dandin* ("You would have it so"). His name and the phrase have become proverbial in allusion to the results of foolish obstinacy.

Dandin, Perrin, a rustic judge in the *Pantagruel* of Rabelais, who decided all cases most expeditiously seated on the trunk of a tree. Racine used the name for a judge in his drama, *Plaideurs* (suitors-at-law), and La Fontaine in his fable of *The Oyster and the Suitors,* where the judge swallows the oyster and gives each suitor a half of the shell.

Dane, The Melancholy, Hamlet, Prince of Denmark.

Dane, William, the villain in George Eliot's novel, *Silas Marner,* who accused Silas falsely of theft and robbed him of his sweetheart.

Dangle, a character in Sheridan's farce, *The Critic,* who forces his worthless advice on the manager of the theater; it is said to have been drawn from Thomas Vaughan, an unsuccessful playwright.

Danisburgh, Lord, a prime minister, friend of Diana, in George Meredith's novel, *Diana of the Crossways.*

Dante, the poet, is supposed to foretell the fortunes of Italy in Byron's poem, *The Prophecy of Dante.* Sardou has a drama entitled *Dante,* and Rossetti a poem, *Dante at Verona.*

Danvers, a character in George Meredith's *Diana of the Crossways.*

Danvers, Sir Charles, the hero of Mary Cholmondeley's novels, *The Danvers Jewels* and *Sir Charles Danvers.*

Daphnaida, the subject of an elegy by Edmund Spenser on Lady Douglas Howard, wife of Arthur Gorges.

Daphne, the heroine of James Lane Allen's *Summer in Arcady.*

Darby and Joan, subjects of a ballad (1735), *The Happy Old Couple,* which has been attributed to Prior, but is generally credited to Henry Woodfall; the originals are supposed to have been John Darby, a printer, to whom Woodfall was apprenticed, and his wife.

Darch, Car and **Nancy,** called the Queen of Spades and the Queen of Hearts in Hardy's novel, *Tess of the D'Urbervilles.*

D'Arcy, a character supposed to be drawn from Dante Gabriel Rossetti, in *Aylwin,* a novel by Theodore Watts-Dunton.

Darcy, Fitzwilliam, the hero of Jane Austen's *Pride and Prejudice.*

Dargo, in a poem by Fergus Fibhevil, supposed to have been written about 290, is slain by Goll.

Darius, the subject of a tragedy (1603) by William Alexander, Lord Stirling.

Dark and Bloody Ground, The, a phrase applied to Kentucky, said to be the signification of its name; it was given because it was the battle-ground of Northern against Southern Indians.

Darleton, Lucy, a character in George Meredith's novel, *The Egoist.*

Darnay, Charles, the Marquis de St. Evrémonde, in Dickens's *A Tale of Two Cities*, for whom Sydney Carton gave his life.

Darnley, Lord, is a character in James Grant's novel, *Bothwell* (1851), and in Maurice Hewlett's romance, *The Queen's Quair* (1904).

D'Artagnan, the dashing hero of Alexandre Dumas's *The Three Musketeers*.

Dar-Thula, heroine of a poem by Ossian (Macpherson), founded on the story of Deirdré (*q. v.*).

Dartle, Rosa, in Dickens's *David Copperfield*, the companion of Mrs. Steerforth, and in love with that lady's son, who does not respond to her affection.

Dashwood, a family in Jane Austen's *Sense and Sensibility*—John, and his sisters, Elinor, who has "sense," and Marianne, all "sensibility."

Dauriat, an editor, and keeper of a bookshop frequented by writers and politicians, in Balzac's *A Distinguished Provincial at Paris*, and in *Modeste Mignon*.

Davenant, Sir William, the poet, is a character in Scott's *Woodstock*, claiming descent from Shakespeare.

David, King of Judah, is a character in Peele's drama, *The Love of King David and Fair Bethsabe* (1599); the subject of a poem by Drayton, *David and Goliath* (1630), of one by Abraham Cowley, *Davideis*, and of *Davideis*, by Thomas Ellwood (1712).

David, a character in Balzac's *Seraphita*.

David, St., a legendary character, patron saint of Wales, the uncle of King Arthur. The waters of Bath were believed to owe their virtues to his benediction.

Davy Jones, a name for death among sailors; his "locker" is at the bottom of the sea.

Daw, Marjorie, the subject of a story by Thomas Bailey Aldrich.

Dawkins, a young thief, known as "The Artful Dodger," in Dickens's *Oliver Twist*.

Dawson, Jemmy, the title and hero of a ballad by Shenstone, an officer in the army of Charles Edward Stuart; he was executed in 1745.

Day of Barricades, The, in French history, was May 12, 1588, when the populace rose against the troops of Henri III.

Another was August 27, 1648, at the opening of the War of the Fronde. Other days of barricades were at the beginning of the Revolution of 1630, and that of the insurrection of 1848; also the day of Louis Napoleon's *coup d'état*, December 2, 1851.

Day of the Corn-Sacks, The, January 3, 1591, when officers of Henri IV, disguised as millers with corn-sacks over their shoulders, attempted to take the gate St. Honoré and surprise Paris.

Dazzle, an adventurer in Dion Boucicault's play, *London Assurance* (1841).

Dea, The Men of, are the Tuatha de Danaan of Irish story.

Dean, Ulick, a young composer in George Moore's novels, *Evelyn Innes* and *Sister Teresa.*

Deane, Lucy, the pretty cousin of Maggie Tulliver in George Eliot's novel, *The Mill on the Floss,* from whom Maggie takes her lover, Stephen Guest.

Deans, Davie, the father of Effie (Euphemia) and Jeanie Deans in Scott's *Heart of Midlothian.* Jeanie, who travels from Edinburgh to London to procure a pardon for Effie, convicted of murdering her illegitimate child, is one of the most admired characters in fiction. The original of the character was one Helen Walker. Her monument in the churchyard of Irongrey has an inscription by Sir Walter, in which he says she "practised in real life the virtues with which fiction has invested the imaginary character of Jeanie Deans; refusing the slightest departure from veracity, even to save the life of a sister, she nevertheless showed her kindness and fortitude, in rescuing her from the severity of the law at the expense of personal exertions which the time rendered as difficult as the motive was laudable."

Death, The Ferry of, applied to the ferry of the Irtish, by which political convicts pass to exile in Siberia.

Death-Ride, The, applied to the charge of the Light Brigade at Balaklava, October 25, 1854, celebrated in Tennyson's poem.

Debarry, Sir Maximus, his brother **Augustus,** and his son **Philip,** characters in George Eliot's *Felix Holt.*

Debon, one of the comrades of Brute, the first (legendary) king of Britain. There is a tradition that Devonshire was "Debon's share," the country assigned to Debon.

De Craye, Horace, a friend of Sir Willoughby in George Meredith's *The Egoist.*

Dedlock, Sir Leicester and **Lady Honoria,** important characters in Dickens's *Bleak House.* Lady Dedlock's secret and its revelation are the theme of the story, interwoven with that of the Chancery suit.

Deerslayer, The, in Cooper's novel of the name, is Natty Bumppo (*q. v.*).

Dee's Speculum, a magic mirror which Dr. John Dee said the angels Gabriel and Raphael gave to him. It passed through various hands, was at one time in Horace Walpole's collection at Strawberry Hill, and is said to be now in the British Museum. It is a black, polished, circular disk fitted with a handle.

Defarge, Ernest and **Thérèse,** revolutionists in Dickens's *A Tale of Two Cities.* Madame Defarge sits near the guillotine as victims are led to execution, and counts the heads that fall.

De Gard, the "chaser" in John Fletcher's play, *The Wild-Goose Chase.*

Degoré, Sir, the hero of an old English romance in 996 lines of verse, printed in Garrick's collection. The name is intended, as the author says, to express something almost lost, so should be Dégaré, from *égarer,* to lose temporarily.

Deirdré. See USNACH.

Delada, a tooth of Buddha, preserved in a temple at Kandy. The natives believe that its possession confers the right to govern Ceylon; and they submitted to the English without resistance when in 1815 the tooth passed into the possession of the invaders.

Delamere, Geoffrey, Lord de la Zouche, an important character in Warren's novel, *Ten Thousand a Year.*

Delancy, Jack, the chief character of *The Golden House,* by Charles Dudley Warner.

Delectable Mountains, The, a range of beautiful hills from whose summits the celestial city could be seen, described in Bunyan's *Pilgrim's Progress* (1678).

Della Crusca School. This name, which originated in Florence, as that of a society with the aim of purifying and settling the language, was applied to a coterie in England at the close of the eighteenth century, noted for affectation and mutual admiration. Among the best known of its members are James Boswell, Mrs. Piozzi, Sheridan, Reynolds (dramatist), Holcroft, and Colman the Younger. Robert Merry, who had lived in Florence and been a member of the Italian Academy, signed himself Della Crusca. "While the epidemic malady was spreading from fool to fool, Della Crusca came over and announced himself by a sonnet to Love; Anna Matilda wrote an incomparable piece of nonsense in praise of it; and 'the two great luminaries of the age,' as Mr. Bell [the publisher] calls them, fell desperately in love with each other. From that period not a day passed without an amatory epistle." The society was extinguished by the satire of the critic Gifford in his *Baviad* and *Mæviad* (1794–1795).

Delmare, Indiana, the subject of George Sand's romance, *Indiana*.

Delmour, Frederick, a brilliant and unprincipled man in Miss Ferrier's novel, *The Inheritance*.

Delorme, Marion, a beautiful adventuress (1612–'50), is the subject of a drama by Victor Hugo, the theme of which is that such a woman can be reclaimed by a pure affection.

Delphine, the title and heroine of a novel by Madame de Staël; she is supposed to be an idealized portrait of the author. Delphine is deserted by her lover and dies of a broken heart.

Delville, the haughty and condescending guardian of the heroine in Miss Burney's novel, *Cecilia* (1782).

De Mailly, Charles, the chief character in a novel of the name by the De Goncourts. He is a literary artist whose genius is killed by the unconscious stupidity of his wife, a pretty, heartless actress.

Demetrius, the lover of Hermia, afterward of Helena, in Shakespeare's *A Midsummer Night's Dream*.

Demetrius, a character in Jonson's play, *The Poetaster*, intended for John Marston.

Demiurgus, in Plato's philosophy, the creator-spirit.

Democritus, the laughing philosopher. "To dine with Democritus" is to go without dining.

Democritus Junior, the name under which Robert Burton published *The Anatomy of Melancholy*. It is inscribed on his monument in Christ Church Cathedral.

Dempster, Janet, the heroine of George Eliot's short tale, *Janet's Repentance.*

Dendin, Peter, and his son **Tenot,** characters in the *Pantagruel* of Rabelais. The father interposed in disputes when the litigants were wearied out, and succeeded; the son tried to nip them in the bud, and failed. The same names are used in Racine's *Les Plaideurs* (The Suitors) and in La Fontaine's *Fables.*

Denham, Jenny, an important character in George Meredith's *Beauchamp's Career.*

Denman, Clara, the heroine of *Cecil Dreeme,* by Theodore Winthrop.

Dennis, a hangman in Dickens's *Barnaby Rudge,* who, when he is condemned to death, "discovers that the satisfaction he has felt in turning off his fellow-mortals was probably not shared by them."

Densdeth, the villain of Theodore Winthrop's novel, *Cecil Dreeme.*

Deputy, The, a small boy in Dickens's *Edwin Drood,* hired by Durdles to stone him if he catches him out late. The imp cries a warning rhyme before beginning.

Derby, Charlotte de la Tremouille, Countess of, and Queen of Man, and her son **Philip,** are characters in Scott's *Peveril of the Peak.*

Derby, Earl of. See STANLEY, THOMAS.

Dering, Cuthbert, a character in George Meredith's *Diana of the Crossways.*

Dermat O'Dyna, a character in old Celtic romance, who eloped with the Princess Grainia.

Deronda, Daniel, a young Jew, the hero of George Eliot's novel of the name. He has been brought up as a Christian, and discovers his Jewish parentage by accident after reaching manhood, through the acquaintance of a beautiful Jewess, whom he marries.

Derrydown Triangle, The, a sobriquet given to Lord Castlereagh, Marquis of Londonderry, in a parody on the Athanasian Creed, by William Hone. The first word is from his title; the other refers to his oratory, the triangle being a thing with three sides, the meanest and feeblest of musical instruments.

Derwentwater, The Earl of, who was executed for participating in the attempt to restore the Stuarts to the throne after the accession of George I, in 1715, is a character in Walter Besant's novel, *Dorothy Forster*, and in A. E. W. Mason's *Lawrence Clavering*.

Desborough, Lucy, the wife of Richard in George Meredith's *The Ordeal of Richard Feverel*, who falls a victim to Sir Austin's "system" of the proper education of youth.

Deschappelles, Pauline, the heroine of Bulwer's play, *The Lady of Lyons*.

Descoings, a grocer in Balzac's novel, *A Bachelor's Establishment*, who was sent to the scaffold with André Chenier, in 1794. The grocer's death caused a greater sensation than that of the poet. His widow had a mania for lottery and always for the same number; she "nursed a trey." But after many failures the trey turned up just after her savings had been stolen, so that she had not renewed her chance; and she died of grief.

Desdemona, the wife of Othello in Shakespeare's tragedy of the name, daughter of Brabantio, a Venetian senator; she is killed by her husband, inspired by Iago to believe in her infidelity.

Deserted Village, The, of Goldsmith's poem, called Sweet Auburn, is identified as Lissoy, where his father was pastor.

Desmarets, Jules, and his beautiful wife **Clemence,** who died mortally wounded by a doubt of her faithfulness entertained for only a short time by her husband, are characters in Balzac's short story, *The Thirteen*.

Desmas, the name of the penitent thief in some apocryphal gospels. In Longfellow's *The Golden Legend* he is called Dumachus.

Desmond. See TERENCE.

Desmond of Kilmallock, the head of the family, who perished in the time of Elizabeth, still keeps his state, according to tradition, under the waters of Lough Gur, rides around the lake in the early morning once every seventh year in full armor, and will some time return to take his own again.

Despair, Giant, in Bunyan's *Pilgrim's Progress*, lived in Doubting Castle, from which Christian and Hopeful escaped by means of the key called Promise.

Desplein, a famous Parisian surgeon, sprung from a poor Parisian family, appears professionally in many of Balzac's stories. In *The Atheist's Mass,* he established and attended a quarterly mass for a poor water-carrier who had been kind to him in his early struggles, although he was himself a pronounced atheist.

De Vere, John. See OXFORD, EARL OF.

Devereux, the title and hero's name of a novel by Bulwer-Lytton.

Devereux, Louise and **Wardour,** characters in Meredith's novel, *Beauchamp's Career.*

Devil, The: the barber and tool of Louis XI, Olivier Ledain, was so called for his evil deeds.

Devil, Robert the, of Normandy, whose father was said to have been a fiend in form of a knight. He forms the subject of an opera by Meyerbeer.

Devil, The Printer's: Aldus Manutius, the celebrated Venetian printer, had a little negro boy to help in his office, who was believed by the populace to be an imp of Satan.

Devil, Son of the, the cruel Eccelino, Governor of Vicenza and chief of the Ghibellines.

Devil on Two Sticks, The. See ASMODEUS and CLEOFAS.

Devil's Parliament, The: that assembled by Henry VI at Coventry, in 1459, was so called because it passed attainders on the Duke of York and his chief supporters.

De Witt, Jorian and **Bramham,** characters in Meredith's *The Adventures of Harry Richmond.*

De Witte, John and **Cornelius,** statesmen of Holland, are introduced in *The Black Tulip* (1850) by Dumas.

Dewlap, The Duke and Duchess of, characters in Meredith's *The Tale of Chloe.*

Dewsbury, Anastasia and **Elizabeth,** characters in Meredith's *The Adventures of Harry Richmond.*

Dewy, Dick, the hero of Hardy's novel, *Under the Greenwood Tree.*

Dhulkarnein (the two-horned), in the Koran, is said to have built the famous rampart against the incursions of Gog and Magog. The wall was made of pieces of iron filled in with melted metal. Dhulkarnein is generally supposed to be Alexander the Great, but some suppose him to have been a much earlier Alexander, contemporary with Abraham. The word in the form *Dulcarnon* is used for a dilemma.

Diaforus, Thomas, father and son, physicians in Molière's *Le Malade Imaginaire.* The name is proverbial for an ignorant and pretentious doctor.

Diamond Jousts, The Nine, instituted by Arthur. The prizes, diamonds, were all won by Launcelot, who gave them to Guinevere, and she in a pet threw them into the river, as told in Tennyson's *Elaine.*

Diana, the subject of the "excellent conceitful sonnets of H. C." (Henry Constable), 1584.

Diana of the Crossways, Diana Warwick, in George Meredith's novel of the name, a beautiful young woman of good society, innocent of evil-doing, though indiscreet enough to set envious women's tongues wagging over her every impetuous action.

Diana the Second of Salmantin, the subject of a pastoral romance by Gil Polo.

Diana Vernon, one of the heroines of Scott's *Rob Roy.*

Diane de Poitiers, a character in *The Two Dianas,* by Dumas.

Dianora, the heroine of one of Boccaccio's stories, which has substantially the same plot as Chaucer's *The Franklin's Tale.*

Diarmaid, the hero of *Diarmaid and Grainne* in Campbell's *Tales of the Highlands*—the same as *Dermat O'Dyna,* or Diarmid. See GRANIA.

Dibutades, a potter of Sicyon, whose daughter traced her lover's shadow on the wall, suggesting the process to her father, which he used in his trade, said to be the origin of sculpture in relief and portrait painting.

Diccon, an itinerant beggar pretending madness, in the early English comedy, *Gammer Gurton's Needle,* attributed to Bishop Still.

Dick, Mr., Richard Babley, a mild lunatic in Dickens's *David Copperfield,* who was forever engaged in writing a memorial to "one of those people that are paid to be memorialized."

Dickon, applied to the King in Shakespeare's *Richard III*, in a paper sent to Norfolk, "Dickon thy master is bought and sold."

Dickson, Thomas, and his son, **Charles,** characters in Scott's *Castle Dangerous*. When Charles is slain, his father will not waver in his task of guarding Lady Augusta: "A time will come for recollection and an hour for revenge!"

Diddler, Jeremy, a clever witty swindler in Kenney's farce, *Raising the Wind*.

Didier, Henri, the lover of Julie in Stirling's drama, *The Courier of Lyons* (1852).

Dido, Queen, the legendary founder of Carthage; in Virgil's *Æneid* she entertains the shipwrecked Æneas, and falls in love with him; and when he sails away kills herself in despair. Many plays, operas, and poems have been founded on her story, among them a tragedy (1734) by Reed; an opera (1783) by Marmontel; a tragedy by Marlowe and Nash (1594); and operas by Metastasio (1724) and Purcell (1657).

Dieppe, Captain, a bold, adroit adventurer with a touch of chivalry, in Anthony Hope's novel of the name.

Dietrich, in the *Nibelungenlied*, is Theodoric the Great.

Diggon, Davie, a shepherd in Spenser's *The Shepearde's Calendar*, who talks of the bad shepherds he found in foreign countries, referring to the Roman Catholic clergy.

Diggory, in Goldsmith's comedy, *She Stoops to Conquer*, is a barn-servant taken into the house "to make a show at the side-table."

Dimanche, Monsieur, a character in Molière's comedy, *Don Juan* (1665), a type of the timid creditors who are disarmed by an impudent show of politeness on the part of their debtors.

Dimmesdale, Arthur, in Hawthorne's *The Scarlet Letter*, a Puritan clergyman, reverenced as a saint, but secretly racked by remorse for a concealed sin. He appears in the play based upon the romance, also in an opera by Walter Damrosch.

Dinah, the colored cook of the St. Clairs in Mrs. Stowe's novel, *Uncle Tom's Cabin*.

Dinas Emrys, a fort on Snowdon, which was building by Vortigern; every night the part built during the day was swallowed up. Merlin found the cause to be two serpents, one white and one red, struggling continually at the bottom of a pool below the works. The white serpent, he said, stood for the Saxons, the red for the Britons; and the red should ultimately conquer. Merlin was then called Ambrose; and the name meant Fort of Ambrose (Embres).

Dingwall, Davie, an attorney employed to resist the claims of the Lords of Ravenswood in Scott's *The Bride of Lammermoor.*

Dinias, the hero of an old Greek novel, *The Wanderings, Adventures, and Loves of Dinias and Dercyllis.*

Dining on Nothing: For this several phrases have been used: to dine with Duke Humphrey, said to be because loungers in St. Paul's who had no dinner to go to were facetiously said to be looking for the tomb of Duke Humphrey, son of Henry IV, which was not there; to dine with Sir Thomas Gresham, alluding to loungers at the Royal Exchange; to dine with the Cross-Legged Knights, because lawyers at one time met their clients at the Temple Church, where are effigies of Crusaders, and men out of employment frequented the place in the hope of some small earnings. Dining with Mahomet means dying.

Dinmont, Dandie (Andrew), an eccentric store-farmer in Scott's *Guy Mannering.*

Diomedes, one of the Greek heroes at the siege of Troy, a character in Shakespeare's *Troilus and Cressida.*

Dione, the subject of a pastoral tragedy by John Gay (1720).

Dionysius the Areopagite, one of the judges of that tribunal in the time of St. Paul, to whom certain writings of the fifth century were erroneously ascribed.

> "Those doctrines so vicious
> Of the old Areopagite Dionysius."
> —Longfellow's *The Golden Legend.*

Dionysius the Younger, a character in Murphy's drama, *The Grecian Daughter,* where he is slain by Euphrasia.

Dioscuri, The, Castor and Pollux, or Polydeuces, called also Tydaridæ. *The Dioscuri* is a celebrated idyl of Theocritus.

Diotima, the teacher of Socrates in Plato's *Symposium,* the priestess of Mantineia.

Dipsodes, the people of Dipsody, subjugated by the hero of Rabelais's *Pantagruel*.

Dipsychus, subject of a poem by Arthur Hugh Clough—conversations between Dipsychus and Spirit.

Dirk Hatteraick, a smuggler in Scott's *Guy Mannering*.

Dirkovitch, Colonel, a Russian soldier and spy, in Kipling's story, *Life's Handicap*.

Dishart, Gavin, the title character of Barrie's novel, *The Little Minister*.

Distaff's Day, the day after Twelfth Night, when women returned to their distaffs; also called Rock Day, one name of a distaff being rock.

Dityrambus, a name of Bacchus; hence, a kind of song in honor of the god of wine, of which Arion was the reputed originator.

Divine, The, is a title of St. John the Evangelist, but has been applied to many. Raphael is sometimes called the divine painter, and likewise the Spaniard Luis Moralês; Ferdinand de Herrera, the divine poet; Jean de Ruysbroek, the divine doctor; Tyrtamos, or Theophrastus, the divine speaker; Ariosto, the divine Lodovico.

Djabal, in Browning's drama, *The Return of the Druses*, claims to be Hakeem, their incarnate god, sent to lead them back to Lebanon from the small island they have colonized, where they are under a prefect belonging to the Knights of Rhodes, who has become their oppressor. Djabal's plans fail; but his ally, Lois, a young Breton, has secured the removal of the tyrant and been appointed in his place, just at the time that Anael, whom they both love, has murdered the prefect. Djabal and Anael die, but Djabal is still Hakeem for his Druses; and Lois leads them back to Syria. See DRUSES.

Dobbin, William, a colonel in Thackeray's *Vanity Fair*, a disinterested friend of the wealthy Osborne family, who marries Amelia Sedley after she has been George Osborne's widow for ten years.

Doboobie, Dr. Demetrius, an astrologer in Scott's *Kenilworth*, who assumes the name Alasco.

Doctor of the Incarnation, a title given to St. Cyril of Alexandria for his defense of that doctrine against Nestorius.

Dodger, The Artful. See DAWKINS.

Dods, Meg, in Scott's *St. Ronan's Well*, the landlady of the Cleikum inn, regarded as "one of the best low comic characters in fiction."

Dodson and Fogg, the lawyers in Mrs. Bardell's suit for breach of promise against Mr. Pickwick in Dickens's *The Pickwick Papers*.

Doeg, the herdsman of King Saul who slew fourscore and five priests. Dryden applies the name in his *Absalom and Achitophel* to Elkanah Settle, who had made an attack upon him. Settle was a dramatist, now known only by the satires upon him.

Dogberry, a "solemn ass" of a constable in Shakespeare's *Much Ado about Nothing*.

Dog, The, a surname applied to Diogenes.

Dog, The Thracian: Loilus, the grammarian, was so called for his critical barkings at Homer and Plato.

Dogs. Among dogs noted in literature, history, and legend are the following: Arthur's was named Carall; Lord Byron's Boatswain has an epitaph by the poet over his grave at Newstead; Cuchulain's was a hound, Luath; Douglas in *The Lady of the Lake* has a dog, Luffra; Erigone's dog, Mœra, is the star canis; Fingal's was Bran; Hercules killed Geryon's dogs, Orthros, the two-headed, and Gargittos; Landseer painted his dog Brutus in his picture, "The Invader of the Larder"; the greyhound in the pathetic story of Llewellyn's dog was Gelert; a greyhound named Master M'Grath won three Waterloo cups and was presented at court in 1871; the dog of Montargis, Dragon, was the means of detecting his master's murderer, Lieutenant Macaire, by the aversion he exhibited. Two French plays, *The Dog of Montargis* and *The Dog of Aubry*, are founded upon the incident, and the former has been adapted in English; this follows a somewhat different version of the story: the victim's sweetheart recognizes her lover's sash in Macaire's possession, and his accomplice is killed by Dragon; Orion's dogs are Arctophonos and Pto-ophagos; Sir Walter Scott had a deerhound Maida, and a black hound, Hamlet; the dog of *The Seven Sleepers*, which spoke with a human voice, was Katmir; in Dickens's *Hard Times* is a performing dog, Merrylegs; the most famous of the Mt. St. Bernard dogs, which saved forty lives, was Barry; his stuffed skin is preserved in the Berne museum. Mrs. Browning wrote a poem to her dog, Flush; Richard Watson Gilder celebrated his Leo; Bob, son of Battle, is the hero of an exciting novel. Rab, a mastiff, is the hero of a famous true story by Dr. John Brown. Rip Van Winkle's dog Snyder is familiar to theater-goers. Alcibiades said he cut off his dog's tail to give the Athenians something to talk about besides himself.

Dogs of War, The: Famine, Fire, and Sword.

Dolabella, a friend of Cæsar and Antony, a character in Shakespeare's *Antony and Cleopatra* and in Dryden's *All for Love.*

Dollalolla, Queen, in the burlesque opera, *Tom Thumb,* by Fielding, altered by O'Hara, opposes Tom's marriage with her daughter, Huncamunca.

Dolla Murrey, a character in Crabbe's *The Borough,* who died while playing cards.

Dolliver, Doctor, in Hawthorne's *The Dolliver Romance,* an honest old apothecary who has come into possession of the elixir of life. He is said to have been modeled after Seymour Kirkup, whom the author knew in Florence.

Dolly Varden, a character in Dickens's *Barnaby Rudge,* a bright little coquette, noted for her gay dress.

Dombey, Mr. Paul, his first and second wives **Fanny** and **Edith,** his daughter **Florence,** and **Little Paul,** characters in Dickens's novel, *Dombey and Son.*

Dom-Daniel, in the *Continuation of the Arabian Nights,* a magic establishment under the ocean near Tunis, begun by Hal-il-Maugraby and finished by his son. It had four entrances, each with 4,000 stairs, and Satan was worshiped there by sorcerers and magicians. It was destroyed by Habed-il-Rouman. In Southey's *Thalaba* Domdaniel is a cave of enchanters destroyed by Thalaba.

Domestic Poultry, in Dryden's *The Hind and the Panther,* stands for the Roman Catholic clergy.

Dominie Sampson, a poor scholar, and a noted character in Scott's *Guy Mannering.*

Domizia, in Browning's drama, *Luria,* a noble lady of Florence, who hopes that Luria will avenge on the Republic its ingratitude toward her two brothers.

Don Adriano de Armado. See ADRIANO.

Donalbain, the younger son of King Duncan, who succeeded his brother Malcolm on the throne of Scotland in 1093, a character in Shakespeare's *Macbeth.*

Donald, a faithful steward in Holcroft's comedy, *The Deserted Daughter,* altered into *The Steward* (1785).

Donald, subject of a poem by Browning founded upon an incident related to him by the man concerned. The chivalry of the deer is contrasted with the treachery of the sportsman.

Donald of the Hammer, a Highlander so strong that he could work for hours with a fore-hammer in each hand; he "filled the banks of Lochawe with mourning and clamor."

Donatello, Count of Monte Beni, a character in Hawthorne's *The Marble Faun,* who resembles the Faun of Praxiteles in appearance and is simple, natural, and joyous, till after he has committed a murder on impulse, when he loses his faun-like character.

Don Juan, a legendary character, a type of the libertine, who appears in the literature of various countries. The original is supposed to be one Don Juan Tenorio of Seville, who killed in a duel the father of a girl whom he had tried to ruin. A statue of the murdered man was placed in the family tomb; and Don Juan breaks into the tomb and invites the statue to a feast he is to give. The statue appears at the feast, compels Don Juan to follow him, and leads him to hell. The story was used by Gabriel Tellez in a drama; Goldoni founded a play upon it; Corneille and Molière made use of it; in music it was treated by Glück in his ballet *Don Juan* (1765), and by Mozart in *Don Giovanni* (1787). Byron's character of *Don Juan* is from the same source. Browning gives the name to the principal character in his *Fifine at the Fair.*

Donne, The Rev. Mr., one of the curates in Charlotte Brontë's novel, *Shirley,* said to have been drawn from one of her father's assistants.

Donnerhugel, Rudolph and **Theodore,** characters in Scott's *Anne of Geierstein.*

Donnithorne, Arthur, a character in George Eliot's *Adam Bede,* who ruined a farmer's girl, Hetty Sorrel, and brought a reprieve just as she was about to be executed for the murder of her child, of which he was the father.

Donovan, the hero of Edna Lyall's novel of the name.

Don Quixote, the hero of Cervantes's celebrated romance of the name.

Dony, Florimel's dwarf in Spenser's *The Faerie Queene.*

Donzel del Phebo, The, "that wandering knight so fair," in a Spanish romance in *The Mirror of Princely Deeds and Knighthood.* Translation by Richard Percival. (Donzel here means a young man.)

Dooley, Mr., a character created by Finley Peter Dunne. His opinions on current events, addressed to Mr. Hennessey, are reported in newspaper articles and published in book-form. His comments are an amusing combination of native shrewdness, Irish wit, and apparent ignorance; their peculiarity is the satire on public measures and popular opinions under the guise of the speculations of an ignorant but clever saloon-keeper, who hears all manner of creeds, philosophies, policies, arts, and events discussed day after day, and falls into the habit of oracular opinion and decision.

Doolin of Mayence, the hero of an old French romance of chivalry, the ancestor of Ogier the Dane.

Doone, Lorna, a girl belonging to a family of well-born outlaws living in Exmoor, England; the heroine of a novel of the name by Richard D. Blackmore.

Doorm, an earl in Tennyson's *Enid,* slain by Geraint for striking Enid on the cheek.

Dora, the heroine of an idyl by Tennyson.

Dora Spenlow, David's "child-wife" in Dickens's *David Copperfield.*

Dorastus, the lover of Fawnia in a romance (1588) by Robert Greene, *Pandosto, the Triumph of Time,* upon which Shakespeare's *A Winter's Tale* is founded. It was afterward published under the title, *The History of Dorastus and Fawnia.* In the "history," Hermione is actually dead, and the love of Leontes for Perdita drives him to suicide.

Dorax, in Dryden's tragedy, *Don Sebastian* (1690), is the assumed name of Don Alonzo, who turned renegade and joined the Emperor of Barbary because King Sebastian of Portugal gave Violante, his betrothed, to Henriquez. Dorax is regarded as the greatest of Dryden's tragic characters.

Doricles, a name assumed by Florizel in Shakespeare's *A Winter's Tale.*

Dorimant, a witty rake in Etherege's *The Man of Mode* (1676); the original of the character was the notorious profligate, the Earl of Rochester.

Dorinda, a name applied in the Earl of Dorset's verses to Catherine Sedley, mistress of James II.

Dorine, a maid of Marianne in Molière's *Tartuffe* (1664).

Dorlange, a character in Balzac's *Member for Arcis.*

D'Ormeo, the prime minister in Browning's drama, *King Victor and King Charles.*

Doron, a character in Greene's *Menaphon,* which has been supposed to be intended for Shakespeare.

Dorothea, the heroine of Goethe's poem, *Herrmann and Dorothea.*

Dorothea, the heroine of Massinger's *The Virgin Martyr* (1622); she is attended by an angel, to whom she had given alms when he wore the form of a beggar-boy.

Dorothea Brooke. See BROOKE.

Dorrit, William, a prisoner for debt, known as the Father of the Marshalsea, in Dickens's *Little Dorrit.* His brother Frederick, his good-for-nothing son Edward, and his daughter Fanny, a ballet-dancer, are characters in the book. The younger daughter, Amy, is Little Dorrit, the heroine. William becomes heir to a large estate, pays his debts, and leaves the Marshalsea in glory.

Dot. See PEERYBINGLE.

Dotheboys Hall, Squeers's school in Dickens's *Nicholas Nickleby,* to which children who were uncared for or under a cloud were sent, and were bullied, starved, and beaten, until Nicholas breaks up the establishment.

Doubting Castle, the castle of Giant Despair in Bunyan's *Pilgrim's Progress.*

Douglas, the title and hero of a tragedy by the Rev. John Home, first played in Edinburgh in 1756, by which the presbytery was so scandalized that Home left the ministry.

Douglas, the name of a family in Miss Ferrier's novel called *Marriage.* Mary Douglas is the heroine.

Douglas, Anne, the heroine of Constance Fenimore Woolson's novel, *Anne.*

Douglas, Archibald, Earl, and **Margery,** his daughter, are characters in Scott's *The Fair Maid of Perth.*

Douglas, Archibald, Earl, called **Tineman** (the loser), who lost the battles of Homildon Hill, Shrewsbury, and Verneuil, is a character in Shakespeare's *Henry IV*, Part II.

Douglas, Archibald, Earl of Angus, surnamed "Bell the Cat," is a character in Scott's poem, *Marmion.*

Douglas, Archibald, Laird of Kilspindie, who had been banished, returned, braving the King's displeasure, to ask pardon; he had been a favorite of the King when a child. The King sent him to France, where he died soon afterward. The story is the subject of a ballad by Finley.

Douglas, Clara, a character in Bulwer-Lytton's play, *Money.*

Douglas, Ellen, the heroine of Scott's poem, *The Lady of the Lake.*

Douglas, George, in Scott's *The Abbot,* effects the rescue of Queen Mary from confinement.

Douglas, James, a character in Scott's poem, *The Lady of the Lake,* is an imaginary personage, a supposed uncle of the banished Earl of Angus.

Douglas, James, the Black, a character in Scott's *Castle Dangerous* (Castle of Douglas), where he presents himself to Lady Augusta Berkeley as the "Knight of the Tomb."

Douglas, John Sholto, a brave Englishman who takes part in the defense of Delhi, in Flora Annie Steel's novel, *On the Face of the Waters,* a tale of the Sepoy mutiny.

Douglas, Lady Margaret, is the heroine of a ballad, *The Douglas Tragedy,* in *The Border Minstrelsy.* Lord William stealing her away, was pursued by her father and brothers, with whom he fought and left them dying or grievously wounded. He himself was so wounded that he died as soon as he reached his mother's house, and before morning his lady also was dead.

Douloureuse Garde, The, a castle at Berwick-upon-Tweed, where Launcelot of the Lake defended Queen Guinevere against the charge of Mador that she had poisoned his brother. King

Arthur in gratitude gave the castle to Launcelot and it was named La Joyeuse Garde.

Dounce, John, the hero of Dickens's sketch, *The Misplaced Attachment of Mr. John Dounce.*

Dousterswivel, in Scott's *The Antiquary,* a German who uses a divining rod in search of hidden treasure for getting money from the credulous.

Dowlas, Daniel, his wife **Deborah** and his son **Dick,** characters in the comedy by George Colman the Younger, *The Heir-at-Law* (1797), afterward called *The Lord's Warming-pan* (1825). He is raised to the peerage as Lord Duberly by the supposed death of the heir, Henry Morland, who appears shortly after Dowlas has entered upon possession.

Downer, Billy, a shoeblack and philosopher from whom Selby's play, *The Unfinished Gentleman,* takes its name.

Doyce, Daniel, an engineer and inventor in Dickens's *Little Dorrit.*

Doyle, Laurence, a civil engineer in George B. Shaw's play, *John Bull's Other Island.*

Dragon, the device on the banner of the old British kings. Pendragon means something like great dragon, and was applied to a warrior who slew a dragon or chief; for the word came to be applied to the chief warriors. Geoffrey of Monmouth tells a story of a star that appeared at Winchester when Aurelius was king, which sent forth a ray ending in a dragon-shaped flame. Uther caused two golden dragons to be made, one of which he gave to Winchester, and the other he used as a royal standard. Henry VII took a red dragon for his device at Bosworth Field.

Dragon of Wantley, The (Warncliff, a lodge and wood in Penniston, Yorkshire), is the subject of an old burlesque ballad, included in Percy's *Reliques.* The hero, More, of More Hall, killed the monster by kicking him in the mouth, where only he was vulnerable. Henry Carey founded upon it a burlesque opera (1737), with the same name, the music by Lamke; and the following year as equel, *Margery: or, The Dragoness,* was produced at Covent Garden.

Dragon's Hill, Berkshire, according to legend, the place where St. George killed the dragon, though other traditions give

"Sylenê in Libya" and Berytus or Beyrut. According to Saxon annals, Cedric of the West Saxons slew the pendragon Naud with five thousand men, at Dragon's Hill.

Dragon-Slayers. Dragons were killed, according to legends of the saints, by St. Philip, the Apostle, St. Martha, St. Cado, St. Florent, St. Paull, St. Maudet, St. Keyne of Cornwall, St. George, St. Margaret, St. Clement of Metz, St. Michael, St. Samson, St. Romain, and by Donatus and Pope Sylvester.

Drapier, M.D., signature of Dean Swift to a series of letters (1724) to the people of Ireland, advising them not to accept the copper money coined by William Wood under a patent granted by George I for his mistress, the Duchess of Kendal, who was to share the profits with Wood. The logic and brilliancy of the letters, for the discovery of whose authorship a reward of £300 had been offered, caused the withdrawal of the patent and the collapse of the scheme. In verses on his own death Swift wrote:

> "Can we the Drapier then forget?
> Is not our nation in his debt?"

Drawcansir, a celebrated character in a burlesque play, *The Rehearsal* (1671), by George Villiers, Duke of Buckingham, and others; he is a swaggering bully, who is represented as killing all the combatants on both sides in a battle, and making a boastful speech after it. The name has become a synonym for a braggart. Carlyle calls actors in the French Revolution, "Drawcansir-figures, of enormous whiskerage, unlimited command of gunpowder; not without ferocity and even a certain heroism, stage heroism, in them."

Dred, a fugitive slave hiding in the Dismal Swamp in Virginia, in Harriet Beecher Stowe's novel of the name, afterward called *Nina Gordon.*

Dreddlington, Lord, a character in Warren's *Ten Thousand a Year.*

Dreeme, Cecil, the subject of a novel by Theodore Winthrop.

Dren, Philip, the hero of *The Monarch of Mincing Lane,* by William Black.

Dromios, The Two, twin brothers, in Shakespeare's *The Comedy of Errors,* attendants on the two Antipholuses.

Drood, Edwin, the title and hero's name of the novel which Dickens left half finished at his death. Edwin disappears mysteriously and is believed to have been murdered. The indications are that his uncle, John Jasper, was to be revealed as his murderer. Jasper was in love with the girl to whom Edwin had been betrothed, though they had agreed to give up the marriage, which was agreeable to neither of them, being an arrangement of their parents; but of this they had spoken to no one but the young girl's guardian.

Drowne, the hero of Hawthorne's short story, *Drowne's Wooden Image,* the theme of which is the inspiration given by love to work that is otherwise purely mechanical.

Drugger, Abel, a tobacco merchant in Jonson's comedy, *The Alchemist* (1610), who goes to Subtle to find out how to arrange his new shop to bring luck. It was a favorite rôle of Garrick's. *The Tobacconist* is a farce made from this comedy.

Druid, Dr., a pedantic Welsh tutor in Cumberland's comedy, *The Fashionable Lover* (1772).

Drum, John (sometimes **Tom**), a name used in the phrase "John Drum's entertainment," used by Shakespeare and others to signify ill treatment of an unwelcome guest, "to hale a man in by the heade and thrust him out by both the shoulders." *Jack Drum's Entertainment* is the title of an anonymous comedy (1601).

Drummle, Bentley, called "The Spider," a surly, niggardly fellow in Dickens's *Great Expectations,* who marries Estella, the heroine, and ill-treats her.

Drunken Parliament, The, a name given to the Parliament of 1661 at Edinburgh at a time "when the men of affairs were almost perpetually drunk."

Druses, a sect whose home was originally in Egypt; they were driven out by persecution and settled in Syria, whence they were driven and lived under the Knights of Rhodes in an island of the Sporades. The founder was the Hakeem Biamr Allah, believed to be incarnate God and the last divine prophet. The head of the sect was called the Hakeem. In the fifteenth century Lois de Dreux, a Breton and a convert, led them back to Syria. Browning's drama, *The Return of the Druses,* deals with imagined incidents leading up to this event. See DJABAL.

Dry-as-Dust, Rev. Dr., an imaginary personage, the author of prefatory letters in some of Scott's novels. His name is often applied to a dull, plodding author.

Dryfesdale, Jasper, an old steward at Lochleven Castle who tries to poison Mary Stuart and her retinue, in Scott's *The Abbot.*

Du Barry, Countess, the subject of a play, *Du Barry,* by David Belasco, and a character in *The Queen's Necklace, Joseph Balsamo,* and *The Memoirs of a Physician,* by Dumas, all these being representations of one of the mistresses of Louis XV.

Dubric, St., or **Dubricius,** the archbishop that crowned Prince Arthur when he was fifteen years old, mentioned in Drayton's *Polyolbion* and Tennyson's *The Coming of Arthur.*

Duchess May, The, heroine of Mrs. Browning's poem, *The Rhyme of the Duchess May.*

Duchomar, in Ossian's *Fingal,* was in love with Morna, daughter of Cormac, King of Ireland, and slew his successful rival. Morna stabbed him then with his own sword, and he, taking it from her, slew her with it.

Ducie, Vivian, a character in Meredith's novel, *Beauchamp's Career.*

Du Croisy and **La Grange,** in Molière's *Les Précieuses Ridicules* (1659), court two romantic girls who think their manners too plain; they therefore send their lackeys with high-flown titles to woo the girls, who are at first enchanted, but in the end are undeceived.

Dudgeon, Richard, the title-character of Shaw's play, *The Devil's Disciple.*

Dudley, Esther, the title and heroine of a short tale by Hawthorne.

Dudley, Lord, a "profoundly immoral" English peer living in Paris, a character in several of Balzac's novels, *The Lily of the Valley* and others. His wife, **Lady Arabella,** appears also in that novel, in *A Daughter of Eve* and others.

Dudu, one of the three beauties of the harem in Byron's *Don Juan.*

Duenda, a Spanish goblin or house-spirit. The title of a comedy by Calderón is *La Dama Duenda.*

Duessa, in Spenser's *The Faerie Queene*, the daughter of Falsehood and Shame, who assumes various disguises to beguile the Red Cross Knight. She is supposed in the first book to personify the Roman Catholic Church; while Duessa in the fifth book is intended for Mary Stuart, arraigned before Queen Elizabeth, as Mercilla.

Duffian, the Honorable and Reverend Herbert, a character in Meredith's novel, *Evan Harrington.*

Du Guesclin, the famous Constable of France, appears in Conan Doyle's romance, *The White Company.*

Duke, The, in Shakespeare's *As You Like It*, banished by his usurping brother, is living contentedly in the Forest of Arden with his friends.

Dulcinea del Toboso, the country girl whom Don Quixote chose for the object of his chivalrous devotion. Her name was Aldonza Lorenza; and the Knight gave her the name Dulcinea (now used as a synonym for sweetheart) as being something like her own but finer, and added the name of her birthplace, making a title, "to his thinking, harmonious, uncommon and significant."

Dull, a constable in Shakespeare's *Love's Labor's Lost.*

Dumachus, name given to the impenitent thief in Longfellow's *The Golden Legend*, where the penitent thief is Titus. In the *Gospel of Nicodemus*, they are, respectively, Gestas and Dysmas, and in *Joseph of Arimathea*, Gesmas and Dismas.

Dumaine, one of the lords attending the King in *Love's Labor's Lost*, described as handsome and witty.

Dumbello, Lady, a pretty simpleton in Anthony Trollope's novel, *The Small House at Allington.*

Dumbiedikes, The Laird of, a grasping landlord in Scott's *The Heart of Midlothian.* The young laird is in love with Jeanie Deans.

Dumb Ox, The, of Sicily, a name given to St. Thomas Aquinas by his fellow-students at Cologne, on account of his taciturnity and abstraction and his heavy body. The story is, that his teacher remarked that if that ox should begin to bellow the world would be filled with the noise. Longfellow speaks of the "Dumb Ox of Cologne" in *The Golden Legend.* St. Thomas was afterward called the Angelic Doctor and the Angel of the Schools.

Dun, a hangman in Charles Cotton's *Scarronides,* which is a travesty on *The Æneid* (1672).

Dun, Joe, a bailiff of Lincoln in the time of Henry VII, from whose name the verb "to dun" is said to have come.

Duncan, King of Scotland, a character in Shakespeare's tragedy, *Macbeth.* The circumstances of his murder by his host are taken from the account of the assassination of King Duff. The real Duncan, whose death resulted from the treachery of Macbeth, Mormaer of Moray, in 1040, is on record as an unjust and weak sovereign, unlike the gracious Duncan of the tragedy.

Dun Cow, The, a fabulous beast kept by a giant in Shropshire. It wandered to Dunsmore Heath, where it was killed by Sir Guy of Warwick.

Dundee. See CLAVERHOUSE.

Dundreary, Lord, in Tom Taylor's comedy, *Our American Cousin,* originally a subordinate character, but made the principal rôle by the actor, Edward A. Sothern, who virtually created the unique personality of Dundreary.

Dunkle, Doctor Ginery, an American "gentleman of great poetical elements" in Dickens's *Martin Chuzzlewit.*

Dunois, the hero of a famous French song, *Dunois the Brave,* first called *Partant pour la Syrie.* The music was composed by Queen Hortense, mother of Napoleon III. The words are attributed to Monsieur de Laborde. It became the national air of the French Empire. Sir Walter Scott made an English translation.

Dunois, Count. See BASTARD OF ORLEANS.

Dunsinane, the scene of a battle in Shakespeare's *Macbeth,* is a hill nine miles northeast of Perth.

Dunstan, St., the patron of smiths, who in his cell near Glastonbury Church was visited by Satan while at his metal-working, and caught his guest by the nose with red-hot forceps.

Dunstane, Captain Luken, and **Lady Emma,** characters in Meredith's *Diana of the Crossways.*

Durance, Colney, a cynical friend of the Radnors in Meredith's novel, *One of Our Conquerors.*

Durandarte, a fabulous Spanish hero in the romances of chivalry. He is introduced in *Don Quixote,* in the Knight's adventure in the cave of Montesinos.

Durbeyfield, Tess, heroine of Thomas Hardy's *Tess of the D'Urbervilles.*

Durden, Dame, a notable housewife, heroine of an English song. The name was applied to Esther Summerson in Dickens's *Bleak House,* by her housemates.

Durdles, a stone-mason in Dickens's *Edwin Drood,* who is more familiar than anyone else with the cathedral crypt, for which he has the keys in order to make repairs. Jasper, the villain, makes use of him to explore the crypt for some sinister purpose, which would have appeared if the author had finished the novel.

Duroy, Georges, the title-character of De Maupassant's novel, *Bel Ami.*

Durrance, John, an important character in A. E. W. Mason's novel, *Four Feathers.*

Durward, Quentin, the title and hero of a novel by Sir Walter Scott. Quentin is in the Scottish guards in the pay of Louis XI of France and saves the King's life in a boar-hunt.

Dutocq, a clerk in the Department of Finance, a spying hypocrite in Balzac's novel, *The Middle Classes.*

Duval, Armand, the hero of Dumas's drama, *La dame aux Camélias.*

Duval, Catherine, the title-character of Ludovic Halévy's story, *Mademoiselle Duval.*

Duval, Denis, the title and hero of a novel which Thackeray left unfinished.

Duvidney, Dorothea and **Virginia,** characters in George Meredith's *One of Our Conquerors.*

Dvalin, a dwarf in Oehlenschläger's *The Dwarfs,* who spun new golden hair for Sif, Thor's wife, after Loki had cut off her own.

Dwarfs: in the story, *Valentine and Orson* (fifteenth century), Lady Clerimond has a dwarf, Pacolet, who has a winged horse. In Scott's *The Black Dwarf,* he is a malignant fairy. The guardian of the Nibelungen hoard is Dwarf Alberich, whose cloak of invisibility is captured by Siegfried. A castle specter who gives malicious advice is the subject of an allegorical romance by Ludwig Tieck, *Dwarf Peter*. A short, amusing story by Dickens is entitled *Chops the Dwarf*.

Dysmas. See DUMACHUS.

Earthly Paradise, The, a legendary land sought by a company of gentlemen and sailors, who in their old age arrive at a western land before unknown, where they pass the time in telling stories from the old mythologies, which make up the poem, *The Earthly Paradise*, by William Morris.

East Lynne, scene and title of a novel (1861) by Mrs. Henry Wood, the dramatic version of which has been popular for many years.

Easy, Midshipman, the title and hero of a novel by Captain Marryat.

Ebbeson, Niels, the subject of a Norwegian patriotic tragedy by Christian Levin Sander (1756–1819).

Echephron, an old soldier in the *Pantagruel* of Rabelais, who tells the tale of *The Man and "His Hapworth of Milk,"* one of the many stories of those who, in imagining a great fortune to come, lose what is to be the foundation of it.

Echetlos (holder of the plowshare), the hero of a legend of the Battle of Marathon, who plowed down the ranks of the enemy, appearing wherever the Grecian lines were weakening. He disappeared after the battle, and the oracle, being consulted, gave him no name but the Holder of the Plowshare, "The great deed ne'er grows small." Browning has made him the subject of his poem, *Echetlos*.

Eckhardt, the faithful, in German legend, is the friend of Tannhäuser, who tried to prevent him from exposing himself to the enchantments of the sorceress. In another legend he is an old man who on the evening of Maundy Thursday drives all the people of Eisleben indoors to save them from a dreadful procession of headless bodies, dead men, and two-legged horses that is to pass by. A story by Tieck, translated by Carlyle, is founded upon a legend that makes Eckhardt warn travelers from the fatal delights of the Venusberg.

Eden, City of, in Dickens's *Martin Chuzzlewit*, a city on paper only, in reality a dreary and malarial marsh with a dozen log-cabins.

Edenhall, in Cumberland, the scene of the story of the fairy goblet left on St. Cuthbert's Well, whose loss or destruction will take away all good luck from the family. Uhland's poem, *The Luck of Edenhall,* is translated by Longfellow. The goblet is in the possession of Sir Christopher Musgrave, Bart., of Eden Hall, Cumberland, not so entirely shattered as the ballad represents.

Edgar, the son of Gloucester in Shakespeare's *King Lear.*

Edgar, master of Ravenswood in Scott's *The Bride of Lammermoor.*

Edgarmond, Corinne, the subject of Madame de Staël's *Corinne.*

Edie Ochiltree, in Scott's novel, *The Antiquary,* is called by Irving, "that mirror of philosophic vagabonds and Nestor of beggars."

Edith, a character in Scott's poem, *The Lord of the Isles,* who, in disguise as a page, had many adventures.

Edmonstone, the name of a family figuring in *The Heir of Redclyffe,* by Charlotte M. Yonge.

Edmund, the natural son of Gloucester in Shakespeare's *King Lear.*

Edward, the hero of James Thomson's tragedy, *Edward and Eleanora* (1739), which was refused a license after its first production, "on account of its political allusions, and more especially because it contained a too flattering portrait of the Prince of Wales, who was not in good odor with the Court or Ministry."

Edward I, the hero of a drama in blank verse by George Peele (1593).

Edward II, the subject of a tragedy by Christopher Marlowe, his "troublesome raigne and lamentable death."

Edward III, the subject of Rev. Dr. Joshua Barnes's drama of that name (1688).

Edward IV, a character in Shakespeare's *Henry VI,* Parts II and III, and in *Richard III.* He is introduced in Scott's *Anne of Geierstein,* and also appears in an old ballad, *Edward IV and the Tanner of Tamworth.*

Edward, the Black Prince, the subject of a tragedy by Shirley (1640).

Edward, Prince of Wales, the son of Henry VI, a character in Shakespeare's *Henry VI*, Part III.

Edward, Prince of Wales (Edward V), son of Edward IV, one of the "Princes in the Tower," appears in Shakespeare's *Richard III*.

Edward, Prince of Wales, afterward Edward VI, a character in Mark Twain's *The Prince and the Pauper*, and in the play by Abby S. Richardson.

Edwardes, Murray, a character in Mrs. Humphry Ward's *Robert Elsmere*, who carries out Elsmere's plans after his death.

Edwards, Desire, the heroine of Edward Bellamy's novel *The Duke of Stockbridge*, a descendant of Jonathan Edwards.

Edwin, the hero of Parnell's tale, *Edwin of the Green*, who is changed from deformity to beauty by fairies.

Edwin, the hero of Beattie's poem, *The Minstrel* (1773).

Edwin, the hero of Sir Henry Taylor's play, *Edwin the Fair*.

Edwin, the hero of Goldsmith's ballad, *The Hermit*.

Edwin, the hero of Fanny Burney's tragedy, *Edwin and Elgitha*.

Edwin, the hero of Mallet's ballad, *Edwin and Emma*.

Edwin, the hero of Alexander Smith's poem, *Edwin of Deira*.

Effiat, Henri d', Marquis of Cinq-Mars (*q. v.*).

Égalité, a title assumed by Louis Philippe Joseph, Duke of Orleans, to indicate his adherence to the cause of the people in the Revolution. He was called Philippe Égalité; was guillotined in 1793. His son, Louis Philippe, was king of France, 1830–1848.

Eger, Sir, one of three heroes of an old English romance in verse, Sir Eger, Sir Grahame, and Sir Graysteel.

Egerton, Audley, a statesman in Bulwer's *My Novel*, a rival in love of Harley L'Estrange.

Eglantine, the daughter of Pepin and bride of Valentine in *Valentine and Orson* (fifteenth century).

Eglantine, Madame, the prioress in Chaucer's *Canterbury Tales*, celebrated for her French accent after the school "of Stratford-atte-Bowe."

Eglett, Lady Charlotte, in George Meredith's *Lord Ormont and His Aminta*, is the sister of Lord Ormont.

Egmont, Lamoral, Count of, a patriot of the Low Countries (1522–1568), executed by order of the Duke of Alva for opposition to the policy of Spain. Goethe's tragedy, *Egmont*, is founded on his career.

Eikon Basilike, The (Royal Image), in reply to which Milton wrote his celebrated *Eikonoclastes* (Image-breaker), was supposed to be the work of Charles I, but is now admitted to be by Dr. John Gauden, whose loyalty to the Stuarts was rewarded after the Restoration with the bishopric of Exeter and afterward that of Worcester.

Eire, one of the Tuatha de Danaan in Irish legend, from whom Ireland takes the name Erin.

Eivir, in Scott's *Harold the Dauntless*, is a Danish maid who waits on Harold in the disguise of a page and afterward marries him.

Ekdal, Hjalmar, in Ibsen's *The Wild Duck*, a weak, vain, boastful, shiftless idealist. **Gina Ekdal,** a child, is a pathetic character, who, grieved at her father's repelling her, shoots herself.

Elaine, the subject of one of Tennyson's *Idyls of the King*, in love with Sir Launcelot. She is called "the lily maid of Astolat."

Elbow, a Malapropian constable in Shakespeare's *Measure for Measure*, who arrests "two notorious benefactors, void of all profanation in the world that good Christians ought to have."

Elburne, Countess, a character in Meredith's novel, *Evan Harrington*.

Eldorado, an imaginary country abounding in gold, which Francis Orellana, a companion of Pizarro, professed to have discovered between the Amazon and the Orinoco.

Eleanor Cobham, Duchess of Gloucester, celebrated for her beauty and immorality, a character in Shakespeare's *Henry VI*, Part II.

Eleanor de Bohun, Duchess of Gloucester, a character in Shakespeare's *Richard II*.

Eleazar, a bloodthirsty, brutal Moor in Marlowe's tragedy (finished by Dekker), *Lust's Dominion* (1588).

Elector, The Great, Frederick William of Brandenburg (1620–1688).

Elena, the heroine of the second part of Sir Henry Taylor's *Philip Van Artevelde.*

Elene, subject of a poem attributed to Cynewulf, on the finding of the cross by St. Helena.

Eleven Thousand Virgins, The, the subject of a medieval legend, according to which St. Ursula, to escape marriage with a pagan prince, fled in company with ten noble companions, each attended by one thousand virgins. They were captured and killed at Cologne by a party of Huns, and their alleged bones are exhibited in the church built in their honor at Cologne. The earlier forms of the legend do not specify the number, and various conjectures have been formed as to the origin of the "eleven thousand" statement. One is that it arose from one of the virgins being named Undecimella; a more probable one that the M standing for martyrs in the notice of them in the Freisingen codex—"SS. M. XI. Virginum" (eleven virgin martyrs)—was mistaken for M, the numeral.

Elfrida, the subject of a tragedy (1753) by William Mason, with the chorus in imitation of the Greek drama.

Elfthryth, the beautiful daughter of Ordgar, to whom King Edgar sent Ethelwald to see whether she were as beautiful as she was said to be. Ethelwald fell in love with her, and, representing to the King that her beauty had been overpraised, married her himself; but when the King discovered the deception he slew Ethelwald and made Elfthryth his wife.

Elginbrod, David, the title and hero of a novel by George Macdonald.

Elia, the well-known pseudonym of Charles Lamb, first used as a signature to his first paper in the *London Magazine.* "Remembering," Talfourd says, "the name of a gay, light-hearted foreigner who fluttered there for a time," he signed it to the contribution. The second paper he sent unsigned and the printer added the Elia, which Lamb then adopted.

Eliacin, a character in Racine's tragedy, *Athalie,* the same as Joas. The name has become proverbial in France to designate one of illustrious birth destined to a brilliant career after encountering great dangers.

Eliakim, a name applied to the Duke of York (afterward James II), in a poem by Samuel Pordage, *Azaria and Hushai,* written as a reply to Dryden's *Absalom and Achitophel.*

Elisabeth, the heroine of *The Exiles of Siberia,* by Madame Cottin (1773–1807).

Elizabeth, daughter of the King of Hungary, the heroine of Charles Kingsley's dramatic poem, *The Saint's Tragedy.*

Elizabeth, Princess, daughter of Elizabeth Woodville, is betrothed to Richmond in the last act of *Richard III,* when he becomes the victor.

Elizabeth, Queen, is introduced in Scott's *Kenilworth,* in Henry Jones's tragedy *The Earl of Essex* (1745), and other works. *Elizabetha Triumphans* (1588), a poem in blank verse by James Aske, commemorates the defeat of the Spanish Armada. Her birth and christening and prophecies concerning her are related in Shakespeare's *Henry VIII,* and a passage in the second act of *A Midsummer Night's Dream,* beginning "That very time I saw," is regarded as an allusion to her. Mercilla in *The Faerie Queene* represents her. She is a character in Schiller's drama, *Mary Stuart;* and is introduced in Charles Major's *Dorothy Vernon of Haddon Hall.*

Elizabeth Woodville, Queen of Edward IV, a character in Shakespeare's *Richard III.*

Ellenwood, Mr., the hero of Hawthorne's tale, *The Wedding Knell.*

Elliott, Anne, the heroine of Jane Austen's novel, *Persuasion.*

Elliott, Hobbie, a character in Scott's *The Black Dwarf.*

Elliston, Roderick, the subject of Hawthorne's tale, *Egotism.*

Eloisa, the supposed writer in Pope's poem, *Eloisa to Abélard,* founded on the story of Abélard and Héloïse.

Elsa, the title and heroine's name of a novel by Alexander Lange Kjelland.

Else, the heroine of the Danish ballad, *Aager and Else,* which has been translated by Longfellow; the dead Aager tells Else that when she rejoices, his grave is lined with roses, but filled with black blood when she grieves.

Elshender, The Recluse, the hero of Scott's *The Black Dwarf.*

Elsie, the heroine of Longfellow's poem, *The Golden Legend,* who offers her life for Prince Henry of Hoheneck.

Elsie Venner, the title and heroine of a novel by Oliver Wendell Holmes, treating of the power of heredity.

Elspie, the heroine of Clough's poem, *Bothie of Toberna-Vuolich.*

Elton, Mr., a vulgar clergyman in Jane Austen's novel, *Emma.*

Elvire, a name used by Lamartine in his *Meditations* and *Harmonies,* for the lady addressed in them.

Elvire, the wife of Don Juan in Browning's *Fifine at the Fair.*

Ely, John Morton, Bishop of, a character in Shakespeare's *Richard III.* The marriage of Richmond (Henry VII) and Elizabeth, uniting the York and Lancaster families, was suggested by him.

Emelie, in Chaucer's *The Knight's Tale,* the wife of Palamon, "fairer than the lilie on hire stalkes greene." The story is introduced into the play, *Two Noble Kinsmen,* and Dryden's *Palamon and Arcite* has Emilia as its heroine.

Emerald Isle, The, a name first applied to Ireland in a poem, *Erin,* by Dr. William Drennan (1754–1820).

Émile, the subject of Jean Jacques Rousseau's novel of the same name.

Emilia, the wife of Iago in Shakespeare's *Othello,* of "thorough vulgarity and loose principles united to a high degree of spirit, energetic feeling, strong sense, and low cunning."

Emilia Viviani, the "noble and unfortunate lady now imprisoned in the convent of St. Anne, Pisa," to whom Shelley addressed the poem, *Epipsychidion.*

Em'ly, Little, the niece of Dan'l Peggotty in Dickens's *David Copperfield,* who elopes with David's friend Steerforth on the eve of her intended marriage to her Cousin Ham, a longshoreman.

Empedocles, a famous Sicilian philosopher, about 444 B.C., who, according to tradition, threw himself into the crater of Mt. Ætna to give the impression that the gods had carried him to heaven; but an eruption threw out one of his iron sandals and exposed the fraud. He is the subject of a dramatic poem by Matthew Arnold, *Empedocles on Etna.*

Endicott, John, Governor of Massachusetts, appears in Hawthorne's tale, *The Maypole of Merry Mount.*

Endymion. Keats's poem, *Endymion,* is the one criticized in an article in *The Quarterly Review,* which was supposed to have hastened his death. Endymion is the subject of a romance (1624) in French by Gombaud, of a lyric by Longfellow, and a play (1592) by John Lyly.

Endymion, the title and hero of a novel by Disraeli.

Enfilden, Domini, the heroine and chief female character of Robert Hichens's novel, *The Garden of Allah.*

Engaddi, The Hermit of, an enthusiast in Scott's *The Talisman.*

England, Clothier of, a title given to John Winchcomb, also called Jack of Newbury, who in the time of Henry VIII kept one hundred looms, and armed and clothed one hundred of his men to march against the Scots in the army that overthrew them at Flodden Field.

Enid, a lady of King Arthur's court, wife of Geraint, the subject of Tennyson's idyl, *Geraint and Enid.*

Ennius (239–169 B.C.), sometimes called the father of Latin poetry, whose name has been applied to early poets of other countries as a title.

Enobarbus, a character in Shakespeare's *Antony and Cleopatra,* who kills himself in remorse at having wronged his master.

Entelachy, in the *Pantagruel* of Rabelais, is the kingdom of Queen Quintessence (land of speculative science) visited by Pantagruel and his companions in their search for the holy bottle.

Epicene, a supposed young woman, subject of Ben Jonson's comedy, *Epicene: or, The Silent Woman.*

Epicharis, a Roman woman who entered into a conspiracy against Nero, and strangled herself, after submitting to torture rather than reveal her accomplices. She is the subject of a fine French tragedy by Legouvé, *Epicharis et Néron* (1794).

Epicurus of China, The: Tao-tse, whose "Potion of Immortality" is said to have caused the death of several emperors seeking deathlessness.

Epidicus, a faithful slave, title and subject of a comedy by Plautus, his own favorite among his works.

Epimenides, of Crete, a poet and philosopher contemporary with Solon, who, according to the legend, slept in a cave fifty-seven years, during which time his soul had been studying medicine and philosophy, so that he was possessed of great wisdom when he waked; he lived 289 years. Goethe has a poem, *The Awakening of Epimenides.*

Eppie, the child adopted by the miser in George Eliot's novel, *Silas Marner.*

Equity, The Father of: Heneage Finch, Earl of Nottingham (1621–1682), called Amri in *Absalom and Achitophel.*

Eraclius, an Emperor of whom a story is told in the *Gesta Romanorum* and by the summoner in Chaucer, to the effect that when a knight who had been condemned to death for murder was proved innocent by the appearance of the supposed victim, the Emperor ordered the knight to death in order that his former command should be carried out; the man who brought him back, because he had not carried out the order; and the supposed victim, because he was the cause of the deaths of the other two. The story is told also of Cornelius Piso.

Erceldoune, Thomas of, or Thomas the Rhymer, a legendary character, who was taken by an elf to an underground place beneath the Eildon tree; after seven years he was allowed to visit the upper world on his promise to return when summoned. One day when he was making merry with his friends he was told that a hart and a hind were parading the street; he knew it was his summons and went at once to the Eildon tree, disappeared, and has never since been heard from. In Scott's *Castle Dangerous* a vision of Thomas of Erceldoune is seen by Hugo Hugonet.

Erl-king, The, a spirit or goblin, fabled to lure persons away, especially children. One of its haunts was the Black Forest in Thuringia. He is sometimes called King of the Elves. Herder translated into German the Danish ballad, *Sir Olaf and the Erl-king's Daughter;* and Goethe's poem, *Erl-König,* which has been set to music, is widely known.

Ermenrich, in *The Sigurd Saga,* was a king of Gothland, who from false information that his son, Randwer, had tried to win the love of his father's bride, Swanhild, ordered Randwer to be hanged and Swanhild to be trampled to death by wild horses. But the daughter of Sigurd and Gudrun was so beautiful that the beasts would not harm her till she was hidden under a blanket, when she was trodden to death. Her brothers avenged her by cutting off the hands and feet of Ermenrich.

Ermengarde, of Baldringham, a character in Scott's *The Betrothed.*

Erminia, the heroine of Tasso's *Jerusalem Delivered,* in love with Tancred.

Ernani, the hero of Verdi's opera *Ernani* (1844), founded on Hugo's novel, *Hernani* (1830).

Ernest, the hero of Hawthorne's short story, *The Great Stone Face.*

Ernest, Duke, the subject of a twelfth-century poem, *Duke Ernest,* by a minnesinger, Henry von Veldig. It is the story of his pilgrimage to expiate his crime in murdering his feudal lord.

Ernest de Fridberg, the hero of Stirling's drama, *The Prisoner of State* (1847).

Eros, a freed slave of Antony. When Antony after the battle of Actium feared that he might fall into the hands of Octavius he ordered Eros to kill him, as the slave had sworn to do at his command. Eros drew his sword, but, unable to slay his master, thrust it into his own side and fell dead at Antony's feet. The story is told by Plutarch, and is introduced by Shakespeare in his *Antony and Cleopatra.* Eros is a character in Dryden's play, *All for Love.*

Erpingham, Sir Thomas, a character in Shakespeare's *Henry V.* He gave the signal for attack at Agincourt by throwing his truncheon in the air, calling, "Now strike!"

Escarbagnas, Countess of, the subject of a one-act farcical comedy by Molière. The name is sometimes applied to one absurdly vain of rank.

Escot, Mr., the "deteriorationist" at the house-party in Thomas Love Peacock's novel, *Headlong Hall.*

Esgrignon, Marquis Carol d', commander of the Order of Saint-Louis, a Royalist, ruined by the Revolution, is a character in Balzac's *The Chouans* and also in *Jealousies of a Country Town.*

Esmeralda, a beautiful gipsy girl in Hugo's *Notre Dame de Paris*, accused of being a witch and executed.

Esmeralda, the heroine of a story by Frances H. Burnett, and a play founded on it by William Gillette.

Esmond, Henry, the hero of Thackeray's novel, *Esmond*, a cavalier in the time of Queen Anne, who emigrates to Virginia.

Espard, Marquis d', a character in Balzac's *The Commission in Lunacy*, whose wife tried to have a guardian appointed for him because he had paid back to a Protestant family the amount of money of which they had been despoiled by his ancestor after the Revocation of the Edict of Nantes. This money he had accumulated by economy and from the proceeds of a book he wrote, *The Picturesque History of China*, after losing most of his inherited fortune by his wife's extravagance. She was aided by his brother in the scheme, which failed. She is a character in *A Distinguished Provincial at Paris* and in several other novels of Balzac.

Esquart, Lord and **Lady,** characters in Meredith's novel, *Diana of the Crossways*.

Essex, The Earl of, in the time of Queen Elizabeth, Robert Devereaux, is the subject of a tragedy in English by Henry Jones (1745) and of French tragedies by Thomas Corneille (brother of Pierre), La Calprenède, and the Abbé Boyer. *The Unhappy Favorite: or, The Earl of Essex,* a play by John Banks, was produced in 1682.

Estella, the heroine of Dickens's *Great Expectations*.

Esther, the subject of a tragedy by Racine (1689).

Esther, the heroine of *Ben Hur*, by Lew Wallace.

Esther Hawdon, or **Summerson,** the heroine of Dickens's novel, *Bleak House*.

Esther Lyon, a character in George Eliot's *Felix Holt*.

Estifania. See COPPER CAPTAIN.

Est-il-possible? (Is it possible?), a nickname given by James II to his son-in-law, Prince George of Denmark, husband of Anne, who made the exclamation whenever any defection from James was mentioned.

Estrildis. See GUENDOLEN.

Etange, Julie d', the chief character of Rousseau's novel, *The New Héloïse*.

Ethan Brand, the title and hero of a short story by Hawthorne. Brooding over the subject of the unpardonable sin, he wanders away to find how to commit it.

Etherege, Sylph, the title and heroine of a short story by Hawthorne.

Etherington, Lord, an important character in Scott's novel, *St. Ronan's Well.*

Ethnic Plot: so the "Popish Plot" is called in Dryden's *Absalom and Achitophel.*

Etiquette, Madame, name applied to Marie Antoinette's mistress of ceremonies, the Duchesse de Noailles, a martinet in enforcing ceremonial rules. She appears in Mühlbach's *Marie Antoinette and Her Son.*

Étoile, a name under which the Countess of Avesnes was known, in Ouida's novel, *Friendship;* an author and artist supposed to be a portrayal of Ouida herself.

Ettarre, the false lady loved by Pelleas in Tennyson's *Pelleas and Ettarre,* one of the *Idyls of the King.*

Ettrick Shepherd, The, a pseudonym of the poet, James Hogg, who was born in the forest of Ettrick in Somersetshire, and was a shepherd in early life.

Euarchus, in Sir Philip Sidney's *Arcadia,* is supposed to be a portrait of the author's father.

Eucharis, in Fénélon's *Télémaque,* one of the nymphs of Calypso, with whom Telemachus fell in love. She is said to have been intended for Mademoiselle de Fontange, a maid of honor to Madame de Montespan, a favorite for a few months of Louis XIV, discarded when she lost her good looks. She died at twenty.

Eulalie, St., a maiden martyred at the age of twenty, about 292 A.D. *The Canticle of Eulalie* is the most ancient poem extant in the *langue d'oïl.*

Eumnestes, the personification of Memory in Spenser's *The Faerie Queene.*

Euphrasia, a girl in Beaumont and Fletcher's *Philaster,* who enters Philaster's service as a page.

Euphrasia, daughter of Evander, in Murphy's *The Grecian Daughter,* embodying the story of the daughter that saved her father's life by feeding him from her breast.

Euphrasia, a depraved beauty in Balzac's *Melmoth Reconciled* and also in *The Magic Skin.*

Euphues, an elegant Athenian gentleman, the chief character in John Lyly's famous works, *Euphues: or, The Anatomy of Wit* (1579), and *Euphues and his England* (1580). It was designed as a satire upon the fashions of manners and speech then being imported from Italy into England.

Eustace, Ethne, the heroine of A. E. W. Mason's novel, *The Four Feathers.*

Eustace, Father, abbot of St. Mary's, plays an important part in Scott's *The Monastery.*

Eustace, Jack, Lucinda's lover in Bickerstaff's *Love in a Village,* who gains admission to her father's house as a music-master.

Eva, the daughter of Torquil in Scott's *The Fair Maid of Perth.*

Evadne, in Beaumont and Fletcher's *The Maid's Tragedy,* is married to Amintor, who is compelled to discard Aspasia, his betrothed, and marry Evadne.

Evadne, the heroine of Sheil's drama, *Evadne: or, The Statue.*

Evandale, Lord, a suitor of Edith Bellenden, in Scott's *Old Mortality.*

Evan Dhu of Lochiel, a Highland chief in Scott's *The Legend of Montrose.*

Evan Dhu M'Combich, a character in Scott's *Waverley.*

Evangeline Bellefontaine, the heroine of Longfellow's poem, *Evangeline,* founded on an incident in the exile of the French inhabitants of Acadia, now Nova Scotia, in 1755, by order of George II.

Evangeline St. Clair, usually called Eva, a beautiful child in Mrs. Stowe's *Uncle Tom's Cabin.*

Evangelist, a character in Bunyan's *Pilgrim's Progress.*

Evangelista, Madame, a Creole descended from a great Spanish family, in Balzac's *A Marriage Settlement.*

Evans, Sir Hugh, a Welsh parson and schoolmaster in Shakespeare's *The Merry Wives of Windsor.*

Evelina, the heroine of Fanny Burney's novel of the name, afterward Lady Orville.

Evelyn, Alfred, the lover of Clara Douglas in Bulwer's play, *Money*.

Evelyn, Sir George, a character in Mrs. Inchbald's *Wives as They Were and Maids as They Are*.

Evelyn Hope, the subject of an elegiac poem by Robert Browning.

Everard, Colonel Markham, and his father, of the Commonwealth party, characters in Scott's *Woodstock*.

Everdene, Bathsheba, the heroine of Thomas Hardy's novel, *Far from the Madding Crowd*.

Everyman, subject of a Morality, defined in the title as "A Treatise how the hye Fader of Heven sendeth Dethe to somon every creature to come and gyve a counte of theyr lyves in this Worlde." Everyman stands for the entire human race. It dates from the reign of Edward IV. The original is in the library of Lincoln Cathedral. It has been played with great success in recent years.

Evil May-Day, The. May 1, 1517, was so called on account of a riot in London, beginning in Cheapside with an attack upon foreigners by apprentices; the rioters were fired upon from cannon in the Tower.

Evremonde, Evelyn and **Captain Lawson,** characters in George Meredith's novel, *Evan Harrington*.

Ewart, Nanty, the skipper of the *Jumping Jenny* in Scott's *Redgauntlet*.

Excalibur, the sword of King Arthur, which he drew from a stone, and on which was an inscription saying that he who drew it out should be King of Britain. The final disposal of the sword is described in Tennyson's *Morte d'Arthur*. The name is also given Escalibor and Caliburn.

Exeter, Henry Holland, Duke of, a faithful Lancastrian introduced in the third part of Shakespeare's *Henry VI*.

Exeter, Thomas Beaufort, Duke of, who defended Harfleur against the French, is a character in Shakespeare's *Henry V*.

Exterminator, The, so Montbars (b. Languedoc, 1645) was called by the Spaniards for his severities in the Antilles and Honduras, which, it is said, were to avenge the cruelties of the Spaniards themselves.

Exton, Sir Pierce of, the murderer of the King in Shakespeare's *Richard II.*

Eyre, Jane, the title and heroine of Charlotte Brontë's novel (1847).

Ezechias, the subject of a drama (1564) by Nicholas Udall, founded on the story of Hezekiah in the Second Book of Kings.

Ezzelin, Sir, in Byron's *Lara,* the knight that charges Lara with being Conrad the corsair.

F.'s Aunt, Mr., an old lady in Dickens's *Little Dorrit,* who occasionally interrupted the grim taciturnity that characterized her, to offer a brief remark, in a deep warning voice, entirely foreign to the subject of conversation and traceable to no association of ideas.

Fabian, a witty servant of Ophelia in Shakespeare's *Twelfth Night.*

Fabii, The, the subject of a play of the sixteenth century, mentioned in Stephen Gosson's work, *Plays Confuted: Showing that They Are not to be Suffered in a Christian Commonweale* (1581).

Fabiola, the subject of a romance (1854) of the early history of the Church, by Cardinal Wiseman.

Fabius Maximus (d. 203 B.C.), the Roman general who has given his name to the policy of wearying out an enemy by delays. Washington has been called the Fabius of America, and the Duke of Montmorency (1493–1567) the Fabius of France.

Fabius, Quintus, the subject of a play acted before Queen Elizabeth, 1573.

Fabricius, an author in Le Sage's *Gil Blas,* who makes a merit of obscurity. "The natural and simple won't do for sonnets, odes, and the sublime," he says.

Fabricius, a Roman consul (282 B.C.), celebrated for the simplicity of his life, his probity, and disinterestedness. In a piece which has become a classic, Rousseau invokes his shade, to testify that the Roman Republic fell through luxury.

Fadladeen, the chamberlain of the harem in Thomas Moore's poem, *Lalla Rookh* (1817), a severe critic of the young poet, who, to his mortification, turns out to be his king.

Fafnir, in northern epic poetry a dragon that slew his father, Hreidmar, to gain possession of the golden treasure. He was slain by Sigurd. He is regarded as the personification of cold or darkness, who has stolen the golden hoard of the summer sunshine.

Fagin, a noted character in Dickens's *Oliver Twist,* a Jew that trains boys to steal and takes their booty.

Fainéant, Le Noir (The Black Idler): so, in Scott's *Ivanhoe,* the disguised King Richard (Cœur de Lion) was called by the onlookers, on account of his seeming indifference, until he finally roused himself and gained the victory.

Fainéants, Les Rois (The Royal Do-Nothings), a name given to the last kings of the Merovingian dynasty, who left all authority to the Mayors of the Palace. The term is often applied to kings who allow others to exercise the power nominally their own. Louis V, last of the Carlovingian dynasty, was called *Le Roi Fainéant.*

Fair Geraldine, a lady celebrated in poems of the Earl of Surrey (1516–1547), supposed to be one of the Fitzgeralds (Geraldines), daughter of the Earl of Kildare, afterward Countess of Lincoln.

Fair Magalona, the heroine of an old French romance of chivalry, *The History of the Fair Magalona, daughter of the King of Naples, and Peter, son of the Count of Provence.*

Fair Maid of Anjou, The: Edith Plantagenet, an attendant of Queen Berengaria.

Fair Maid of Galloway, The: Margaret, daughter of Archibald V, Earl Douglas.

Fair Maid of Kent, The: Joan, daughter of the Earl of Kent, wife of the Black Prince, and mother of Richard II.

Fair Maid of Perth, The: Catherine Glover in Scott's novel of that name.

Fair Rosamond, the mistress of Henry II of England before his accession to the throne, and, according to the story, poisoned by Eleanor, his Queen, who discovered her in a secret bower at Woodstock; this was set in a labyrinth to which the King found his way by a thread. Her story is the subject of an old ballad, *The Complaint of Rosamond,* a poem by Samuel

Daniel (1594). She is mentioned in Tennyson's *A Dream of Fair Women.*

Fairstar, Princess, the heroine of a fairy tale of the name by the Comtesse D'Aulnoy.

Faithful, the companion of Christian in Bunyan's *Pilgrim's Progress,* who was burned to death at Vanity Fair.

Faithful, Jacob, the title and hero of a sea-story by Captain Frederick Marryat.

Faithful, John, the hero of a German folk-tale. On the journey with the Prince his master, who is taking home his bride, John hears some crows talking of three dangers impending over his master; but learns, too, that if anyone shall warn the master he will be turned into stone. Nevertheless, John saves the Prince from all; but at the last, his motive is misunderstood and he is ordered to the scaffold, where he tells his story, and while the Prince suffers agonies of remorse, the faithful servitor turns to stone.

Faithful Shepherdess, The, is Corin, in John Fletcher's pastoral drama (1610), which was an imitation of Guarini's *Pastor Fido,* and which Milton used in his *Comus,* a part being, it is said, literally transcribed.

Falcon, Cornelia, a famous operatic singer, appears in Balzac's *Béatrix;* and Emmanuel Gonzalès has used certain incidents of her career in *La Vierge de l'Opéra.*

Falconara, Theodore de, the hero of Horace Walpole's romance, *The Castle of Otranto.*

Falconer, Jessica, the heroine of James Lane Allen's novel, *The Choir Invisible,* and the drama from it.

Falconer, Robert, the hero and title of a novel by George Macdonald.

Falkland, a character in Godwin's novel, *Caleb Williams.* Originally of noble nature, he commits murder under great provocation, is tried and acquitted. The dramatized version is called *The Iron Chest.*

Falkland, the hero of Bulwer's first novel, which he afterward suppressed. See also FAULKLAND.

Falleix, Jacques and **Martin,** brothers, financiers, characters in Balzac's *The Firm of Nucingen, The Government Clerks,* and others.

Falstaff, Sir John, one of Shakespeare's most famous characters, perhaps the greatest comic character in dramatic writing, appears in *The Merry Wives of Windsor* and in both parts of *King Henry IV*. The name as originally given in the play was Sir John Oldcastle; but it was changed because of the supposition that the character was intended for a real John Oldcastle, who, as Lord Cobham, fell a martyr to his faith as a Lollard or Wicliffite.

Fang, a bullying police-magistrate in Dickens's *Oliver Twist,* intended as a portrait of one A. S. Laing, of Hatton Garden Police Court. The likeness was so true that Mr. Laing was compelled to resign his office.

Fanny, Lord, a nickname applied to Lord Hervey by Pope on account of his foppery and effeminacy.

Fanshawe, a poor student, the hero of Hawthorne's first novel (1828).

Fantine, a pathetic character in Victor Hugo's *Les Misérables.* She becomes a woman of the streets, being first a poor working-girl; her lover deserts her, and in order to provide food for her child she sells her hair and her teeth, and finally dies of starvation.

Fardorougha, the title and hero of a novel by William Carleton (1798–1869), in which are given descriptions of Ribbonism.

Farebrother, The Rev. Camden, an unpopular rector in George Eliot's *Middlemarch.*

Farina, the subject of a novel by George Meredith.

Farinata degli Uberti, a noble Florentine, leader of the Ghibellines. Dante saw him in the Inferno, in an open fiery tomb, not to be closed till the judgment-day. He recalls to Dante that he saved Florence from being razed to the ground after its capture, when all the others of the council consented to its destruction.

Farmer George, a name applied to George III of England, for his homely tastes and manners, and also, it is said, because he kept a farm at Windsor for the small profit it yielded.

Farrant, Donovan, the chief character in Edna Lyall's novel, *Donovan* (1882).

Farrell, Aminta, married to Lord Ormont in Meredith's *Lord Ormont and his Aminta.* He neglects her and she elopes with Weyburn.

Farringdon, Elizabeth, the heroine of *The Farringdons,* by Ellen Thorneycroft Fowler.

Fashion, Sir Novelty, the hero of Cibber's *Love's Last Shift.* In the sequel to it by Vanbrugh, *The Relapse,* he is Lord Foppington.

Fastolfe, Sir John, a character in Shakespeare's *Henry VI,* Part I, who "played the coward" at the siege of Orleans.

Fata Alcina, sister of Fata Morgana in Boiardo's and Ariosto's *Orlando,* who carried off Astolfo and afterward turned him into a myrtle-tree.

Fata Morgana, better known as Morgan le Fay, a fairy that appears in the romances of chivalry. In Boiardo's *Orlando Innamorato,* she is represented as living at the bottom of a lake and acting as a sort of goddess of Fortune. In the Arthurian romances she is the sister of Arthur and reveals to him the misconduct of Guinevere. According to Malory's *History of Arthur,* she tried to have Arthur murdered, designing to murder her husband, King Vrience, and marry Sir Accolon, her paramour, whom she would make king of Britain after Arthur's death. In *The Earthly Paradise,* William Morris makes her the bride of Ogier the Dane after the end of his earthly career.

Fathom, a famous villain, the subject of Smollett's novel, *The Adventures of Ferdinand, Count Fathom.*

Fatima, the daughter of Mohammed, one of the "four perfect women." It is the name of a hermitess and miracle-worker, and of the mother of Prince Camaralzaman, both in the *Arabian Nights.*

Fatima, the last of Bluebeard's wives, saved by the arrival of her brothers, in Perrault's *Contes de Fées* (1697).

Faulconbridge, Philip, a natural son of Richard I, appears in Shakespeare's *King John,* coarse and reckless, but brave and patriotic.

Faulkland, Julia's anxious and jealous lover in Sheridan's comedy, *The Rivals* (1775).

Faultless Painter, The, Andrea del Sarto; he is the subject of one of Browning's poems.

Faun, The Marble. See DONATELLO.

Faust, or **Faustus, Dr.,** believed to be a real person who lived at the close of the fifteenth and early part of the sixteenth centuries. His legendary character is that of a necromancer who sold himself to the devil in consideration of the gift of magic powers. A history of him in German was published in 1587–88, and the same year one in English by Bishop Aylmer. He is the hero of Marlowe's most famous drama, *The Tragical History of Dr. Faustus* (1600–1601), much admired by Goethe, who said he had thought of translating it; but he wrote instead his original drama, *Faust,* his most celebrated work, in which Faust is first a student ambitious of knowledge beyond human reach, and then makes a contract with Mephistopheles, who is to enable him to gratify all his desires for the specified time, and then receive his soul. The second part of the work shows him redeemed.

Fauntleroy, a character in Hawthorne's *The Blithedale Romance.*

Fauntleroy, Cedric Erroll, Lord, the subject of Mrs. Burnett's story, *Little Lord Fauntleroy,* and of a drama founded upon it.

Favorita, La, of Donizetti's opera of the name, is Leonora de Guzman, a favorite of Alfonzo XI of Castile.

Fawnia, the heroine of Greene's Romance, *Pandosto: the Triumph of Time,* upon which Shakespeare founded his comedy, *A Winter's Tale.*

Fazio, a Florentine, the subject of Dean Milman's tragedy of the name, first produced in 1815 under the title, *The Italian Wife.*

Fear Fortress, in the romance of *Croquemitaine,* is an imaginary stronghold that vanishes when boldly approached and attacked.

Feathernest, Mr., the name under which the poet Southey is satirized in Peacock's novel, *Melincourt.*

Featherstonhaugh, the subject of a ballad by Robert Surtees (1779–1834), *The Death of Featherstonhaugh,* which he palmed off as a medieval production upon Sir Walter Scott, who quoted it in the notes to *Marmion.*

Fedalma, the heroine of George Eliot's dramatic poem, *The Spanish Gypsy.*

Fedora, the heroine of a drama of the name by Sardou.

Feeble, Francis, a tailor, one of Falstaff's recruits in Shakespeare's *Henry IV*, Part II. Falstaff calls him "most forcible Feeble," an epithet which is proverbial.

Felician, Father, the priest and schoolmaster, in Longfellow's *Evangeline*.

Felicians, The, Utopians described as living under a strict reign of law in *L'heureuse nation* (*The Happy Nation*), by Mercier de la Rivière, a French economist (1720–1794).

Feliciano de Sylva, a favorite author of *Don Quixote*.

Felix, a character in Balzac's *The Lily of the Valley*.

Felix, in Corneille's tragedy, *Polyeucte*, the governor of Armenia, a type of the timid office-holder.

Felix, in Longfellow's *The Golden Legend*, is the Monk of Hildesheim, who, doubting how a thousand years could be as one day with God, listened to the singing of a milk-white bird for three minutes, as he supposed, but found that it had been a hundred years.

Felixmarte of Hyrcania, the hero of a Spanish romance of chivalry, a book condemned to be burned by the curate in Cervantes's *Don Quixote*.

Fell, Doctor, a dean of Christ Church (1625–1686), immortalized by a quatrain translated from Martial by a student in disgrace, who substituted Dr. Fell for Zabidi in the original:

> "I do not like thee, Doctor Fell;
> The reason why I cannot tell;
> But this I know, and know full well,
> I do not like thee, Doctor Fell."

Fellingham, General, Mary, and **Herbert,** characters in Meredith's tale, *The House on the Beach*.

Felton, Septimius, subject of the last novel written by Hawthorne and left unfinished at his death. Septimius seeks the *Elixir of Life*.

Female Quixote, The, the subject of a novel (1752) by Charlotte Lennox.

Fenellan, Dartrey, and **Simeon,** brothers, characters in Meredith's *One of Our Conquerors*.

Fenia and **Menia,** two giantesses of Sweden, bought as slaves by King Frodi of Denmark to work in his enchanted mill.

They ground out gold, peace, and prosperity for him, till he became so greedy that he would allow them no rest. Then they changed their song and ground out armed men, and by their spells brought the Viking Mysinger, who landed with his troops and slew the sleeping Danes. The story is in Longfellow's translation of the *Grotta Savngr*. The Viking placed the magic millstones on his vessel and bade the giantesses grind salt; but when he, too, kept them at work without rest, they ground so much salt that it sank the ship.

Fenton, a suitor of Anne Page in Shakespeare's *The Merry Wives of Windsor,* afterward her husband.

Feramorz, in Moore's *Lalla Rookh,* the poet who tells stories to the Princess on her way to be married to the King of Bucharia. On the wedding morning she finds that the King is Feramorz himself, with whom she has fallen in love on the way.

Ferdinand, in Shakespeare's *The Tempest,* is the son of the King of Naples, in love with Miranda.

Ferdinand, the King of Navarre in Shakespeare's *Love's Labor's Lost.*

Fergus, a Red Branch knight in Irish legend.

Fergus, Ferragus, Ferran, or **Ferracute,** a giant in the Charlemagne romances, twenty cubits high and strong as forty men, slain by Orlando in a combat to decide between the faith of Orlando and that of the pagan giant.

Ferishtah, a Dervish, the imaginary author of the poetic fables in Browning's volume, *Ferishtah's Fancies.*

Ferney, The Patriarch of: Voltaire, who lived at Ferney, near Geneva.

Ferrar, Nicholas, the founder of a religious society in Shorthouse's novel, *John Inglesant.*

Ferrars, Pamela, the heroine of Mrs. Croker's novel, *The Cat's-Paw,* an English girl who has strange adventures in India.

Ferrex and **Porrex.** See GORBODUC.

Feste, the jester in Shakespeare's *Twelfth Night,* one of the airiest and wittiest of his clowns.

Festus, the subject of a dramatic poem by Philip James Bailey (1839).

Festus, the friend of Paracelsus in Browning's dramatic poem, *Paracelsus.*

Feverel, Sir Austin, and his son **Richard,** characters in Meredith's novel, *The Ordeal of Richard Feverel,* which shows how the carefully planned system of the father for bringing up his boy worked in practise.

Feversham, Harry, the hero of A. E. W. Mason's novel, *The Four Feathers.*

Fezziwig, Mr., a kind old merchant, who appears to Scrooge, his former employé, in his vision—in Dickens's *A Christmas Carol.* Mrs. Fezziwig is famous for her party, when she was "one vast, substantial smile."

Fiammetta, a lady whose name is used in many of Boccaccio's works, supposed to have been Maria, natural daughter of Robert, King of Naples, and beloved by the author. Fiammetta means a little flame. She is the heroine of a novel by Boccaccio, told in the first person by La Fiammetta herself.

Fidele, a name assumed by Imogen in Shakespeare's *Cymbeline.*

Fidele and **Fortunio,** the heroes of a rhymed drama by Anthony Munday (1554–1633), *The Two Italian Gentlemen.*

Fides, the mother of John of Leyden, who sacrificed herself for him, a character in Meyerbeer's opera, *The Prophet* (1849).

Fidessa, the companion of Sansfoy (Faithless) in Spenser's *The Faerie Queene,* who was in reality Duessa, daughter of Falsehood and Shame.

Field, Jane, the subject of a novel by Mary E. Wilkins.

Field of the Cloth of Gold, The, a field between Ardres and Guisnes, where Henry VIII of England and Francis I of France met in 1520, in a pavilion of cloth of gold.

Field of the Forty Footsteps, The, a place back of the British Museum, once called Southampton Fields. The story is that two brothers who took opposite sides in Monmouth's Rebellion fought there, and both were killed. Forty impressions of their footsteps remained, and for many years no grass would grow upon them. The subject was taken for a novel by the Misses Porter and a melodrama by Mayhew.

Fielding, Mrs., and her daughter, **May,** characters in Dickens's *The Cricket on the Hearth.* The mother is "very genteel and patronizing, in consequence of having once been better off, or of laboring under an impression that she might have been, if something had happened (in the indigo trade) which never did happen, and seemed to have never been particularly likely to happen."

Fierabras, a Saracen in the Charlemagne romances, who made himself master of Rome and carried away the crown of thorns and the balsam used to embalm the body of Jesus, one drop of which would restore the most badly wounded. He slew the giant that guarded the marble bridge of Mantible. Ferumbras is the name given him in an English translation.

Fierabras of Alexandria, a legendary giant, master of Babylon and Jerusalem, Seigneur of Russia and Lord of Cologne.

Fiesco, the subject of a historical tragedy by Schiller (1783).

Fifine, a gipsy rope-dancer, the subject of Browning's poem, *Fifine at the Fair*.

Figaro, the clever intriguer, hero of the comedies *The Barber of Seville* and *The Marriage of Figaro*, by Caron de Beaumarchais (1732–1799). In the former he is a barber, in the latter a valet. Mozart has an opera, *The Marriage of Figaro* (1786), and Pasiello and Rossini have each founded an opera upon *The Barber of Seville* (1810 and 1816), with the same title.

Fighting Prelate, The, a sobriquet of Henry Spencer, Bishop of Norwich, who fought against the rebels under Wat Tyler, and then absolved them before their execution. In 1383 he led an army into Flanders to support the cause of Urban VI.

Filia Dolorosa, the Duchess of Angoulême, daughter of Louis XVI (1778–1851), also called the Modern Antigone.

Filomena, St., a healer of the sick and wounded. Longfellow's poem, *Santa Filomena*, is on Florence Nightingale.

Finching, Flora, a rich widow in Dickens's *Little Dorrit*, the first love of Arthur Clennam, said to be the portrait of a married woman with whom Dickens had been in love in his early years and whom as a young girl he had introduced in *David Copperfield* as Dora.

Findabair of the Fair Eyebrows, the daughter of Queen Maeve, who promised her to each of the heroes whose aid she desired in her quarrel. When Findabair saw the slaughter and learned of her mother's trick, she fell dead.

Finn, one of the great heroes of Irish legend, the father of Ossian, and leader of the Fianna. He learned the three ways of poetry, was a king, a seer, and a poet, and a Druid—just, generous, and terrible in battle. After the battle of Gabhra with the High King, the Fianna were much weakened and finally disappeared. Finn and his warriors are sleeping in a great cave; and when the trumpet of the Fianna is blown they will awake with their old strength.

Finn, Phineas, the subject of one of Anthony Trollope's *Parliamentary Novels.*

Finot, Andoche, a journalist in Balzac's *César Birotteau,* and other novels, who hid a "brutal nature under a mild aspect."

Finucane, Jack, sub-editor of the *Pall Mall Gazette* in Thackeray's *Pendennis.*

Fion, in Gaelic story, a giant who could dip his hand in the River Lubar when standing with one foot on each of the mountains between which it runs. A series of poems on Fion and heroes connected with his story is called *Fiona.*

Fionnuala, a swan-daughter of Lir, who was sentenced to wander over the waters of Ireland till the Irish became Christians, but to be released at the sound of the first bell summoning to mass. In Moore's *Irish Melodies* is a poem, *The Song of Fionnuala.*

Fir-bolg, The—men of the bog—a colony of Belgæ from Britain settled in Ireland before the Tuatha de Danaan.

Firmilian, the subject of "a spasmodic tragedy" (1854), published under the name, T. Percy Jones, a burlesque by William E. Aytoun on some of his contemporary poets.

Firmin, Philip, the hero of Thackeray's novel, *The Adventures of Philip.* His father, George Brand Firmin, is the chief character in *A Shabby-Genteel Story,* where he goes by the name George Brandon.

First Gentleman of Europe, The: George IV of England was so called; also Louis d'Artois of France.

Fisbee, Helen, known as Helen Sherwood, the heroine of Booth Tarkington's novel, *The Gentleman from Indiana.*

Fischer, Lisbeth, the subject of Balzac's novel, *Cousin Bette.*

Fitzborn, in Disraeli's novel, *Vivian Grey,* is intended for Sir Robert Peel.

Fitzgerald, Burgo, a character in Trollope's novel, *Can You Forgive Her?*

Fitz-Stephen, the pilot, owner of the White Ship that carried Prince Henry, son of Henry I of England. The ship was wrecked, the Prince was lost, and Fitz-Stephen would not survive him. The story is told in Rossetti's poem, *The White Ship.*

Fitzurse, Lord Waldemar, a character in Scott's *Ivanhoe.*

Flanders, Moll, the subject of a novel by Daniel De Foe.

Flavia, a woman in whom the passion of love yields to the honor and obligation of royalty, the heroine of Anthony Hope's novels, *The Prisoner of Zenda* and *Rupert of Hentzau.*

Fleance, a son of Banquo in Shakespeare's *Macbeth,* the imaginary ancestor of the Stuart kings.

Fleetwood, the hero of *Fleetwood; or, The New Man of Feeling,* by William Godwin.

Fleming, Marjorie, a brilliant child whose story is told by Dr. John Brown.

Fleming, Rhoda, her father, and her sister **Dahlia,** characters of Meredith's novel, *Rhoda Fleming.*

Flemming, Paul, the hero of Longfellow's prose tale, *Hyperion.*

Fleshly School of Poetry, The, a name applied by Robert Buchanan to the sensuous verse of Swinburne and Rossetti.

Fletcher, a family in Miss Baylor's *On Both Sides.*

Flibbertigibbet, a foul fiend in Shakespeare's *King Lear.* This and the other names of fiends in the scene are said to be taken from the *Declaration of Popish Impostures* (1603) by one Horsnet, where Flibberdigibet is cast out of Edmund Peckham by a Jesuit. In Scott's *Kenilworth,* Dickie Sludge acts the part of an imp in Leicester's play and is called Flibbertigibbet.

Flite, Miss, a little woman in Dickens's *Bleak House,* who haunts the Court of Chancery for years in the hope of gaining a judgment.

Flodden Field, where the Scots were defeated in 1513, is the subject of a famous old ballad; also of Campbell's *Lochiel's Warning* and of *The Flowers of the Forest,* by Jane Elliott; and Scott's *Marmion* is a "tale of Flodden Field."

Flor and **Blancheflor,** the subject of a fourteenth-century tale in verse by Conrad Fleck, of two children who are married, after Flor has rescued Blancheflor from the palace of a sorcerer-sultan in Babylon.

Flordelice, or **Fordelis** (Fiordiligi in the original), in Ariosto's *Orlando Furioso* (1516), the wife of Brandimart, King of the Distant Islands.

Florentius, a knight in Gower's *Confessio Amantis,* whose life depended on his finding the answer to a question; during the year given him he sought everywhere and at last learned it from an old hag who exacted in return a promise of marriage from him. Substantially the same story is told by Chaucer's *Wife of Bath,* but no name is given to the knight. Shakespeare mentions Florentius in *The Taming of the Shrew.*

Floreski, Count, the Polish hero of Kemble's drama, *Lodoiska.*

Florimel, a character in Spenser's *The Faerie Queene,* who loved Marinel. He did not return her love, but when he was reported dead she set out to learn whether the report was true, was taken prisoner, freed by Marinel, and became his bride. "The False Florimel" was made by a witch from snow and wax. "Florimel's girdle" was a test of chastity, once worn by Venus.

Florizel, the lover of Perdita in Shakespeare's *A Winter's Tale.*

Flosky, Mr., a transcendentalist in Peacock's *Nightmare Abbey,* said to be intended for Coleridge.

Flowery Kingdom, The: China.

Fluellen, a Welshman in Shakespeare's *Henry V,* affected in his speech, but having "much care and valor."

Flute. See QUINCE.

Flutter, Sir Fopling, the hero of Etherege's comedy, *The Man of Mode.*

Flying Dutchman, The, a phantom ship, the legend of which is told in various ways. As given by Sir Walter Scott, it is the specter of a ship on which a horrible crime was committed, after which the plague broke out among the sailors; and on account of it they were driven away from every port they tried to enter, and, as ghosts, still haunt the seas in their ghostly ship. By another version it is the ship of a Dutch captain who, when beaten back by winds off the Cape of Good Hope, swore with a horrible oath that he would double the Cape if it took him till the Day of Judgment; and he was taken at his word and roams over those waters awaiting the coming of Doomsday. Wagner's opera, *The Flying Dutchman*, is founded on this story; but the captain has received a promise that his punishment shall end when he finds a woman whose love to him is faithful unto death. In Dr. John Leyden's *Scenes of Infancy*, the ship is doomed for having been the first to engage in the slave-trade. Captain Marryat founded his novel, *The Phantom Ship*, upon this legend.

Flying Highwayman, The, one William Harrow, executed in 1763, at Hertford, England, whose practise was to take flying leaps with his horse over the turnpikes.

Fœdora, Countess, a beautiful Russian in Balzac's *The Magic Skin*.

Folliard, Helen, called the "Colleen Bawn," the heroine of William Carleton's *Willy Reilly* (1840).

Folliott, The Rev. Dr., a muscular Christian, jovial and sincere, in Peacock's *Crotchet Castle*, said to have been drawn to atone to the clergy for some satires on the profession in the drawing of clergymen in other novels of his.

Fontaine, Madame, a Paris fortune-teller in Balzac's *The Unconscious Humorists*.

Fontanow, Abbé, a bigoted and meddlesome priest in Balzac's novels. He was canon of Bayeux Cathedral, afterward a vicar in Paris.

Fool, The, in Shakespeare's *King Lear*, is, Coleridge says, "as wonderful a creation as Caliban; his wild babblings and inspired idiocy articulate and gage the horrors of the scene."

Fool of Quality, The, the subject of a novel by Henry Brooke (1706–1783).

Foppington, Lord, a character in Sir John Vanbrugh's comedy, *The Relapse* (1697), and Sheridan's adaptation of it, *A Trip to Scarborough* (1777). Colley Cibber's comedy, *The Careless Husband* (1704), has the same Lord Foppington as a character.

Forbonius and **Prisceria,** the subject of a work by Thomas Lodge (1584), "with the lamentable Complaint of Truth over England."

Forester, Lady Jemima, wife of **Sir Philip,** whose evil deeds are revealed to her by the magic mirror in Scott's tale, *Aunt Margaret's Mirror.*

Formosa. See PSALMANAZAR.

Fornarina, La, the daughter of a baker (*fornaio*), of whom several portraits were painted by Raphael, and who was the model for some of his other works.

Forrester, Sir, the hero of a legend in Hawthorne's *Septimius Felton.*

Forster, Dorothy, heroine of a novel by Walter Besant, whose brother was concerned with Lord Derwentwater in the attempt to restore the Stuarts after the death of Anne.

Fortinbras, Prince, in Shakespeare's *Hamlet,* nephew of the King of Norway.

Fortuna, the blind goddess of luck. Sir Thomas More published about 1540 "Lady Fortune: The Boke of the fayre Gentylwoman that no man shulde put his truste or confydence in."

Fortunate Isles, The, or Islands of the Blest, imaginary islands in the western ocean, the abode of the happy dead. Ben Jonson's masque, *The Fortunate Isles,* was produced in 1627.

Fortunatus, the hero of certain old legends, and of a romance in Italian by Straparola. There are German and French versions. The goddess Fortuna gave him an inexhaustible purse, and he came into possession also of a wishing-cap that took him at once to any place he might desire to visit. These gifts ultimately caused his ruin. Hans Sachs made the story the subject of a drama (1553), and Thomas Dekker used it in his *Old Fortunatus* (1600); it is the basis of Ludwig Tieck's *Phantasus* (1816).

Fortunio, in the *Fairy Tales* (1682) of the Countess d'Aulnoy, a girl who joined the army in place of her aged father, and was supplied by fairies with an incredibly swift horse, Comrade, having the gift of speech.

Forty Thieves, The, characters in a famous tale in *The Arabian Nights,* who dwelt in a secret cave, the door of which would open only at the password "Sesamé." James R. Planché gave the title to a burlesque.

Forwards, Marshal, a title given to General Blücher by the Russians in 1813, on account of the swiftness of his advances, and adopted all over Europe as his pseudonym.

Foscari, Francis, Doge of Venice, who was deposed at the age of eighty-four. He dropped dead on the "Grand Staircase" on hearing the bell announce the election of his successor, as he was going down to take leave of his only remaining son, sentenced to banishment for taking bribes. Lord Byron founded upon this his tragedy, *The Two Foscari* (1811); Mary Russell Mitford's tragedy, *Foscari,* was produced in 1826; and Verdi made it the subject of an opera.

Fosseuse, La, so called because she was a grave-digger's daughter, a fine character in Balzac's *The Country Doctor.*

Foster, Dolly, afterward Lady Mickleham, the heroine of Anthony Hope's *The Dolly Dialogues,* an innocent but sophisticated shepherdess of the Arcadia of the fast set in London.

Foster, Silas, a farmer in Hawthorne's *The Blithedale Romance,* who has the direction of the outdoor work of the community.

Fotheringay, Miss, the stage name of Emily Costigan in Thackeray's *Pendennis.*

Fouché, Joseph, Duc d'Otrante (1753–1820), a member of the National Convention and minister of police under the Consulate and Empire, was dismissed by the Emperor and died in exile after the return of the Bourbons. He is a character in Balzac's *The Chouans.*

Fougas, the title character of Edmond About's novel, *The Man with the Broken Ear.*

Foul-Weather Jack, a name given to the unlucky Commodore Byron (1723–1786) and also to Admiral Sir John Norris (d. 1749).

Foulon, who had once told the starving people to eat grass, appears in Dickens's *A Tale of Two Cities,* where he is hanged after a brief trial by the revolutionists.

Fountain of Youth, The, a fabled fountain, supposed to be in the island of Bimini, one of the Bahamas, or in Florida, which could restore their youth to the old. It is the subject of Hawthorne's tale, *Dr. Heidegger's Experiment.*

Four Masters, The, a name given to the authors of the *Annals of Donegal:* Michael and Cucoirighe O'Clerighe and Maurice and Fearfeafa Conry.

Fracasse, Captain (Baron de Sigognac), the subject of a romance (1863) by Théophile Gautier. The name has become a synonym for a swaggering soldier.

Fra Diavolo, the subject of an opera by Auber, the book by Scribe. The chief character is an Italian brigand, and the name is taken from the sobriquet of a Calabrian robber, Michele Pozza or Pezza, who by some accounts had been a monk under the name Fra Angelo. The opera does not follow the events of his history. He was pardoned and admitted into the Neapolitan army, but was taken prisoner and hanged at Naples in 1806.

Fradubio (Brother Doubt), in Spenser's *The Faerie Queene,* was changed into a tree by Duessa, who had previously changed his lady-love Frælissa into a tree. They were planted side by side; and when the Red Cross Knight broke a bough from one, he saw that it dripped blood and learned the tale of the metamorphosis.

Fra Lippo Lippi, the painter, is the subject of a poem by Robert Browning, which follows closely the facts of his life, and suggests a reason for the contrast between his life and his work.

Frampul, Lord, or **Goodstock,** host of the "Light Heart" in Ben Jonson's *The New Inn.*

France, King of, a fine character in Shakespeare's *All's Well that Ends Well.*

France, Princess of, one of the principal characters in Shakespeare's *Love's Labor's Lost.*

Francesca, a Venetian girl, daughter of the Governor of Corinth in Byron's drama, *The Siege of Corinth* (1816).

Francesca da Rimini, daughter of the Lord of Ravenna, married to Lanciotto, son of Malatesta, Lord of Rimini, a deformed man, who, discovering the love of Francesca and his handsome brother Paolo, put them both to death. Their story has been made famous by Dante, whose description of their punishment and Francesca's story of their death is one of the most beautiful episodes in *The Divine Comedy.* The Italian author, Silvio Pellico, has founded a tragedy upon the story. Leigh

Hunt made the story the subject of a dramatic poem, and an opera by Herman Götz, finished by Brahms and Franck, has the same title (1877). Later dramas are by D'Annunzio, F. Marion Crawford, and Stephen Phillips.

Franceschini, Guido, the husband and murderer of Pompilia in Browning's poem, *The Ring and the Book.*

Francesco, the hero of a novel by Robert Greene, *Francesco's Fortunes* (1590).

Francesco, a character in Massinger's *The Duke of Milan* (1622), who plays a part like that of Iago in *Othello.*

Franchi, Louis dei and **Fabian dei,** the twins in a French play translated by Boucicault, *The Corsican Brothers.*

Frankenstein, the subject of a romance by Mary Godwin Shelley.

Fraud, is portrayed by Dante as a person in the *Inferno,* with a kind and gracious human face exposed to view, and the body of a serpent kept out of sight.

Frayling, Evadne, a character in Sarah Grand's novel, *The Heavenly Twins.*

Frederick, the usurping Duke in Shakespeare's *As You Like It.*

Frederick Barbarossa (Redbeard), Frederick II of Germany, the subject of many legends. One of these makes him the Wild Huntsman who appears before a great calamity, flying through the air, followed by his train; but this has been applied to Charlemagne, Arthur, and other famous leaders. By another legend Barbarossa sits in a cave, leaning upon a table through which his beard has grown, awaiting the hour of his country's need, when he will arise to make her victorious.

Freeport, Sir Andrew, a merchant belonging to the imaginary club responsible for *The Spectator.*

Freiherr von Güttingen, The, the subject of one version of the story of the rich man who was pursued by mice in consequence of his cruelty to the poor. For having collected them in a barn and burned them to death, he was pursued to his castle on Lake Constance and eaten alive, after which the castle sank into the water. Other versions of the story are those of Archbishop Hatto, Bishops Adolf and Widerolf, and William of Malmesbury.

Freischütz, Der, a legendary marksman in league with the devil. The story is told in Apel's *Ghost-Book* (1810) and is used in Weber's opera (1821).

Freitchie, Barbara, an old woman who flung out the American flag in Frederick, Md., before the Confederate troops in the Civil War (1862); the subject of a poem by Whittier, and of a play by Clyde Fitch.

French-Pindar, The: Jean Dorat, for whom Charles IX created the office of Poète Royal, was so called (d. 1582).

Friar Dominic, the subject of Dryden's play, *The Spanish Friar*, satirizing the vices of the priesthood.

Friar Gerund, a popular preacher in Padre Isla's Spanish romance, a satire on the sensational pulpit oratory of his day (1703–1781).

Friar John, a character in the *Pantagruel* of Rabelais, reckless, witty, enterprising, and profane.

Friar Laurence, the Franciscan that marries the lovers in Shakespeare's *Romeo and Juliet.*

Friar of Orders Grey, A, the subject of a ballad compiled from fragments in Shakespeare and other dramatists.

Friar Rush (German, *Bruder Rausch*), the subject of an old tale, in which the friar was sent from hell by the devil to encourage the monks in their evil lives and make them even worse—one of the many satires upon the priesthood.

Friar Tuck, one of the company of *Robin Hood.* He appears in *Ivanhoe* as the Clerk of Copmanhurst.

Friars of Berwick, The, the subject of a comic story by William Dunbar.

Friday, a young savage saved from death by Robinson Crusoe and afterward his servant.

Friend of Man, The, title of a book by the Marquis de Mirabeau (1715–1789), father of the famous orator, and applied to the author as a sobriquet.

Frithiof, or **Frithjof,** the hero of an Icelandic story of the thirteenth century, and of Bishop Tegnér's poem founded upon it, *Frithjof's Saga.* He married Ingeborg, daughter of a Norwegian king. The poem has been translated into nearly every European tongue; twenty-one versions in English have been made, and nineteen in German.

Fritz, Old, a sobriquet of Frederick II, the Great, of Prussia.

Frollo, Claude, an archdeacon in Victor Hugo's *Notre Dame de Paris,* a sanctimonious hypocrite.

Fromont, the younger partner in Alphonse Daudet's novel, *Fromont Jeune et Risler Aîné* (Fromont Junior and Risler Senior) (1874).

Front de Bœuf, Reginald, a follower of Prince John of Anjou in Scott's *Ivanhoe.*

Froth, a foolish gentleman in Shakespeare's *Measure for Measure,* discharged after arrest, on account of his evident mental incapacity.

Froth, Lord and **Lady,** a conceited dupe and a literary lady in Congreve's play, *The Double Dealer* (1700).

Frugal, Luke, a hypocrite in Massinger's *The City Madam.*

Ftatateeta, Cleopatra's nurse in Shaw's *Cæsar and Cleopatra.*

Fudge, Captain, the master of a ship, the *Black Eagle,* described as a phenomenal liar in *A Collection of William Crouch's Papers* (1712), suggested as the origin of the exclamation.

Fudge, Foaming, in Disraeli's *Vivian Grey,* is said to be meant for a likeness of Lord Brougham.

Fudge Family, The, the imaginary authors of a series of poems in the form of letters, *The Fudge Family in Paris,* by Thomas Moore, satirizing the toadyism of some British travelers. A sequel was published, *The Fudge Family in England.*

Fum the Fourth: so Byron calls George IV in *Don Juan.* "Fum" in Chinese is said to be a combination of the snake, cock, goose, and stag.

Fungus, the leading character in Foote's play, *The Commissary.*

Funk, Peter, a name said to be used for a person engaged to bid up articles at auctions.

Fusbos, in Rhodes's *Bombastes Furioso,* is Minister of State to the King of Utopia.

Fusbos, a pseudonym of Henry Plunkett, one of the first contributors to *Punch.*

Fuseli is addressed by Mary Wollstonecraft in a short poem of Browning, an expression of despairing love.

Fyrapel, in the epic *Reynard the Fox* (1498), is the leopard.

Gaberlunzie Man, The, a wandering beggar, subject of a ballad in which James V of Scotland (1512–1542), the reputed author, describes a love-adventure of his own. James Ballantine published *The Gaberlunzie's Wallet.* "Gaberlunzie" is defined as a coarse gown worn by the king's bedesmen.

Gabler, Hedda, the title of a play by Ibsen and the heroine's name. She is married to George Tesman, is interested in a depraved genius, Ejlert Lövberg, and commits suicide.

Gabriel, The Angel, is an actor in many of the Mohammedan legends. He gave the Koran to the prophet; at the Battle of Bedr he caused the army of the faithful to appear twice its size, which seems to have been unnecessary in view of the other miracle, the bringing of three thousand angels whom he led against the enemy, mounted upon his horse, Haïzûm. In Longfellow's *The Golden Legend,* Gabriel is the angel of the moon, who brings to men the gift of hope.

Gabriel Lajeunesse, the fiancé of the heroine of Longfellow's *Evangeline,* who was separated from her when the French were exiled from Acadia, and whom she found, after long search, dying in a hospital in Philadelphia.

Gabriel's Hounds, a name sometimes given to the pack of the Wild Huntsman, whose passing presages disaster. Wild geese are sometimes called so from the resemblance of their cry to the voice of hounds in chase.

Gadsbys, The, the family of an officer of Hussars in India, subject of Kipling's novel, *The Story of the Gadsbys.*

Gadshill, a companion of Falstaff in Shakespeare's *Henry IV,* Part I. The place, Gadshill, in Kent, was noted as a place of many robberies.

Gaheris, Sir, a nephew of King Arthur, of whom it is related in Malory's *History of Prince Arthur* that the King banished him from the court for having slain his mother in wrath at her illicit relations with Sir Lamorake.

Gaillard, Theodore, a journalist, and his wife **Suzanne,** a courtesan, characters in *The Unconscious Humorists,* and other novels of Balzac.

Gainsborough, Cecily, the heroine of Anthony Hope's novel, *Tristram of Blent*, a cousin of the hero, who, recognizing in her the peculiar beauty and wonderful charm of his mother, voluntarily resigns his inheritance to her as the rightful heir.

Gainsford, a character in George Meredith's *Sandra Belloni.*

Galahad, Sir, the son of Sir Launcelot and Elaine in the Arthur romances, the purest and noblest of all the knights. His shield was snow-white, with a cross upon it, which Joseph of Arimathea had made with his blood before giving it to King Evelake, from whom Sir Galahad received it. He drew his sword from a rock whence no other knight could force it, and was the only one who could sit in the *Siege Perilous*, the seat at the Round Table destined for the knight who was to find the Holy Grail. This he found when he went upon the quest, and, according to the story, when he was about to take the sacrament, he saw a "figure in the likeness of a child; and the visage was as red and as bright as fire; and he smote himself into that bread"; so that Sir Galahad saw the actual physical process of transubstantiation. His quest is the subject of Tennyson's idyl, *The Holy Grail*, and of his poem *Sir Galahad.*

Galatea, a sea-nymph beloved by Polyphemus, but in love with Acis. The giant crushed his rival under a rock, and Galatea in her grief was changed into a fountain. *Acis and Galatea* is the subject of an opera by Handel (1710).

Galatea, the name of the heroine of one of Virgil's eclogues, a shepherdess, and of a pastoral by Cervantes (1584), imitated by Florian; also of a comic opera by Victor Massé (1852).

Galatea, a statue modeled by Pygmalion, which was animated with life, when the artist fell in love with his work. The story is told by William Morris in *The Earthly Paradise.* W. S. Gilbert's "mythological comedy," *Pygmalion and Galatea*, is founded upon this story.

Gale, Dr. Rhoda, an important character in Reade's *A Woman-Hater.*

Galeotti, the Italian astrologer of Louis XI of France. In *Quentin Durward* he gives the King the answer recorded of the soothsayer Thrasullus to Tiberius when the Emperor told him to predict the day of his own death—that he could only tell that it would be just twenty-four hours before that of the Emperor.

Galotti, Emilia, the title and heroine of a tragedy by Gotthold Ephraim Lessing.

Galuppi, an old Venetian composer, celebrated in Browning's poem, *A Toccata of Galuppi's.*

Gama, Vasco da, the Portuguese navigator who discovered the route to the Indies around the Cape of Good Hope, is the hero of the *Lusiad,* the epic of Camoëns. Da Gama is also the hero of the opera *L'Africaine,* by Meyerbeer, the libretto by Scribe (1865).

Gambara, Paolo, a wandering, poverty-stricken musician, whose wife maintained them both for a time with her needle, subjects of Balzac's novel, *Gambara.*

Gambier, Captain Augustus Frederick, a character in two of George Meredith's novels, *Sandra Belloni* and *Vittoria.*

Gambrinus, a legendary character, the inventor, by the aid of Satan, of chiming-bells and lager beer. The Holy Roman Emperor made him Duke of Brabant and Count of Flanders, in his delight with the new beverage; and the imp whom the devil sent to bring him to hell drank so much that he fell asleep, overstayed his time, and dared not go back to hell at all. So Gambrinus was left in peace and finally was turned into a beer-barrel.

Gammon, Oily, a hypocritical lawyer in Warren's novel, *Ten Thousand a Year.*

Gamp, Sarah, a monthly nurse in Dickens's *Martin Chuzzlewit,* who was constantly quoting compliments made to her by the mythical Mrs. Harris.

Ganabim, the island of thieves in the *Pantagruel* of Rabelais.

Gander, Sir Gregory, a pen-name under which George Ellis published *Poetical Tales and Trifles* (1778).

Gandercleugh, an imaginary town in Scotland, the residence of Jedediah Cleishbotham, the imaginary editor of Scott's *Tales of My Landlord.* It was on the river Gander. Cleugh means cliff.

Gandia, Duke of. See BORGIA, FRANCESCO.

Gandolf, a Viking in Ibsen's early play, *The Warrior's Tomb.* He becomes a Christian through the influence of Blanca, whom he meets on a voyage undertaken to avenge his father's death.

Gandolphini, Prince and **Princesse,** characters in a story in Balzac's novel, *Albert Savarus,* by the hero. In this story, *L'Ambitieux par amour,* by Balzac's character, he is represented as relating his own adventures under the name Rodolphe.

Ganem, the hero of the tale in *The Arabian Nights, The Slave of Love,* who rescued the Caliph's favorite from the grave where she had been buried alive by the order of the jealous Sultana.

Ganlesse, Richard, an *alias* of Edward Christian in Scott's *Peveril of the Peak.*

Gann, Caroline, the heroine of Thackeray's *A Shabby-Genteel Story,* a character in his *The Adventures of Philip* also, where she is called the "Little Sister."

Gannett, Dr., a character in Meredith's novel, *Beauchamp's Career.*

Gannius, Delphica and **Dr.,** appear in *One of Our Conquerors,* by George Meredith.

Ganor, Ganora, variations of the name of Guinevere, King Arthur's wife.

Garagantua, a giant that swallowed five pilgrims in a salad, hero of an old story dating earlier than 1575, *The History of Garagantua.* Shakespeare's reference in *As You Like It* is probably to this. See GARGANTUA.

Garcias, Pedro, mentioned in the preface to Le Sage's *Gil Blas.* Two scholars found on the way to Salamanca, inscribed upon a fountain, "Here lies the soul of the licentiate Pedro Garcias." One of them merely laughed at the notion of burying a soul; but the other pried out the stone and found under it a bag of one hundred ducats.

Gardiner, Stephen, Bishop of Winchester, an unscrupulous prelate introduced by Shakespeare in *King Henry VIII* and by Tennyson in *Queen Mary.*

Gareth, the son of Lot, King of the Orkneys and of Morgause or Bellicent. His mother, wishing to keep him with her, consented to let him go to Arthur's court only on condition that he should serve a year in Arthur's kitchen, concealing his name, not supposing he would go on such terms. He did, however, and was called ironically by the steward Fairhands (*Beaumains*). He freed Lyonors, the sister of Lynette, from Castle Perilous; and at the close of the idyl, *Gareth and Lynette*, Tennyson says:

> "And he that told the tale in older times
> Says that Sir Gareth wedded Lyonors,
> But he that told it later says Lynette."

Garfield, Rose, a pretty girl in Hawthorne's *Septimius Felton*.

Gargamelle, the wife of Grandgousier and mother of Gargantua (*q.v.*), a monster with an enormous appetite, interpreted as referring to the extravagant cost of queens.

Gargantua, the subject of the famous romance of the name by Rabelais. The name and character are taken from the older story of Garagantua.

Gargery, Joe, a blacksmith in Dickens's *Great Expectations*, married to a termagant.

Garland, Mr. and **Mrs.** and their son **Abel,** a kind-hearted family in Dickens's *The Old Curiosity Shop*. They are said to be portraits of a family with whom Dickens when a boy had lodgings when his father was confined in the Marshalsea.

Garrett, Edward, the pen-name of Isabella F. Mayo, author of *The Occupations of a Retired Life*.

Garrick, David, the chief character in a play of his name by Robertson and in *The Love of David Garrick;* he is a character in *Pretty Peggy*, a play by Frances A. Matthews.

Garth, Caleb, an upright yeoman, and **Mary,** his daughter, characters in George Eliot's *Middlemarch*.

Gas, Charlatan, a character in Disraeli's *Vivian Grey*, supposed to be intended for Canning.

Gascoigne, Sir William, the Lord Chief Justice who sent Prince Hal to prison, appears in Shakespeare's *King Henry IV*, Part II.

Gashford, a fawning sneak in Dickens's *Barnaby Rudge*, Lord George Gordon's secretary.

Gastibelza, the subject of one of Victor Hugo's works. Monpon composed music for an opera from it.

Gaston, Lady May, the heroine of Hope's *Quisante.*

Gaston, Marie, a poet and playwright in Balzac's *Letters of Two Brides, La Grenadière,* and *The Member for Arcis.*

Gatty, Charles, the painter who marries Christie in Reade's novel, *Christie Johnstone.*

Gaudin, Pauline, a character in Balzac's *The Magic Skin.*

Gaudissart, Felix, a commercial traveler, afterward a theater manager, the hero of Balzac's *Gaudissart the Great,* appears in several other of his novels.

Gaultier, Bon, Ballads, parodies on modern poetry by Aytoun and Martin.

Gaultier, Marguerite, the chief character in a play by Dumas *fils, La Dame aux Camélias,* the play and the character both known in the English version as Camille.

Gaunt, Griffith, the subject of a novel by Charles Reade.

Gaunt, John of, Duke of Lancaster (1339–1399) is a character in Shakespeare's *King Richard II.*

Gaunt, Rev. Dr. John, the leading character in William J. Dawson's novel, *A Prophet in Babylon.*

Gauntlett, Emilia, the heroine of Smollett's *Peregrine Pickle.*

Gaussin, Jean, the hero of Daudet's *Sappho* and its dramatization.

Gautama, the historic Buddha, subject of Sir Edwin Arnold's poem, *The Light of Asia.*

Gautier et Garguille, names used in French to signify everybody, equivalent to "all the world and his wife."

Gavroche, a Paris gamin in Hugo's *Les Misérables.*

Gawain, one of Arthur's knights, and his nephew, called "The Courteous"; in Tennyson's idyl, *Pelleas and Ettarre,* he is trusted by Pelleas and betrays him. *The Adventures of Sir Gawain* is an old metrical romance by Clerk of Tranent, of which only two cantos remain. *The Marriage of Sir Gawain* is an old ballad.

Gawky, Lord, a nickname of Richard Grenville, Lord Temple (1711–1770).

Gawreys. See WILKINS, PETER.

Gay, Lucien, in Disraeli's *Coningsby* is said to be intended for Theodore Hook.

Gay, Walter, the lover of Florence in Dickens's *Dombey and Son.*

Gazette, Sir Gregory, in Foote's play, *The Knights,* is fond of news about politics, which he does not comprehend.

Geddes, Joshua, a Quaker and his sister **Rachel,** in Scott's *Redgauntlet,* befriend Darsie Latimer and Alan Fairford.

Geierstein (the Rock of Vultures), **Castle of,** the seat of the family of the heroine of Scott's *Anne of Geierstein.* She is the daughter of Count Albert of Geierstein and Baroness of Arnheim. Count Arnold is her uncle.

Geith, George, the subject of Mrs. Trafford Riddell's novel of the name, a man of great strength of character and courage.

Gelert, or **Gellert,** the name of Llewellyn's hound in the well-known Welsh story, which, being left in charge of an infant, killed a wolf that would have devoured it; the master came, and seeing the cradle overturned and the dog's mouth bloody, hastily assumed the guilt of the dog and killed him, only to find the body of the wolf under the bed and the child beneath the cradle. Gelert's tomb, called Beth-Gelert, is shown at Snowdon. But the story is only one version of a tale common to the folklore of nearly every Aryan people, though with variations. Usually the hero is a dog, but sometimes it is an ichneumon, in one version a weasel, in others a cat or an otter; and the intruder is sometimes a snake. According to one authority, the place Beth-Gelert was named in honor of a Welsh saint of the fifth century, Celert.

Gem of Normandy, The, Emma, daughter of Richard the Fearless, Duke of Normandy, married to Ethelred II of England and afterward to Canute. According to the legend, she proved her innocence of charges brought against her, by the ordeal of walking blindfold unhurt over red-hot plowshares.

Gemmels, Andrew. See OCHILTREE, EDIE.

General Undertaker (Entrepreneur), **The,** a nickname given to the Emperor Napoleon Bonaparte, on account of the many great public works he undertook but did not complete.

Genestas, Pierre, a character in Balzac's, *The Country Doctor.*

Genevieve, the heroine of Coleridge's ballad *Genevieve,* and of his poem *Love.* Romances by Alphonse Karr (1838) and by Lamartine (1851) have this title, the name of their respective heroines.

Genevieve or **Genovefa,** of Brabant, is the heroine of a popular German story told by Tieck and Müller, and dramatized by Raupach, according to which she was suspected of infidelity and escaped from death into the Forest of Ardennes, where she gave birth to a son who was suckled by a white doe. Her innocence was afterward made clear and she was received back in her home by her husband, the Count Palatine Siegfried of Mayenfeld, in the time of Charles Martel.

Genevieve, St. (422–512), the patron saint of Paris, which was saved by her prayers from destruction by Attila (451). She was a shepherdess from Nanterre.

Gentilhomme, René. See MAILLARD.

Gentle Boy, The, subject of a tale by Hawthorne of the time of the persecution of Quakers in Massachusetts colony.

Gentle Shepherd, The, a nickname applied to George Grenville (1712–1770), who exclaimed, "Tell me where!" in a speech in Parliament, when William Pitt hummed the line of the song, "Gentle Shepherd, tell me where." The incident fastened the name upon Grenville.

Geoffrey Crayon, the pen-name under which Irving published his *Sketch Book.*

George, Mr., a big, generous man, the proprietor of a shooting-gallery, in Dickens's *Bleak House,* whose real name was George Rouncewell.

George, St., and the Dragon. The legend says he was a son of Lord Albert of Coventry. He fought against the Saracens, and rescued Sabra, a king's daughter, from a dragon. She went to England and they were married and lived in Coventry. There are two old ballads on the subject, *St. George and the Dragon,* and *The Birth of St. George.*

George-a Greene, subject of a drama (1587) of the name by Robert Green. He was a companion of Robin Hood and the pinner or pound-keeper of Wakefield. The drama seems to have been founded upon an old prose romance, *The History of George a-Green.*

Geraint, Sir, a knight of the Round Table, hero of Tennyson's idyl, *Geraint and Enid.*

Geraldine, Fair, the lady to whom Henry Howard, Earl of Surrey, wrote love sonnets, supposed to be Lady Elizabeth Fitzgerald.

Geraldine, Lady, the earl's daughter in Mrs. Browning's poem, *Lady Geraldine's Courtship.*

Geraldine, the Lady, the "serpent-woman" in Coleridge's poem, *Christabel.*

Gérard, the chief character of Reade's *The Cloister and the Hearth.* Also a character in Balzac's *The Chouans.*

Gerard, Lucy, the heroine of Payn's novel, *Lost Sir Massingberd.*

Gerhard the Good, subject of a thirteenth-century romance by the minnesinger, Rudolph of Ems. Gerhard, a merchant of Cologne, buys with his own cargo of goods a cargo of Christian slaves in order to free them.

Géronte, a name used in old French comedy for old men, carrying at first no hint of ridicule, but gradually becoming a designation for a hard, miserly, conceited old man, yet narrow, credulous, and easily deceived. Molière has used it for persons of this character.

Gertrude, Hamlet's mother in Shakespeare's drama. In the original *Historie of Hamblett,* her name is Gerutha.

Gertrude of Wyoming, subject of Thomas Campbell's poem (1809), founded on the destruction of Wyoming by the Indians.

Geryon, in mythology, a king of Hesperia, having three bodies. Dante gives the name Geryon to a monster, personating Fraud, having the face of a just man, while his body, concealed under water, was that of a serpent. At the command of Virgil, Geryon carried him and Dante on his back from the seventh to the eighth circle in the Inferno.

Gesmas, the traditional name of the impertinent thief on Calvary.

Gessler, Albrecht, the Austrian governor of Switzerland, shot by William Tell. The tradition is embodied in Schiller's drama, *Wilhelm Tell,* and Rossini's opera, *Guglielmo Tell.*

Giaffir, the pasha of Abydos, father of the heroine of Byron's poem, *The Bride of Abydos.*

Giallar, Göillar, or **Gjallar,** the bridge on the boundary of Niflheim, hung by a single hair. Heimdall, the watchman of the gods, is stationed there, with the Giallar-horn, upon which he will blow a terrible blast when Ragnavok comes and brings the great battle between the gods and the evil forces of Loki.

Giants: These monsters abound in mythology, fable and allegory. Among the giants of classic mythology were the Titans, the one-eyed Cyclops, Orion, Ephialtes, Cacus, Euceladus, buried under Mount Etna, Atlas with the world on his back, Typhæus of the hundred heads, and Briareus of the hundred hands. The Northern mythology has the dwellers in Jötunheim, land of giants, the frost giants and the flame giants. In Christian legend, the giant St. Christopher carried the child Christ across a ford. In medieval fable there were the giants Colbrand and Amerant slain by Guy of Warwick, Ascapart by Sir Bevis of Southampton, and Coulin destroyed by Debon, Galapas slain by Arthur. Rabelais mentions the giants of Chalbroth, Gargantua, Erix, Grangousia, Pantagruel, Gabbara, and others. Pulci's Morgante died from the bite of a crab, and Margutte laughed himself to death at seeing a monkey putting on his boots. Camoëns describes the giant Adamastor guarding the Cape of Good Hope. Swift takes Gulliver to Brobdingnag, the country of giants. Don Quixote encountered Malambruns, Caraculiambo, and Alifanfaron and the giantess Giralda. Ariosto's Egyptian giant, Caligorant, caught travelers in an invisible net. Bunyan's Pilgrim encountered Giant Despair, Giant Grim, Giant Slay-good, and Maul, the giant of sophistry. The nursery tale makes Jack the slayer of Galligantus, Cormoran, Blunderbore, and others. According to a legend, the tower of Pisa was bent by the Saracen giant, Angoulaffre, who leaned against it to rest. In *The Faerie Queene* are the giants Cormorant, Corflambo, and Orgoglio, three times the size of an ordinary man. Gogmagog or Goëmagot, was king of giants in Britain; he wrestled with Corineus and was thrown into the sea from the Cornish coast at a place called the Giant's Leap. The story of the giant who had no heart in his body and was tricked by Boots, who found out that his heart was in an egg inside a duck swimming in a well within a church standing on an island in a far-away lake, is one of a large family of similar stories.

Giaour (jowr), the subject of Byron's poem, who wished to be known by no other name.

Gibbie Goose, a half-witted servant in Scott's novel, *Old Mortality.*

Gibon, Madam, a coarse, clever, mercenary woman in Henri Monnier's *Scènes Populaires* (1852).

Gigadibs, the young man to whom the churchman's answer is addressed in Browning's poem, *Bishop Blougram's Apology.*

Giggleswick, a nymph who was pursued by a satyr and changed, in answer to her prayer to the gods, into a fountain.

Giglio, Prince of Paflagonia, hero of Thackeray's fairy tale *The Rose and the Ring.*

Giguet, Colonel, and his son **Simon,** characters in Balzac's *The Member for Arcis.*

Gilbert, Dr., a character in Dumas's historical novels.

Gilbert, Sir, a knight of the Round Table, whose sword and cerecloth had power to heal wounds by a touch.

Gil Blas, the hero of Le Sage's famous novel (1715), a clever and kind but unscrupulous fellow, the hero of many adventures.

Gilderoy, the hero of an old Scottish ballad, a famous robber said to have plundered Cardinal Richelieu and Oliver Cromwell. Another ballad places Gilderoy in the time of Mary Queen of Scots, and still another in the eighteenth century. One of the ballads is by Thomas Campbell.

Gildippe, an English baroness in Tasso's *Jerusalem Delivered,* who went to the Holy Land with her husband and after many brave deeds was slain with him by Solyman.

Gilfil, Rev. Maynard, the hero of George Eliot's tale, *Mr. Gilfil's Love-Story.*

Gilfillan, Habakkuk, called "Gifted Gilfillan," an enthusiastic Cameronian in Scott's *Waverley.*

Gill, Harry, the farmer in Wordsworth's ballad, *Goody Blake and Harry Gill,* doomed never to be warm again, by the curse of the old woman whom he had forbidden to carry home a few sticks from his wood.

Gil Morrice, the hero and title of an old Scottish ballad, on which Home's tragedy, *Douglas,* was founded. Gil is said to be a form of Childe, an old title given to the eldest son of a noble family.

Gilpin, John, the "train-band captain" of Cowper's ballad, which was first published, anonymously, in 1782. The original is said to have been one Bayer, a linen-draper in Paternoster Row, London.

Gines de Passamonte, a galley-slave freed by Don Quixote and afterward manager of a puppet-show.

Ginevra, the subject of one of the poems in Rogers's *Italy*, a bride who on her wedding-day hid herself in play in a chest, which, having a spring lock, buried her alive.

Gingerbread, Giles, the hero of an old English nursery tale.

Gingerpop School, a nickname applied by David Macbeth Moir to a species of poetry lightly humorous, at times pathetic, at times farcical. Examples given were Byron's *Beppo* and *Don Juan* and Procter's *The Ring of Gyges* and *A Spanish Story*.

Ginns, a race of beings corresponding to the fallen angels.

Ginx's Baby, the subject of Jenkins's once popular story, called "the Protestant baby"; it had been cared for by a Catholic Sister, and was the occasion of an absurd religious controversy.

Gioconda, La. See LUCIO and SILVIA.

Giraud, Léon, a philosopher who predicted the downfall of Christianity and of the family, in Balzac's *A Distinguished Provincial at Paris*, appearing also in others of his novels.

Girder, Gibbie, a cooper in Scott's *The Bride of Lammermoor*, appointed queen's cooper.

Girnington, The Laird of, Frank Hayston, laird of Bucklaw, in Scott's *The Bride of Lammermoor*.

Gitche Manito, the Great Spirit, deity of the North American Indians.

Gladiator, The, a tragedy in verse (1841) by Alexander Soumet—the struggle of dying paganism with Christianity.

Glamis, Thane of, a title inherited by Macbeth.

Glasher, Lydia, the mother of Grandcourt's children in George Eliot's *Daniel Deronda*.

Glasse, Mrs. Hannah, pseudonym of the author of a cookbook (1747) supposed to be by Dr. John Hill. The famous direction, "First catch your hare, then cook it," is credited to this book; but catch may have been *scatch*, that is, *skin*.

Glastonbury, the traditional burial-place of King Arthur; and also of St. Joseph of Arimathea. The legend says that St. Joseph thrust his staff into the ground there and that it blossoms every Christmas—the "Glastonbury thorn."

Glatisant, a monster in Malory's *Prince Arthur*, pursued by Sir Palomides. It was called the "questing beast," because there was a noise in its body like that of hounds questing, that is, in full cry.

Glaucus, a character in Bulwer's *The Last Days of Pompeii*.

Glee-Maiden, The, poor Louise in Scott's *The Fair Maid of Perth*.

Glegg, Mrs., one of Maggie Tulliver's aunts in George Eliot's *The Mill on the Floss*.

Glenallan, the Earl of, a character in Scott's *The Antiquary*.

Glenallan, Lord, a suitor of Mary Douglas in Miss Ferrier's novel, *Marriage*.

Glenalvon, a son of Lady Randolph in Home's tragedy, *Douglas* (1757).

Glenarvon, the hero of a novel by Lady Caroline Lamb, supposed to be intended for Lord Byron.

Glencoe, scene of the murder of thirty-eight Macdonalds in 1692 by the soldiers of Captain Campbell. It is the subject of a tragedy (1839) by Thomas Noon Talfourd and a poem by Thomas Campbell, *The Pilgrim of Glencoe* (1842).

Glendinning, Sir Halbert, the knight of Avenel in Scott's *The Abbot*.

Glendower, Owen, a Welsh nobleman in Shakespeare's *Henry IV*, Part I.

Glenthorn, Lord, the chief character in Miss Edgeworth's *Ennui*.

Glenvarloch, Lord, the title of Nigel Olifaunt in Scott's *The Fortunes of Nigel*.

Gloriana, the queen of fairy-land in Spenser's *The Faerie Queene*, meaning, as the author says, glory in the general intention, Queen Elizabeth in particular.

Glorious John, the poet John Dryden (1631–1701).

Glory, Old, a popular name in the United States for the national flag.

Glossin, Gilbert, a rascally lawyer in Scott's *Guy Mannering*.

Gloucester, Duchess of. See ELEANOR.

Gloucester, Duke of, a coarse and fiery but loyal character in Shakespeare's *King Lear*.

Glover, Catherine, the heroine of Scott's *The Fair Maid of Perth*.

Glowrowrum, Lady, a guest at Burgh-Westra in Scott's *The Pirate*.

Glowry, Scythrop, in Peacock's *Nightmare Abbey*, in love with two women at the same time, is meant for the poet Shelley, who, it is said, admitted the truth of the portrait and was amused by it.

Glubdubdrib, a sorcerers' island visited by Gulliver, in Swift's *Gulliver's Travels*.

Glumdalca, the queen of the giants and in love with Tom in Fielding's burlesque, *Tom Thumb the Great*.

Glumdalclitch (little nurse), a child nine years old and forty feet high who had charge of Gulliver in Brobdingnag, in Swift's *Gulliver's Travels*.

Glumms. See WILKINS, PETER.

Glycine, an orphan girl in Coleridge's dramatic poem, *Zapolya* (1817).

Glyde, Sir Percival, the villain in Wilkie Collins's *The Woman in White*.

Gnotho, an old man in *The Old Law* by Middleton, Massinger, and Rowley, who thinks the Old Law should enable him to exchange an old wife for a young one.

Gobbo, Launcelot, Shylock's servant in Shakespeare's *The Merchant of Venice*, son of a blind old man who also appears in the play.

Gobseck, an unscrupulous usurer in Balzac's novel of the name, appearing also in others. His grandniece and her daughter, both courtesans, are characters in several of the novels of the *Comédie Humaine*.

Goddard, Mary, the heroine of Crawford's *A Tale of a Lonely Parish*.

Godefroid, a character in Balzac's *The Seamy Side of History.*

Godfrey of Bouillon, the wise and brave chief of the crusaders, a character in Tasso's *Jerusalem Delivered,* also in Scott's *Count Robert of Paris.*

Godiva, or **Godgifu,** subject of a popular legend. When she importuned her husband, Earl Leofric, to relieve the people of Coventry from a burden of taxation, he agreed to do it if she would ride naked through the town. This she did, covering herself with her long hair, after sending word to all the people to remain indoors and not to look out. All kept faith with her except one, who has come down as Peeping Tom of Coventry, and who is represented by a figure in the niche of a house in the town. A periodical procession was instituted to commemorate the event. The story is the subject of a poem by Tennyson.

Godless Florias, The, a name given to an issue of English two-shilling coins in 1849, from which F. D., defender of the faith, was omitted by the master of the mint, Shiel, a Catholic. They were called in the same year.

Godly Queen Hester, the subject of a miracle-play (1561).

Godolphin, title and hero's name of a novel by Bulwer.

Goëmagot, or **Goëmot,** a legendary British giant, who was tossed into the sea by Corineus at Goëmagot's Leap, or Giant's Leap at Haw, near Plymouth. Corineus is supposed to have given its name to Cornwall. The story is told in Geoffrey's *British History* and Spenser's *The Faerie Queene.* Gogmagog is another form of the name.

Goetz von Berlichingen, or **Goetz of the Iron Hand,** a German burgrave who lost his hand at the siege of Laudshut, and had it replaced by an iron one, which is still shown at Jaxthausen, his birthplace. He is the subject of a historical drama by Goethe (1773).

Goffe, Matthew, a character in Shakespeare's *Henry VI,* Part II.

Gog and Magog, the popular names of two colossal statues in the Guildhall, London. The original figures were burned in the great fire of 1666; the new ones were made in 1708. They are supposed to have been intended for Corineus and Goëmagot.

Gogo, a character in *Robert Macaire,* type of the victims of the "promoter," always ready to take the bait of a fraudulent investment.

Gold of the Nibelungen, and **Gold of Toulouse,** expressions used for ill-gotten and unlucky gains. The latter refers to a Roman consul who seized consecrated gold and silver from the Druids at Toulouse and was defeated with great loss, B.C. 106.

Goldemar, King, or **Vollmar,** a kobold or house-spirit of German legend, who lived three years with Neveling von Hardenberg.

Golden Age, the first age, fabled to have been simple, innocent, and happy, succeeded by ages of silver, brass, and iron, but some time to return, corresponding to the millennium.

Golden Ass, The, the subject of a celebrated romance of Apuleius of the second century. The hero, Lucien, was accidentally changed into an ass, and after undergoing much ill-treatment was restored to his human form. The romance has been borrowed from, imitated, and translated into many languages.

Golden Bull, The, an edict of the Emperor Charles IV (1336) settling the law of procedure in imperial elections, said to have been so called from its gold *bulla* or seal. The expression has been applied also to an edict of Andrew II in the thirteenth century, changing the government from an absolute monarchy to an aristocracy.

Golden Dragon of Bruges, The, was taken by crusaders from St. Sophia at Constantinople and placed on the belfry at Bruges, whence it was taken to Ghent by Philip van Artevelde.

Golden Dustman, The. See BOFFIN.

Golden Gate, The, the entrance to the harbor of San Francisco is so called. The Golden Gate of Constantinople is a triumphal arch surmounted by a statue of Victory raised by Theodosius.

Golden Horn, The, an arm of the Bosporus at Constantinople.

Golden House, The, Nero's palace at Rome.

Golden Legend, The, a collection of lives of saints made by Jacques de Voragine in the thirteenth century. It is the subject of a dramatic poem by Longfellow.

Golden-Mouthed, The, St. John Chrysostom.

Golden Rose, The, a cluster of roses and buds beautifully made of gold and blessed by the Pope the fourth Sunday in Lent. It is given to a lady who has shown devoted piety and zeal, or, if no one eminent enough is found, the rose is laid up in the Vatican. The ex-Empress Eugénie of France and ex-Queen Isabella of Spain (1868) have been among the recipients.

Golden Verses, applied to precepts attributed to Pythagoras, advising a review every night of the acts of the day.

Golden Water, The, enchanted water sought by Princess Parizade in the *Arabian Nights*. A small quantity in a basin would make a perpetual fountain.

Goldilind, the heroine of William Morris's story, *Child Christopher and Goldilind the Fair*.

Goldsmith, Oliver, the chief character in the comedy of his name, by Augustus Thomas, and in F. Frankfort Moore's play of the same name, and a character in his novel, *The Jessamy Bride*.

Golgotha (the place of a skull), name of a place of execution outside Jerusalem. It was applied to a church gallery in Cambridge where heads of the colleges sat. Temple Bar, where heads of criminals were set, was sometimes called the "City Golgotha."

Goll. See DARGO.

Gondibert, Duke, of the royal line of Lombardy, hero of Davenant's unfinished heroic poem of the name (1651).

Gondreville, Malin, grandson of a mason who rose to be tribune, councilor of state, count of the empire, and senator, a character in several of Balzac's novels, *The Gondreville Mystery*, *Domestic Peace*, and others.

Goneril, Duchess of Albany, one of the false and cruel daughters of Lear in Shakespeare's *King Lear*, who poisons her sister from jealousy.

Gonnella, a celebrated buffoon, jester to the Estes of Ferrara. His *Jests* were published in 1506.

Gonsalez Fernan, a Spanish hero of the tenth century, celebrated in ballad literature.

Gonzago: *The Murder of Gonzago* was the play selected by Hamlet for the actors to play before the King.

Gonzalvo de Cordova, called the Great Captain (1443–1515), subject of a romance by Claris de Florian (1791).

Goodchild, Charlotte, a wealthy orphan in Macklin's *Love-à-la Mode,* all of whose suitors except Sir Callaghan O'Brallaghan desert when they hear that her fortune is lost.

Goodfellow, Robin, or **Puck,** a merry, jesting sprite whose tricks are recorded in the ballad *From Oberon in Fairyland.*

Goodman of Ballengeich. The name assumed by King James V of Scotland on his incognito excursions about Edinburgh and Stirling. Ballengeich is a pass leading down behind the Castle of Stirling.

Good Parliament, that of 1376, so called from its remonstrance against the appointment of ecclesiastics to all great offices and the remittance of great sums of money to Rome.

Goodstock, the Host, Lord Frampul, the pretended landlord in Jonson's play, *The New Inn.*

Goodwillie, Professor, the chief character of J. M. Barrie's comedy, *The Professor's Love-Story.*

Goodwin, Colonel and **Clara,** characters in Meredith's novel, *The Adventures of Harry Richmond.*

Goodwin, Morton, the hero of Edward Eggleston's novel, *The Circuit Rider.*

Goody Two-Shoes, the heroine of a nursery tale first published by Newberry (1765), and supposed to have been written by Oliver Goldsmith.

Goorelka, a character in Meredith's novel, *The Shaving of Shagpat.*

Goosey Goderich, name given by Cobbett to Frederick Robinson, created Earl of Ripon in 1833. He was Premier in 1827–1828. Cobbett had nicknamed him Prosperity Robinson because he had argued from the great number of joint-stock companies that the country was in a state of unexampled prosperity, and this just before the financial crisis of 1825. His subsequent career as a statesman made the second nickname popular.

Gorboduc, King of Britain, subject of the first tragedy in English blank verse, by Thomas Norton and Thomas Sackville, afterward Lord Buckhurst (1561); first printed in 1565. The play is sometimes called Ferrex and Porrux, from the two sons of Gorboduc. The story is told in brief in the second book of *The Faerie Queene,* and the clown in *Twelfth Night* mentions a niece of King Gorboduc, to whom the old hermit of Prague "wittily said, 'That that is, is.'" Written also **Gordodug** and **Gorbogud.** See FERREX.

Gordian Knot, The, so called from Gordius, a Phrygian laborer who became king by reason of an oracle promising the kingship to him who should first enter the temple of Jupiter at Gordium. His son Midas consecrated to the god the chariot that had enabled him to carry off the prize. The knot that held the yoke to the body of the chariot was seemingly inextricable, and an oracle declared that whoever untied it should reign over all Asia. Alexander the Great cut the knot with his sword and declared that he had thus fulfilled the prophecy—hence the common phrase, to "cut the Gordian knot."

Gordon, Francis, a trooper of the Royal Guards, whose death is the subject of an amusing paragraph in a note to Scott's *The Heart of Midlothian.*

Gordon, Lord George, the chief instigator of the "No Popery" riots in London in 1780, consequent upon an act of Parliament removing certain disabilities and penalties from Catholics. Lord George was arrested on a charge of high treason and acquitted. The riots play an important part in Dickens's *Barnaby Rudge,* where the author follows historical fact in relation to them.

Gordon, Honor, the heroine of Mrs. Croker's novel, *Mr. Jervis.*

Goren, Mr., a character in Meredith's novel, *Evan Harrington.*

Gorgibus, a plain citizen in Molière's *Les Précieuses Ridicules* (1659), who is distressed at the affectations of his daughter and his niece.

Gorgibus, the father of a romantic girl in Molière's *Sganerelle* (1660).

Goriot, Jean Joachim, one of Balzac's most famous characters, the subject of *Père Goriot,* a father who gives up everything for his ungrateful daughters.

Gorlois, in the Arthur romances, lord of Tintagel and husband of Igrayne, who was the mother of Arthur.

Goslett, Harry, the hero of Besant's novel, *All Sorts and Conditions of Men.*

Gosling, Adeline, a character in Meredith's *Rhoda Fleming.*

Gosling, Giles, landlord of the Black Bear, in Scott's *Kenilworth.*

Gospeller, The Hot. Dr. Barnes, burned at Smithfield, 1540.

Gossamer (God's seam or thread), according to the legend, was the ravelings of Mary's winding-sheet, which fell away as she ascended to heaven.

Gotham, a parish in Nottinghamshire, England, the people of which had a traditionary reputation for stupidity. *The Merry Tales of the Mad Men of Gotham* was popular in the time of the Tudors. Gotham is now chiefly remembered by the three wise men who went to sea in a bowl. In *Salmagundi,* by Washington and William Irving and James K. Paulding, the name was applied to New York and it is now a popular nickname for that city.

Gottlieb, a cotter with whom Prince Henry of Hoheneck lived while he was a leper. Elsie, Gottlieb's daughter, in Longfellow's *The Golden Legend,* offered to give her life for the cure of the Prince, and ultimately became his wife.

Gouraud, Baron, a general under the Empire and ultimately a peer, a character in Balzac's *Pierrette* and *Cousin Pons.*

Gourmaz, Don, a type of the Spanish noble in Corneille's drama, *The Cid.* It was criticized by the French Academy, subservient to Richelieu.

Gow, Henry, or **Henry Smith,** Hal of the Wynd, an armorer, the hero of Scott's *The Fair Maid of Perth.*

Gowan, Henry, an artist in Dickens's *Little Dorrit,* belonging to a family distantly related to the Barnacles.

Gower, John, the poet, author of *Confessio Amantis,* from which the story of Shakespeare's *Pericles* is taken, and therefore introduced as the chorus in that play. He was called by Chaucer "The Moral Gower" in the dedication of *Troylus and Crysede.*

Gowkthrapple, Maister, a preacher of the Covenanters in Scott's *Waverley.*

Graalburg, described in Wolfram von Eschenbach's *Parzival* as a gorgeous temple founded by King Titurel on Mount Salvage, Spain, to contain the Holy Grail.

Grace, Lady, an unpretentious, sensible woman in the comedy *The Provoked Husband* (1726), partly written by Van Brugh, finished by Cibber.

Grace, The Pilgrimage of, a revolt in York, England, in 1536 upon the suppression of small monasteries.

Gradasso, a king of Sericana in Boiardo's *Orlando Innamorato* (1495) and Ariosto's *Orlando Furioso* (1516), who fought against Charlemagne. His vassals, "discrowned kings," dared address him only on their knees. The name is applied in Italy to a bully.

Gradgrind, Thomas, a famous character in Dickens's *Hard Times,* who "mentally introduced himself" as "a man of realities."

Graeme, Adam, the hero of Mrs. Oliphant's novel, *Adam Graeme of Mossgray.*

Graeme, Magdalen, formerly the Lady of Heathergill and appearing toward the end of the story as Mother Nicneven, the grandmother of Roland Graeme in Scott's *The Abbot.*

Graeme, Roland, an important character in Scott's *The Abbot,* a partizan of Queen Mary of Scots.

Graham, Mary, the protégée of Old Martin and fiancée of Young Martin in Dickens's *Martin Chuzzlewit.*

Grahame, Colonel John, and his nephew, Cornet Richard, in the Duke of Monmouth's army, introduced in Scott's *Old Mortality.* Grahame of Claverhouse was afterward Viscount Dundee.

Grail, The Holy, or **Sangreal,** the subject of many legends. It is generally understood to be the cup from which Jesus drank at the Last Supper, and which was filled with the blood from his wounds at the Crucifixion, preserved by Joseph of Arimathea and carried by him to Glastonbury. According to other accounts, it was the platter on which the paschal lamb was served at the last celebration of the Passover by Jesus with His disciples. The Grail could be in charge only of keepers pure in deed, word, and thought; and it disappeared when that condition was broken. Thereafter many knights went in search of it; and Sir Galahad, of the Round Table, was successful.

Grammarian, The, subject of Browning's poem, *A Grammarian's Funeral*, describing the last honors to one who was content to spend his life in the conscientious pursuit of one small fraction of truth.

Grammont, the chief character of Fitch's comedy, *His Grace de Grammont.*

Granby, the subject of a novel of fashionable life by T. H. Lister (1826).

Grandamour or **Graunde Amoure,** a knight whose adventures are told in Stephen Hawes's allegory, *The Passe-Tyme of Pleasure* (1515), "containing the knowledge of the Seven Sciences and the course of Man's Life in this Worlde."

Grandcourt, Henleigh Mallinger, Gwendolen's husband in George Eliot's *Daniel Deronda.*

Grande Mademoiselle, The, Anne Marie Louise d'Orléans, Duchesse de Montpensier, in the time of Louis XIV.

Grandet, Eugénie, a great heiress, heroine of Balzac's novel of the name. The incidents of her life were used by Bayard in a drama, *The Miser's Daughter.*

Grandgousier, or **Grangousier,** the father of the giant Gargantua in Rabelais's romance of that name, a personification of gluttony. The word means great gullet. The character has been supposed to be intended for King Louis XII.

Grandison Cromwell, a nickname given to Lafayette by Mirabeau.

Grandison, Sir Charles, the hero of Richardson's famous novel (1753), endowed with all the virtues and graces and gifts of fortune.

Grandissimes, The, a Creole family, subject of a novel by George W. Cable (1880).

Grand Monarque, The, Louis XIV (1638–1715), who centralized the government of France.

Grandmother's Review, My, a nickname given to the *British Review* by Lord Byron.

Grand Old Man, The, William Ewart Gladstone.

Grand Pendu, The, in cartomancy, the king of diamonds, which bodes death by execution to him who draws it.

Grane, the swift horse of Siegfried.

Graneangowl, the chaplain at Ardenvohn Castle in Scott's *The Legend of Montrose.*

Grania, daughter of the High King of Ireland, betrothed to Finn but in love with Diarmid, with whom she ran away. When, years after, Diarmid fell a victim to Finn's treachery, she married Finn.

Grant, Barbara, a character in Stevenson's novel, *David Balfour.*

Grantly, Bishop, of Barchester, "a bland and kind old man," the father of Archdeacon Grantly; both are characters in Anthony Trollope's novel, *The Warden.*

Grantorto, a giant personifying rebellion, in Spenser's allegory, *The Faerie Queene.*

Gratiano, a character in Shakespeare's *The Merchant of Venice.*

Gratiano, a character in the Italian *commedia dell' arte,* a pedantic doctor in a grotesque mask.

Graustark, the subject of a novel by George Barr McCutcheon.

Graves, Priscilla, a character in Meredith's *One of Our Conquerors.*

Gray, Auld Robin. See AULD ROBIN GRAY.

Gray, Crailey, the chief character in Tarkington's *The Two Vanrevels* (1902).

Gray, Dorian, the subject of Oscar Wilde's novel, *The Picture of Dorian Gray.*

Gray, Duncan, the subject of a humorous ballad (1792), by Robert Burns.

Gray, Gideon, the village doctor at Middlemas in Scott's novel, *The Surgeon's Daughter.*

Gray, Lucy, the subject of a ballad by Wordsworth.

Gray, Rosamund, the heroine of a tale by Charles Lamb.

Graziella, the subject of a story by Lamartine.

Great-heart, Mr., the guide of Christian's wife and children in *Pilgrim's Progress.*

Great Magician, The, Sir Walter Scott, also called The Wizard of the North.

Great Mogul, The, chief of the Mogul Empire, which ended in 1806. The name is often applied in derision to one that assumes superiority or authority.

Great Witch of Balwery, The, Margaret Aiken of Scotland, accused of witchcraft in the sixteenth century, who confessed and saved herself by turning informer, alleging that she knew a witch by a secret mark in the eyes. She was taken about to act as a witch-detective.

Greaves, Sir Launcelot, the hero of a novel of the name by Smollett, a sort of English Don Quixote.

Greek Kalends, The. There were no kalends in the Greek system, therefore "at the Greek Kalends" means never.

Green, Verdant, the hero of a story by Cuthbert Bede.

Green-Bag Inquiry, The, an investigation in England concerning the documents contained in a green bag that were laid before Parliament in 1817. The statement that they were seditious seems to be true from the fact that after secret investigation the Habeas Corpus Act was suspended and political meetings of suspected character were forbidden.

Greenwich, The Archbishop of, in Dickens's *Our Mutual Friend,* head waiter in a Greenwich hotel, solemn and dignified.

Gregory, the name of a fagot-maker who plays the physician in Fielding's farce, *The Mock Doctor* (1733), which is a version of Molière's *Le Médecin Malgré Lui* in which this character is Sganarelle.

Gregory, Father, a character in George Meredith's *Farina.*

Gregsbury, Mr., a member of Parliament in Dickens's *Nicholas Nickleby.*

Grenat, Émile, a character in Meredith's *Lord Ormont and His Aminta.*

Grendel, a fiendish monster in the old romance, *Beowulf.*

Grenville, Arthur, a character in Balzac's *A Woman of Thirty.*

Grenville, Sir Richard, the commander of *The Revenge* in the time of Elizabeth, celebrated in Tennyson's poem, *The*

Revenge. Sir Richard is drawn in Charles Kingsley's ***Westward Ho!***

Gresham, Sir Thomas. See DINING.

Grethel, Gammer, the supposed narrator of Grimm's *Fairy Tales,* said to be Frau Viehmänin.

Grettir, title character of a novel by Baring-Gould.

Greville, Henri, the pen-name of Alice Durant-Fleury.

Grewgious, Hiram, the guardian of Rosa Bud in Dickens's novel, *The Mystery of Edwin Drood.*

Grey, Agnes, a governess in Anne Brontë's novel of the name (1847).

Grey, Alice, the heroine of Barrie's comedy, *Alice Sit-by-the-Fire.*

Grey, Elliott, the chief character in Wallack's play, *Rosedale.*

Grey, Henry, Provost of St. Anselm's, a philosopher, in Mrs. Humphry Ward's *Robert Elsmere.*

Grey, John, the hero of Anthony Trollope's *Can You Forgive Her?*

Grey, John, the hero of James Lane Allen's *The Choir Invisible.*

Grey, Lady Jane (1537–1554), the subject of tragedies by Nicholas Rowe, Ross Neill, Tennyson, and, in French, Madame de Staël, Laplace, Brifaut, and Soumet.

Grey, Sir Thomas, executed for conspiracy to murder the King, a character in Shakespeare's *Henry V.*

Grey, Valentine de, a character in Knowles's play, ***Woman's*** *Wit* (1838).

Grey, Vivian, the hero of Disraeli's novel of the name; it is supposed that he drew the character as his own portrait.

Greyslaer, Max, the subject of a novel, *Greyslaer,* by Charles Fenno Hoffman.

Gribouille, a popular name in France for one who does everything *à contretemps,* illustrated by the man that jumped into the river for fear of getting wet by the rain.

Gridley, Mr., known as "the man from Shropshire," one of the Chancery victims in Dickens's *Bleak House.*

Grieux, The Chevalier de, the hero of the Abbé Prévost's novel, *Manon Lescaut.*

Grieve, David, the subject of a novel by Mrs. Humphry Ward.

Grig, Tom, the lamplighter in Dickens's tale, *The Lamplighter's Story,* a narrative version of a farce he had written earlier.

Grildrig (mannikin), a name given to Gulliver in *Brobdingnag.*

Grim, the hero of an old comedy (1662), *Grim, the Collier of Craydon,* by J. T.

Grim, Giant, who stopped pilgrims on their way to the Celestial City, in Bunyan's *Pilgrim's Progress,* was slain by Great-heart.

Grimello, the subject of *Grimello's Fortunes* by Nicholas Breton (1604).

Grimes, Old, the subject of a well-known ballad by Albert G. Greene.

Grimes, Peter, a drunken criminal, whose story is told in Crabbe's *The Borough* (1810).

Grimwig, Mr., a friend of Mr. Brownlow, in Dickens's *Oliver Twist.*

Gringo, Harry, a pen-name of Henry Augustus Wise, author of *Los Gringos* (The Unintelligible Ones).

Gringoire, Pierre, the chief character of a comedy, *Gringoire,* and a character in Hugo's *The Hunchback of Notre Dame,* and in a drama from it, *The Egyptian.*

Grinioff, Peter, tells the story in Pushkin's *The Captain's Daughter.*

Griselda, Grizzell, or **Griseldis, the Patient,** a character in Chaucer's *The Clerk of Oxenford's Tale.* She is a model of patience and resignation.

Griskinessa, the wife of the King of Utopia in Rhodes's *Bombastes Furioso.*

Gros-Jean, a popular name in France for one that assumes to teach another who knows better than himself. La Fontaine, however, gave it a different significance in the fable of *The Dairyman and the Pot of Milk*—that is, one who loses what he has dreamed of as the foundation of a great fortune.

Gros-René, Molière's type of a valet, care-free and joyous.

Grouch, Sophy, the title character of Anthony Hope's romance, *Sophy of Kravonia.*

Groveby, Sir Harry, and his uncle, of Gloomstock Hall, characters of Burgoyne's play, *The Maid of the Oaks.*

Grub, Gabriel, a surly fellow reformed by his Christmas Eve experience, in a story told by Mr. Wardle in Dickens's *The Pickwick Papers.*

Grub, Jonathan, his wife, and his daughter **Emily,** characters in William O'Brien's farce, *Cross Purposes* (1842).

Grub Street, now Milton Street, near Moorfields, London, figures in literature as the home of hack-writers who ground out heavy or worthless productions.

Grumbletonians, or the "Country Party," in the time of William and Mary, were so called in distinction from the court party.

Grumbo, a giant in the tale of *Tom Thumb.*

Grumio, a clever servant of Petruchio in Shakespeare's *The Taming of the Shrew.*

Grün, Anastasius, the pen-name of Anton Alexander von Auersperg, a German poet (1806–1876).

Grundy, Mrs., in Morton's comedy, *Speed the Plough,* is often referred to, but does not appear as a character. Her neighbor, Dame Ashfield, is constantly asking, "What will Mrs. Grundy say?" which has given rise to the use of the name as a synonym for the conventional world.

Gryphon or **Griffin,** a fabulous animal with an eagle's head and a lion's body.

Guadiana, The River, according to a story told to Don Quixote, was formerly a squire of Durandarte, who, grieving for his master, was changed by enchantment into a river of his name.

Guard, Theodore de la, a pen-name of Nathaniel Ward.

Guardian Angel, The, the subject of a poem by Browning, suggested by a picture of Guercino in the church of St. Augustine at Fano, Italy. Also the title of a novel by Oliver Wendell Holmes.

Guary Miracle, The, described as a kind of miracle-play in the Cornish dialect.

Gudrun, a character in the Edda of Samund Sigfusson, married to Sigurd and after his death to King Atti, whom she came to hate for his cruelty and murdered, after killing their two children. She then threw herself into the sea, but was rescued and married to another king. **Gudrun** is the name of the heroine of a North Saxon poem of the thirteenth century, and of the last poem in the third part of William Morris's *The Earthly Paradise.*

Guelpho, a crusader, next in command to Godfrey, in Tasso's *Jerusalem Delivered* (1575).

Guendolen, in an Arthur romance, the mother of his son, Gyneth.

Guendolen, a legendary character, wife of Locrine, who divorced her, upon which she collected an army and attacked him. He was killed and she threw her rival Estrildis and her daughter Sabre into a river, which was therefore called Sabrina or Sabren, now Severn.

Guenevra, the wife of Necbatanus in Scott's *The Talisman.*

Guénic, Baron du, a brave soldier devoted to the Royalist cause, the head of an ancient Breton house, in Balzac's *The Chouans and Beatrix.*

Guest, Stephen. See DEANE, LUCY.

Guidascarpi, Angelo, Clelia, and **Renaldo,** characters in Meredith's novel, *Vittoria.*

Guiderius, a character in Shakespeare's *Cymbeline.*

Guido, the brother of Rinaldo in Ariosto's *Orlando Furioso,* was taken by the Amazons and forced to marry ten of them, but escaped to Charlemagne's army.

Guildenstern and **Rosencrantz,** characters in Shakespeare's *Hamlet.*

Guillot, in La Fontaine's fable, *The Wolf Turned Shepherd,* would have it written upon his hat that he was "Guillot shepherd of this flock"—a quotation applied to one who makes a display of his titles, rank, or riches.

Guinevere, Guenever, or **Guanhumara,** the wife of King Arthur. There are different versions of her story; but all are agreed that she was false to Arthur and that she spent her closing years in a nunnery.

Guiscardo, the squire of Tancred, King of Salerno, in Dryden's *Sigismunda and Guiscardo,* to whom Tancred's daughter is clandestinely married.

Guise, The Duke of, is the subject of a drama by Webster, *Guise: or, The Massacre of France* (1620) and of *The Duke of Guise,* by Dryden and Lee. He is a character in some of Dumas's historical novels.

Gulchenrous, a beautiful, esthetic youth in Beckford's *Vathek* (1784).

Gulistan (the rose-garden), the title of a collection of tales and verses by Saadi, of Shiraz, Persia.

Gulliver, Lemuel, the supposed narrator of *Gulliver's Travels* (1726) by Jonathan Swift.

Gulnare, the daughter of a king of the under-sea people, mother of Beder in the *Arabian Nights* tale, Beder and Giauharê.

Gulnare, wife of the Sultan, who helps the corsair to escape in Byron's poem, *The Corsair.*

Gulveraz, a character in Meredith's novel, *The Shaving of Shagpat.*

Gummer's Ore, a fabulous floating island in the northern seas, near the Scandinavian peninsula.

Gummidge, the widow of Peggotty's partner in Dickens's *David Copperfield.*

Gunther, in the *Nibelungenlied,* King of Burgundy and husband of Brunhild; he was slain by his sister, Kriemhild, in the dungeon of Etzel (Attila).

Gurney, Gilbert, the hero and title of a novel by Theodore Hook, supposed to be autobiographical.

Gurth, in Scott's *Ivanhoe,* a Saxon swineherd.

Gurth, a brother of the King in Bulwer's *Harold.*

Gurton, Gammer, the heroine of an English comedy, second in point of age to *Ralph Roister Doister.* The subject is the loss of a needle and the title *Gammer Gurton's Needle.* The authorship has been attributed to John Still, Bishop of Bath and Wells (1561).

Gushington, Angelina, the pen-name of Lady Dufferin.

Gusley, Hester, the chief character of Mary Cholmondeley's *Red Pottage.*

Gustavus Vasa, King of Sweden, the subject of a play by Henry Brooke (1730), which was not allowed to be acted on account of its reflections upon Sir Robert Walpole, then Premier.

It was printed by the author, and Brooke realized a thousand guineas from the sale.

Gutter Lyrist, The, a nickname applied to Robert Buchanan, on account of his choice of subjects.

Guy of Warwick, Sir, the hero of an ancient romance, a crusader who slew the giant Amerant in the Holy Land and after his return to England fought the Danish giant Colbrand and slew the Dun Cow of Dunsmore and a winged dragon. At last he became a hermit and begged bread daily from his wife Phelis, who did not know him until he revealed himself to her upon his deathbed. He is the subject of *Guy and Amarant* (1649).

Guyon, Sir, the personification of temperance in Spenser's *The Faerie Queene.*

Guzman d' Alfarache, the hero of a Spanish romance, supposed to have suggested to Le Sage *The Life of Gil Blas.*

Gwenwyn, a character in Scott's *The Betrothed.*

Gwynn, Nell, the title character of a novel by F. Frankfort Moore, of Paul Kester's play, *Sweet Nell of Old Drury,* and *Mistress Nell,* by George C. Hazelton. She is a character, also, in W. H. Ainsworth's novel of her name, and in Anthony Hope's *Simon Dale.*

Gwynplaine, the name character of Hugo's *The Man Who Laughs.*

Gyges, the ring of, was found on the finger of a gigantic corpse in the flanks of a brazen horse. It rendered the bearer invisible.

Gyneth, a daughter of Arthur whom Merlin threw into a trance that lasted five hundred years.

Gynt, Peer, the chief character in Ibsen's drama of the name. He has been brought up on fairy tales and stories of his family's past grandeur, is a visionary, a liar, and boaster, a moral coward and compromiser, with something of attractiveness about him withal.

Hackler, Jim, the title character of George Ade's comedy, *The County Chairman.*

Hadgi, Stavros, a Greek brigand, the title character of Edmond About's novel, *The King of the Mountains* (1856).

Hafiz, the pen-name of "Stott of Dromore," abused in Byron's *English Bards and Scotch Reviewers* (1809).

Hafner, Fanny, the daughter of a Jewish swindler in Bourget's novel, *Cosmopolis* (1892).

Hagan, or **Hagen,** in the *Nibelungenlied* (1210), murdered Siegfried and was killed by Kriemhild.

Hagenbach, Archibald von, the Governor of La Ferette in Scott's *Anne of Geierstein.*

Hagenbach, Joseph, the hero of *Geier Wally,* by Wilhelmine von Hillern.

Haidee, "the beauty of the Cyclades," daughter of a Greek pirate, heroine of an episode in Byron's *Don Juan.*

Haizum. See GABRIEL.

Hajji Baba, tells his story in James Morier's *The Adventures of Hajji Baba of Ispahan.*

Hakeem. See DJABAL.

Hakkadosh, Jochanan, a rabbi, subject of a poem by Browning, whose life is extended fifteen months by the gift of time from the lives of a lover, a warrior, a poet, a statesman, and a child.

Hakon, Hakonsson, a historical character introduced in Ibsen's *The Pretenders.* He is confident of his power to carry out his "great King-thoughts" of uniting all Norway into one peaceful nation.

Halcombe, Marion, one of the chief characters in Collins's novel, *The Woman in White.*

Halgaver, The Mayor of, an imaginary person to be haled before whom is a threat made to the slovenly. Halgaver is a moor in Cornwall famous for a carnival held there in July.

Halifax, John, the hero of a novel by Dinah Maria Mulock (Mrs. Craik).

Halkett, Cecilia, an heiress, friend of Nevil in George Meredith's *Beauchamp's Career.*

Hall, Cyril, Vicar of Nunnely in Charlotte Brontë's *Shirley.*

Hall, Father, a name assumed by Father St. Clare in Shorthouse's *John Inglesant.*

Halcro, Claud, a minstrel in Scott's *The Pirate.*

Hale, Nathan, the Revolutionary hero, is the subject of a play by Clyde Fitch, a character in *Brinton Eliot,* a novel by James E. Farmer, and the subject of a poem by Francis M. Finch.

Hallam, Arthur Henry (1811–1833), son of Henry Hallam, the historian, a young man of great promise, a friend of Tennyson and subject of his poem, *In Memoriam.*

Haller, Mrs., the assumed name of the Countess of Waldbourg, heroine of Benjamin Thompson's play, *The Stranger* (1797), adapted from Kotzebue, a favorite character of the famous actress, Miss O'Neill.

Halley, Lord and **Lady Grace,** characters in Meredith's novel, *One of Our Conquerors.*

Hallward, Basil, the painter in Oscar Wilde's novel, *The Picture of Dorian Gray.*

Hamet Benengeli, Cid, the imaginary Moor to whom Cervantes attributes the writing of *Don Quixote.*

Hamilcar is a character in Flaubert's *Salammbô.*

Hamilton, Alfred, the hero of *The Initials,* by Baroness Tautphœus.

Hamilton-Wells, Angelica and **Theodore,** called **Diavolo,** the title characters of Sarah Grand's novel, *The Heavenly Twins* (1893).

Hamlet, Prince of Denmark, the hero of Shakespeare's drama of the name. Amlettus, Amleth, and Hamblet are older forms of the name. It was first published under the title *The Revenge of Hamlett, Prince of Denmark,* in 1603. *Hamlet* is the subject of an opera in French (1868) by Ambroise Thomas, the music of which is said to be fine, but the text "a horrid mutilation" of Shakespeare's tragedy.

Hamlin, Perez, the title character of Edward Bellamy's novel, *The Duke of Stockbridge.*

Hammer, The, Judas Asmonæus, surnamed Maccabæus the Hammer (B.C. 166–136); and Charles Martel (Hammer) (689–741).

Hammer of England, The, William Wallace (1270–1305).

Hammer of Heretics, a name that has been applied to St. Augustine (395–430); Pierre d'Ailly (1350–1425), president of the council that condemned John Huss; John Faber (1470–1541), author of *The Hammer of Heretics;* and St. Hilary (350–367), Hammer of the Arians.

Hammer of Scotland, The, Edward I (1272–1307), upon whose tomb in Westminster Abbey is inscribed in Latin, "Here is Long Edward, Hammer of the Scots." He was also called "Longshanks" and "The English Justinian."

Hampole, The Hermit of, Richard Rolle, religious poet (about 1290–1349), an Augustinian monk who lived solitary near Hampole, Doncaster.

Hampton-Evey, Rev. Stephen, a character in Meredith's *Lord Ormont and His Aminta* (1894).

Handsome Englishman, The, so John Churchill, Duke of Marlborough (1650–1722), was called by Turenne's troops.

Handsome Swordsman, The, Joachim Murat (1767–1815).

Handy Andy, the hero of Samuel Lover's Irish story of the name.

Handy, Abel, a pensioner in Anthony Trollope's *The Warden.*

Handy, Sir Abel, an inventor whose patents would not work, a character in Morton's comedy, *Speed the Plough* (1798).

Hanging Judge, The, a name given to Sir Francis Page (Judge 1718–1741) and to the Earl of Norbury, Justice of the Common Pleas in Ireland, 1820–1827, who was in the habit of jesting when pronouncing sentence of death.

Hannele, the chief character in Hauptmann's play of the name. She is a little outcast child who, just before her death, has delirious trances in which the personages and events of her unhappy life become objective visions and are seen by the audience.

Hannibal, the Carthaginian general, a character in Thomas Nabbes's tragedy, *Hannibal and Scipio* (1637).

Hanno, a slave in Dr. John Moore's novel, *Zeluco* (1789), the description of whose death is highly praised.

Hans Chapel of Our Lady of the Ferry, The, legend of, in Scott's *Anne of Geierstein.*

Hans of Iceland, the subject of a novel by Victor Hugo.

Hans von Rippach, a non-existent character, inquired for as a joke by German students.

Hanswurst, a clown of the old German comedy, corresponding to the English *Jack Pudding*, the French *Jean Potage*, the Italian *Macaroni*, and the Dutch *Pickel hering*, gluttons.

Hapgood, Penn, a leading character in Trowbridge's *Cudjo's Cave.*

Hapmouche, in the *Pantagruel* of Rabelais, a giant that invented the process of smoking meats.

Happer, Mysie, in Scott's *The Monastery,* helps Sir Piercie to escape, and becomes his wife.

Happy Valley, The, in Dr. Johnson's *Rasselas,* the kingdom of Amhara in Abyssinia.

Hapsburg or **Habsburg,** the Imperial House of Austria. The first emperor (1273–'91) of the family, Rudolph, is the subject of a poem by Schiller.

Harapha, a giant in Milton's *Samson Agonistes,* who mocked Samson at a safe distance.

Harcourt, a character in Shakespeare's *Henry IV,* Part II.

Hardcastle, Kate, the heroine of Goldsmith's comedy, *She Stoops to Conquer* (1773).

Harden, Lucia, the scholarly heroine of May Sinclair's *The Divine Fire.*

Harding Septimus, the hero of Anthony Trollope's novel, *The Warden,* who resigns his office on conscientious grounds. His daughter **Eleanor** is the heroine.

Haredale, Emma, Reuben, her father, and **Geoffrey,** her uncle, characters in Dickens's *Barnaby Rudge.*

Harefoot, Harold, a sobriquet of Harold I, referring to his swiftness of foot.

Harewood, James, a war-correspondent in Chambers's novel, *The Ashes of Empire* (1899).

Hargrave, a man of fashion, hero and title of a novel by Mrs. Trollope (1843).

Harkaway, Grace, an heiress in Boucicault's play, *London Assurance.*

Harkless, John, the chief personage of Booth Tarkington's novel, *The Gentleman from Indiana.*

Harland, Elfrida, the principal character of Ellen T. Fowler's novel, *A Double Thread,* and the drama founded upon it.

Harlequin, a character of old popular Italian comedy, servant of Pantaloon and lover of Columbine—otherwise Arlecchino and Arlechinetta. He appears in England in pantomime and puppet-show.

Harlequin, a nickname applied to Robert Harley, Earl of Oxford and Mortimer (1661–1724).

Harleth, Gwendolen, the heroine of George Eliot's *Daniel Deronda*.

Harley, a man of excessive diffidence and sensitiveness who gives the name to Mackenzie's novel, *The Man of Feeling* (1771).

Harley, Adrian, called "the Wise Youth," in Meredith's novel, *The Ordeal of Richard Feverel* (1859).

Harlow, Miss, the heroine of Murphy's farce, *The Old Maid*.

Harlowe, Clarissa, the unfortunate heroine of Richardson's novel of the name, regarded as one of the most beautiful characters in fiction.

Harmachis, a descendant of the Pharaohs in Rider Haggard's *Cleopatra*.

Harmon, John, the heir to the estate held by the Golden Dustman in Dickens's *Our Mutual Friend*.

Harold, the last Saxon king of England, is the subject of a novel by Bulwer and of a play by Tennyson.

Harold, Childe, the hero of Byron's poem, *Childe Harold's Pilgrimage,* a blasé man of the world, seeking diversion in travel.

Haroun al Raschid, a caliph (765–809). Many of the tales of the *Arabian Nights* are laid in his reign, and he is an actor in some of them and in other Eastern tales.

Harpagon, the miser of Molière's comedy, *L'Avare*.

Harpalus, the hero of an old pastoral. The name is used in Spenser's *Colin Clout's Come Home Again* for a character supposed to be intended for the Earl of Dorset.

Harrington, the hero of Maria Edgeworth's novel, *Harrington*.

Harrington, Evan, the son of a country tailor in Meredith's novel, *Evan Harrington* (1861).

Harris, Mrs., in Dickens's *Martin Chuzzlewit*, the imaginary friend of Sairey Gamp.

Harrison, one of the parliamentary commissioners in Scott's *Woodstock*.

Harry, Sir, the servant of a baronet, so nicknamed on account of his airs in Townley's *High Life Below Stairs* (1759).

Hart, King, the subject of an allegorical poem by Bishop Gawain Douglas of Dunkeld, in which the heart is the king of the man.

Hartford Wits, The, were Joel Barlow, John Trumbull, David Humphreys, and Lemuel Hopkins originally; afterward also Richard Alsop, Theodore Dwight, Nathan Cogswell, Elihu Smith, and others.

Harthouse, James, a bored young man in Dickens's *Hard Times.*

Hartley, Adam, a character in Scott's novel, *The Surgeon's Daughter.*

Hartright, Walter, one of the chief characters in Wilkie Collins's *The Woman in White.*

Hartwell, a widow in John Fletcher's play, *Wit Without Money* (1639).

Hartwig, George, tells the story in Spielhagen's *Hammer and Anvil* (1869).

Harum, David, the subject of a novel by Edward Noyes Westcott and a play (1900) from it by R. and M. Hitchcock and E. E. Rose. He is a type of American country life more than a generation ago, created out of carefully studied realities; a man trained in straitened circumstances and developing with success, keen, skeptical, not overscrupulous where the hypocritical and tricky are concerned, but kindly with the simple and straightforward, living up to his Golden Rule: "Find out what the other fellow means to do to you, and do it to him first."

Hassan, in Byron's poem, *The Giaour* (1813), is a caliph slain by the Giaour in revenge for the death of Leila, a beautiful slave in the caliph's seraglio, beloved by the Giaour.

Hassan, Abu, hero of the *Arabian Nights* tale, The Sleeper Awakened.

Hassal Alhabbal, Cogia, whose History is one of the *Arabian Nights* tales, has many losses; then his wife finds a splendid diamond in a fish, which makes their fortune.

Hastings, in Goldsmith's play, *She Stoops to Conquer,* one of the two young men that mistook Mr. Hardcastle's house for an inn.

Hastings, Lord Reginald, the chief character in Robert Hichens's novel, *The Green Carnation* (1894).

Hastings, William, Lord, appears in Shakespeare's *Henry VI*, Part III, and in *Richard III*.

Haswell, a physician in Mrs. Inchbald's play, *Such Things Are* (1786), that gave himself to work in Indian prisons.

Hat, Gessler's, Herrmann Gessler, an Austrian governor in Switzerland, ordered a hat set up in Altdorf, to be saluted by all who passed by. William Tell, according to the tradition, refused and was condemned to shoot an apple from the head of his son. He did it successfully and afterward shot Gessler himself, in an uprising that ended in liberty for the Four Forest Cantons. Schiller has a drama, *William Tell*, and Rossini an opera, *Guglielmo Tell*.

Hatch, Mrs., the chief character of Mrs. Burton Harrison's play and novel, *The Unwelcome Mrs. Hatch*.

Hats and Caps, names given to two political parties in Sweden in the eighteenth century; those favoring the French wore hats, and the partizans of Russia made a badge of the Russian cap.

Hatteraick, Dirk, a smuggler, in Scott's *Guy Mannering*.

Hatto, Archbishop of Mainz in 914, according to the legend not only refused to relieve the poor in time of famine from his abundant store, but decoyed a multitude of them into a great barn and burned them in it. As a punishment he was pursued by a great army of mice; he took refuge in a tower on an island in the Rhine near Bingen; but they swam after him and devoured him. One version of the story makes them the souls of the peasants in the form of mice. The same story, substantially, has been told of others who were cruel to the poor: Bishop Adolf of Cologne (1112); Freiherr von Güttingen, who was devoured by mice at his castle in the Lake of Constance which sank into the lake and may still be seen at times; and Count Graaf, owner of a tower on the Rhine. Widerolf, Bishop of Strasburg in 997, met a similar fate because he suppressed the convent of Seltzen.

Haunted Man, The. See REDLAW.

Hauteserre, Adrien, and **Robert d',** brothers, in Balzac's *The Gondreville Mystery*.

Hautlieu, Lady Margaret de, a character in Scott's *Castle Dangerous*.

Hautlieu, the Marquis of, in the introduction to Scott's *Quentin Durward,* is visited by the author.

Haut-Ton, Sir Oran, an orang in Peacock's novel, *Melencourt* (1817), prepared by his patron to represent the borough of Onevote in Parliament, "such an excellent fellow," Saintsbury says, "that one almost wishes he could have been discovered to be no Orang at all, but a baby lost early in the woods, could have recovered his speech, improved his good looks, and married Anthelia."

Havelaar, Max, the title character of a novel of the name by Edouard Douwes Dekker.

Havelok the Dane, the hero of a legend in old romance, the earliest known form of which is in French; it was put into rhyme by a trouvère in the twelfth century and afterward was translated into English. Havelok was the son of a Danish king set adrift by his guardians, and rescued and reared by a fisherman of Lincolnshire. About twenty years later some usurping English nobles wishing to get rid of the rightful heir, a princess, married her to Havelok, a peasant as they thought. But by the aid of his father Havelok defeated them and became king in his wife's right of that part of England and later of Denmark.

Havisham, Miss, a spinster in Dickens's *Great Expectations.*

Hawdon, Esther, known as Esther Summerson, the heroine of Dickens's *Bleak House.*

Hawk, Sir Mulberry, the bear-leader of a young lord in Dickens's *Nicholas Nickleby.*

Hawkeye, an Indian name for Natty Bumppo, hero of Cooper's *Leatherstocking Tales.*

Hawkeye State, The, Iowa, so called from an Indian chief.

Hawkyard, Brother, an exhorter in Dickens's tale, *George Silverman's Explanation,* who says: "The Lord has had a good servant in me, and He knows it."

Hayraddin, a treacherous Bohemian in Scott's *Quentin Durward.*

Hayston, Frank, laird of Bucklaw, married to Lucia in Scott's *The Bride of Lammermoor.* In Donizetti's opera, *Lucia di Lammermoor,* the character is called Arturio.

Hazard, Myrtle, the heroine of *The Guardian Angel,* by Oliver Wendell Holmes.

Hazeldean, Jock o', the subject of a well-known old ballad, modernized by Sir Walter Scott.

Headlong, Squire Harry, the owner of *Headlong Hall* in Peacock's novel of that name.

Headrigg, Cuddie, the plowman at Tillietudlem in Scott's *Old Mortality.*

Headstone, Bradley, a schoolmaster in Dickens's *Our Mutual Friend.*

Heart of Midlothian, The, the old jail or Tolbooth at Edinburgh. It was taken down in 1817; the site is marked with a heart in the pavement. It gives the name to Scott's novel, as being the scene of Effie Deans's imprisonment.

Heath, Sir Massingberd, the title character of Payn's *Lost Sir Massingberd.*

Heathcliff, the principal character in Emily Brontë's novel, *Wuthering Heights.*

Heathcote, Ward, a leading character in Miss Woolson's *Anne.*

Heathen Chinee, The, subject of a famous poem by Francis Bret Harte, entitled *Plain Language from Truthful James.*

Hecate, a mysterious divinity, one of the Titans, appears with the witches in Shakespeare's *Macbeth,* and in William Morris's *An Epic of Hades.*

Hector, the Trojan hero of the *Iliad,* is a character in Shakespeare's *Troilus and Cressida.*

Hector of the Mist, an outlaw in Scott's *The Legend of Montrose.*

Hecuba, the second wife of Priam, is the subject of a tragedy by Euripides. Hamlet says of the actor's simulated grief at the sight of Hecuba at the death of Priam: "What's Hecuba to him, or he to Hecuba?" an expression become proverbial.

Heep, Uriah, a character in Dickens's *David Copperfield.*

Heinrich, the hero and title of a poem by Hartmann von der Ane, whose story is the subject of Longfellow's *The Golden Legend.*

Heinrich, the bell-founder, the chief character in Hauptmann's play, *The Sunken Bell,* the type of the struggling, aspiring artist, who, cast down by defeat, is led to more remote and loftier heights by a new ideal, whence the inevitable fall.

Heinrich, Kaiser, is introduced in Meredith's novel, *Farina.*

Heinrich, Princess, a character in *The King's Mirror* by Anthony Hope.

Helbeck, Alan, the subject of a novel by Mrs. Humphry Ward, *Helbeck of Bannisdale.*

Heldar, Dick, the chief character of Kipling's *The Light that Failed.*

Helen, Lady, the heroine of Colman's drama, *The Iron Chest* (1796), founded on Godwin's *Caleb Williams.*

Helen of Kirconnell, subject of an old ballad, of which many versions have been made. Helen Irving, daughter of the Laird of Kirconnell, threw herself in front of her lover to receive a bullet from the gun of a rival.

Helen, Sister, the subject of a poem by Dante Gabriel Rossetti. Sister Helen is destroying a faithless lover by melting a waxen image before the fire.

Helena, in love with Demetrius in Shakespeare's *A Midsummer Night's Dream* (1594).

Helena, the heroine of Shakespeare's *All's Well that Ends Well.*

Hélène d'Aiglemont, a character in Balzac's *A Woman of Thirty.*

Helenus, a son of Priam, introduced in Shakespeare's *Troilus and Cressida.*

Helge, the subject of a romance by the Danish poet Oehlenschläger.

Helicanus, a lord of Tyre in Shakespeare's *Pericles.*

Hel Keplein, a mantle of invisibility in the *Heldenbuch* (book of heroes) of the thirteenth century.

Helmer, Nora, the heroine of Ibsen's *A Doll's House.*

Héloïse. See ELOISA.

Héloïse, the New, the subject of a romance by Rousseau.

Helstone, Rev. Matthewson, and his niece **Caroline,** characters in Charlotte Brontë's *Shirley.*

Hemjunah, daughter of the sultan Zebenezer in Ridley's *The Princess of Cassimir;* changed by enchantment into a toad, she became acquainted with another toad; he proved to be the sultan of India, to whom she had been betrothed when very young; they were married after being released from the enchantment.

Henchard, Michael, the title character of Thomas Hardy's *The Mayor of Casterbridge.*

Henjumhei, Gunnar, the chief character of H. H. Boyesen's *Gunnar.*

Henri, Mademoiselle, the pupil and afterward the wife of the hero of Charlotte Brontë's novel, *The Professor.*

Henriel, Comte Henri d', a character in Meredith's *Beauchamp's Career.*

Henrietta, Maria, the widow of King Charles I, is introduced in Scott's *Peveril of the Peak,* and in Dumas's *Twenty Years After.*

Henriette, the "womanly woman" in Molière's *Les Femmes Savantes.*

Henry II of France is introduced in Dumas's *The Two Dianas* and *The Page of the Duke of Savoy.*

Henry III is in *Chicot the Jester* and the *Forty-Five Guardsmen* of Dumas, and in Weyman's *A Gentleman of France.*

Henry IV (1366–1413), **Henry V** (1388–1422), **Henry VI** (1421–1471), Lancastrian kings of England, and **Henry VIII,** second of the Tudor kings, are subjects of plays by Shakespeare. King John's son, Prince Henry, who became Henry III, appears in the drama *King John* as a man, though he was but nine when John died. Henry V, as Prince Hal, is a character in both parts of *King Henry IV.* Henry IV is a character in *King Richard II.* Henry VII as Richmond, is a character in the third part of *King Henry VI,* and in *Richard III.* By his marriage with the daughter of Edward IV the claims of the houses of York and Lancaster were united. He was the first of the Tudors. Henry II appears in Scott's *The Betrothed.* Henry VIII is the subject of a novel by Miss Mühlbach, and is a character in Charles Major's *When Knighthood Was in Flower* and the drama from it; also in an opera by Saint-Saëns.

Henry IV of France is a character in Dumas's *Marguerite of Valois* and *The Forty-five Guardsmen,* and in Weyman's *A Gentleman of France.* King Henry IV and the Ligue under the Duke of Guise are the subjects of Voltaire's epic poem, *The Henriade.* Henry of Navarre is also the hero of Macaulay's poem, *Ivry*. In Barclay's *Argenis* he is called Poliarchus.

Henry, Peter, the title character of Émile Souvestre's *The Confessions of a Workingman.*

Henry, the Young, the subject of an opera by Méhul, noted for the beautiful hunting symphony that forms the overture.

Henschel, the chief character in Hauptmann's play, *Teamster Henschel.*

Hentzau, Rupert of, appears in Anthony Hope's *The Prisoner of Zenda,* and is the chief actor in its sequel, which bears his name.

Heorot, the palace of Hrothgar, King of Denmark, celebrated in *Beowulf,* the Anglo-Saxon epic of the sixth century.

Heraclidæ, supposed descendants of Hercules. A tragedy of Euripides is entitled *The Heraclidæ.*

Heraclius, the name of two emperors of the East, father (610–642), and son, who reigned three and a half months. Calderon and Corneille have each a tragedy, *Heraclius.*

Heraud, Sir, a character in the romance, *Guy of Warwick.*

Herbert, Sir Walter, a character in Shakespeare's *Richard III.*

Herculaneum, the subject of an opera by Félicien David.

Hercules Secundus, a title assumed by the Roman Emperor, Commodus, who is said to have killed one hundred lions and defeated one thousand gladiators.

Hercules, or **Alcides,** is the subject of a tragedy by Euripides (408 B.C.) and two by Seneca (first century A.D.). *The Judgment of Hercules* is a moral poem (1741) by Shenstone.

Hereford, Henry of (Bolingbroke, afterward Henry IV), is introduced in Shakespeare's *King Richard II.*

Heretic's Tragedy, The, the subject of a poem by Browning. The heretic is Jacques du Bourg-Molay, last Grand Master of the Order of Knights Templars, burned at Paris in 1314.

Hereward, a character in Scott's *Count Robert of Paris,* one of the Varangian Guard, afterward a crusader with Count Robert.

Hereward, the Wake, "the last of the English," the subject of a novel by Charles Kingsley.

Heriot, George, jeweler to the king in Scott's novel, *The Fortunes of Nigel.*

Heriot, Walter, a character in Meredith's *The Adventures of Harry Richmond.*

Hermadec, Ives, a character in Loti's novel, *Mon Frère Ives.*

Hermann, the hero of Goethe's poem, *Hermann and Dorothea.*

Hermann, Prince, a character in Meredith's novel, *The Adventures of Harry Richmond.*

Hermegyld, a convert of Constaunce in Chaucer's *The Man of Law's Tale.*

Hermensul, an idol worshiped in Westphalia, broken by Charlemagne, who made its temple into a Christian church.

Hermes, St., an electric light sometimes seen to play about a ship's masts, called by sailors St. Elmo's or St. Helme's fire, the fires of St. Peter and St. Nicholas, as well as St. Hermes.

Hermes Trismegistus (thrice greatest), the Egyptian god Thoth.

Hermia, one of the heroines of Shakespeare's *A Midsummer Night's Dream.*

Hermil, Tullio, and **Juliana,** the chief characters in D'Annunzio's novel, *The Intruder* (1872).

Hermione, in Shakespeare's *A Winter's Tale,* is the wife of the jealous Leontes and mother of Perdita.

Hermione, the Lady, a character in Scott's *The Fortunes of Nigel.*

Hermit, The, a poem by Thomas Parnell (1679–1718), in which the hermit was traveling with a youth who committed several seeming crimes without any apparent motive. When the hermit began to curse him, the youth showed himself as an angel and explained his acts, all of which were shown to be interventions to prevent greater evil. This is one form of a legend that is known in many literatures.

Hermstrong, the hero and title of a novel (1796) by Robert Bage, of which the subtitle is *Man as He Is Not.*

Hernani, the subject of a tragic drama by Victor Hugo. Its first representation in 1830 was signalized by a veritable struggle, in the parterre, between the classicists and the romanticists.

Herne, the Hunter, a traditional character, whose oak is mentioned in *The Merry Wives of Windsor*. The oak was cut down in 1795.

Hero, a priestess of Venus, whose lover Leander was drowned in the Hellespont, when swimming across to her. *Hero and Leander* is the subject of a Greek romance of the fifth or sixth century attributed to Musæus. A poem by Marlowe and Chapman (1598) has the same subject; also one by Thomas Hood (1827) and a translation by Edwin Arnold (1873).

Hero, one of the principal characters in Shakespeare's *Much Ado about Nothing*.

Herod, called the Great, to whom is attributed the massacre of the innocents, is a frequent character in the miracle plays.

Herod, Antipas, son of the preceding, who ordered the execution of John the Baptist. *Le Herodiade* is the title of an opera by Massenet (1881).

Heronville, Duc d', a dwarfish and vicious descendant of an ancient house in Balzac's *The Hated Son*.

Herrick, Lenore, the heroine of Rhoda Broughton's *Good-bye, Sweetheart*.

Herries of Birrenswork, Laird of the Solway Locks, a partizan of Charles Edward in Scott's *Redgauntlet*.

Her Trippa, a character in the *Pantagruel* of Rabelais—Henricus Cornelius Agrippa, a philosopher and physician of Nettesheim.

Herwig, King of Heligoland, defeated Hartmuth, who had carried away Gudrun, his betrothed, liberated and married her.

Hesperus, the evening star, fabled to have been a youth that climbed Mount Atlas to observe the stars and was seen no more on earth.

Hesperus is the subject of a romance by Jean Paul Richter (1795).

Hesperus, The Wreck of the, is the subject of a poem by Longfellow.

Hessel, Lena, a character in Ibsen's *The Pillars of Society*.

Hester Savory, a young Quakeress admired by Charles Lamb, who wrote a poem on her death.

Hexam, Lizzie, a fine character in Dickens's *Our Mutual Friend.*

Heywood, Thomas, the title character of W. E. Norris's novel, *The Rogue.*

Hiawatha, the hero of an "Indian Edda" by Longfellow. It is founded on a tradition of the North American Indians of a personage of miraculous birth who was sent among them to teach them the arts of peace. He was known by different names among the various tribes—beside Hiawatha, Tarenyawagon, Chiabo, Manabozo, and Michabou. The scene of the poem is among the Ojibways on the southern shore of Lake Superior. Hiawatha is the son of the West Wind, Mudjekee'wis, and Wenonah, daughter of Nokomis. He taught his nation to cultivate maize, to navigate the waters, to extract oil, and to use medicine.

Hibbins, Mistress, an old lady in Hawthorne's *The Scarlet Letter*, sister of Governor Bellingham.

Hickathrift, Tom, or **Jack,** a legendary character, said to have killed a huge giant living in a marsh at Tylney, in Norfolk. He was knighted and appointed governor of Thanet. The story gives his date at the time of the Norman conquest.

Hick Scorner, title and chief character of an old morality play, a scoffer at religion.

Higden, Betty, the proprietor of a minding-school and a mangle, in Dickens's *Our Mutual Friend.*

High-heels and Low-heels, opposing parties in Lilliput, by which Swift in *Gulliver's Travels* satirized the Conservative and High Church party as the High-heels and their opponents as Low-heels.

Highland Mary, the subject of Burns's poem, generally supposed to be Mary Campbell.

Hilary, the hero of James Lane Allen's *Summer in Arcady.*

Hilda, a young New England girl in Hawthorne's *The Marble Faun*, or *Transformation*, an art student in Rome.

Hildebrand, Meister, a champion with magic powers in old German romance.

Hildebrod, Duke, grand protector of the liberties of Alsatia, in Scott's *The Fortunes of Nigel.*

Hill, Sir John (1716–1775), an author, satirized by Christopher Smart in a poem, *The Hilliad*, in which he is called Hillario.

Hillary, Tom, a rascal in Scott's *The Surgeon's Daughter.*

Hillmer, Amalie, the heroine of a novel by the erratic Swedish writer, Johan Ludwig Almquist (1793–1866).

Hinchcliffe, Henry Salt, a resourceful engineer in Kipling's *Their Lawful Occasions.*

Hind and Panther, The, in Dryden's poem of the name (1687) stand for the Church of Rome and that of England.

Hinda, in Moore's *Lalla Rookh*, is the daughter of the Emir of Persia. She cast herself into the sea in her grief for the death of her lover, Hafed, the fire-worshiper.

Hinzelmann, a famous kobold of German legend, who lived in the old Castle Hudemühlen.

Hiördis, in Ibsen's drama, *The Vikings*, is the "very incarnation of violence, of the lust of conquest, of hate, of revenge." She brings in the tragic events of the play.

Hippocrene, the fountain of the Muses, which gushed from the hoof-print of Pegasus.

Hippolyta, the Queen of the Amazons, introduced in Shakespeare's *A Midsummer Night's Dream.*

Hippolyta, the heroine of D'Annunzio's novel, *The Triumph of Death.*

Hippolytus was falsely accused by Phædra, his stepmother, and his father caused his death. Artemis induced Æsculapius to restore him to life. Browning's poem, *Artemis Prologizes*, is a monologue of Diana as she watches him while he lies unconscious on his way back to life. Euripides and Seneca treated the subject in tragedies, and Racine's *Phèdre* is based on the same story. An English tragedy by Edmund Smith, *Phædra*, was acted in 1708 and highly praised.

Hirlas Horn, The, a drinking goblet, subject of a poem of the twelfth century by Owain Kyveiliog, Prince of Powis. As the horn passes around a group of warriors, their deeds are recounted in turn.

Hiroux, Jean, a type of the habitual convict in Henri Monnier's *Popular Scenes* (1825).

Histrio-Mastix, was the title of a tract against theatrical performances (1633) by William Prynne, for which, at the instigation of Laud, he was condemned by the Star Chamber to pay £5,000, stand in the pillory and lose his ears and be imprisoned for life, while his book was burned by the common hangman.

Hjalmar, Prince, in Maeterlinck's early drama, *Princess Maleine*, kills her murderer and then takes his own life.

Hjort, Daniel, the subject of a national tragedy, considered one of the very best in Swedish literature, by Julius Vecksell (b. 1838).

Hoamen, an Indian tribe near the Missouri, conquered by the Aztecs, whom Madoc, in Southey's work of that name (1805), assisted in regaining their rights.

Hoax, Stanislaus, in Disraeli's *Vivian Grey*, is supposed to be intended for Theodore Hook, said also to be the original of Lucien Gay in *Coningsby*.

Hobbinal, in Spenser's *The Shepherd's Calendar*, is the learned writer Gabriel Harvey (1545–1630), his friend.

Hobbler, The, the translation of *Clopinel* was applied to the lame French poet Jean de Meung (1260–1320). The same word was applied to the Greek poet, Tyrtæus, for an innovation in meter.

Hobbs, Henrietta, the heroine of Jerome K. Jerome's *Miss Hobbs*.

Hobnelia, a shepherdess in Gay's pastorals, who tried spells to win the love of the indifferent Lubberkin.

Hobson, Tobias, a Cambridge liveryman of the seventeenth century, whose rule of making each customer take the next horse in line gave rise to the expression, "Hobson's Choice."

Hocus, Humphry, in Arbuthnot's *History of John Bull*, is the Duke of Marlborough, represented as the attorney who carried on John's lawsuit against Lewis Baboon (Louis XIV).

Hödeken (little hat), a German kobold who wore a little hat pulled down over his face.

Hohenstiel-Schwangau, Prince, in Browning's poem with that title, is Napoleon III.

Holbeach, Henry, one of the pen-names of W. B. Rands, author of *The Shoemakers' Village*.

Holden, Eben, the title and hero of a novel by Irving Bacheller (1900).

Holdenough, Nehemiah, a Presbyterian minister in Scott's *Woodstock.*

Holgrave, a radical young man in Hawthorne's *The House of the Seven Gables.*

Hollingsworth, a philanthropist in Hawthorne's *The Blithedale Romance,* intensely earnest, but narrow in the pursuit of his aim, which is to found an institution for reforming criminals.

Holmes, Sherlock, a famous detective in Arthur Conan Doyle's *The Adventures of Sherlock Holmes.* A play based on the several stories in which he appears, was written and is acted by William Gillette.

Holofernes, a pedant in Shakespeare's *Love's Labor's Lost.* He is supposed to be intended for an Italian teacher in London, John Florio, who had criticized English dramas as "neither right comedies nor right tragedies, but perverted histories without decorum."

Holroyd, Vincent, a character in Anstey's *The Giant's Robe.*

Holt, Felix, title and hero of George Eliot's *Felix Holt, Radical.*

Holy Bottle, in Rabelais's *Pantagruel,* was sought by Pantagruel and Panurge on account of its oracular powers, and was found in Lanternland in an alabaster fount within a magnificent temple.

Holy Island, The, Lindisfarne on the northeastern coast of England, associated with St. Cuthbert. Ireland, Guernsey, and Rügen have been so called also.

Holy Maid of Kent, The: Elizabeth Barton, who claimed divine inspiration, and was beheaded in 1534 for having prophesied that Henry VIII would die a sudden and violent death if he should persist in divorcing Queen Katherine.

Holy Willie, in Burns's satirical poem *Holy Willie's Prayer,* was one William Fisher, an elder in the Kirk, who afterward, it is said, was found guilty of appropriating the church funds and died in a ditch into which he had fallen while intoxicated.

Homais, Monsieur, a pharmacist and free-thinker in Flaubert's novel *Madame Bovary*.

Homespun, Zekiel and **Cicely,** brother and sister in Colman's *The Heir-at-Law* (1797), who find their fortune in London.

Hominy, Mrs., a character in Dickens's *Martin Chuzzlewit*.

Honeycomb, Will, one of the members of the imaginary club of *The Spectator;* he was the authority on all matters pertaining to the gay world.

Honeycombe, the name of an unpleasant family in Colman's play *Polly Honeycombe* (1760).

Honeyman, Charles, a fashionable clergyman of social habits in Thackeray's *The Newcomes* (1855).

Honeythunder, Luke, a philanthropist in Dickens's *The Mystery of Edwin Drood*.

Honeywood, the hero of Goldsmith's comedy *The Good-Natured Man*, undiscriminating in his friendships and charities.

Honeywood, Patty, the heroine in *Verdant Green* by Cuthbert Bede.

Honour and Glory Griffiths, the nickname of one Captain Griffiths, who sent letters to the Admiralty office addressed to "Their Honours and Glories at the Admiralty."

Hood, Robin, a famous outlaw who lived in England, according to Stow, his historian, in the reign of Richard I; but others place him somewhat later. The scene of his exploits was Sherwood Forest, in Nottinghamshire, and in his band were Maid Marian, Friar Tuck, Mutch, the miller's son, Will Stutly, Will Scarlett, and Little John. The legends credit him with great courage, skill in archery, kindness to the weak, and—what probably contributed most toward making him a popular hero—with robbing the rich to give to the poor. One supposition is that he was Robert Fitzooth, heir to the Earldom of Huntingdon. Thomas Love Peacock has a romance, *Maid Marian* (1822). The Yeoman Archer in Scott's *Ivanhoe* is revealed at last as Robin Hood. *The Downfall of Robert, Earl of Huntingdon* (1601), by Chettle and Munday, was on the same subject; also an anonymous comedy (1661) and an opera, each entitled *Robin Hood*. In 1795 Joseph Ritson made a collection of songs, ballads, and other poems relating to him. He is the hero of Tennyson's poetic comedy *The Foresters*.

Hope, Evelyn, the subject of a poem by Robert Browning.

Hope, The Bard of: Thomas Campbell, author of *The Pleasures of Hope*.

Hopeful, a companion of Christian in Bunyan's *Pilgrim's Progress*.

Hope-on-High Bomby, a burlesque Puritan.

Hopkins, Captain, a prisoner for debt in Dickens's *David Copperfield*.

Horatio, the friend of Hamlet in Shakespeare's tragedy.

Horatius, the last of the three Horatii that fought for Rome against the three Curiatii, champions of Alba. When his brothers were slain and their three opponents wounded he pretended flight, and as they pursued he turned suddenly and killed them one by one. The story is the subject of a tragedy by Corneille, in which the sister of the hero, Camille, fiancée of one of the Curiatii, utters imprecations upon her brother, which so exasperate him that he runs her through with his sword. In the English tragedy by Whitehead, Camille is called Horatia.

Horatius Cocles, one of the three that kept the bridge over the Tiber against Porsena; his heroism is celebrated in Macaulay's *Lays of Ancient Rome*.

Horicon, the name given to Lake George by James Fenimore Cooper, commonly regarded as the Indian name.

Horn, King, the hero of an old French romance in verse, attributed to Mestre Thomas. An English version of perhaps the twelfth century is called *The Geste of King Horn*, ascribed to a poet, Kendale. A ballad made from the story is called *Hynd Horn*.

Hornbook, Adam, the pen-name of Thomas Cooper, author of *Alderman Ralph*.

Hornbook, Doctor, the subject of a satirical poem by Burns, *Death and Doctor Hornbook*, founded on an actual occurrence. The subject of it, John Wilson, was driven from the place by the attention it excited.

Horneck, Mary, the title character of Frank F. Moore's novel *The Jessamy Bride;* and a character in the play *Oliver Goldsmith* by Augustus Thomas. She was the original Jessamy Bride.

Horner, Jack, hero of a nursery rhyme. There is a story that Jack Horner was a steward sent by the Abbot of Glastonbury to deliver the title-deeds of twelve manors to Henry VIII, who, as he had reason to believe, was displeased with him; that the deeds were put under a crust and made to look like a great pie; and that Jack, lifting up a corner of the crust, saw what was under it and took out one of the parchments, which happened to be the deed to the manor of Wells.

Horn Gate, one of the two gates of sleep in the underworld, through which dreams are sent to sleepers. The other gate is of ivory.

Horse, The Enchanted, the subject of one of the *Arabian Nights* tales. It took the rider through the air, where he wished to go.

Horse Latitudes, a calm belt in the North Atlantic between 30° and 35°, where vessels loaded with horses, being becalmed, were sometimes under the necessity, for lack of water, to throw some of them overboard.

Hortense, Mademoiselle, the French maid of Lady Dedlock in Dickens's *Bleak House* (1853), the murderer of Mr. Tulkinghorn. The character is taken from Mrs. Manning, whose trial on a charge of murder the author attended.

Hortensio, an unsuccessful suitor of Bianca in Shakespeare's *The Taming of the Shrew.*

Hosier, Admiral, the subject of a ballad, *Hosier's Ghost,* by Richard Glover. He was sent to blockade the Spanish at the West Indies and was ordered not to attack. His men died off with disease, and he died of grief. After Vernon's victory with six ships, the ghosts of Hosier and his men rose in their hammock-shrouds lamenting the fate to which they were doomed instead of the brilliant victory they might have won.

Hotspur, Henry Percy, son of the Earl of Northumberland, so called for his fiery and impetuous temper. He is a character in Shakespeare's *Richard II* and *Henry IV*, Part I.

Hotspur of Debate, The: so the Earl of Derby (1799–1869) was called by Macaulay.

House of Fame, The, a splendid palace built on a mountain of ice, with names of illustrious poets on its pillars—the subject and title of a poem by Chaucer.

House of Socrates, The, often referred to, was criticised as too small, when he said: "May it please the gods that it be filled with true friends."

Houssain, Prince, the owner of a magic carpet, which could carry him instantly wherever he wished to go—in the *Arabian Nights* tale, *Ahmed and Paribanou.*

Houyhnhnms, a race of horses in *Gulliver's Travels,* endowed with reason and ruling over men.

Howadji, The, a name by which George William Curtis is sometimes called, from his book *The Howadji in Syria.* The word means a traveler.

Howden, Mrs., one of the disappointed ones at the reprieve of Porteous in Scott's *The Heart of Midlothian.*

Howleglas, the Abbot of Unreason, a disguise of Adam Woodcock in Scott's *The Abbot.*

Howler, The Reverend Melchisedech, a ranting minister in Dickens's *Dombey and Son.*

Hoyden, Miss, a romping country girl in Vanbrugh's *The Relapse* (1697), and Sheridan's version of the same play, *A Trip to Scarborough* (1777).

Hubbard, Bartley, the chief character of Howells's *A Modern Instance.*

Hubbard, Mother, the proprietor of a dog in a well-known nursery rhyme.

Hubberd, Mother, the supposed narrator of a fable of an ape and a fox to the poet during an illness, in Spenser's *Prosopopoia: or Mother Hubberd's Tale* (1591).

Hubble, Mr. and **Mrs.,** an elderly wheelwright and his wife in Dickens's *Great Expectations.*

Hubert de Burgh, Earl of Kent, introduced in Shakespeare's *King John* as conspiring with the King for the murder of Prince Arthur.

Hub of the Universe: Dr. Holmes said the people of Boston thought the dome of their State-house the Hub of the Universe; and the phrase is applied to the State-house and to the city itself.

Huddibras, Sir, in Spenser's *The Faerie Queene,* was "not so good of deeds as great of name."

Hudiage, a Shah of Persia to whom the girl Moradbak told, to wile away his sleepless hours, *The Oriental Tales* of Comte de Caylus.

Hudibras, a Presbyterian justice in the time of the Commonwealth, the subject of Samuel Butler's famous poem satirizing the Puritans, many of whom—Cromwell, Calny, Prynne, Lambert, Desborough, Fleetwood, and others—are brought in by name; and incidentally the follies and pretensions current at the time are also satirized.

Hudibras Redivivus, an imitation of Butler, was published by Edward Ward in 1705; the author was fined and pilloried.

Hudson, Sir Geoffrey, the celebrated dwarf and page of Queen Henrietta Maria, is a character in Scott's *Peveril of the Peak.*

Hugh, a leader in the Gordon riots in Dickens's *Barnaby Rudge.*

Hugh of Lincoln, the subject of a legend related in Matthew Paris's (d. 1259) *History*—that a boy named Hugh, eight years old, was stolen by the Jews of Lincoln, who tortured and crucified him. The occupant of the house where his body was found confessed that the Jews killed a child every year, whereupon eighteen of the richest Jews were hanged. The story is the subject of an old ballad and of Chaucer's *The Prioress's Tale,* of which Wordsworth made a modernized version. A similar ballad relates the murder of a boy named Hew by a Jewish girl.

Hugo, the leader of the Franks in the First Crusade, appears in Tasso's *Jerusalem Delivered* (1575). He was Count of Vermandois and brother of Philippe I of France.

Hugo, a natural son of the Marquis of Este, beheaded at the command of his father, who discovered that his wife Parisina was in love with Hugo. The story is the subject of Byron's poem *Parisina.*

Huguenot Pope, The, a name given to Philippe de Mornay (1549–1623), a French nobleman distinguished for his zeal and influence in favor of the French Protestants.

Huguenots, The, title of a noted opera by Meyerbeer (1836).

Hugues, Master, of Saxe Gotha, an imaginary composer, one of whose fugues is the subject of comment by an organist playing it in a poem by Browning.

Hulot, Baron Hector, held several offices under the Empire, which made him a baron, but sank through immorality into dishonor and ruin. He is a character in Balzac's *Cousin Betty.*

Humgudgeon, Grace-be-here, one of Cromwell's corporals in Scott's *Woodstock.*

Humma, a fabulous Indian bird, the shadow of whose wings falling on a head is a sure augury that it will wear a crown.

Humphrey, Duke of Gloucester, called the good Duke Humphrey, is a character in Shakespeare's *Henry IV*, Part II, where he is Prince Humphrey and plays an unimportant part, and in the first two parts of *Henry VI.* He was the uncle and protector of the young King.

Humphrey, Master, an old gentleman living in an ancient house in a suburb of London, where a sort of club met every week at ten in the evening. A quaint old clock stood in one corner of their room; in the lower part of its case the club members placed manuscript stories which were taken out and read at the meetings. These were to be published in a serial miscellany, *Master Humphrey's Clock*, begun in April, 1840, and continuing nearly two years; and *The Old Curiosity Shop* and *Barnaby Rudge* were published in it, as well as a sort of sequel to *The Pickwick Papers.* The clock is said to have been suggested by a large clock-face with the name Humphrey surrounding it used as a watch and clock maker's sign in the town of Barnard Castle, Durham, opposite a hotel where Dickens spent some weeks collecting material for *Nicholas Nickleby.*

Huncamunca, a princess in Fielding's burlesque opera *Tom Thumb* (1730).

Hundred Days, The, the interval between March 20, 1815, when Napoleon entered Paris after escaping from Elba, and June 22d, when he abdicated.

Hundred Fights, the hero of a, Conn, King of Ireland.

Hunter, Mr. and **Mrs. Leo,** characters in Dickens's *The Pickwick Papers.*

Huntingdon, David, Earl of, Prince Royal of Scotland, a character in Scott's novel *The Talisman.*

Huntinglen, the father of Lord Dalgarno in Scott's novel *The Fortunes of Nigel.*

Huntworth, Lady, the chief character in R. C. Carton's play, *Lady Huntworth's Experiment.*

Huon, the chief character of Sheridan Knowles's play *Love* (1840), a serf who becomes a prince by distinguishing himself in war.

Huon de Bordeaux, a hero of a romance of chivalry that bears his name. He succeeded Oberon as Fairy King when Oberon was taken to Paradise. Wieland's famous poem *Oberon* is founded upon this story.

Hurgonel, Count, betrothed to Orna in Davenant's *Gondibert.*

Hurlo-Thrumbo, the subject of a burlesque, *Hurlo-Thrumbo: or, The Supernatural* (1730), by the dramatist and actor Samuel Johnson (1705–1773), which had extraordinary popularity by reason of its extravagance and oddity.

Hurst, Lady Caroline, a character in Robert Hichens's *Felix.*

Hurtali, a giant who at the time of the Deluge sat upon the roof of the ark astride, being too big to go into it. This honor is claimed also for Og.

Hushai, in Dryden's *Absalom and Achitophel,* is Hyde, Earl of Rochester, friend and adviser of Charles II.

Hutchinson, Thomas, Governor of Massachusetts, is seen in the procession in Hawthorne's tale *Howe's Masquerade;* is also in *Edward Randolph's Portrait.*

Hyanisbe, a character in Barclay's *Argênis* that has been supposed to be intended for Queen Elizabeth.

Hy Brassail, islands of the blest in Gaelic fiction, the land of perpetual youth.

Hyde, Mr. See JEKYLL, DR.

Hyder Ali, a character in Scott's *The Surgeon's Daughter.*

Hypatia, a celebrated woman, a lecturer on philosophy at Alexandria, murdered by fanatical Christians. She is the subject of a novel by Charles Kingsley.

Hyperaphanii, the Huguenots in the once famous allegory *Argênis,* by John Barclay (1582–1621). It was written in Latin and has been several times translated. Clara Reeve's version is called *The Phœnix.*

Hyperion, a Titan, father of the sun; sometimes Helios, the sun, is so called. *Hyperion* is the title of a fragmentary poem by Keats, and of a romance by Longfellow.

Hythloday, Raphael, an imaginary traveler whom Sir Thomas More gives as his authority in reference to the Island of Utopia.

Iachimo, an Italian scoundrel in Shakespeare's *Cymbeline,* whose insinuations against Imogen arouse her husband to murderous fury.

Iago, the "ancient" or ensign of Othello in Shakespeare's play of the latter name, probably the most famous villain in literature. His hints regarding the virtue of Desdemona, Othello's wife, cause the Moor to kill her.

Ianthe, a leading character in Sir William Davenant's play *The Siege of Rhodes.* Pepys was so charmed with Mrs. Betterton's acting in the part that he called her Ianthe.

Ianthe, the child to whom Byron's *Childe Harold's Pilgrimage* was dedicated, was Lady Charlotte Harley, then eleven years old.

Ibbetson, Peter, the subject of a novel by George Du Maurier.

I Braesil. See HY BRASSAIL.

Ibrahim, the subject of a romance by Mademoiselle de Scudéry (1607–1701).

Ibycus, a lyric poet of Greece, who, being mortally wounded by robbers, called upon a passing flock of cranes as he was dying to witness against his murderers. Not long afterward, one of the robbers at a public game saw some cranes passing over and was surprised into saying: "Look! the cranes of Ibycus!" which led to the punishment of the crime. "The Cranes of Ibycus" has become a proverbial expression for the detection of crime in some singular way. Schiller has made the story the subject of a poem.

Ida, the heroine of Tennyson's poem *The Princess.*

Ilchester, Janet, in Meredith's *The Adventures of Harry Richmond,* marries Harry, who has been disinherited in her favor.

Ildico, a Burgundian princess, the heroine of Laurence Binyon's poetic drama *Attila.*

Iliad, The, of Homer, the epic of the siege of Troy or Ilium. The name has been applied to heroic poems celebrating the legendary history of other nations: the German Iliad is a name sometimes given to the *Nibelungenlied;* the French Iliad, *The Romaunt of the Rose;* the Portuguese, the *Lusiad* of Camoëns; the Scotch, William Wilkie's *Epigoniad.* The Knight's Tale, *Palamon and Arcite,* by Chaucer, has been called the Old English Iliad.

Illuminated Doctor (**Doctor illuminatus**), a title bestowed upon Raymond Lully (1235–1315), a Spanish writer, author of a system, *Ars Lulliana,* aiming to reconcile faith with reason. The same title was given to the celebrated German mystic, John Tauler (1294–1361).

Imasen, Grantley, the hero of Anthony Hope's novel *In Double Harness.*

Imis, a princess in the Countess d'Aulnay's *Fairy Tales,* who chose her cousin Philax in preference to a fay named Pagan. Pagan then shut them up in a splendid palace, the Palace of Revenge, where they could have every wish gratified except the wish to leave it; and after a time the strongest desire they had was to get out and separate.

Imlac, a traveler and poet, companion of the hero of Dr. Johnson's *Rasselas.*

Imogen, the heroine of Shakespeare's drama *Cymbeline.*

Imogene, in Matthew Gregory Lewis's ballad, *Alonzo the Brave and the Fair Imogene* (1795), said to Alonzo on his departure to the war: "If ever I marry another, may thy ghost be present at the bridal feast and carry me off to the grave." He fell in battle; and he appeared at her bridal feast and carried her away.

Imoinda, the daughter of a white man who has gone to Angola, where she marries the black Prince Oroonoko, in a novel by Aphra Behn, dramatized by Thomas Southerne under the same title *Oroonoko* (1696).

Inca, The, a surname of Garcilaso, whose mother belonged to the royal family of Peru; his father was a lieutenant of Alvarado and Pizarro. He wrote a history of the laws and government of the Incas, which was translated into English by Sir Paul Rycaut.

Ines, Christopher, a character in Meredith's novel *The Amazing Marriage* (1895).

Inez, Donna, the mother of *Don Juan* in Byron's poem of that name, a learned lady, "a walking calculation."

Inez de Castro, called "the beauty of Castile," was privately married in 1345 to Pedro, heir of Alfonso IV of Portugal. When his father found it out he caused Inez to be put to death. Two years later he died; and Pedro caused the body of Inez to be exhumed and crowned. The story has appeared often in literature; Camoens introduced it in the *Lusiad;* one of the earliest tragedies of the modern stage was by Ferreira, a Portuguese poet, on this subject (1554), which was also used by the French dramatists Lamotte (1723) and Guiraud (1826), and the English Ross Neil, in *Inez de Castro: or, The Bride of Portugal.*

Inger, Lady, a great personage in Norway in her day, is the subject of Ibsen's *Lady Inger of Ostrat.*

Ingham, Colonel Frederic, a pen-name of Edward Everett Hale's.

Inglesant, John, the subject of a philosophical novel (1881) by Joseph Henry Shorthouse.

Ingoldsby, Thomas, a pseudonym of the Rev. Richard Harris Barham (1788–1845), author of *The Ingoldsby Legends* —droll stories and legends quaintly told in musical verse.

Ingomar, the hero and title of a poetic drama by Friedrich Halm.

Ingot, Ada, a character in Robertson's play, *David Garrick,* and heroine of *The Love of David Garrick.*

Ingram, Edward, a character in William Black's novel *The Princess of Thule.*

Inkle, Thomas, subject of the story, *Inkle and Yarico* in *The Spectator,* by Richard Steele. Inkle was a young Englishman who fell in love with an Indian girl in one of the Spanish colonies, and after living with her for some months sold her into slavery in Barbados. The story is the subject of a drama by George Colman (1787). Steele drew the story from a book by Richard Ligon, who had lived at Barbados. Yarico was one of his slaves.

Innes, Evelyn, an opera-singer in George Moore's novel of the name and its sequel, *Sister Theresa.*

Innisfail, an old name of Ireland, signifying *Isle of Destiny.*

Interpreter, Mr., in Bunyan's *Pilgrim's Progress*, at whose house Christian stopped on his way to the Celestial City, is designed to represent the Holy Spirit.

Invalid, An, a pseudonym of Harriet Martineau under which she published *Life in the Sick Room* (1844).

Invincible Doctor, The, a title given to William of Occam (1270–1347), the "greatest leader of Nominalism in the Middle Ages." He was called also *Doctor Singularis.*

Invisibles, The: the Rosicrucians were so called because they dared not appear in public. A sect denying the perpetual visibility of the Church also was so called.

Ion, King of Argos, the subject of a tragedy (1835) by Thomas Noon Talfourd.

Iona's Saint, St. Columba, of whom it is fabled that on certain evenings of every year he is seen on church towers counting the islands "from Kilda to the green Ierne's shore," to see that none of them have been taken away by witchcraft.

Ioris, Prince Ireneo, the hero of Ouida's novel *Friendship.*

Iphigenia, who was rescued from the altar of sacrifice and taken to Tauris, is the subject of two tragedies by Euripides. A French drama on the subject was written by Potrou in 1640, and Racine's *Iphigenie in Aulis* in 1674; Dennis had one acted in London, 1700; and Goethe's *Iphigenie in Tauris* was represented at Berlin in 1786. Glück wrote two operas on the subject.

Ipomydon, the subject of an early English romance in verse.

Ipsden, Viscount, a character in Reade's *Christie Johnstone.*

Iras, an attendant of Cleopatra in Shakespeare's *Antony and Cleopatra.*

Irem, the Garden of, an earthly paradise spoken of in the Koran. It was built for Shedad, King of Ad; but as soon as it was finished an angel struck it and it vanished.

Irena, in Spenser's allegory, is a personification of Ireland.

Irene, the subject of a tragedy by Dr. Samuel Johnson (1709–1784); it was produced by Garrick in 1749, but ran only nine nights.

Irene, the subject of a tragedy in verse by Voltaire (1778).

Ireson, Floyd, a skipper whose hard heart is the occasion of Whittier's poem *Skipper Ireson's Ride.*

Iris, the subject of a play by Pinero.

Irish Night, a night of terror in London after the flight of James II, caused by the report that Irish soldiery were let loose to murder all the Protestants.

Irma, Countess of Wildenort, the chief character of Auerbach's novel *On the Heights* (1865).

Iron Age, The, the last of the four ages in human history into which the ancients divided it, the age of Pluto, characterized by crime, injustice, and impiety.

Iron Arm (Bras de Fer), a Huguenot captain, François de Lanoue, killed at the siege of Lamballe (1591).

Iron Crown of Lombardy, The, has a band of iron within it, said to have been made from a nail of the true Cross, given to Constantine by his mother, Helena, who discovered the cross.

Iron Duke, The, a name applied to the Duke of Wellington, said not to refer at all to his characteristics, but to have arisen from his name having been given to an iron steamboat that plied between Dublin and Liverpool.

Iron Hand, Goetz of the, Goetz von Berlichingen, the subject of a drama by Goethe, a burgrave of the sixteenth century, who lost his right hand at the siege of Landshut, and had it replaced by an iron one.

Iron Mask, The, or, **The Man in the Iron Mask,** an unknown French prisoner whose identity has been the subject of much conjecture. He was taken secretly to the fortress of Pignerol in 1662; he was next taken to the Isle of Ste. Marguerite, and lastly to the Bastille, where he died in 1703, having always worn the mask, not of iron, but of black velvet. One supposition is that he was a twin brother of Louis XIV, his existence having been kept secret for fear of a claim he might make on the throne. It has been suggested that he was a young foreigner who acted as chamberlain to Queen Anne and was the real father of Louis XIV. It is more generally believed now that he was Count Matthioli, agent of the Duke of Mantua, who had deceived Louis in a treaty for the purchase of the fortress of Casale, and whom Louis, in disregard of international law, had seized and held when he discovered the deception, and had kept him concealed to hide the breach of law. He was buried under the name of Marchiali. He is the subject of a French tragedy by Fournier and one in German by Zschokke, and of a novel by the elder Dumas, all under the assumption that he was brother to the King. This was the opinion of Voltaire.

Ironside, or **Ironsides,** a surname given to Edmund II (989–1016), King of the Anglo-Saxons, on account of his iron armor.

Ironside, Sir, one of the knights of the Round Table, called the Knight of the Red Lands, who kept the Lady Liones captive in Castle Perilous. He is supposed to represent Death. Sir Gareth fights the fight of faith and overcomes him.

Ironsides, a name applied to the soldiers of Cromwell after the victory of Marston Moor.

Ironsides, Old, a popular name for the United States frigate Constitution, which took part in the bombardment of Tripoli in 1804 and made a record in the war of 1812.

Irrefragable Doctor, The, Alexander Hales, an English scholastic philosopher of the thirteenth century.

Irtish, The, a river crossed by exiles to Siberia; hence "to cross the Irtish" is to pass off the stage of action.

Irus, a beggar in Ithaca, whose name is used as a proverbial standard of poverty.

Irwin, Hannah, the companion of Clara Mowbray in Scott's *St. Ronan's Well,* who has drawn her into a false marriage.

Isaac, a Portuguese Jew in Sheridan's play *The Duenna,* who mistakes the duenna for Louisa and elopes with her.

Isaac of York, the father of Rebecca in Scott's *Ivanhoe,* a rich Jew.

Isaacs, Mr., the hero of a novel by F. Marion Crawford.

Isabel, Queen of France, a character in Shakespeare's *Henry V.*

Isabella, the subject of a poem by Keats, *Isabella: or, The Pot of Basil,* a story from Boccaccio.

Isabella, the sister of Claudio, and heroine of Shakespeare's *Measure for Measure.*

Isabella, a nun in Thomas Southern's *The Fatal Marriage* (1692). She is married to Biron, whose father, Count Baldwin, disinherits him on that account, and he is reported to have been killed at the siege of Candy. His wife has just been married to Villeroy when he returns; and his brother Carlos, who has supplanted him, has him murdered and charges Villeroy with the crime; but the truth is discovered, Carlos suffers, and Isabella goes mad. The part of Isabella was a favorite with Mrs. Siddons.

Isabella, Donna, in Mrs. Centlivre's play *The Wonder* (1714), jumps from a window to escape a marriage her father has planned for her, and is caught by an English officer, whom she marries.

Isabella, The Lady, subject of a ballad in Percy's *Réliques*, whose stepmother caused her to be killed and served up to her father in a pie. The stepmother is burned alive, the cook is made to stand in boiling lead; and the scullion boy, who tried vainly to save Isabella, and revealed the crime, becomes the heir of the father.

Isabella, a pagan princess in Ariosto's *Orlando Furioso* (1516), in love with Zerbino, who could not marry a pagan.

Isabella, Queen of Richard II in Shakespeare's *King Richard II.*

Isabella, Princess of Sicily, a character in Meyerbeer's opera *Robert le Diable* (1831), in love with Robert.

Isabelle, in Molière's play *L'École des Maris* (1661), is brought up by Sganerelle to make him a useful wife. She dupes him and marries Valère.

Isabelle, the daughter of Philip II, who, according to the story, made a vow not to change her linen till the fall of Ostend. The siege lasted three years, and the yellowish brown of her linen gave the name to the color, which was called *Isabelle.*

Isenbras, Ysenbras, or **Isumbras, Sir,** a character of medieval romances of chivalry, punished for his haughty spirit and made humble by adversity. An incident of his later career, when he carried two poor children on his horse across a ford, is the subject of a painting by Millais.

Isengrin, or **Isengrim, Sir,** in *Reynard the Fox* (1498), is the wolf, standing for the barons, who are outwitted by Reynard, the Church.

Ishban, a name applied to one "as good a saint as usurer e'er made," said to have been intended for Sir Robert Clayton, in Dryden's *Absalom and Achitophel* (1682).

Ishbosheth, son of King Saul. In Dryden's *Absalom and Achitophel* his name is applied to Richard Cromwell.

Iskander, or **Scanderbeg** (*q.v.*), is the subject of Disraeli's *The Rise of Iskander.* In *The Tailor's Story* in the *Arabian Nights,* Alexander the Great is called "Iskander with the Two Horns."

Island of Lanterns, The, in the *Pantagruel* of Rabelais, was inhabited by pretenders to learning called *Lanternois.*

Island of St. Brandan, The, an imaginary island named for the Irish saint of the sixth century, who went in search of the Islands of the Blest. On old maps it was laid down west of the Canaries, appearing on a map as late as 1755.

Island of the Seven Cities, The, an imaginary island in the west, discovered by seven bishops, who set sail from Spain at the time of the Moorish domination, and founded seven cities upon it with splendid houses and temples. According to the legend, navigators who visited it were never allowed to return.

Islands of the Blest, or **Fortunate Isles, The,** in mythology, islands where the favorites of the gods were taken at their death. Many allusions to them are found in poetry and romance.

Ismael, the subject of an Oriental tale by Bulwer (1820).

Ismene and **Ismenias,** characters in a twelfth-century romance by one Eustathius, which Gower used in his *Confessio Amantis,* and Shakespeare in his *Pericles.*

Ismeno, an infidel magician in Tasso's *Jerusalem Delivered.*

Ismey, Valeria, one of the chief characters of Robert Hichens's novel *Felix* (1902).

Isolda, Iseult, Yseult, Isoude, Isolt, Ysolt, or **Ysoude,** of Ireland, called **the Fair** or **La Belle Isolde,** the wife of King Mark of Cornwall, but in love with Sir Tristram, his nephew. Their story is told in the Arthurian romances, in Tennyson's *The Last Tournament,* Matthew Arnold's *Tristram and Iseult,* and Wagner's opera, *Tristan und Isolde,* varying much in the incidents.

Isolde or **Yseult,** of Brittany, called Iseult of the White Hands, was married to Sir Tristram after he was driven from

King Mark's court. She, as well as the preceding, is a personage of Matthew Arnold's poem *Tristram and Iseult.*

Isoline, of Messina, a character in Knowles's play, *John of Procida* (1840), who died of grief after her husband and her father had fallen at the "Sicilian Vespers" (1282).

Isoult, the heroine of *The Forest Lovers,* by Maurice Hewlett, and the drama by A. E. Lancaster.

Israfil, or **Israfeel,** in Mohammedan mythology, the angel who is to sound the resurrection trumpet.

Italian Molière, The, Carlo Goldoni, dramatist (1707–1793).

Italian Pindar, The, Gabriello Chiabrera, lyric poet (1552–1637).

Ithuriel, an angel in Milton's *Paradise Lost,* whose spear at once detected falsehood by a touch.

Ivan, called the Terrible, Ivan IV of Russia, the first to take the title Tsar (1529–1584).

Ivanhoe, the disinherited son of Cedric of Rotherwood in Scott's novel *Ivanhoe.*

Ivan Ivanovitch, the subject of a poem by Browning. A popular Russian story called *The Judgment of God* supplied the incidents of the tale. The name Ivan Ivanovitch stands in a general way for the Russian people.

Ivory Gate, The, one of the gates of dreams; the delusive dreams come through this gate. See HORN GATE.

Iwain, the Knight of the Lion in the romances of chivalry. A lion that he helped against a dragon became his companion, and with the lion's help he killed several giants and freed three hundred virgins from dangers.

Ixion: Robert Browning, in his poem *Ixion,* imagines a protest of Ixion against the excessive punishment, in which he denounces the gods for their vindictiveness and predicts their final fall.

Jack, an unfortunate boy, the subject of a novel by Daudet.

Jack, Colonel, so the hero of DeFoe's *Adventures of the Truly Honorable Colonel Jacque* was "vulgarly called," a thief who goes to Virginia and becomes a land- and slave-owner.

Jack Amend-all, a nickname given to Jack Cade (d. 1450) on account of his promised "reforms."

Jack and the Bean-Stalk, the subject of a nursery tale found in various forms among all Aryan peoples and also the North American Indians.

Jack-a-Vale, the hero of an old popular tale, known only by allusions.

Jackman, Major Jemmy, in Dickens's *Mrs. Lirriper's Lodgings,* cultivated her boy's mind on a system of his own, which she thought "ought to be known to the throne and lords and commons."

Jack o' Lantern, the ignis fatuus, so called from a superstition that it was an evil spirit carrying a light to lead travelers astray.

Jack-o'-Lent, a puppet thrown at in Lent for amusement; and hence, a stupid fellow.

Jack of Newbury, John Winchcomb, a rich clothier in the time of Henry VIII, who armed and clothed one hundred men for the army that fought the Scots at Flodden Field.

Jack the Giant-Killer, a valiant Cornishman who overcame stupid giants by clever stratagems.

Jackwood, Neighbor, the subject of a novel by John T. Trowbridge, which has been dramatized.

Jacob's Stone: so the Inisfail or "stone of fortune" is sometimes called. It was used in Ireland as a coronation stone, was brought to England from Scone by Edward I, and is enclosed in the coronation chair of England. The tradition is that it is the stone on which Jacob rested his head in Bethel when he saw the angels ascending and descending the ladder let down from heaven.

Jacobites, The, a historic drama by François Coppée (1885).

Jacques, the servant of the Duke of Aranza in Tobin's play *The Honeymoon,* who, at the Duke's desire, plays his part in order to tame the spirit of his bride.

Jacques, One, Two, Three, Four and **Five,** names given to himself and some of his associate revolutionists by Defarge in Dickens's *A Tale of Two Cities.*

Jacques Bonhomme, a general name for the French people.

Jadwin, Curtis, the chief character of Frank Norris's novel *The Pit,* and the drama by Channing Pollock

Jaffier, one of the conspirators in Otway's tragedy *Venice Preserved* (1682).

James I of England is introduced in Scott's *The Fortunes of Nigel* (1822).

James V of Scotland, the hero of Scott's poem *The Lady of the Lake,* "Snowdoun's Knight."

James Stuart, called James III, a character in A. E. W. Mason's *Lawrence Clavering* and *Clementina.*

James, Truthful, the supposed narrator of the story of the "heathen Chinee" in Bret Harte's poem *Truthful James.*

Jamshid, King of the genii, whose hidden jeweled cup filled with life's elixir is spoken of in *Paradise and the Peri* in Moore's *Lalla Rookh* (1817).

Janes, The War of the Two: so is called the contest in the fourteenth century between Jane of Flanders and Jane of Penthièvre, after the captivity of their husbands.

Jane I (Jeanne) of Naples, who caused her husband, Andrew of Hungary, to be murdered and then married the assassin, is the subject of a tragedy by La Harpe, *Jeanne de Naples.*

Janfaries, Katherine, the subject of an old ballad on which is founded Scott's *Young Lochinvar,* a character called Lamington in the original.

Japhet, Baron, a chemist in Balzac's *The Magic Skin.*

Jaques, the melancholy, a famous character in Shakespeare's *As You Like It.*

Jarley, Mrs., the owner of the wax-work show in which Little Nell in Dickens's *The Old Curiosity Shop* points out the figures to visitors.

Jarndyce, John, one of the parties in the Chancery suit of Jarndyce and Jarndyce in Dickens's *Bleak House.*

Jarvie, Baillie Nicol, a noted character in Scott's *Rob Roy.*

Jasper, John, a choirmaster in Cloisterham Cathedral, the uncle of Edwin in Dickens's *Edwin Drood.*

Javert, an officer of the law in Hugo's novel *Les Misérables.*

Jeames de la Pluche, a footman who inherits a fortune, subject of Thackeray's *Diary of Jeames de la Pluche.* Jeames (James) has become a general name for a flunky.

Jean Jacques, the Christian names of Rousseau (1712–1778), by which he is often mentioned without the surname.

Jeanjean, general name for a conscript.

Jeanne d'Arc. See JOAN OF ARC.

Jeannot, in popular French farce, a type of the simple and credulous peasant.

Jeannot, a character in Voltaire's tale *Jeannot and Colin,* designed to show the advantage of a solid education in view of the uncertainties of fortune.

Jean Paul, a name by which Jean Paul Friedrich Richter (1763–1825) wrote and is generally known; also called "the only one."

Jeddler, Dr. Anthony, in Dickens's tale *The Battle of Life* (1846), in whose philosophy the world is "a great practical joke."

Jehane Saint-Pol, the heroine of Maurice Hewlett's novel *Richard Yea-and-Nay* (1900).

Jekyll, Dr., the better phase of the dual character of the gentleman who is the subject of Robert Louis Stevenson's novel *The Strange Case of Dr. Jekyll and Mr. Hyde.*

Jellyby, Mrs., a type of the busybody of useless philanthropy in Dickens's *Bleak House.*

Jenkins, a name for a society reporter, first used by *Punch* for a writer in the London *Morning Post,* who gave snobbish reports of society events.

Jenkins, Winifred, in Smollett's *Humphry Clinker,* a predecessor of Mrs. Malaprop.

Jenkinson, Ephraim, a swindler who imposes upon Moses and the Vicar in Goldsmith's novel *The Vicar of Wakefield.*

Jenkinson, Mrs. Mountstuart, a rich woman in Meredith's novel *The Egoist.*

Jennico, Basil, the hero of *The Pride of Jennico,* by Agnes and Egerton Castle, novel and play.

Jenny, a girl of the street, the subject of a noted poem by Rossetti.

Jenny Wren, a doll's dressmaker in Dickens's *Our Mutual Friend,* whose real name is Fanny Cleaver.

Jephthah is the subject of plays by John Christopherson about 1546 and George Buchanan (1554) and of a song quoted by Hamlet. *Jephthah* is the title of an opera by Handel (1752).

Jeremy Diddler, a swindler in Kenney's farce *Raising the Wind* (1772–1849).

Jeronimo, or **Hieronymo,** the leading character in Kyd's *The Spanish Tragedy* (1597). It is recorded that his expression to himself when he found his application to the King ill-timed, "Go-by, Jeronimo," became a common phrase of the street. The part was played by Ben Jonson. Sly's allusion to "St. Jeronimy" in the induction to *The Taming of the Shrew* is supposed to be a blunder for a phrase from the play the subtitle of which was *Hieronymo is Mad Again.*

Jerusalem, in Dryden's *Absalom and Achitophel,* stands for London; *The Destruction of Jerusalem* is an old poem; *The Battell of Jerusalem* is a poem of Adam Davie, about 1312; *Jerusalem Delivered* (from the Mohammedans), by Tasso, appeared in 1581. William Blake has a poem, *Jerusalem, the Emanation of the Giant Albion.* Dean Milman's *The Fall of Jerusalem* was published in 1820.

Jerusalem Chamber, The, the room where Henry IV of England died in Westminster Abbey. It had been predicted that he would die in Jerusalem, and he supposed that it would be on a crusade or a pilgrimage.

Jervis, Mark, the hero of Mrs. B. M. Croker's novel *Mr. Jervis.*

Jess, a character in James M. Barrie's *A Window in Thrums,* who looked upon the world through her cottage window for twenty years.

Jess, the title and heroine of a novel by H. Rider Haggard.

Jessamy Bride, The, a name by which Mary Horneck, afterward Mrs. Gwyn, was known. Goldsmith is supposed to have been in love with her. *The Jessamy Bride* is the title of a novel by Frank F. Moore.

Jessica, in Shakespeare's *The Merchant of Venice,* is the daughter of Shylock and elopes with Lorenzo—"a most beautiful pagan, a most sweet Jew."

Jessie, "the flower o' Dumblane," the subject of a song by Robert Tannahill.

Jessier, Michael, the subject of a novel by Edward Rod.

Jesus is a personage of Rostand's poetic drama *La Samaritaine.*

Jew, The Wandering, is the subject of several legends. He is sometimes identified with the Wild Huntsman of German legend, who, when Jesus was thirsty, bade him drink from the water standing in the print of a horse's foot.

Jewdwine, Horace, a critical journalist in May Sinclair's novel *The Divine Fire.*

Jezebel, the wicked wife of Ahab, King of Israel, figures in the famous dream of her daughter Athaliah in Racine's drama *Athalie.*

Jim Crow, a general name for a negro; railroad carriages for negro passengers are called Jim-Crow cars. According to an account by William Winter, the name is said to have come from one Jim Cuff, owned by a man named Crow, who used to sing a queer song of his own making with the refrain:

> "Wheel about, turn about, do jes so,
> An' ebery time I wheel about
> I jump Jim Crow,——"

at the end of which he gave a little jump and as he came down "set his heel a-rockin'." He was seen by Thomas D. Rice, well known as a delineator of negro character, who learned the song, added to it, changed the air somewhat, and sang it to his audiences just as the old negro did, to their immense delight.

Jingle, Alfred, an amusing liar and swindler in Dickens's *Pickwick Papers.*

Jingoes, a name given to the war-party in England in 1878, from a popular music-hall song:

> "We don't want to fight; but, by Jingo, if we do,
> We've got the ships, we've got the men, we've got the money, too."

Hence the boastful cry for war and conquest is called **Jingoism.**

J. J., in Thackeray's *The Newcomes,* was J. J. Ridley, an artist and friend of Clive Newcome.

Jo, a friendless boy in Dickens's *Bleak House,* living in a London slum called "Tom All-alone's."

Joan of Arc is the subject of Voltaire's *La Pucelle,* of tragedies by Soumet, and Schiller, *The Maid of Orleans,* of a romance by Mark Twain, and is a character in Andrew Lang's novel *A Monk of Fife.*

Joan, Pope, the traditionary English girl who was elected and served as Pope for two years before her sex was discovered, is the subject of a German miracle play, once popular, *The Canonization of Pope Joan* (1480).

Jobling, Tony, a law-writer in Dickens's *Bleak House.*

Jocasta, mother of Œdipus, is the subject of a drama taken from the Phœnissæ of Euripides, by George Gascoigne, Francis Kinwelmersh, and Christopher Yelverton. It was the first Greek play, so far as is known, put upon the English stage, and the second in blank verse.

Jocelyn, Rose, the heroine of George Meredith's novel *Evan Harrington.*

Jock o' Hazeldean, the subject of a familiar song by Sir Walter Scott, modernized from an ancient ballad, *Jock o' Hazelgreen.*

Jockey of Norfolk, John Howard, Duke of Norfolk, an adherent of Richard III, who fell on Bosworth Field, the first Howard to be Duke of Norfolk. The warning rhyme which he found in his tent the night before the battle is given in Shakespeare's *Richard III.* The incident is historical.

Joconde, La, a name given in France to the wife of Francesco del Giocondo, of Florence, the subject of the celebrated picture by Leonardo da Vinci in the Louvre known as Mona Lisa.

Jocrisse, a character in the old French farces, a credulous simpleton, the laughing-stock of his companions.

John, Don, the villain of Shakespeare's play *Much Ado about Nothing.*

John, King of England from 1199 to 1216, subject of Shakespeare's play *King John* (1508). There was an older play, *Kynge Johan,* where historical characters were mingled with allegorical personages, as Treason, Sedition, Civil Order, Widowed Britannia. As Prince John he is introduced in Scott's novel *The Talisman.*

John, Little. See Robin Hood.

John, Prester, a traditional Eastern sovereign said by one authority to be descended from Ogier the Dane, by another to be of the family of the Magi and to rule over their country, though his country is variously given as Abyssinia, India, and Ethiopia. In Ariosto's *Orlando Furioso,* Senapus, supposed to be the same personage, is King of Ethiopia, is blind and always hungry because his food is carried away by harpies before he can touch it; and this had to go on till a stranger should come to his rescue on a flying horse. Astolpho came on a griffin and chased the harpies into Cocytus.

John-a-Dreams, a name used by Hamlet for a fellow lacking the power of action.

John Bull's Other Island (Ireland), a comedy by George Bernard Shaw.

John Company: the old East India Company was so called by the natives, who could not comprehend a corporation.

John de Matha, founder of the order of the Trinitaires, devoted to the ransom of captives. A poem by Whittier is entitled *The Mantle of John de Matha*, founded on the legend that the ship in which he was bringing away "seven-score Christian souls" whose ransom he had paid, lost rudder and sails in a fight with Moors; but when the saint gave his "cross-wrought mantle" to be raised for a sail, the ship took a swift course to the Christian port of Ostia.

Johnny Crapaud, a nickname for a Frenchman.

Johnny Rebs, a nickname given to the Confederate soldiers in the War of Secession (1861–1865).

John of Leyden, John Bockhold (1510–1536), leader of the Anabaptists, the subject of Meyerbeer's opera *The Prophet.*

Johns, Doctor, the subject of a novel by Donald Grant Mitchell.

Johnson, a clever Bohemian in *The Adventures of Mr. Ledbury*, by Albert Smith, said to have had an original in one Jack Johnson, who figured in London society in the early years of the nineteenth century.

Johnson, Esther. See STELLA.

John the Baptist is the subject of a Latin tragedy by Nicholas Grimbold, written in 1547, and probably acted the same year at Oxford—*Archipropheta.* He is the subject of a drama bearing his name, by Sudermann.

Jones, John Paul, the hero of a novel by Allan Cunningham, *Paul Jones*, and of *The Pilot*, by Cooper.

Jones, Tom, the hero of Fielding's novel *The History of Tom Jones, a Foundling.*

Jonson, Ben, the poet, is introduced in Scott's *Woodstock*, and in Theodore Watts-Dunton's *Christmas at the Mermaid.*

Jorkins, Mr., a mild man in Dickens's *David Copperfield,* was represented by his partner Spenlow, who spoke for him as an exacting and merciless man who would have his bond; and though Mr. Spenlow was grieved when he could not raise a clerk's salary or give more time on a bill to a client, he could not move his obdurate partner.

Josaphat, in *Balaam and Josaphat* (eighth century), by John Damascenus, was an Indian prince, whose father tried to defeat the prediction that he would become a Christian and a devotee, by keeping him from all knowledge of misery, and giving him only pleasures. But in three drives which he took he saw Old Age, Sickness, and Death; this caused him to become a Christian hermit; and at his death he was canonized.

Joseph, the son of Jacob, is the subject of an opera, *Joseph in Egypt.*

Joseph, a canting hypocrite, servant of Heathcliff, in Emily Brontë's *Wuthering Heights.*

Josephine, the wife of Werner in Byron's tragedy *Werner.*

Josephine, The Empress, is the subject of a drama by Albert R. Havens.

Joseph of Arimathea, legends concerning. See GRAIL and GLASTONBURY. A forged confession purporting to be his, which was placed in an inscription, with the object of disproving the resurrection of Jesus, is the theme of Guy Thorne's novel *When it was Dark.*

Joshua, one of the nine worthies represented in Shakespeare's *Love's Labor's Lost.*

Josse, a jeweler in Molière's comedy *L'Amour Médecin.* "You are a jeweler, Monsieur Josse," is a phrase used by writers to indicate that a man's views are referable to his interest, as Josse gave advice in the interest of his business.

Jour, King of Mambrant, a legendary person who carried away Josian, wife of Sir Bevis, and his sword and steed.

Jourdain, Margery, a witch in Shakespeare's *Henry VI,* Part II.

Jourdain, Monsieur, a famous character, hero of Molière's *Le Bourgeois Gentilhomme,* who, having become suddenly rich, wishes to acquire education and culture, and engages masters for all accomplishments, who cheat him and turn him into ridicule. His most celebrated saying expresses his wonder at learning from his master of philosophy that he had been talking prose all his life and never knew it.

Jowler, the name under which Smollett satirized the Earl of Chatham in *The Adventures of an Atom* (1769).

Joyeuse, Charlemagne's sword, which was buried with him.

Joyeuse Garde, La, the estate given by Arthur to Launcelot of the Lake, for defending the Queen from Sir Mador's accusation of having poisoned his brother.

Juan, Don, usually called Don John of Austria, a natural son of Charles V (1545–1578), who gained the victory of Lepanto, and defeated the Moors in Spain, is the subject of a drama by Casimir Delavigne, *Don Juan of Austria* (1835). He is introduced in Crawford's *In the Palace of the King* and the drama from it; also in Ebers's *Barbara Blomberg.*

Juan Fernandez, the Island of, is in the Pacific off the coast of Chili. Alexander Selkirk, a buccaneer, lived there alone for four years; and *Robinson Crusoe* is supposed to have been suggested by his adventures, though DeFoe places his island in the Caribbean Sea, and it is much more probable that he got the idea from a story in Garcilaso's *Royal Commentaries of Peru.*

Juba, a prince of Numidia in Addison's tragedy *Cato.*

Judas Iscariot, a miracle-play (1848) by Richard H. Horne, founded on the idea that the object of Judas was to force Jesus to show his divine power and so hasten his triumph. He is a character of Paul Heyse's drama *Mary of Magdala.*

Judas Maccabæus, introduced as one of the Nine Worthies in Shakespeare's *Love's Labor's Lost.* Longfellow has a dramatic poem, *Judas Maccabæus,* and Rubinstein an opera, *The Maccabees.*

Judi, Al, according to the Koran, the mountain on which the ark rested.

Judith, the Jewess who cut off the head of Holofernes to save her town, is the heroine of an oratorio (1764) by Isaac Bickerstaff, the music by Dr. Arne.

Julia, a character in Shakespeare's *Two Gentlemen of Verona.*

Julian, the subject of a tragedy by Miss Mitford, produced in 1823 with Macready in the leading part.

Julian, said to be intended for Lord Byron, in Shelley's poem *Julian and Maddalo: a Conversation*, while Maddalo is Shelley himself.

Julian, Count, the hero of Landor's tragedy *Count Julian.*

Julian the Apostate, the chief character in Ibsen's double drama, *Emperor and Galilean.*

Juliana, the saintly heroine of Fletcher's play *The Double Marriage.*

Julie, the subject of Rousseau's novel *Julie: ou la Nouvelle Héloïse.* The original was the Comtesse d'Houdetot, Rousseau's love for whom is avowed in his *Confessions.*

Julie, the title character of Strindberg's drama *Countess Julie.* A neurotic, bored by a colorless life and fevered by a midsummer madness, she "throws herself at the head" of her father's valet, who becomes brutal under his triumph.

Juliet, the daughter of the Capulets in Shakespeare's *Romeo and Juliet.*

Juliet, loved by Claudio in Shakespeare's comedy *Measure for Measure.*

Julio of Harancour, the subject of Holcroft's comedy *The Deaf and Dumb*, a waif who proves to be a count.

Julius Cæsar, the subject of Shakespeare's tragedy of the name. *A Play on the Death of Julius Cæsar*, by Lord Stirling, was published in 1607.

Jumping Frog of Calaveras, The, the subject of a popular sketch by Mark Twain (Samuel L. Clemens), said to have first made him known in England.

Jumps, Jemmy, a character in *The Farmer*, an opera by Shield (1788).

Junius, the pen-name of the writer of a series of forty-four celebrated letters on political subjects, which appeared in the London *Public Advertiser* at intervals from 1769 to 1772. The identity of the author has never been discovered with certainty, though the most generally received opinion points to Sir Philip Francis (1740–1818); Macaulay in his essay on Warren Hastings cites the circumstantial evidence pointing to that theory. The letters attacked the Government of the day and even the King, with the greatest vigor and brilliancy, and roused intense interest all over England and the greatest curiosity as to the writer, which has not wholly died out after more than a century since their publication. The author is quoted as writing to the publisher of the newspaper: "It is not in the nature of things that you or anyone else should know me unless I make myself known. . . . I am the sole depository of my secret, and it shall die with me."

Junto, The, a small number of English Whigs in the time of William and Mary, who ruled their party for twenty years; Somers, Russell, and Montague were among the members.

Jupe, Cecilia or **Sissy,** daughter of a circus clown in Dickens's *Hard Times.*

Jupiter Carlyle: so Rev. Alexander Carlyle (1722–1805) of Inveresk, Scotland, was called, on account of his fine head, taken as a model for Jupiter Tonans.

Jupiter Scapin, a nickname given to Napoleon I by the Abbé de Pradt, on account of the mingled greatness and meanness in his character.

Just, The, has been added to the names of several historic characters, notably Aristides (d. 468 B.C.), who was ostracized by the votes of people tired of hearing him called the Just; and Haroun-al-Raschid (765–808), the greatest of the caliphs of the Abasside dynasty.

Juvenal of Painters, The: William Hogarth (1697–1764) was so called from the satire expressed in his paintings.

Juxon, Charles James, a character in Crawford's *A Tale of a Lonely Parish.*

Kadr, Al, the night supposed to be the third from the end of Ramadân, when the Koran was sent down to Mahomet.

Kaf, a fountain of immortality.

Kail, a prince sent to Mecca to pray for rain. Offered his choice among three clouds, white, red, and black, he chose the black, which sent a flash of lightning that killed him.

Kailyard School, The, a nickname applied to the idealizing of Scottish life that appeared toward the close of the nineteenth century.

Kamal, an outlaw chief in Kipling's *East and West.*

Kampen, Arne, the chief character in Björnson's novel *Arne.*

Karénina, Anna, the title character of Tolstoi's romance and of the drama of that name.

Karl Heinrich, Prince, of Sachsen-Karlsburg, the hero of Wilhelm Meyer-Förster's novel *Old Heidelberg*, of the plays, and the sequel.

Karski, Irma di, a character in Meredith's *Vittoria*.

Karûn, a traditional uncle of Moses, a proverbial Crœsus of the Arabs and Jews.

Katerfelto, a quack in Cowper's poem *The Task*. The name was adopted as the title of a novel by J. G. Whyte-Melville.

Katharine, one of the ladies of the Princess in Shakespeare's *Love's Labor's Lost*, betrothed to Dumain.

Katherina, the shrew in Shakespeare's *The Taming of the Shrew*.

Katherine, daughter of Charies VI of France and wife of Henry V of England, a character in Shakespeare's *Henry V*.

Katherine of Aragon, the first wife of Henry VIII, is drawn as a fine and noble character in Shakespeare's *Henry VIII*.

Katherine, St., is said to have been the subject of a play acted at Dunstable before 1119. Her *Life* was written in English verse by John Capgrave (1393–1464), founded upon verses by a priest, Arreck, of St. Pancras, London.

Katinka, a Georgian girl, one of the three beauties of the harem that Don Juan, in Byron's poem of the name, entered disguised as a young woman.

Katmîr, the dog of the Seven Sleepers.

Katusha, an innocent girl exiled to Siberia in Tolstoi's *Resurrection*.

Kavanagh, a clergyman, subject of Longfellow's tale of that name.

Kay, Sir, in the Arthurian romances, the foster-brother of Arthur. He fails in whatever he undertakes.

Kearney, Kate, the subject of an Irish song of the name, by Lady Morgan.

Kecksey, a foolish old man in Garrick's play *The Irish Widow* (1757), who professes to like a flirt and vixen for a wife.

Keegan, Father, an unfrocked priest in Shaw's play *John Bull's Other Island*.

Keeldar, Shirley, the heroine of Charlotte Brontë's novel *Shirley*.

Keezar, Cobbler, a German immigrant in colonial America who had a lapstone made by the magician Agrippa, which showed him a vision of the future of the country, in Whittier's poem *Cobbler Keezar's Vision.*

Kehama, a powerful rajah, the subject of Southey's *The Curse of Kehama* (1809).

Keith, The Wise Wife of, Agnes Simpson, accused of conspiracy against James VI, and executed for witchcraft.

Keller, François, a Parisian banker in Balzac's *Domestic Peace* and other novels.

Kempfer-Hausen, one of the speakers in the *Noctes Ambrosianæ,* and the signature of Robert P. Gillies in *Blackwood's Magazine.*

Kempion, the subject of an old ballad in which a damsel enchanted into the form of a serpent was released by three kisses from her lover. *Kemp Osvain* and *The Laidly Worm of Spindlestonheugh* give the same story.

Kenelm, St., the subject of a tradition of the Middle Ages, that his murder in Gloucestershire was made known by a scroll carried to an altar in St. Peter's by a white dove.

Kenge. See CONVERSATION KENGE.

Kenilworth, the castle, now in ruins, of the Earl of Leicester, a favorite of Queen Elizabeth, which gives the name to one of Scott's novels. Henry VI retired to it in times of adversity and it is the scene of Shakespeare's *Henry VI,* Part II.

Kenna, a daughter of King Oberon in *Kensington Garden,* an allegorical poem by Thomas Tickell (1686–1740).

Kennedy, Oswald, a magnanimous gentleman in W. E. Norris's *The Rogue.*

Kenneth, Sir, Knight of the Crouching Leopard, a leading character in Scott's novel *The Talisman,* is David, Prince Royal of Scotland.

Kent, the Earl of, a character in Shakespeare's *King Lear.*

Kenwigs, the name of a devotedly united family in Dickens's *Nicholas Nickleby.*

Kenyon, an American sculptor in Rome, a leading character in Hawthorne's *The Marble Faun* (*Transformation*).

Kergarouët, a rich count of the Bretagne nobility, a character in Balzac's *The Purse* and other novels.

Kerival, Inys de, the heroine of Fiona Macleod's *Green Fire.*

Kerka, the wife of Attila in Laurence Binyon's poetic drama *Attila.*

Kerniguy, Louis, in Scott's *Woodstock,* a name assumed by Charles II.

Kerr, Lewis, a character in Egerton Castle's novel *Consequences.*

Ketch, Jack, a general name for an executioner, from one who executed many of those sentenced by Jeffreys during the "Bloody Assizes."

Kettledrummle, Gabriel, a preacher of the Covenanters in Scott's *Old Mortality.*

Kevin, St., celebrated in a poem in Moore's *Irish Melodies,* so holy that he threw Kathleen into the sea lest he might not resist her fascinations.

Keyne, St., at whose prayer the serpents in the valley of the Severn were turned into Ammonites, which may be found at this day. It was at her prayer, also, that the fountain burst forth at Mt. St. Michael; the husband or wife who drinks first from its waters after marriage will rule the household.

Kezia, a peppery servant in George Eliot's *The Mill on the Floss.*

Keziah, a witchlike old aunt of the hero of Hawthorne's *Septimius Felton.*

Kickleburys, The, subject of Thackeray's novelette *The Kickleburys on the Rhine.*

Kidd, Robert, an alleged pirate, subject of a once popular song. His real name was William Kidd, and it has been proved that he was not a pirate.

Killigrew, Delia, the heroine of *The Splendid Spur,* by Arthur Quiller-Couch.

Kilmansegg, Miss, an heiress with an artificial leg of gold, subject of a poem by Hood.

Kilmeny, the subject of a tale in verse by James Hogg, and of a novel by William Black.

Kim, the subject of a story by Rudyard Kipling. He was the son of an English soldier in India.

Kimberley, Bolsover, the hero of *The Way of the World,* by David C. Murray.

King and the Beggar, The, Cophetua and Penelophon (called by Shakespeare Zenelophon) in the old ballad.

King and the Cobbler, The, Henry VIII and a subject, in a story of his adventures in disguise.

King Cotton, a personification of the chief staple of the Gulf States. The sentence "Cotton is king" was used by a South Carolinian in the Senate in 1858.

King Estermere. There is an old romance, *How the King of Estmureland married the daughter of the King of Westmureland.*

King Franconi, a nickname given to General Murat (1767–1815) for his love of showy dress. Franconi was a noted mountebank.

King Log, the subject of Æsop's noted fable with the moral: "Those that are dissatisfied when they are well off, must not complain when they get what they ask for."

King-Maker, The, a title given to Richard Neville, Earl of Warwick. He was at first on the side of the House of York, but was offended at Edward's marriage with Lady Grey and went over to Lancaster. He was killed fighting for Henry VI at Barnet in 1471.

King Nibelung, a mythical king, who was owner of an immense treasure, and who gave his name to the famous epic of Germany.

King Nodel: so the lion is called in *Reynard the Fox.*

King of Bark: Christopher III (d. 1448), King of Sweden, Norway, and Denmark, received the name at a time of famine, when bark had to be mixed with meal for food.

King of Bath, a title given to Richard (Beau) Nash (1674–1751), master of ceremonies at Bath for fifteen years.

King of Reptiles, a nickname given with a double meaning to Count Lacépede (1756–1825), a naturalist to whom Buffon entrusted the completing of his Natural History, and who was most subservient to Napoleon.

King of Yvetot, The, was sovereign of a small principality in France, who retained the title of king till the sixteenth century. It became a synonym for one with large pretensions and small authority, and is familiar from Beranger's satire *Le Roi d'Yvetot.*

King, The Snow: Gustavus Adolphus (d. 1632) was called so in Vienna, because, it was said, he melted away like a snowball as he went southward to warmer regions.

King, The White, the sovereign of the old kingdom of Muscovy, who wore a white robe.

King Pecheur (Sinner), in one of the legends of the Holy Grail, was a descendant of Joseph of Arimathea, entrusted with the care of the grail and the sacred lance on condition of perfect purity. Having sinned, in thought only, he was punished by the sacred lance falling upon and wounding him mortally.

King Pétaud, the presiding officer of an assembly of beggars, is used in the phrase, "the court of King Pétaud," to signify an assembly of disorder.

King Victor and **King Charles.** See CHARLES EMMANUEL and VICTOR.

Kingscote, Violet, a character in Black's *The Monarch of Mincing Lane.*

Kingsearle, Wolf, the hero of Jerome K. Jerome's comedy *Miss Hobbs.*

Kinmont, Willie, the hero of a ballad, *William Armstrong,* a notorious freebooter, who was confined in Carlisle Castle, from which he was released by a force of mounted men under the Laird of Buccleuch.

Kirby, Corinthia Jane, an English girl in Meredith's *The Amazing Marriage.*

Kirke, Hazel, title character of a popular play by Steele Mackaye.

Kirkpatrick, Cynthia, a character in Mrs. Gaskell's novel *Wives and Daughters.*

Kirsanov, Arkady, a leading character in Turgéniev's *Fathers and Sons.*

Kirkwood, Maurice, the hero of O. W. Holmes's novel *A Mortal Antipathy.*

Kit-Cat Club, a famous literary society in the time of Queen Anne, which took its name from Christopher Cat, a pastry-cook at the tavern in King Street, London, where the club met. The portraits of the members were painted by Sir Godfrey Kneller in three-quarter lengths, hence called kit-cats. Sir Richard Blackmore published in 1708 a poem, *The Kit-Kats.*

Kite, Sergeant, the hero of Farquhar's comedy *The Recruiting Officer* (1705).

Klabotérmann, a kobold believed to be sometimes seen in the Baltic sitting smoking on the bowsprit of a phantom ship, the *Carmilhan.*

Klaus, Peter, a goatherd of German tradition, who was led by a mysterious young man into a dell where he found twelve knights silently playing skittles. He drank from a can of wine he saw there and went to sleep. When he awoke he found everything changed and strange, and discovered that he had slept twenty years.

Klosking, Ina, a singer in *A Woman-Hater,* by Charles Reade.

Kmita, Pan Andrea, the hero of Sienkiewicz's novel *The Deluge.*

Knickerbocker, Diedrich, the imaginary author of Irving's humorous *History of New York* (1809).

Knight of Arts and Industry, The, the hero of Thomson's poem *The Castle of Indolence.*

Knight of La Mancha, The, Don Quixote.

Knight of the Burning Lamp, Bardolph in Shakespeare's *Henry IV,* Part I.

Knight of the Ebon Spear, Britomart in Spenser's *The Faerie Queene.*

Knight of the Invincible Sword, Amadis de Gaul's title for himself.

Knight of the Leopard. See KENNETH.

Knight of the Lions, a title assumed by Don Quixote after his attack on the lions.

Knight of the Sorrowful Countenance, Don Quixote.

Knight of the Swan, Lohengrin, son of Parsifal.

Knight of the Tomb, the "Black Douglas" in Scott's *Castle Dangerous.*

Knight of the White Moon, Simon Carrasco in Cervantes's *Don Quixote.*

Knightley, George, the hero of Jane Austen's novel *Emma.*

Knights, Prentice, a secret society in Dickens's *Barnaby Rudge.*

Knowell, an old man in Ben Jonson's *Every Man in His Humor,* a character supposed to have been acted by Shakespeare.

Koëldwithout, Baron von, the hero of a tale told in Dickens's *Nicholas Nickleby.*

Kolao, a man in a Chinese tale who, upon his prayer, received back the soul of his dead son in a leathern bag which was not to be opened till he had laid the body in a new hut; then the bag was to be opened so that the soul might enter the boy's mouth. But while he was building the hut, his wife opened the bag and the soul flew away.

Koranzzo, the subject of a tragedy, *Koranzzo's Feast* (1811), by one Hayes, a footman of Lord Belgrave, a very strange, apparently insane production. Only 150 copies were printed, and all but sixteen were destroyed in a fire.

Korrigans, a kind of mermaids of Breton superstition.

Krause, Hélène, the heroine of Hauptmann's play *Before Sunrise.*

Kriss Kringle, originally *Christkindlein,* the Christ-child, is now used as a name for St. Nicholas.

Kristiansen, Salve, the chief character in Jonas Lie's novel *The Pilot and His Wife.*

Krogstad, Nils, a character in Ibsen's *A Doll's House.*

Krook, a junk-dealer in Dickens's *Bleak House,* whose death, apparently by spontaneous combustion, excited much controversy as to its possibility.

Kruitzner, the subject of one of Miss Lee's *Canterbury Tales,* to which Lord Byron acknowledged his indebtedness for "the characters, the plan, and even the language," in some parts of his tragedy *Werner* (1822).

Kubla Khan, the builder of the palace described in Coleridge's fragmentary dream-poem.

Kurtsevichi, Princess, the heroine of Sienkiewicz's novel *Fire and Sword.*

La Balafré. See LESLY, LUDOVIC.

La Bastie la Brière, Ernest de, married to the heroine of Balzac's *Modeste Mignon.*

La Baudraye, Dinah Piëdefer, in Balzac's *The Muse of the Department,* wrote a novel, *A Prince of Bohemia.*

Labarum, The, the standard of the Roman Empire for the time of Constantine. Scott says: "Ducange fills half a column of his huge page with the mere names of the authors who have written at length on the Labarum," and describes it as a "spear of silver, having suspended from a cross beam below the spoke a small square silken banner, with portraits of the reigning family, and over these the famous monogram which expresses at once the figure of the cross and the initial letters of the name of Christ."

Lacerteux, Germinie, the heroine of *Lacerteux: the Tale of an Unhappy Servant*, by the De Goncourts.

Lacy, Miriam, the heroine of Kipling's tale *The Brushwood Boy* (1899).

Lacy, Damian de, the hero of Scott's novel *The Betrothed.*

Ladies' Peace, The: so a peace concluded in 1529 at Cambrai was called because it was mainly negotiated by the mother of Francis I and the aunt of Charles V.

Ladislaus, an amusing cynic in Massinger's play *The Picture* (1629).

Ladislaw, Will, an artist in George Eliot's novel *Middlemarch.*

Lady Bountiful, a title said to have been originated by Farquhar, whose play *The Beaux' Stratagem* has a character of that name.

Lady in the Sacque, The, in Scott's tale *The Tapestried Chamber* is an apparition that appears to a guest of Lord Woodville in a chamber long disused.

Lady of England or of the English, The, a title conferred by the council of Winchester, 1141, upon Matilda, or Maud, daughter of Henry I (*Domina Anglorum*).

Lady of Shalott, The, the subject of a poem by Tennyson, whose story is much like that of Elaine in *The Idyls of the King.*

Lady of the Bleeding Heart, The, Ellen Douglas in Scott's poem *The Lady of the Lake.*

Lady of the Lake, The, in Malory's *Prince Arthur*, was Nineve, or Nimue, with whom the enchanter Merlin fell in love. After learning his magic secrets she buried him under a stone.

Lady of the Lake, in Tennyson's *Idyls of the King*, is Vivien, who shut Merlin in a hollow oak where he was "lost to life, and use, and name, and fame."

Lady of the Lake, The, in Scott's poem of the name, is Ellen Douglas, and the lake is Loch Katrine, in which is Ellen's Isle.

Lady of the Sun, The, a title given to Alice Perrers, or Pierce, a mistress of Edward III of England, on account of her great beauty.

Lady of Threadneedle Street, The Old, the Bank of England.

Ladylift, Elinor, a character in Mrs. Archer Clive's novel *Paul Ferroll* (1855).

Laertes, the brother of Ophelia in Shakespeare's *Hamlet*.

Lafayette, General, is introduced into Dumas's *Taking the Bastile* and others of his novels.

Lafeu, a wordy old lord in Shakespeare's *All's Well that Ends Well*.

Lagado, in Swift's *Gulliver's Travels*, the capital city of Balnibarbi.

Laird, The, a character in Du Maurier's *Trilby*.

Laird of Cockpen, The, a name of a companion of Charles II in his exile, Mark Caross, owner of Cockpen, near Edinburgh.

Lajeunesse, Gabriel, the lover of Evangeline Bellefontaine in Longfellow's *Evangeline*.

Lake Poets, Lake School, or Lakers, The, a name given to several writers who, in the opening years of the nineteenth century, lived about the lakes of Cumberland. Wordsworth, Southey, and Coleridge are the poets brought to mind by the name, but Lamb, Lloyd, and Wilson were also included in what Jeffrey called that "sect of poets." The fact is now recognized that they are not a "school" in the sense of having a common method, but the term is conveniently used to designate Wordsworth, Southey, and Coleridge as associated with the Lake Country.

Lalla Rookh, the heroine of Thomas Moore's poem of the name.

La Luc, Theodore, the hero of Mrs. Radcliffe's *The Romance of the Forest*.

Lamare, Jenane de, the heroine of De Maupassant's story *A Life.*

Lambert, Sir John, the dupe of Dr. Cantwell in Bickerstaff's play *The Hypocrite,* which is an English version of Molière's *Tartuffe.*

Lambert, Hetty, in Thackeray's *The Virginians,* marries Henry Warrington.

Lambert, Louis, the title and name of the hero of one of Balzac's novels.

Lambourne, Michael, a villain in the service of the Earl of Leicester in Scott's *Kenilworth.*

Lamia, a serpent-woman, the subject of a poem by Keats.

Lammermoor, Lucia di, subject of an opera by Donizetti founded on Scott's novel *The Bride of Lammermoor.*

Lammeter, Nancy, a character in George Eliot's *Silas Marner.*

Lammle, an adventurer and fortune-hunter in Dickens's *Our Mutual Friend.*

Lamorake, Sir, one of the Knights of the Round Table.

Lamourette's Kiss, a proverbial expression for an emotional and transient reconciliation. The reference is to an incident in the Legislative Assembly at Paris, July 7, 1792, when the various factions were in fiercest opposition; Adrien Lamourette, a prelate and member of the Assembly, made such an eloquent plea for concord that the political enemies rushed into one another's arms with promises of peace, and a deputation headed by Lamourette, whose name signifies "the little sweetheart," went to inform the King. But the reconciliation did not outlast the night.

Lancaster, John, Prince of, a character in both parts of Shakespeare's *Henry IV,* and, under the title Duke of Bedford, in *Henry V* and the first part of *Henry VI.*

Lancelot, or **Launcelot of the Lake,** the most famous of the Knights of the Round Table. He was the son of King Ban of Brittany and was called "of the Lake" from having been stolen in his infancy by Vivien, the Lady of the Lake, and brought up there. Sir Galahad was his son. Lancelot is represented as splendidly brave and generous, the one stain upon his character being his guilty love for Queen Guinevere.

Lanceor, in Maeterlinck's drama *Joyzelle,* is saved by the perfect love between him and Joyzelle.

Landless, Helena, and her twin brother Neville, characters in Dickens's *Edwin Drood.*

Land of Beulah, The, spoken of in Isaiah lxii, 4, is, in Bunyan's *Pilgrim's Progress,* a land of rest where pilgrims paused before entering the Celestial City.

Langeais, Duchesse Antoinette de, a beautiful woman who reigned in Paris at the beginning of the Restoration. She is a character in Balzac's *The Thirteen* and *Père Goriot.* Plays founded on her life were produced in Paris in 1834 and 1868.

Langham, Alice and **Hope,** characters in Richard Harding Davis's novel *Soldiers of Fortune* and the drama from it by Augustus Thomas.

Langham, Edward, an Oxford tutor in Mrs. Humphry Ward's *Robert Elsmere.*

Langley, Sir Frederick, in Scott's novel *The Black Dwarf.*

Langstaff, Launcelot, the pen-name under which *Salmagundi* (1809) was published by Washington and William Irving and James K. Paulding.

Langton, Ellen, the heroine of Hawthorne's novel *Fanshawe.*

Languish, Lydia, the heroine of Sheridan's comedy *The Rivals.*

Laodamia, the wife of Protesilaus, a Greek slain by Hector at the opening of the siege of Troy.

La Palice, a French captain killed at the battle of Pavia in 1523. His soldiers composed a song in his honor, in which were the lines:

> "A quarter-hour before his death
> He was still alive,"

meaning that he was fighting to the last; but taken in its literal sense it gave rise to the proverbial expression for a self-evident fact, "a truth of La Palice."

Lapet, Monsieur, a swaggering coward, author of a book on dueling in Fletcher's play *Nice Valour* (1647).

Lapham, Silas, the chief character of Howells's novel *The Rise of Silas Lapham* (1884).

Laputa, in Swift's *Gulliver's Travels,* a flying island inhabited by philosophers.

Lara, the title and hero's name of a poem by Byron, identical with Conrad in *The Corsair.*

Lara, The Count of, a character in Longfellow's dramatic poem *The Spanish Student.*

Lara, The Seven Sons of, were sons of Gustios de Lara of Castile. They were slain in an ambush set by the brother-in-law of Gustios, and were avenged in after years by their young half-brother, Mudarra. The story, whose date is 993, is the subject of a drama by Lope de Vega.

Laridon, a name given by La Fontaine in his fable on *Education* to a degenerate dog; so that those rendered by luxury unworthy of their ancestors are called Laridons.

L'Arlesienne, in Daudet's novel of the name, is a girl always present, though never appearing in visible shape.

Larondie, Dulcie, the heroine of Henry A. Jones's play *The Masqueraders.*

Laroque, Marguerite, the heroine of Feuillet's *The Romance of a Poor Young Man.*

Larrian, General, a character in Meredith's *Diana of the Crossways.*

Larsen, Wolf, the title character in Jack London's *The Sea-Wolf.*

Larynx, Rev. Mr., a jovial divine in Peacock's novel *Nightmare Abbey.*

La Saisiaz (Savoyard for "the sun"), the name of a villa that gives the title to a long poem of Browning's.

Las Casas, in Sheridan's *Pizarro,* is an old Spanish gentleman who tried vainly to stop the cruelties practised by his countrymen.

Last Man, The: so Charles I was called by the Parliamentary party, who supposed him to be the last king that would reign in England. They called Charles II the "last man's son."

Last Man, The, who shall see the destruction of the world, is the subject of a poem by Thomas Campbell.

Last of the Goths, The, Roderick, whose reign as last of the Visigothic kings ended in 711.

Last of the Greeks, The, Philopœmen (d. 183 B.C.), the last great military leader of the ancient Greeks.

Last of the Mohicans, in Cooper's novel, is their chief, Uncas.

Last of the Romans, The: Aëtius has been so called, at whose death, in 454, the resistance to Attila failed. Caius Cassius was so called by Brutus. The title has been applied to remarkable Latin scholars; to Rienzi, to Charles James Fox, to Horace Walpole.

Last of the Saxon Kings, Harold, The, hero of Bulwer-Lytton's novel of that title.

Last of the Tribunes, The, Rienzi, the subject of Bulwer's novel of the name.

Last of the Troubadours, The, the Gascon poet, Jacques Jasmin (1798–1864).

Laszlo, Marsa, the gipsy heroine of *Prince Zilah* by Jules Claretie.

Latimer, Darsie, in Scott's *Redgauntlet,* the name by which Sir Arthur Darsie Redgauntlet is known.

Laughing Philosopher, The, Democritus of Abdera, who made a jest of the tragedies of life. Heraclitus was the weeping Philosopher.

Launce, the servant of Proteus in Shakespeare's *Two Gentlemen of Verona.*

Launcelot Gobbo, the servant of Shylock in Shakespeare's *The Merchant of Venice.*

Launfal, Sir, the steward of King Arthur, the subject of a romance in verse by Thomas Chestre of the time of Henry VI. Also the subject of James Russell Lowell's poem *The Vision of Sir Launfal.*

Laura, immortalized by Petrarch, was the wife, it is supposed, of Hugues de Sade, of Avignon, who died in 1348.

Laurence, Theodore, the hero of Louisa M. Alcott's *Little Women* and its sequels.

Lauretta di Guardino, a character in *John Inglesant* by J. H. Shorthouse.

La Vallière, The Duchess de, subject of a drama by Bulwer, one of the favorites of Louis XIV; also in Dumas's *The Vicomte de Bragelonne.*

Lavender, Frank, an artist in William Black's *A Princess of Thule.*

Lavender, Rev. Dr., a character in Mrs. Deland's stories *Old Chester Tales, Dr. Lavender's People, The Awakening of Helena Richie,* and the play from the last-named work.

Lavengro, the subject of a work by George Borrow, descriptive of gipsy life and character.

Lavington, Argemone, a beautiful, spiritual character in Charles Kingsley's novel *Yeast.*

Lavinia, the heroine of a tale in Thomson's poem *The Seasons,* a gleaner in the fields of Palémon.

Law's Bubble, a great speculation projected by John Law (1671–1729) of Edinburgh, who had a bank in France and in connection with it the "Mississippi Company," from which great profits were expected. The shares of the bank rose to twenty times the original value. Then came a collapse (1720), which caused great financial distress. The episode forms the plot of Emerson Hough's novel *The Mississippi Bubble.*

Laxley, Ferdinand, a character in Meredith's *Evan Harrington.*

Lazarillo de Tormès, the hero of a Spanish romance (1553) by Diego de Mendoza, a poor hidalgo who hides his poverty, wearing a ruffle to suggest a shirt and covering his want of clothes by his cloak.

Lazarus, the subject of a mystery play by Hilarius, of the time of King Stephen.

Lazie, Sir Lawrence, the subject of an old story, the earliest known copy of which is dated 1670. It tells how he broke the laws of Lubberland by serving several masters, and was tried for high treason.

Leader, The Lost, in Robert Browning's poem so entitled, was suggested by Wordsworth's defection from the Liberal cause.

League, The Grey, a combination of Swiss peasants in 1424 to resist tyranny, so called from their homespun dress.

League and Covenant, The Solemn, was formed in 1638 in Scotland against prelatical government in the church.

League of the Public Welfare, The, an alliance against Louis XI of France formed by the powerful dukes of the kingdom.

Leandro, a generic name in Italian comedy for a young man in love with his own good looks and his personal adornments.

Leandro the Fair, the hero of one part of *The Romance of Romances* concerning Amadis de Gaul—the part by Pedro de Lujan.

Lear, a mythical king of Britain whose date is fixed by the chronicles at 800 B.C., made famous by Shakespeare's tragedy *King Lear* (1605).

Learnèd Blacksmith, The, Elihu Burritt, an American linguist (1811–1879).

Learnèd Painter, The, Charles Lebrun (1619–1690), noted for historic accuracy.

Learnèd Tailor, The, Henry Wild, linguist, of Norwich (1684–1734).

Learoyd, John, a heavy-footed Yorkshireman in Kipling's stories.

Leatherhead, in Ben Jonson's comedy *Bartholomew Fair* (1614), is identified by some with the noted architect Inigo Jones.

Leather-Stocking, a celebrated character, Natty or Nathaniel Bumppo, in Cooper's novels *The Deerslayer*, *The Pathfinder*, *The Pioneers*, *The Prairie*, and *The Last of the Mohicans*.

Le Beau, a character in Shakespeare's *As You Like It.*

Lecoq, Monsieur, a remarkable detective, the creation of Émile Gaboriau in a novel of that title.

Lecoulteur, Fabienne, the chief character of Sardou's drama *Thermidor* (1891).

Lecouvreur, Adrienne, a celebrated tragedienne, the subject of a novel and of a popular drama by Eugène Scribe.

Ledbrain, Mr., in Dickens's tale *The Mudfog Association*, reads a paper showing the total number of legs in a Yorkshire town to be in round numbers 40,000; while the total number of chair and stool legs is only 30,000; hence, allowing three legs to a seat as a conservative estimate, it appears that 10,000 individuals, one half the population, either never sit down at all, or pass their leisure time sitting on boxes.

Leddy, Grippy, the heroine of Galt's novel *The Entail.*

Lee, Albert, a character in Scott's *Woodstock.*

Leek, the, is worn by Welshmen on St. David's day, March 1st, said to be in commemoration of King Cadwallader's victory over the Saxons in 640, when, by the recommendation of the saint his soldiers wore leeks in their caps that they might know one another. Drayton, in his *Polyolbion*, says it was because the saint in his hermitage lived upon leeks, which he gathered in the fields.

Lefèbvre, Abbé, a character in Balzac's novels *Louis Lambert* and *A Seaside Tragedy.*

Le Fevre, Lieutenant, the subject of a pathetic story in Sterne's *Tristram Shandy* (1759).

Léganès, Marquis de, a Spanish grandee in Balzac's *El Verdugo* (The Executioner).

Legend, Sir Sampson, a lying old man in Congreve's *Love for Love* (1695).

Leg-of-Mutton School, The, a title given to writers who seek patronage from the great by servile flattery, the leg of mutton signifying the material reward they have in view. It was first used by Lockhart in reviewing a poem.

Legrand, Fanny, the title character of Daudet's *Sappho* and its dramatizations.

Legree, Simon, a cruel slave-driver, overseer of a plantation, in Mrs. Stowe's *Uncle Tom's Cabin.*

Leicester, The Earl and Countess of, characters in Scott's *Kenilworth.* The Earl appears also in Schiller's *Mary Stuart.*

Leigh, Amyas, the hero of Charles Kingsley's novel *Westward Ho!*

Leigh, Aurora, the heroine of Mrs. Browning's poem of the name, "through whom are exemplified the noble ends and the high office of true art." Romney Leigh, her cousin, also is a character in the poem.

Leila, the heroine of Byron's poem *The Giaour.*

Leila, the heroine and title of a novel by Bulwer.

Leilah, a heroine of Mohammedan romance. Leilah and Mejnoun are the typical lovers.

Lelia, the title and heroine of a novel by George Sand.

Lelio, the typical lover in popular Italian comedy.

Le Mesurier, Paul, the hero of Rhoda Broughton's *Good-Bye, Sweetheart!*

Lennox, Colonel Charles, the hero of Miss Ferrier's novel *Marriage.*

Lenore, the subject of a ballad by Gottfried August Bürger, who was carried away by the ghost of her lover, Wilhelm. The idea was taken from an old Dutch ballad, which may have been also the original of a similar old English ballad, *The Suffolk Miracle.*

Lenore, the name of the lost maiden in Poe's poem *The Raven.*

Leodogran or **Leodograunce,** the King of Camelliard in the Arthurian romances, who had "one fair daughter, fairest of all flesh on earth," Guinevere.

Leon, in Ariosto's *Orlando Furioso* (1516), is the son of the Greek Emperor, betrothed to Bradamant.

Leon, the hero of Fletcher's play *Rule a Wife and Have a Wife* (1640).

Leon, Raphael, the hero of Zangwill's *Children of the Ghetto.*

Leona, the page in Dumas's *The Page of the Duke of Savoy.*

Leonardo, Duke of Mantua, the hero of Knowles's play *The Wife* (1833).

Leonidas, subject of a once much-lauded poem (1737) by Richard Glover.

Leonidas of Modern Greece, The: Marco Bozarris received this title for his successful attack with twelve hundred men upon four thousand Turco-Albanians at Kerpenisi in 1823. He lost his life in that engagement.

Leonidas Wedell: so Frederick the Great called one of his officers, General Wedell, for his heroic defense of the Elbe at Teinitz in 1744.

Leono's Head: Porto Leono, the ancient Piræus, was so called from a great lion of white marble, which the Venetians carried to their arsenal.

Leonora, the usurping Queen of Aragon in Dryden's play *The Spanish Fryar* (1680).

Leonora, in Beethoven's opera *Fidelio* (1791), disguises herself as a man under the name Fidelio in order to effect the release of her husband, a state prisoner in Seville.

Leonora, the heroine of Verdi's opera *Il Trovatore* (1853).

Leonora, the heroine of an episode in Fielding's novel *Joseph Andrews* (1742).

Leonora of Este, the sister of the Duke of Ferrara, for whom Tasso cherished a hopeless passion.

Léonore, in Molière's play *The School for Husbands,* is an orphan brought up by Ariste, who wishes to make her his wife and gains her love by trusting her and leaving her to her own sense of honor.

Leontes, King of Sicily, a character in Shakespeare's *A Winter's Tale.*

Leopard, or **Panther, The,** in Dante's *Inferno,* signifies pleasure, and in a political figure, Florence.

Leopold, Archduke of Austria, a character in Scott's *The Talisman.*

Lesbia, a name given by Catullus (b. 87 B.C.) in his poems to his favorite, Clodia.

Lesbian Poets, Terpander, Arion, Alcæus, and Sappho.

Leslie, Norman, the subject of a novel by Theodore Sedgwick Fay. Also the title character of Andrew Lang's story *A Monk of Fife.*

Lesly, Ludovic, called La Balafré from a saber scar on his face, in Scott's *Quentin Durward.*

Lespel, Grancey, a character in Meredith's *Beauchamp's Career.*

L'Estrange, Harley, a shy and dreamy young nobleman in Bulwer's *My Novel.*

Lesurques, the chief personage in Stirling's play *The Courier of Lyons* (1852).

Leucadia's Rock, the promontory from which Sappho leaped into the Ionian Sea.

Leuchtenstein, Count, the hero of Weyman's novel *My Lady Rotha.*

Leucippe, an Athenian soldier in W. S. Gilbert's play *Pygmalion and Galatea.*

Lever of Archimedes, The: the famous mathematician of Syracuse in Sicily, speaking of the mechanical power of the lever, said: "If I had but a point of support, I could move the earth." Balzac says Peter the Hermit, Calvin and Robespierre were "levers of Archimedes," finding each his "point of support in the interests and desires of men."

Levett, Dr. Robert, the subject of a fine elegy (1782) by Dr. Samuel Johnson.

Leviathan of Literature, The, Dr. Samuel Johnson (1709–1784).

Levison, Francis, the villain of Mrs. Wood's novel *East Lynne* and of its dramatization.

Levites, The, in Dryden's *Absalom and Achitophel*, are the nonconformist ministers expelled by the Act of Conformity (1681–1682).

Lewis, Landgrave of Thuringia, husband of Elizabeth in Charles Kingsley's *The Saint's Tragedy* (1846).

Lewis, Don, the uncle of a bookworm, no scholar himself, but doting on scholarship, in Cibber's play *Love Makes a Man* (1700).

Lewis, "Monk": so Matthew Gregory Lewis was called because of his famous novel, *The Monk*.

Lewiston, Jacob, an impostor and blackmailer in Miss Ferrier's novel *The Inheritance*.

Leyburn, Catherine, the wife of the hero of Mrs. Humphry Ward's *Robert Elsmere*.

Leycippes and **Clitophanta,** chief characters and title of a Greek romance of the fifth century by Achilles Tatius.

Libni, in Pordage's satire *Azaria and Hushai*, is Titus Oates.

Lieschen, Teufelsdröckh's maid-of-all-work in Carlyle's *Sartor Resartus*.

Ligarius, a character in Shakespeare's *Julius Cæsar*.

Light-Horse Harry, General Henry Lee (1756–1816), a brave cavalry officer in the American Revolutionary War. In an oration on the death of Washington he used the famous phrase, "First in war, first in peace, and first in the hearts of his countrymen."

Light of Asia, The, Buddha, the subject of Sir Edwin Arnold's poem *The Light of Asia*.

Light of the Harem, Nourmahal, sultana, bride of Selim, celebrated in Moore's *Lalla Rookh*.

Lightwood, Mortimer, a character in Dickens's *Our Mutual Friend*.

Lili, one of the favorites of Goethe, was Anna Elisabeth Schönemann, of Frankfort.

Lilian, the heroine of Charles Kingsley's novel *Alton Locke.*

Lilis or **Lilith,** in Jewish tradition, the wife of Adam before he married Eve, by whom he had demon children. She was supposed to be especially hostile to the newly married and to young children. In the superstitions of the Middle Ages she was a witch. She appears in the Walpurgis-night scene in Goethe's *Faust. Adam, Lilith, and Eve* is the title of a poem by Browning.

Lilliput, the country of the Lilliputians, a race of pygmies whom Gulliver found in his *Travels.*

Lillyvick, Mr., a collector of water-rates in Dickens's *Nicholas Nickleby.*

Limbo, in theology, that abode of the dead into which Christ descended when he preached to the "spirits in prison," supposed to be those that died without knowledge of the Gospel, not deserving of hell, but not redeemed. Thus "limbo" is used for a neutral land. The limbo of the moon, according to Ariosto, holds time misspent, counsel thrown away, unfulfilled desires, unpaid vows, deathbed alms, and all things vain and insincere.

Limmason, Lieutenant, a Hussar in Kipling's *Life's Handicap.*

Limp, the initials of Louis, James, Mary, and Prince. It is said to have been a sign of a Jacobite in the time of William III to limp, signifying his loyalty to James II, his wife Mary, and the Prince, afterward called the Pretender. Louis, of course, was the French King.

Lincoln, John Langland, Bishop of, a character in Shakespeare's *Henry VIII.*

Lind, Marian, the heroine of George B. Shaw's novel *The Irrational Knot.*

Lindabrides, the heroine of a once popular romance, *The Mirror of Knighthood.*

Linden, Christina, a character in Ibsen's *A Doll's House.*

Lindesay, Lord, of the Byres, a character in Scott's novel *The Abbot.*

Lindore, Lord, and his daughter, Lady Emily, are characters in Miss Ferrier's novel *Marriage.*

Lingon, a parson in George Eliot's novel *Felix Holt.*

Linkinwater, Tim, the chief clerk of the Cheeryble Brothers in Dickens's *Nicholas Nickleby,* who had served them forty-four years.

Linklater, Laurie, a character in Scott's *The Fortunes of Nigel,* is one of the Yeomen of the Royal Kitchen.

Linne, The Heir of, a great spendthrift, the subject of an old ballad.

Linnet, Kitty, an actress, the heroine of Foote's play *The Maid of Bath.*

Lion of God, Ali (597–660), a valiant defender of the faith of Mahomet.

Lion of the North, Gustavus Adolphus of Sweden (1594–1632).

Lioness, in Malory's *History of Prince Arthur,* was held captive in Castle Perilous by Sir Ironside, and freed by Sir Gareth, whom she married.

Liris, in Moore's *Loves of the Angels,* one of the daughters of men, beloved by the angel Rubi. At her entreaty he appeared before her in all his glory, when she fell into his arms, burned to ashes by the intensity of his brightness.

Lirriper, Mrs. Emma, a good-hearted widow, the supposed narrator of Dickens's Christmas story *Mrs. Lirriper's Lodgings* and its sequel *Mrs. Lirriper's Legacy.*

Lisa, an unpleasant character in Bellini's opera *La Sonnambula* (1831).

Lisette, the subject of a noted song by Béranger, *Les Infidelités de Lisette.*

Lismahago, Captain, a half-pay officer in Smollett's *Humphry Clinker* (1771), a rude, conceited, and disputatious Scotchman, who marries Tabitha Bramble for her four thousand pounds.

Litterly, Viscount Barrington, the hero of Pinero's play *The Amazons.*

Little Comedy, a name given to Catherine Horneck, afterward Mrs. Bunbury, a friend of Goldsmith.

Little-Endians and **Big-Endians,** in Swift's *Gulliver's Travels,* were two warring religious factions, the one distinction between them being that the Little-Endians broke their eggs at the little end and the Big-Endians theirs at the big end.

Little Englanders, a nickname applied to English people opposed to extension of the empire by conquest.

Little Gentleman in Velvet, The, a favorite toast of the Jacobites after the death of William III—meaning the mole that raised the hill against which his horse stumbled in the park at Hampton Court, causing the King's death.

Little, Henry, the hero of Reade's *Put Yourself in His Place.*

Little-John, Hugh, in Scott's *Tales of a Grandfather,* is his grandson, John Hugh Lockhart.

Little Master, The: Sebald Beham, sixteenth century, was so called on account of the smallness of his engravings and paintings.

Little Red Riding-Hood, the heroine of a nursery tale, known in many countries in varying versions. The English version ends tragically; but in the German the child and her grandmother are swallowed by the wolf, but come out well and whole when the hunter cuts the wolf open in the morning.

Litvinov, Grigory, the chief character in Turgéniev's *Smoke.*

Livingstone, Guy, the hero of a novel of the name by George A. Lawrence (1827–1876).

Lizard Islands, The, fabulous islands of refuge for unfortunate damsels.

Llewellyn, David, the supposed narrator of the story of Blackmore's *The Maid of Sker.*

Loadstone, Lady, a character in Ben Jonson's play *The Magnetic Lady.*

Lochaw, the original seat of the Campbells, whose lands were very extensive; hence the saying, "a far cry to Lochaw."

Lochiel, the Lord of, a Cameron, who fought at Culloden for the "Young Pretender," is the subject of Thomas Campbell's poem *Lochiel's Warning.*

Lochinvar, the hero of a ballad sung by Lady Heron in Scott's *Marmion,* who carries off the "bride of Enderby" as she is about to be married to "a laggard in love and a dastard in war."

Lochleven, Lady, a character in Scott's *The Abbot.*

Locke, Alton, a tailor and poet, the subject of a novel by Charles Kingsley.

Lockit, a jailer in Gay's *The Beggars' Opera,* intended for Lord Townshend.

Locksley, an outlaw (Robin Hood) in Scott's *Ivanhoe.*

Locksley Hall, the subject of a famous poem by Tennyson.

Lodore, The Falls of, made famous by Southey's poem, are in the Tarn in France.

Lodowick, Friar, a name assumed by the Duke in Shakespeare's *Measure for Measure.*

Logistilla, a fairy in Ariosto's *Orlando Furioso.*

Lohengrin, Knight of the Swan, the subject of a thirteenth-century German poem by the minnesinger Wolfram von Eschenbach, and of an opera by Wagner.

L'Oiseleur, a character in Mozart's opera *The Magic Flute.*

Lone Star State, The, Texas, which has a single star in its escutcheon.

Longaville, one of the lords attending the King in Shakespeare's *Love's Labor's Lost,* his only fault, "a sharp wit matched with too blunt a will."

Longbeard, William, "the most famous and wittie English traitor," is the subject of a "pleasant and prettie historie" (1593) by Thomas Lodge.

Longius, the traditionary name of the soldier that pierced the side of Jesus.

Long Parliament, a common designation of the Parliament extending from 1640 to 1653, when it was dissolved by Cromwell.

Longueville, name of a family, characters in Balzac's *The Ball at Sçeaux.*

Loose-Coat Field, the battle of Stamford (1470), where the pursued forces threw off their coats to hasten their flight.

Lopez, the curate of Beaumont and Fletcher's play *The Spanish Curate* (1622).

Lora, Leon de, an illustrious landscape and marine painter, and a "prince of repartee and dissipation," a character in seven of Balzac's novels, *The Unconscious Humorists* and others.

Lorbrulgrud, the capital of Brobdingnag in Swift's *Gulliver's Travels.*

Lord Burleigh, a character in Mr. Puff's drama *The Spanish Armada,* and in Sheridan's farce *The Critic.*

Lord of Crazy Castle, The, John Hall Stevenson (1718–1785), author of *Crazy Tales* (1762), who lived at Skelton Castle.

Loredano, a character in Byron's tragedy *The Two Foscari.*

Lorelei, The, a siren on the Rhine that lures men to their death, the subject of a famous poem of Heine's.

Lorle, the heroine of an opera by Foerster (b. 1849) founded on Auerbach's story *Die Frau Professorin.*

Lorenzo, the lover of Jessica, with whom she elopes, in Shakespeare's *The Merchant of Venice.*

Lorenzo, an atheist in Young's *Night Thoughts.*

Loring, Dorothy and **Sir John,** characters in Meredith's *Evan Harrington.*

Lorrain, Pierrette, the heroine of Balzac's novel *Pierrette.*

Lorraine, Alice, the title and heroine's name of a novel by Richard D. Blackmore.

Lorraine, Mrs. Felix, in Disraeli's *Vivian Grey,* is supposed to be a portrait of Lady Caroline Lamb.

Lorrequer, Harry, the hero of a novel of the name by Charles Lever.

Lossell, Elias, the title character of *God's Fool,* by Maarten Maartens.

Lot, King of Orkney in the Arthurian legends.

Lot Parson, a pen-name under which Charles Kingsley published a pamphlet, *Cheap Clothes and Nasty,* aimed at the sweating system.

Lothair, the hero of a novel of the name by Disraeli.

Lothario, a character in the tale *The Curious Impertinent* in *Don Quixote.* His friend Anselmo had such confidence in the faithfulness of his wife Camilla that he induced Lothario to try to overcome it; the result was that she eloped with Lothario; Anselmo died of grief, Lothario was killed in battle, and Camilla betook herself to a convent.

Lotte, the heroine of *The Sorrows of Young Werther* (1774) by Goethe. Charlotte Buff, the original of the character, married Goethe's friend, Kestner, the Albert of the story.

Lotus-Eaters, or **Lotophagi, The,** who ate of the fruit of the lotus-tree, forgot their friends and homes, and lived in a state of dreamy, idle content, described in Homer's *Odyssey.*

Louden, Joseph, the hero of Booth Tarkington's *The Conquest of Canaan.*

Lougher, Colonel Henry, a character in Blackmore's novel *The Maid of Sker.*

Louis Charles, the Dauphin, appears in Mühlbach's novel *Marie Antoinette and her Son.*

Louis of Bourbon, Bishop of Liège, a character in Scott's *Quentin Durward.*

Louis the Dauphin, a braggart, appears in Shakespeare's *Henry V.*

Louis VIII, of France, when the Dauphin, is a character in Shakespeare's *King John.*

Louis XI, of France, a character in Scott's *Quentin Durward,* introduced also in *Anne of Geierstein;* and appears in Shakespeare's *Henry VI,* Part III. He appears in Justin H. McCarthy's play and novel *If I Were King.*

Louis XIII, of France, introduced in Bulwer's play *Richelieu,* in Alfred de Vigny's novel *Cinq-Mars,* and in Dumas's *The Three Musketeers,* novel and play.

Louis XIV, of France, appears in Bulwer's *The Duchess de La Vallière,* Dumas's *Twenty Years After,* and *The Vicomte de Bragelonne.*

Louis XV, of France, is in Dumas's *Joseph Balsamo* and *The Memoirs of a Physician,* and Louis XVI also. Louis XV is an important character of the play *Du Barry* by Belasco, and one by Jean Richepin.

Louis XVIII, of France, is introduced in several novels of Balzac's.

Louisa, the heroine of Sheridan's play *The Duenna* (1775).

Louise, the glee-maiden in Scott's *The Fair Maid of Perth.*

Louka, an impudent young woman in Shaw's comedy *Arms and the Man,* who marries her young mistress's discarded fiancé.

Lousteau, Étienne, a clever scoundrel in several of Balzac's novels, *A Daughter of Eve* and others.

Lövberg, Ejlert, a dissipated genius in Ibsen's drama *Hedda Gabler.*

Love, Sir Antony, a woman who goes disguised as a man, the subject and title of a play by Thomas Southerne.

Lovegold, the miser of Fielding's play *The Miser,* after Molière's *L'Avare.*

Lovejoy, Martin, Gregory, and **Mabel,** characters in Blackmore's *Alice Lorraine.*

Lovel, the subject of Thackeray's novel *Lovel, the Widower,* and of his comedy *The Wolves and the Lamb,* dramatized from the novel.

Lovel, Lord, the hero of an old Scottish ballad.

Lovel, Lord, in T. H. Bayly's *The Mistletoe Bough,* a bridegroom whose bride disappears mysteriously. See GINEVRA.

Lovel, Lord Francis, a character in Shakespeare's *Richard III.*

Lovell, Sinfi, a gipsy girl in Theodore Watts-Dunton's *Aylwin.*

Lovelace, the leading character in Richardson's novel *Clarissa Harlowe.*

Lovelace, a young aristocrat in Murphy's *Three Weeks After Marriage* (1776).

Lovewell, the hero of Colman and Garrick's play *The Clandestine Marriage* (1766).

Lovinski, Baron, the villain of Kemble's melodrama *Lodoiska.*

Lowrie, Joan, the title character of Mrs. Burnett's novel *That Lass o' Lowrie's.*

Loyal Derasseur, Monsieur, in Dickens's tale *Our French Watering-Place,* a town-councilor and landlord, an old soldier and admirer of Napoleon, "a gentleman whose true politeness is ingrained, and confirmation of whose word by his bond you would blush to think of."

Lucasta, to whom Richard Lovelace addressed a famous poem, was Lucy Sacheverell.

Lucentio, Bianca's lover in Shakespeare's *The Taming of the Shrew.*

Lucia, the "rambling lady" in male attire in Thomas Southerne's play *Sir Antony Love.*

Lucia d'Orano, Countess, the heroine of Anthony Hope's *Captain Dieppe.*

Lucifer (literally, light-bringer) received its present use as applied to Satan from an interpretation of the words in Isaiah addressed to the fallen King of Babylon: "How art thou fallen from heaven, Lucifer, son of the morning!" It is used by Milton for the demon of pride; and Lucifer is described by Dante as a giant with three faces, expressing anger, envy, and melancholy. Lucifer is a character in Bailey's poem *Festus* and in Longfellow's *The Golden Legend.*

Lucile, the heroine of a romance in verse by Owen Meredith (pen-name of Edward Robert Bulwer-Lytton, the son of Edward Bulwer-Lytton).

Lucinda, spoken of in Thomson's *The Seasons* (Spring), was Lucy Fortescue, wife of Lord George Lyttelton.

Lucinde, the heroine of Molière's *L'Amour Médecin* (1665). Her lover is called in by her maid as a doctor. He tells her father the disease must be reached through the imagination, and suggests a mock marriage with himself, which he takes care to make a legal one.

Lucius, general of the Roman forces in Shakespeare's *Cymbeline.*

Lucius, a mythical king of Britain, who is said to have introduced Christianity, having the pagan temples turned into churches.

Luck of Roaring Camp, The, in Bret Harte's famous story, was an orphan baby adopted by the miners of the camp.

Lucrece, or **Lucretia,** the famous Roman matron who killed herself rather than live after being dishonored, is the subject of a poem by Shakespeare and tragedies by Heywood, Nathaniel Lee, and John H. Payne, and in French by Arnault and Ponsard.

Lucretia, the subject of a novel by Bulwer.

Lucretia, in Disraeli's *Coningsby,* is said to be intended for Madame Zichy, the wife of a Russian diplomatist.

Lucrezia Borgia, of the illustrious Italian family, celebrated for her beauty and her crimes, is the subject of a drama by Victor Hugo and of an opera by Donizetti.

Lucullus, a character in Shakespeare's *Timon of Athens.* Timon's servant calls him "Thou disease of a friend."

Lucy, subject of Tickell's ballad *Lucy and Colin,* which Goldsmith said was "perhaps the best ballad in our language."

Lucy, the heroine of Mackenzie's novel *The Man of the World.*

Lucy, Sir Thomas, who had Shakespeare arrested for stealing deer, is supposed to be caricatured in Justice Shallow in *The Merry Wives of Windsor.*

Lud, a mythical king of Britain. London is said to be Lud's town; and Lud gate, the strong gate that he built at the west. Stow says (1598) that in 1260 the gate was beautified with images of Lud and other kings. The heads were smitten off in the reign of Edward VI, and were restored in the reign of Elizabeth. London is called Lud's town in *Cymbeline.*

Lud, General, a name given to the feigned leader of workingmen in England, who in 1811 tried to prevent the use of power-looms in the place of hand-looms, with the idea that they would lessen the demand for operatives. The leaders wore women's clothes and were called Lud's wives, and all the rioters were named Luddites. The name, it is said, came from a boy named Lud, an imbecile, who had broken two stocking-frames in a passion at being jeered at by other boys.

Luggnagg, an island found in Swift's *Gulliver's Travels,* where the people never die, but, like Tithonus, have not the gift of immortal youth.

Lugh, the god of many arts of the Tuatha de Danaan, in Irish legend.

Luke, in Massinger's *The City Madam,* said to be one of the best two characters of the author. He inherits his brother's great estate, and cuts down the widow, who had scorned him before, to the humble style of living from which his brother's wealth had raised her.

Lukstein, Countess Ilga, the heroine of A. E. W. Mason's *The Courtship of Maurice Buckler.*

Lumpkin, Tony, an awkward booby whose "sense of humor" runs to practical jokes, a leading character in Goldsmith's comedy *She Stoops to Conquer* (1773).

Luna, The Count de, the villain of Verdi's opera *Il Trovatore* (1853).

Lundie, Lizzie, a beautiful girl in Miss Ferrier's novel *The Inheritance.*

Lundin, Dr. Luke, a character in Scott's *The Abbot,* proposes to get Mother Nicneven condemned as a sorceress, regarding her as a professional rival.

Lunel, Albert, the subject of a novel (1844) attributed to Lord Brougham, suppressed on the eve of its publication, reprinted in 1872.

Luria, the hero of Browning's drama of the name. He is a Moorish mercenary who fights against Pisa for Florence.

Lusignan, in Aaron Hill's (1685–1750) tragedy *Zara,* founded upon a work of Voltaire, is "the last of the blood of Christian kings of Jerusalem." He was kept in a dungeon for twenty years by the Saracens.

Lusitania, Portugal, from Lusus, said to have colonized the country; hence the title of the poem by Camoëns, the *Lusiad.*

Lustucru, a personage of the French vaudeville, a type of the simpleton. His master having scored him for some fault, he determines upon suicide and cries, "Let someone bring me a well!"

Lutetia (Lutèce), the ancient Latin name of Paris.

Luther, Martin, is the subject of a drama (1806) by Z. Werner.

Lycidas, the name of a shepherd in Virgil's *Eclogues.* Milton used it for Edward King, who was drowned on the passage to Ireland in 1637, in an elegy in the form of a pastoral.

Lydgate, Dr., a character in George Eliot's *Middlemarch,* wrecks his life by his marriage to Rosamond Vincy, a spoiled beauty.

Lydia, a daughter of the King of Lydia, in Ariosto's *Orlando Furioso,* destroys her lover Alcestes by requiring a treacherous deed of him; and for this she is sentenced to endless perdition.

Lygia, the heroine of Sienkiewicz's novel *Quo Vadis?* and the dramatization of it.

Lykke, Nils, a Danish knight and councilor in Ibsen's *Lady Inger of Ostrat;* the character is historical.

Lyle, in Disraeli's *Coningsby,* is understood to be a portrait of Lord Surrey.

Lyle, Annot, a character in Scott's *A Legend of Montrose.*

Lynborough, Ambrose Coverly, Lord, a character in Anthony Hope's *Helena's Path.*

Lynch Law, "hang first and try afterward," is said to take its name from James Lynch, in Piedmont, Virginia, in 1688, chosen by the community to execute summary justice, there being no law-court within reach.

Lynchnobians, in the *Pantagruel* of Rabelais, are lantern-sellers, that is, book publishers.

Lyndall, the chief character in Olive Schreiner's *The Story of an African Farm.*

Lyndon, Barry, the subject of a novel by Thackeray, an Irish adventurer, written as a burlesque on Bulwer-Lytton's novels about romantic villains.

Lyndsay, Edward, the hero of Miss Ferrier's novel *The Inheritance.*

Lynedale, Lord, a Liberal nobleman in Kingsley's *Alton Locke.*

Lyon, Esther, the heroine of George Eliot's *Felix Holt.*

Lyonnesse, the scene of the final conflict between Arthur and Modred, was west of Camelot and is now "full forty fathoms under water."

Lyonnors, Lady, a captive in Castle Perilous, delivered by Gareth. The story is told in Tennyson's *Gareth and Lynette.*

Lyric Muse, The, a poetess of Tanagra in Bœotia, who defeated Pindar in five music contests.

Lysander, Hermia's lover in Shakespeare's *A Midsummer Night's Dream.*

Lysimachus, a character in Shakespeare's *Pericles.*

Lysistrata, the subject of a satirical comedy of Aristophanes (412 B.C.) in favor of peace.

Mab, Queen of the Fairies, according to English poets; said to have been originally the name of an Irish princess. Queen Mab is described by Shakespeare in a noted passage in Act I, Scene IV, of *Romeo and Juliet.* Ben Jonson and Herrick speak of her as pinching slovenly house-servants. Drayton's *Nymphidia* gives the names of her maids of honor, Hop and Mop, and others, and her waiting-maids, Fib and Tib, etc. *Queen Mab* is the subject of a poem written by Shelley at the age of eighteen, and printed privately in 1813, which was severely condemned for its irreligious tone.

Mabinogion, The (meaning instruction or entertainment for children), a collection of Welsh legends.

Macaber, The Dance, the Dance of Death, the subject of many medieval paintings, especially mural.

Macaire, Robert, or **Richard,** a French knight who in 1371 murdered Aubry de Montdidier, a seigneur of the court of Charles V of France. He was aided by Lieutenant Landry. The murdered man's dog, Dragon, showed such animosity to Macaire, that the King ordered a duel between the dog and Macaire. The man was armed with a great club, but was nevertheless vanquished by the dog, whereupon he confessed his crime and was executed. There are several French plays on the subject, among others *The Dog of Montargis* (the murder took place in a wood near Montargis) and *The Dog of Aubry;* and the former has been presented in an English version, differing somewhat from the original.

McAndrew, a dour Scots engineer, subject of a dramatic monologue by Rudyard Kipling, *McAndrew's Hymn.*

Macamut, in *Purchas's Pilgrimage,* a sultan of Camboya, whose touch and breath were deadly because he lived upon poisons.

Macare, good temper in Voltaire's allegory *Thélème and Macare.*

M'Aulay, Allan, a character in Scott's *A Legend of Montrose.*

Macbeth and **Lady Macbeth,** the chief characters in Shakespeare's famous tragedy. Macbeth, King of Scotland, was killed at Sumphanan in 1057, though in the drama his death takes place at Dunsinane two years earlier. His wife in history was the Lady Guroch, a widow and the granddaughter of Kenneth IV. The mothers of Macbeth and Duncan were sisters, daughters of Malcolm II.

Macbriar, Ephraim, a preacher in Scott's *Old Mortality.*

Macbride, Miss, the subject of a narrative poem by John G. Saxe, *The Proud Miss Macbride.*

Maccabæus, Judas, the Jewish hero, is the subject of a dramatic poem by Longfellow.

M'Cluskie, Lady Glencora, an heiress in Trollope's *Can You Forgive Her?* and other of his "parliamentary novels."

MacCombech, Robin Oig, or **MacGregor,** one of the drovers in Scott's tale *The Two Drovers.*

MacDonell, Edmund and **Eva,** brother and sister in John Banim's novel *Boyne Water.*

McDow, Rev. Duncan, a coarse, self-advertising minister in Miss Ferrier's novel *Destiny.*

Macduff, the Thane of Fife, a character in Shakespeare's *Macbeth.*

McFingal, the subject of a poem by John Trumbull (1750–1831), immensely popular in its day, in the mock-heroic style of *Hudibras.* McFingal is a Scotch-Irish hero, who has long arguments with Honorius, a Whig, and is at last treated by patriots to a coat of tar and feathers. Some of its couplets are taken for Butler's, as for example:

> "A thief ne'er felt the halter draw
> With good opinion of the law."

MacFlecknoe, the subject of a poem by Dryden, a satire on Thomas Shadwell, who considered his plays far superior to Dryden's.

McFlimsey, Flora, the subject of a once popular satiric poem by William Allen Butler, *Nothing to Wear* (1857).

MacGregor, Rob Roy, Robert Campbell, a Highland freebooter, the hero of Scott's novel *Rob Roy.*

MacGuffog, and his wife, a fear-inspiring couple of jailkeepers in Scott's *Guy Mannering.*

Macha, an Irish goddess who had laid a curse upon the warriors of Ulster that made them powerless to fight when they most needed their strength.

Macham, Robert, the discoverer of Madeira Island (1344), and abandoned there by sailors, is the subject of a passage in Drayton's *Polyolbion* and of a poem by Rev. W. L. Bowles.

Macheath, Captain, a leader of highwaymen in Gay's *The Beggars' Opera.*

MacIvor, Flora, the heroine of Scott's *Waverley.*

Mackaye, Sandy, a seller of second-hand books who befriends the hero of Kingsley's *Alton Locke.*

Mackenzie, Rosa, the first wife of Clive Newcome in Thackeray's *The Newcomes.*

Mackenzie, Sheila, the heroine of William Black's *A Princess of Thule.*

Mackrell, John Rose, a character in Meredith's *The Amazing Marriage.*

Maclaughlan, Sir Sampson and **Lady,** characters in Miss Ferrier's novel *Marriage.*

Macleod, Fiona, a pen-name of William Sharp.

Macleod, Lora, the heroine of Fiona Macleod's *Pharais.*

Macleod of Dare, the subject of a novel by William Black.

MacMarres, Captain, a character in Shakespeare's *Henry V.*

Macquart, Jean, an important character of Zola's novels called the *Rougon Macquart Series.*

Macreons: so the British are called in the *Pantagruel* (1545) of Rabelais. It means long-lived, "because no one is put to death for his religious opinions" among them.

MacSarcasm, Sir Archie, a Scotch knight in Macklin's play *Love à la Mode* (1779).

MacSillergrip, a Scotch pawnbroker in Charles Matthews's play *At Home in Multiple.*

MacStinger, Mrs., the vixen landlady of Captain Cuttle in Dickens's *Dombey and Son.*

MacSycophant, Sir Pertinax, a noted character in Macklin's play *The Man of the World,* who "never could stand straight in the presence of a great mon."

MacTab, The Honorable Miss Lucretia, a dependent but proud maiden lady in Colman's comedy *The Poor Gentleman.*

MacTavish Mhov, a Highland outlaw whose widow, Elspat, is the subject of Scott's tale *The Highland Widow.*

MacTurk, Hector, a lieutenant, a great advocate of dueling, in Scott's *St. Ronan's Well.*

Macumer, Baron de, a generous but unfortunate character in Balzac's *Letters of Two Brides.*

Mad Anthony, General Anthony Wayne (1745–1796), an officer in the American Revolutionary War.

Madeline, the heroine of Bulwer's *Eugene Aram.*

Madelon, one of the romantic girls of Molière's comedy *Les Précieuses Ridicules* (1659).

Mademoiselle: Anne Marie Louise d'Orléans, cousin of Louis XIV, is so called, also called *La grande Mademoiselle.*

Madge Wildfire. See MURDOCHSON.

Madoc, a prince of North Wales of the twelfth century, called the Perfect Prince, Lord of the Ocean, subject of Southey's poem of the name, in which he is represented as founding a settlement near the Missouri river.

Mad Parliament, The, a name given by chroniclers to that of 1258; Henry III had accepted the crown of Sicily for his son Edmund, and wasted English money on an adventure of no benefit to the nation. The Mad Parliament, therefore, under the lead of Simon de Montfort, compelled acceptance of the constitution called the "Provisions of Oxford," which practically established an oligarchy of the barons.

Mad Poet, The, Nathaniel Lee, an English dramatic poet, confined as insane (1684–1688); also McDonald Clarke (1798–1842), who died in a New York asylum.

Mæcenas, the liberal patron of Virgil, Horace, Propertius, and other Latin writers, has given his name as a synonym for a patron of literature.

Mævius, a name for a vile poet, taken from the *Eclogues* of Virgil, whence the name of Gifford's satire on the Della Cruscans, *The Mœviad* (1796).

Magalona, a daughter of a king of Naples, the heroine of an old French romance of chivalry, reproduced in German by Ludwig Tieck.

Magda, the heroine of Sudermann's play of the name.

Magician of the North, The, Sir Walter Scott, who was also called the Great Magician and the Wizard of the North.

Magnano, a leader of a rabble in Butler's *Hudibras,* intended for a noted tinker-preacher, Simeon Wait.

Magnetic Mountain, The, in the *Arabian Nights.* It drew out all the nails and other iron from any ship that came near it.

Magnificent, The, a term regularly applied to Lorenzo de' Medici. It has been applied also to Chosroes I (d. 579) of Persia, Robert of Normandy (d. 1035), called *Le Diable*, and the Sultan Soliman I (1493–1566).

Magnus, Peter, a character in Dickens's *Pickwick Papers*, affianced to the lady into whose room Mr. Pickwick blundered by mistake.

Magwitch, Abel, a convict in Dickens's *Great Expectations.*

Mahomet, the subject of a tragedy by Voltaire.

Mahoud, in Ridley's *Tales of the Genii*, servant to a magician.

Maiden King, The: Malcolm IV of Scotland (1141–1465) was called so, on account of his gentle disposition.

Maidens' Castle, The, was on the Severn, held by seven knights, who took captive every maiden that passed, until Sir Galahad expelled the knights from the castle.

Maiden Town, a name once given to Edinburgh, from a tradition that in troubled times the daughters of the Pict kings were sent there for safety.

Maid Marian. See HOOD, ROBIN.

Maid of Athens, Theresa Macri, the subject of Byron's poem, who married and was found twenty-four years later struggling with poverty to feed a large family.

Maid of Bath, The, Miss Linley, a noted beauty, who married Richard Brinsley Sheridan.

Maid of Norway, The, Margaret, daughter of Eric II of Norway, and granddaughter of Alexander III of Scotland. She was to marry the son of Edward I of England, but died on the passage from Norway.

Maid of Orleans, The. See JOAN OF ARC.

Maid of Perth, The Fair, Catherine Glover in Scott's novel of that name.

Maid of Saragossa, The, Augustina, heroine of the siege of Saragossa. When her lover fell she took his place, mounted the battery and worked a gun.

Maillard, Paul, one of *The Two Poets of Croisic* in Browning's poem.

Maironi, Piero, the title character of Fogazzaro's novels *The Sinner* and *The Saint.*

Maisie, the heroine of Kipling's *The Light that Failed.*

Maitland, Cyril, the title character of Maxwell Gray's novel *The Silence of Dean Maitland.*

Maitland, Lincoln, an American painter in Bourget's *Cosmopolis.*

Maitland, Thomas, the pseudonym under which Robert Buchanan attacked the "Fleshly School."

Maître Adam, Adam Billaut, a joiner-poet of Nevers, called the "Virgil of the plane" (d. 1662).

Maître Jacques, in Molière's *L'Avare,* was the coachman and the cook of Harpagon, the miser.

Maître Pierre, the name under which Louis XI meets Quentin in Scott's *Quentin Durward.*

Malagigi, an enchanter in Ariosto's *Orlando Furioso.*

Malagrida, a nickname given to Lord Shelburne (1737–1805), who was very zealous in the opposition during Lord North's administration. Gabriel Malagrida (1689–1761) was an Italian, a Jesuit missionary to Brazil, who was accused of conspiring against the King of Portugal.

Malagrowther, Sir Mungo, a character in Scott's *The Fortunes of Nigel.*

Malabrumno, a giant and wizard in *Don Quixote.*

Malaprop, Mrs., a character in Sheridan's play *The Rivals,* famous for her blunders, especially in using for one word another resembling it in sound.

Malatesta, Guido, the husband of Francesca da Rimini (*q.v.*).

Malavoglia, the name of a family of working people, the subject of a novel of their name, one of the socialistic series, *The Conquered,* by Giovanni Verga. They are conquered by repeated misfortunes in their struggle for existence.

Malbrough, in English translation **Marlbrook,** the subject of a popular French song, *Malbrough s'en va-t-en guerre.* It is thought to refer to Marlborough.

Malbrouk, a legendary child who had attained a man's stature at seven and could assume any form he chose.

Malcolm, surnamed Can More (great head), son of King Duncan, succeeded Macbeth on the throne of Scotland; a character in Shakespeare's *Macbeth.*

Maldonado, a character in Pinero's play *Iris.*

Malecasta, in Spenser's *The Faerie Queene,* the mistress of Joyous Castle and the impersonation of sensual love.

Maledisaunt (evil speaking), a damsel who slandered her lover to keep him from the battlefield. Sir Launcelot forgave her and changed her name to Bienpensaunt (good thinking).

Maléger, a son of the earth like Antæus, whom Arthur could conquer only by throwing him into the lake, since every touch of the earth gave him new vigor.

Maleine, the title character of Maeterlinck's tragedy *Princess Maleine.*

Malfi, The Duchess of, the heroine of a play (1618) by John Webster.

Malgo, a mythical king of Britain who subdued Orkney, Denmark, Norway, Iceland, and Gothland.

Mallard, Ambrose, a character in Meredith's *The Amazing Marriage.*

Malmaison, Archibald, the title character of a novel by Julian Hawthorne (1878).

Malone, Peter Augustus, a curate in Charlotte Brontë's *Shirley,* said to have been drawn from life.

Maltravers, Ernest, the hero of a novel by Bulwer.

Malvil, a character in Murphy's comedy *Know Your Own Mind,* said to have suggested Sheridan's Joseph Surface.

Malvoisin, Sir Albert de, a character in Scott's *Ivanhoe.*

Malvolio, a famous character in Shakespeare's *Twelfth Night.*

Mamamouchi, an imaginary order of knighthood into which Monsieur Jourdain, in Molière's *Le Bourgeois Gentilhomme,* is inducted by a mock ceremony.

Mambrino, a Moorish king, celebrated in the romances of chivalry, whose famous helmet, which rendered the wearer invulnerable, was captured by Rinaldo. It owes its fame to Don Quixote, who took possession of a basin that a barber had put on his head in a rain-storm, and wore it, asserting that it was Mambrino's helmet.

Mamilius, the little prince in Shakespeare's *A Winter's Tale,* who dies in consequence of his mother's disgrace.

Mammon, the god of wealth. Milton makes him one of the fallen angels.

Mammon, Sir Epicure, a character in Jonson's *The Alchemist.*

Managarin, a legendary giant who fills himself with blood and swallows the moon.

Manchester Poet, The, Charles Swain (1803–1874).

Manciple (steward), **The,** one of the pilgrims in Chaucer's *The Canterbury Tales.*

Mandane, the heroine of Mademoiselle Scudéry's romance *Artamène, ou le grand Cyrus.*

Manders, Pastor, a character in Ibsen's *Ghosts,* with a rigid sense of right and wrong, a sure knowledge of what another's duty is, and no human sympathy.

Mandrabul, the discoverer of a gold-mine, offered a golden ram to Juno, the next year a silver one, and gradually decreased his offerings till he stopped them altogether. Hence a Mandrabul offering signifies expiring gratitude.

Mandricardo, King of Tartary in Boiardo's *Orlando Innamorato* and Ariosto's *Orlando Furioso.*

Manduce, the idol of the gluttonous Gastrolaters in the *Pantagruel* of Rabelais.

Manette, Dr., a character in Dickens's *A Tale of Two Cities.*

Manfred, Count, the subject of a poetic drama by Byron, has sold himself to Satan and is served by seven spirits; he dwells in solitude in the mountains, and is wholly without human sympathies.

Mangerton, The Laird of, John Armstrong, hero of Scott's tale *The Laird's Jock.*

Man in Black, The, an odd character in Goldsmith's *Citizen of the World,* supposed to be a portrait of the author's father. His principles are severe, but his heart is soft; he inveighs against pauperism, but cannot deny a beggar. A tale by Washington Irving bears this title.

Man in the Moon: the figure formed by the dark lines in the moon has been the subject of various fancies, fables, and superstitions. In one it is the man spoken of in Numbers xv who was stoned to death for gathering wood upon the Sabbath. The "rude mechanicals" in *A Midsummer Night's Dream* had it a man with a dog and a lantern. In Dante it is Cain with the thorns. Again, it is Endymion beloved by Diana. One German version makes it a man with a woman condemned for churning butter on Sunday. In Icelandic legend, two children were drawing water, when the moon kidnaped them; and they may be seen in the full moon with the bucket on a pole across their shoulders. The rain comes from the bucket they carry.

Manisty, Edward, a character in Mrs. Ward's novel *Eleanor.*

Manito or **Manitou:** the two supreme spirits of the North American Indians are Gitchê-Manitou, the good, and Mitchê-Manitou, the evil spirit.

Manlius Capitolinus, a Roman tribune who defended the capitol against the Gauls, 390 B.C. Lafosse has a tragedy, *Manlius Capitolinus* (1698).

Manly, the title character in Wycherley's play *The Plain Dealer* (1677), said to be copied from Molière's *Le Misanthrope,* and described by the author as of "an honest, surly, nice humor." The play was so popular that the author was called Manly Wycherley.

Manly, a noble and judicious man in Van Brugh and Cibber's play *The Provoked Husband* (1728).

Mann, Mrs., an avaricious and hypocritical woman in Dickens's *Oliver Twist.*

Mannering, Dora, the heroine of Mrs. Oliphant's *A House in Bloomsbury.*

Mannering, Guy, a character in Scott's novel *Guy Mannering.*

Manoa, a fabulous city of El Dorado, on Lake Parime, so rich that the houses were roofed with gold. Many expeditions were undertaken to find Manoa after the account given by Juan Martinez in 1534, who said he was led away from it blindfolded.

Man of Bath, Ralph Allen, who did "good by stealth" and blushed "to have it known," a friend of Pope's.

Man of Blood, The, a name applied by the Puritans to Charles I.

Man of Destiny, The, Napoleon. He himself is said to have believed his career to be guided by supernatural influences.

Man of Feeling, The: Henry Mackenzie was called so from the title of his novel. See HARLEY.

Man of Ross, The, who is immortalized in Pope's *Moral Essays*, was John Kyrle (1664–1754) of Ross, County Hereford, England, distinguished for benevolence.

Man of Sedan, The, Napoleon III (1808–1873), who surrendered there at the fall of Sedan, in September, 1870.

Man of Sin, The, mentioned in II Thessalonians, has been a favorite designation for opponents by people of divers religions. The Fifth Monarchy men applied it to Cromwell.

Man of the People, Charles James Fox (1749–1806).

Manon Lescaut, the heroine of a celebrated French story (1735) by the Abbé Prévost.

Manrico, the hero of Verdi's opera *Il Trovatore* (1853).

Manrique, Rodrigo, a Spanish soldier, well known in Spanish history and made known outside of Spain by the fine Ode on his death by his son, Don Jorge Manrique, translated by Longfellow.

Mänsdotter, Katarina, the wife of Eric XIV of Sweden. Karl Anton Wetterbergh published a collection of lyrics with the title *Leaves from the Journal of Katarina Mänsdotter.*

Mansel, Sir Edward, Lieutenant of the Tower in Scott's *The Fortunes of Nigel.*

Mansfelt, Bruno, a character in Miss Bremer's *The Neighbors* (1835).

Mansfield, The Miller of, the subject of an old ballad in Percy's *Réliques.* His name is Cockle. The story is used in Dodsley's farce *The King and the Miller of Mansfield.*

Mansoni, Coralie, a character in Anthony Hope's *The King's Mirror* (1899).

Mantalini, a fop in Dickens's *Nicholas Nickleby*, supported by his wife, a fashionable milliner.

Mantuan, The: Baptista Spagnolus, a poet surnamed Mantuanus (1443–1516), is mentioned in Shakespeare's *Love's Labor's Lost.*

Mantuan Swan, The, Virgil.

Manuel, the subject of a tragedy (1817) by Charles Robert Maturin.

Manx, Quintin, a character in Meredith's *Diana of the Crossways.*

Maqueda, one of the names of the Queen of Sheba, usually called Balkis.

Mar, Helen, the heroine of Jane Porter's *The Scottish Chiefs.*

Marat, Jean Paul, appears in *Memoirs of a Physician* and *Taking the Bastile,* by Dumas.

Marcas, Géhhirin, the subject of a novel of his name by Balzac.

Marcel, a painter in *Bohemian Life* by Henry Murger.

Marcelia, the innocent wife of the Duke, killed by him in consequence of the false accusation of Francesco, the Iago of Massinger's play *The Duke of Milan* (1622).

Marcella, the heroine of an episode in *Don Quixote.*

Marcella, the subject of a novel by Mrs. Humphry Ward, also a character in her *Sir George Tressady.*

Marcellus, a character in Shakespeare's *Hamlet.* Sir Edward Dyer, a friend of Sir Philip Sidney, is the supposed original of Marcellus.

Marcellus, in Dibdin's *Bibliomania* (1811), is the critic Edmund Malone.

Marcellus, the nephew of Augustus, who died at eighteen (B.C. 23), is the subject of a pathetic episode in Virgil's *Æneid,* Book VI.

March, Earl of, a character in Scott's *The Fair Maid of Perth.*

March, the Earl of, a character in Shakespeare's *Henry VI,* Part III.

March, Edmund Mortimer, a character in Shakespeare's *Henry VI,* Part I.

March, Ursula, marries the hero of Miss Mulock's *John Halifax, Gentleman.*

Marchbanks, Eugene, a character in Shaw's drama *Candida,* is a poet in love with Candida, but goes away disillusioned, contemptuous of the happiness he had desired.

Marchdale, Peter, the hero of Harland's novel *The Cardinal's Snuff-Box.*

Marchioness, The, a name given to the small servant at Sampson Brass's by Dick Swiveller in Dickens's *The Old Curiosity Shop.* The play *Little Nell and the Marchioness* is by Harry P. Manson.

Marcia, in Addison's *Cato,* is loved by Juba and Sempronius.

Marcia, the heroine in Duffield Osborne's novel *The Lion's Brood.*

Marcia, a character in Howells's novel *A Modern Instance.*

Marcius, Caius, afterward Coriolanus, and his son, young **Marcius,** personages of Shakespeare's *Coriolanus.*

Marck, William de la, called the "Boar of Ardennes," a character in Scott's *Quentin Durward.*

Marcliffe, Theophilus, a pseudonym of William Godwin (1756–1836).

Marcos de Obregon, the hero of a Spanish romance by Vicente Espinel (1618), said to have furnished Lesage with many incidents of *Gil Blas.*

Marcus, in Addison's *Cato,* a son of Cato.

Mardyke, Miriam, the heroine of Stephen Phillips's poetic drama *The Sin of David.*

Mareschal, a Jacobite in Scott's *The Black Dwarf.*

Marforio, a statue in Rome, where replies were placed to Pasquin (*q.v.*).

Margarelon or **Margariton,** a character in Shakespeare's *Troilus and Cressida.*

Margaret, title and heroine's name of a novel by the Rev. Sylvester Judd (1813-1853), a story of early New England life.

Margaret, the heroine of Goethe's *Faust,* "a peculiar union of passion, simplicity, homeliness, and witchery." She is often called by the German diminutive of her name, Gretchen, in Gounod's opera *Faust.*

Margaret, Ladye, the heroine of Scott's poem *The Lay of the Last Minstrel* (1805).

Margaret of Anjou, Queen of Henry VI and daughter of René, King of Naples, Sicily, and Jerusalem. She appears in the three parts of Shakespeare's *King Henry VI* and in *Richard III;* also in Scott's novel *Anne of Geierstein;* also the subject of an opera by Meyerbeer.

Margaret's Ghost, the subject of a popular ballad by David Mallet (1724).

Marguerite de Valois, heroine of a novel of the name by Dumas and of five succeeding romances in the series called *La Reine Margot.*

Marguerite, the wife of the hero of William Godwin's novel *St. Leon,* said to be a portrait of the author's wife, Mary Wollstonecraft, and the story of St. Leon's domestic life to be an idealized description of Godwin's own.

Margutte, a gluttonous giant in Pulci's *Morgante Maggiore* (1488).

Maria, a waiting-woman in Shakespeare's *Twelfth Night.*

Maria, a character in Sheridan's *The School for Scandal.*

Maria, a foundling, heroine of Donizetti's opera *The Daughter of the Regiment.*

Mariamne, the wife of Herod the Great. She and her two sons were put to death by Herod. Several tragedies bear the title *Mariamne,* whose authors are: A. Hardy (1623), Pierre Tristan l'Ermite (1640), Voltaire (1724), and Calderon; she is a character in Stephen Phillips's poetic drama *Herod* (1900).

Marian, in Spenser's *Colin Clout's Come Home Again,* is Margaret, Countess of Cumberland.

Marian, a character in Gay's pastorals (1714).

Mariana, a character in Shakespeare's *Measure for Measure.* Tennyson's poem *Mariana in the Moated Grange* gives a wonderful picture of loneliness.

Mariana, a French girl in Shirley's play *Edward the Black Prince* (1640).

Mariana, the heroine of Fielding's play *The Miser.*

Mariana, the heroine of Sheridan Knowles's comedy *The Wife* (1833).

Marianne, the subject of "one of the best French romances for the interest of the situations and the truth of the portraitures," by Marivaux (1728).

Marie Antoinette, Queen of Louis XVI, is the subject of one of Mühlbach's novels and a character in several by Dumas.

Marie de Brabant, tried on a charge of murder and acquitted, the subject of a poem by Ancelot (1825).

Marie Magdalene, *The Life and Repentance of,* a miracle play by Lewis Wager (1567).

Marie Ottilie, of Dornheim, the heroine of a novel by Agnes and Egerton Castle, *The Pride of Jennico*, and of a play from it by Abby S. Richardson and Grace L. Furniss.

Marigold, Doctor, an itinerant auctioneer in a tale of Dickens's that bears his name.

Marikke, the heroine of Sudermann's drama *St. John's Fire.*

Marina, the daughter of Pericles in Shakespeare's *Pericles, Prince of Tyre.*

Marini, Luigi and **Giulia,** characters in Meredith's *Sandra Belloni.*

Marino Faliero, the forty-ninth doge of Venice, elected 1354, the subject of a tragedy by Byron (1821) and of one by Casimir Delavigne (1829).

Marion de Lorme, a character in Bulwer's drama *Richelieu.*

Marita or **Maritana,** the heroine of Gerald du Maurier's play *A Royal Rival.*

Maritana, the heroine of *Don Cæsar de Bazan* in *Don Cæsar's Return* by Victor Mapes and in an opera founded upon the play.

Marius, the Roman general, tribune of the people B.C. 119, is the subject of a drama (1594) by Thomas Lodge, *Wounds of Civil War, Lively Set forth in the True Tragedies of Marius and Sylla;* and of a French tragedy (1791), *Marius à Minturnes,* by Antony Vincent Arnault.

Marius, the title and principal character of the third novel in Hugo's *Les Misérables.*

Marius, the hero of a novel by Walter Pater, *Marius, the Epicurean.*

Marivaux, The English, a name applied to Samuel Richardson. Pierre de Chamblain de Marivaux (1688–1763) was a French novelist of ability, whose tendency to fine-spun metaphysics gave rise to the term *marivaudage.* See MARIANNE.

Mark, King of Cornwall, in the Arthurian romances.

Markleham, Mrs., a character in Dickens's *David Copperfield,* the mother-in-law of Dr. Strong, called by the boys "the Old Soldier" from the way she marshaled a great force of her needy relatives against the doctor.

Marks, Will, the hero of a tale by Mr. Pickwick in Dickens's *Master Humphrey's Clock.*

Marley, Jacob, the former partner of Scrooge in Dickens's *A Christmas Carol.*

Marlow, Sir Charles, an old friend of Mr. Hardcastle in Goldsmith's comedy *She Stoops to Conquer* (1773).

Marlowe, Christopher, the dramatist, is the subject of a drama by Josephine Peabody.

Marmion, Lord, the hero of Scott's poem *Marmion.*

Marmosets, a name given by the dukes of Berry and Burgundy to the able councilors of Charles V and VI (1392).

Marner, Silas, the weaver in George Eliot's *Silas Marner.*

Maro: so Virgil—Publius Virgilius Maro—is sometimes called.

Marphisa, a warrior woman who becomes a Christian after many adventures in *Orlando Furioso.*

Marphurius, a philosopher in Molière's *The Forced Marriage* (1664).

Marplot, the chief character in two of Mrs. Centlivre's comedies, *The Busy-Body* and *Marplot in Lisbon.*

Marplot, Sir Martin, title and hero's name of a translation of Molière's *L'Etourdi,* adapted for the stage by Dryden.

Mar-Prelate, Martin, the pseudonym of the author of a series of tracts against Episcopacy in the reign of Elizabeth, supposed to be John Ap Henry (Penry), executed for seditious words against the Queen in 1593.

Marsac, Gaston de, the title character of Weyman's *A Gentleman of France* and of the drama made from it.

Marsay, Henri de, one of *The Thirteen* in Balzac's novel of that name, and a character in several others.

Marsett, Captain Edward, a personage of Meredith's *One of Our Conquerors.*

Marshal Forwards, a title given to the Prussian general Blücher (1742–1819) on account of the swiftness of his movements.

Marsiglio or **Marsirio,** a Saracen king who figures in the Charlemagne romances.

Marsilia, in Spenser's *Colin Clout's Come Home Again,* was Helena Swavenburgh, Marchioness of Northampton, a Swede.

Martext, Sir Oliver, a vicar in Shakespeare's *As You Like It.*

Martha, the elderly duenna of Margaret in Goethe's *Faust.*

Martha, the title of a popular opera by Flotow and the assumed name of the heroine, Lady Harriet Durham, under which she visits the Fair at Richmond and hires herself out as a servant.

Martia, one of the heroines of Fletcher's play *The Double Marriage.*

Martia, according to Geoffrey's *British History,* was the wife of Guithelin, great-grandson of Mulmutius, who established the Mulmutian laws. These and the laws collected by Martia were translated into the English of his day by Alfred.

Martin, in Swift's *Tale of a Tub,* is Martin Luther. In Dryden's poem *The Hind and the Panther* Martin is used to represent the Lutherans.

Martin-Bellème, Madame, the chief character in *The Red Lily* by Anatole France.

Martin, Jack, the hero of Anthony Hope's novel *A Man of Mark.*

Martin Mar-All, the subject of a play by Dryden.

Martine, the wife of Sganerelle in Molière's *Un Médecin Malgré Lui* (1666), who, when a neighbor interferes with Sganerelle for beating her, turns on him for meddling and says, "I want him to beat me, I do."

Martinsward, Catherine, a character in Meredith's *The Tale of Chloe.*

Martyr King, The, a title applied to Henry VI and Charles I of England and to Louis XVI of France.

Marullus, a character in Shakespeare's *Julius Cæsar.*

Marvel, Ellinor, the heroine of *The Star Dreamer* by Agnes and Egerton Castle.

Marvel, John, tells the story in *The Splendid Spur* by Quiller-Couch.

Marvel, Joshua, the hero of Benjamin L. Farjeon's novel of the name (1872).

Marvelous Boy, The, a name applied by Wordsworth to Thomas Chatterton, the boy-poet (1752–1770).

Marwood, Alice, or **Alice Brown,** a criminal in Dickens's *Dombey and Son.*

Mary Ann, a London slavey who inherits a fortune in Israel Zangwill's story and play *Merely Mary Ann.*

Mary Magdalen, the heroine of Paul Heyse's drama *Mary of Magdala.*

Mary Stuart, Queen of Scots, is the subject of a drama by Schiller, a French version of which was written by Lebrun (1820). James Hogg wrote a long poem, *The Queen's Wake.* One of Alfieri's best tragedies is upon the same theme; and she is a personage of Scott's *The Abbot,* of Dumas's *The Two Dianas,* of James Grant's *Bothwell* (1857), of Charles Major's novel and drama *Dorothy Vernon of Haddon Hall,* and the chief character of Maurice Hewlett's *The Queen's Quair.*

Mary Tudor, Queen of England, is the subject of a drama by Victor Hugo, and one by Tennyson, *Queen Mary.* She is a character in Ainsworth's *The Tower of London.*

Masaniello (Tommaso Aniello), a Neapolitan fisherman who led an insurrection in 1647 against the Duke of Arcos. Caraffa and Auber have operas on the subject.

Mascarillo, a type of the impudent and intriguing valet of the French comedy of the seventeenth and eighteenth centuries.

Maskwell, the title character of Congreve's play *The Double Dealer* (1700).

Maslova, Katusha, the heroine of Tolstoi's novel *Resurrection* and its dramatization. She is a waif brought up as half-servant, half-lady by two rich women, whose nephew, Prince Nehludoff, betrays her.

Mason, Lady, one of the chief characters of Trollope's *Orley Farm.*

Mason and Dixon's Line, a popular name for the boundary between Pennsylvania and Maryland—a free and a former slave State of the American Union. The names were those of the surveyors, and the phrase received its vogue from its use by Randolph of Roanoke.

Massey, Bartle, a conceited bachelor schoolmaster in George Eliot's *Adam Bede,* who rails against women, yet is kind to anyone in trouble.

Master Hugues, an imaginary composer in Browning's poem *Master Hugues of Saxe-Gotha.*

Master Leonard, in medieval demonology, the master of the nocturnal orgies, who presided in the form of a three-horned goat.

Master of Sentences, Peter Lombard (1100–1164), compiler of a book of sentences collected from the fathers.

Matchin, Maud, the chief character in *The Breadwinners*, attributed to John Hay.

Mathis, a miller who murders a Polish Jew for his money, with which he pays his debts and lives in comfort. This character, in Ware's play *The Polish Jew*, was the one in which Henry Irving first gained celebrity.

Matho, the hero of Flaubert's novel *Salammbô* (1862).

Matilda, the evil genius of Ambrosio, the hero of Lewis's romance *The Monk*.

Mauban, Antoinette de, a character in Anthony Hope's *The Prisoner of Zenda* and Edward Rose's dramatization of it.

Maud, the subject of Tennyson's dramatic monologue of the name.

Maufrigneuse, The Duchess de, a character in nine of Balzac's novels, *The Secrets of a Princess, Another Study of Woman*, and others, a woman of many lovers.

Maugis, in French romance a paladin of Charlemagne, called in Italian Malagigi.

Maul, a giant in Bunyan's *Pilgrim's Progress* killed by Greatheart.

Maule, Matthew, the original owner of the land on which stood *The House of the Seven Gables* of Hawthorne's novel.

Maul of Monks (Malleus Monachorum), a title applied to Thomas Cromwell (1490–1540), who was active in suppressing religious houses under Henry VIII.

Maulstatute, a magistrate in Scott's *Peveril of the Peak*.

Mauperin, Renée, in a novel of the name by the De Goncourts, a melancholy rattlepate.

Maupin, Camille, a character in Balzac's *Beatrice*.

Maupin, Mademoiselle de, the subject of a noted novel by Théophile Gautier.

Mauprat, Adrien de, a character in Bulwer's *Richelieu*.

Mauprat, Bernard de, the hero of George Sand's *Mauprat*.

Mause, in Scott's *Old Mortality,* the mother of Cuddie Headrigg, a Covenanter.

Mausolus, a king of Caria, whose tomb, the Mausoleum, was one of the Seven Wonders of the World.

Mauthe Doog, The, an apparition in the shape of a large curly black spaniel, which came into the guard-room of the castle of Peel-town in the Isle of Man every evening at candle-light and lay before the fire till morning.

Mawworm, a sordid, ignorant preacher in Bickerstaff's comedy *The Hypocrite* (1768).

Max, the title character of Weber's opera *Der Freischütz.*

Maxime, a Christian martyr in *The Second Nun's Tale* in Chaucer's *The Canterbury Pilgrims.*

Maximilian I, Emperor of Germany (1493–1519), is the hero of the rhymed epic *Theuerdank,* which combines his adventures with an allegorical romance, in which he woos Queen Ehrenreich, that is, strives after honor, and is tempted by the Devil and his captains, Impudence, Misfortune, and Envy, whom he repels. The epic was written by himself and his secretaries, and published in 1517.

May, Sophie, the pen-name of Rebecca Sophia Clarke.

Mayeux, the name of a hunchback (*ultra-bossu*) in French romance and satire, defined as "a caricature of the bourgeoisie" of the period succeeding the Revolution of 1830.

Maylie, Mrs., a lady who befriends Oliver in Dickens's *Oliver Twist.*

Mazarin, Cardinal, is a character in *Twenty Years After* and *The Vicomte de Bragelonne* (1845) by Dumas.

Mead, Ashley, the hero of Anthony Hope's novel *A Servant of the Public.*

Meadows, Young, a son of Sir William, hero of Bickerstaff's operatic farce *Love in a Village.*

Meagles, Mr., a retired banker, good-humored and benevolent, in Dickens's *Little Dorrit.*

Medley, in Etherege's comedy *The Man of Mode,* has been taken for a portrait of the author.

Medoro, the young Moor in Ariosto's *Orlando Furioso.*

Meiklewham, Saunders, an attorney in Scott's *St. Ronan's Well.*

Meister, Wilhelm, the hero of Goethe's novel *Wilhelm Meister's Apprenticeship.*

Melema, Tito, the husband of Romola in George Eliot's *Romola.*

Melibee, in Spenser's *The Ruins of Time,* is Sir Francis Walsingham.

Melincourt, Authelia, the owner of the castle and heroine of Peacock's novel *Melincourt.*

Melisande, in Maeterlinck's drama *Pelleas and Melisande,* is a little princess whom Goland finds beside a spring and marries.

Melmoth, Dr., in Hawthorne's *Fanshawe,* is president of Harley College.

Melmoth, John, an Irishman, the subject of Balzac's *Melmoth Reconciled,* a "Satanic character" who "died in the odor of sanctity."

Melnotte, Claude, the hero of Bulwer's play *The Lady of Lyons.*

Melusina, a fairy of French legend. She shut her father up in a mountain for some offense to her mother and was condemned to take the form of a serpent every Saturday. *Un cri de Melusine* is used for a shriek of dismay, like that of Melusine on the fatal Saturday.

Melville, Julia, betrothed to the jealous Faulkland in Sheridan's play *The Rivals* (1775).

Memnon, the subject of a novel by Voltaire.

Memnon, the hero of Beaumont and Fletcher's *The Mad Lover.*

Mendoza, Isaac, a rich, conceited, and gullible Jew in Sheridan's play *The Duenna.*

Menenius, Agrippa, a witty and discreet ambassador in Shakespeare's *Coriolanus.*

Menippus, a Greek cynic philosopher and satirist, from whose name is taken the title of a celebrated French satire (1594), *The Menippée,* directed against the Holy League, whose object was to dethrone Henri III and crown the Duc de Guise. The principal authors were P. Pithou, N. Rapin, Passerat, and Leroy.

Menœchmi, The, in the comedy of Plautus, were exactly alike; hence persons so resembling each other are called Menechmians.

Menteith, a thane of Scotland and character in Shakespeare's *Macbeth.*

Menteith, The Earl of, an important character in Scott's novel *The Legend of Montrose.*

Mephistopheles, Mephostophilis, Mephistophilus, or Mephisto, in demonology, was second to Satan in power among the devils, one of the fallen archangels. In Marlowe's tragedy *Dr. Faustus* (1589) he is the attendant demon of the philosopher, and also in Goethe's *Faust* and in Gounod's opera *Marguerite,* or *Faust.*

Mercadet, the type of an unscrupulous stock-jobber drawn by Balzac.

Mercedes, the chief character in a poetic tragedy by Thomas Bailey Aldrich, adapted from the Spanish.

Mercier, Claude, the hero of Weyman's novel *The Long Night.*

Mercutio, a friend of Romeo in Shakespeare's *Romeo and Juliet.*

Mercy, a young pilgrim in Bunyan's *Pilgrim's Progress.*

Merdle, in Dickens's *Little Dorrit,* is a London banker, called the "Master Mind of the Age."

Meredith, Janice, the heroine and title of a novel and drama of the American Revolution by Paul Leicester Ford.

Mergi, the name of a family, characters in Balzac's novel *The Seamy Side of History.*

Meridarpax, in Parnell's *The Battle of the Frogs and Mice* (1712), the Prince of Mice.

Meridies. See PERIMONES.

Merion, Dan, a character in Meredith's *Diana of the Crossways.*

Merlin, a great enchanter, of supernatural origin, who plays an important part in many of the romances of chivalry. *Merlin the Enchanter* is the title of a French "philosophic allegory" (1860) by Edgar Quinet.

Merlin, Hector, an unpleasant but able journalist in Balzac's *A Distinguished Provincial at Paris.*

Merrilies, Meg, a half-insane gipsy, a celebrated character in Scott's *Guy Mannering.*

Merry-Andrew, a street mountebank. The name is attributed to Andrew Borde (1500–1549), who was an itinerant physician, gathering crowds by humorous speeches at fairs and markets.

Merrygreek, Matthew, a servant in Udall's comedy *Ralph Roister Doister.*

Merry Monarch, The, Charles II of England (1630–1685).

Merton, Tommy, a leading character in Thomas Day's once popular work *Sandford and Merton.*

Mertoun, Basil, a pirate in Scott's *The Pirate.*

Mervyn, Arthur, the hero of Charles Brockden Brown's novel *Arthur Mervyn.*

Messala, an important character in *Ben Hur* by Lew Wallace.

Messenger, Angela, the heroine of Besant's *All Sorts and Conditions of Men* (1884).

Metellus Cimber, one of the conspirators, is a character in Shakespeare's *Julius Cæsar.*

Metternich, Prince, a character in Rostand's drama *L'Aiglon.*

Meyrick, the name of a family, characters in George Eliot's *Daniel Deronda.*

Micawber, Wilkins, a celebrated character in Dickens's *David Copperfield,* noted for his improvidence, his mercurial temperament, his high-flown rhetoric, his great schemes which always failed, and his waiting for something "to turn up," which last has become a proverbial expression. Many of his traits are said to have been taken from Dickens's father.

Michael, Cousin, sometimes used as a nickname for the German people, with reference especially to the phlegmatic character usually attributed to them. Michael in Germany is a general name for a rustic.

Michael, in George Lillo's tragedy *Arden of Feversham* (1739), which was altered from an anonymous play of 1592, sometimes attributed to Shakespeare, is a favorite of Arden, but through weakness plays into the hands of his murderers.

Michael, Duke of Strelsau, the villain of Anthony Hope's novel *The Prisoner of Zenda.*

Michael Armstrong, a factory boy, hero of Mrs. Trollope's novel of the name.

Michiela, a character in Meredith's novel *Vittoria.*

Micromegas (Little-great), the title and hero of a philosophic tale by Voltaire, a satire on Fontenelle's *Plurality of Worlds.*

Midas is the subject of a drama by Lyly (1553–1600) and of a burletta (1763) by O'Hara; also of an opera, *The Judgment of Midas,* by Grétry (1741–1813).

Middleham, Mary, the heroine of Maurice Hewlett's novel *Halfway House.*

Middlemas, Matthew, the assumed name of General Witherington in Scott's novel *The Surgeon's Daughter.*

Middleton, Clara, the heroine in George Meredith's *The Egoist,* is engaged to Sir Willoughby Patterne, but finds out his egotistical character in time to break the engagement.

Mignon, a very small but beautiful Italian girl in Goethe's *Wilhelm Meister's Apprenticeship.* The opera *Mignon* (1866) by Ambroise Thomas is based on Goethe's story.

Mignon, Marie-Modeste, an heiress, the heroine of Balzac's *Modeste Mignon.*

Milan, The Duke of, Prospero in Shakespeare's comedy *The Tempest.*

Milan, The Duke of, Silvia's father in Shakespeare's *Two Gentlemen of Verona.*

Milan, Sforza, Duke of, the subject of Massinger's tragedy *The Duke of Milan.*

Mildmay, Frank, the hero and title of a sea-story by Captain Marryat (1792–1848). His adventures are supposed to be taken from the author's own experience.

Mildred, Little, a junior subaltern in Kipling's *The Man Who Was.*

Milford, Jack, one of the youths in danger of ruin in Holcroft's comedy *The Road to Ruin* (1792).

Millamant, a noted character in Congreve's play *The Way of the World* (1700), a brilliant girl.

Millbank, in Disraeli's *Coningsby,* is supposed to be meant for William Ewart Gladstone.

Miller, Daisy, the subject of a story by Henry James, an American girl traveling in Europe.

Miller of Trompington, The, Simon Simkin, the subject of Chaucer's *The Reeve's Tale.*

Millwood, Sarah, the evil genius of the hero of George Lillo's tragedy *George Barnwell* (1732).

Milvey, The Reverend Frank, a curate in Dickens's *Our Mutual Friend.*

Mim, a profane showman in Dickens's *Doctor Marigold,* who sells his little deaf and dumb daughter to Doctor Marigold for six pairs of braces.

Minns, Augustus, the subject of the second part of Dickens's sketch *The Boarding House* (1834).

Minola, Baptista, the father of Katherine in Shakespeare's *The Taming of the Shrew.*

Minoret, Doctor Denis, the guardian of Ursule Mirouet in Balzac's novel of that name, a distinguished physician.

Mirabeau is a character in Dumas's *The Countess of Charny* and in Mühlbach's *Marie Antoinette.*

Mirah, Josepha, a prima donna of loose morals in Balzac's *Cousin Bette.*

Miramont, an ignorant old man but a great admirer of the learned in Fletcher's play *The Elder Brother.*

Miranda, the daughter of Prospero in Shakespeare's *The Tempest,* one of his most admired characters.

Miranda, the heroine of A. E. W. Mason's novel *Miranda of the Balcony.*

Miranda, Léonce, in Browning's *The Red Cotton Nightcap Country,* is the subject of a strange life-drama enacted in Normandy not long before the poem was written. His real name was Mellerio.

Miriam, an artist in Rome, one of the leading characters in Hawthorne's novel *The Marble Faun* (*Transformation*).

Mirouet, Ursule, title and heroine of a novel by Balzac.

Mirrha, the subject of one of Alfieri's best tragedies (1791).

Mirza, an imaginary character whose vision is often alluded to in literature. It is an allegory by Addison in No. 159 of *The Spectator.* Mirza beheld in a trance the river of time rolling through a valley and concealed at each end by a dense mist. Crossing it were many bridges, over which human beings were passing, and beyond were the dwellings of the blest; but when he would penetrate into the secrets of the other land the vision ended, and he saw only the valley of Bagdad.

Misérables, Les, the subject of Victor Hugo's most famous novel.

Mississippi Bubble, The. See LAW'S BUBBLE.

Mitaine, the godchild of Charlemagne in the romance *Croquemitaine*, who went toward Fear Fortress; but it receded and faded into thin air as she approached.

Mite, Sir Matthew, a vulgar, ostentatious, rich man in Foote's farce *The Nabob*, a returned East Indian merchant.

Moddle, Augustus, a character in Dickens's *Martin Chuzzlewit*.

Modish, Lady Betty, a noted character in Cibber's play *The Careless Husband* (1704).

Mohicans, The Last of the, in Cooper's novel of the name, is Uncas, called "Deerfoot."

Mohun, Lord, a dissipated man-about-town in Thackeray's *Esmond.* The original of the character is Lord Mohun, born about 1675, a notorious duelist. He was concerned in an attempt to abduct the actress Anne Bracegirdle, in which his friend Captain Hill killed the actor Will Mountford. He was tried twice for murder, but not convicted. In 1712 he fought in Hyde Park with the Duke of Hamilton over a question of property, and both were mortally wounded.

Molière, the French dramatist, whose real name was Poquelin. Goldoni is called the Italian Molière; Moratin, the Spanish.

Molyneux, Major, the subject of a curious tale of colonial times by Hawthorne.

Monaldi, the title and hero of a romance by Washington Allston (1779–1843).

Monarque, Le Grand, Louis XIV of France.

Monçada, Matthias de, in Scott's *The Surgeon's Daughter*, the grandfather of Richard Middlemas.

Moneytrap, a once popular character in VanBrugh's play *The Confederacy* (1695).

Mongenod, name of a family, important characters in Balzac's *The Seamy Side of History*.

Monimé, a noted character in Racine's tragedy *Mithridates*, one of Rachel's great rôles.

Monimia, the title character of Otway's tragedy *The Or-*

phan (1680); also the tearful heroine of Charlotte Smith's novel *The Old Manor House* (1793).

Moniplies, Richie, a Scotchman, honest and conceited, in Scott's *The Fortunes of Nigel.*

Monk, The, the hero and title of a tale (1794) by Matthew Gregory Lewis.

Monks, a scoundrel in Dickens's *Oliver Twist,* whose real name was *Edward Leeford.*

Monmouth, Lord, in Disraeli's novel *Coningsby,* is "a refined voluptuary," the hero's grandfather.

Monmouth, The Duke of, is a character in Scott's novel *Old Mortality;* also in Anthony Hope's *Simon Dale.* He is the Absalom of Dryden's poem *Absalom and Achitophel.*

Monsieur: This title alone was used to designate Philippe, Duke of Orléans, brother of Louis XIV.

Montalban, Don Kyrie Elyson de, a hero in an old romance, *Tirante the White.*

Montalban, Rinaldo de, a hero in *The Mirror of Knighthood,* a romance of chivalry in Don Quixote's library.

Montargis, The Dog of. See MACAIRE.

Montauran, Marquis de, a royalist at the time of the French Revolution, governor under Louis XVIII of Brittany, Normandy, Maine, and Anjou, a character in Balzac's *The Chouans.*

Montcornet, Maréchal, Comte de, nicknamed "The Upholsterer," because the son of a Parisian cabinet-maker, is a character in many of Balzac's novels, *Domestic Peace, Lost Illusions,* and others.

Montdidier, Aubri de. See MACAIRE.

Monte Cristo, Count of, Edmond Dantes, the hero of the celebrated romance *The Count of Monte Cristo* by Alexandre Dumas (1803–1870). A popular play is founded upon the novel.

Montesinos, a hero of the ballads and romances of chivalry. He lived in a cave in La Mancha, which was visited by Don Quixote.

Montespan, Madame de, a mistress of Louis XIV, is a character in Bulwer's *The Duchesse de la Vallière* (1836).

Montfort, the hero and title of a tragedy (1798) by Joanna Baillie.

Montgomery, Ellen, the heroine of Miss Warner's *The Wide, Wide World.*

Monticello, The Sage of, Thomas Jefferson, whose country-seat in Virginia was named Monticello.

Montoni, the owner of Udolpho Castle in Mrs. Radcliffe's *The Mysteries of Udolpho.*

Montoria, Augustine, the hero of *Saragossa* by Galdós.

Montorio, the hero of Maturin's novel *The Fatal Revenge.*

Montreale, Ginevra di, the heroine of *Ettore Fieramosca* by Massimo Taparelli d' Azeglio.

Montreville, Adela, a begum called the "Queen of Sheba" in Scott's novel *The Surgeon's Daughter.*

Montriveau, General, a soldier of many adventures, in several of Balzac's novels, *The Thirteen* and others.

Montrose, The Duke of, commander of the royal army, appears in Scott's *Rob Roy.*

Montserrat, Conrade, Marquis of, a crusader engaged in many plots in Scott's *The Talisman* (1825).

Monumental City, The, Baltimore.

Moodie, Old, a mysterious character in Hawthorne's *The Blithedale Romance.*

Moore, Hortense, and her brothers, **Louis** and **Robert,** important characters in Charlotte Brontë's *Shirley.*

Moore, Arthur Wellington, the title character of Ralph Connor's *The Sky Pilot* (1899).

Morakanabad, grand vizier of the Caliph in Beckford's *Vathek.*

Morat, an important character in Dryden's *Aurungzebe.*

Mordecai, a Jew in George Eliot's *Daniel Deronda,* who believes it his mission to restore Israel to Palestine.

Mordure, the name given in Spenser's *The Faerie Queene* to the magic sword given to Arthur by Merlin.

More, of More Hall, a legendary hero who slew the Dragon of Wantley. In Corey's burlesque *The Dragon of Wantley* he is called Moore.

More, Sir Thomas (1478–1535), Lord Chancellor under Henry VIII, is the subject of a historical play of unknown authorship, supposed to have been written about 1590. *The Household of Sir Thomas More* (1851) is by Miss Anne Manning.

Moreau, Frederick, the chief character in Flaubert's *Sentimental Education.*

Morell, Candida, the title character of Shaw's drama *Candida.* She is "straight for natural, not conventional reasons," and has the ability to give the impression that she is the ideal "womanly woman."

Morelle, Guy and **Philip,** the chief characters of Miss Yonge's *The Heir of Redclyffe.*

Morgan, the name assumed by Belarius in Shakespeare's *Cymbeline.*

Morgan, The Rev. William, the rector in Mrs. Oliphant's *The Chronicles of Carlingford* and *The Perpetual Curate.*

Morgiana, the cunning slave of Ali Baba in the *Arabian Nights* story *The Forty Thieves.*

Morhault, Moraunt, or **Morhaus, Sir,** a knight of *Meliadus* and other romances of chivalry.

Moria, the guardian of the nymphs, "all voice and air," in Ben Jonson's *Cynthia's Revels.*

Morland, Catharine, the heroine of Jane Austen's *Northanger Abbey.*

Morland, Henry, the title character of Colman's play *The Heir-at-Law.*

Moros, the chief character of a moral play of the time of Elizabeth, *The Longer Thou Livest the More Foole Thou Art.*

Morose, an old miser, successfully tricked by his nephew, Sir Dauphine, in Ben Jonson's *The Silent Woman.*

Morris, in Scott's *Rob Roy,* drowned by order of Helen Campbell when she hears of the capture of her husband, for whom he was hostage.

Morris, Dinah, a Methodist preacher, heroine of George Eliot's *Adam Bede.* The character is said to have been drawn from Elizabeth Evans, the author's aunt.

Morsfield, Adolphus, a personage of Meredith's story *Lord Ormont and His Aminta* (1894).

Mortality, Old, the title and a character of a novel by Sir Walter Scott.

Mortemar, Julie de, the ward of the Cardinal in **Bulwer's** *Richelieu.*

Mortiboy, Richard Matthew, the chief character in *Ready-Money Mortiboy* by Besant and Rice.

Mortimer, Sir Hugh and **Sir John,** characters in Shakespeare's *Henry VI*, Part III.

Mortimer, Mr., in Cumberland's play *The Fashionable Lover*, "did a thousand noble acts without the credit for one."

Morton, the minister of Cairn Vrechan in Scott's *Waverley*.

Morton, Henry, son of Col. Silas and nephew of Ralph, an important character in Scott's *Old Mortality*.

Morton, The Earl of, a character in Scott's novels *The Monastery* and *The Abbot*.

Morton, Ralph, a character in Meredith's *The Ordeal of Richard Feverel*.

Mortsheugh, Johnnie, a grave-digger in Scott's novel *The Bride of Lammermoor*, who says to Edgar: "As brent as your brow is, there is something sitting upon it this day as near akin to death as to wedlock!"

Mosca, in Ben Jonson's play *Volpone* (1605), is the accomplice of "the fox," and afterward betrays him.

Moses, the subject of one of Rossini's best operas (1827).

Moth, the witty page of Don Adriano in Shakespeare's *Love's Labor's Lost*.

Moth, one of the fairies in Shakespeare's *A Midsummer Night's Dream*.

Mother Bunch, the imaginary author of a once popular book (1760) professing to teach "ingenious young men and maids how to get good wives and husbands."

Mother Goose, the fictitious author of Perrault's famous fairy tales.

Mother Goose, a Boston woman whose rhymes as she sang them to her grandchild were taken down and published by her son-in-law, Thomas Fleet, a printer, in 1719.

Mother Nicneven, a leader of witches and elves. The name is assumed by Magdalen Graeme in Scott's novel *The Abbot*.

Mother Shipton, the reputed author of a series of predictions which are often quoted—one, especially, that "carriages without horses shall go."

Motte, La, a character in Mrs. Radcliffe's *Romance of the Forest*.

Mould, Mr., an undertaker in Dickens's *Martin Chuzzlewit.*

Mouillard, the chief character in Bazin's *The Ink-Stain.*

Mouldy, Ralph, a recruit for Falstaff's regiment in Shakespeare's *Henry IV,* Part II.

Mound City, St. Louis, so called from artificial mounds in its vicinity.

Mountfalcon, Lord, a character in Meredith's *The Ordeal of Richard Feverel.*

Mowbray, Clara, and her brother, prominent characters in Scott's *St. Ronan's Well.*

Mowbray, Stella, the heroine of William E. Norris's *The Rogue.*

Mucklebackit, Saunders and **Maggie,** an old fisherman and his wife in Scott's *The Antiquary.*

Muff, Professor, a prominent member of *The Mudfog Association,* a sketch in which Dickens satirized the proceedings of the British Association for the Advancement of Science.

Muff, Sir Henry, one of the candidates for Parliament in Dudley's comedy *The Rival Candidates* (1775).

Muffat de Beuville, Count, a character in Zola's *Nana.*

Mug, Matthew, in Foote's farce *The Mayor of Garratt* (1763), is said to be a caricature of the Duke of Newcastle.

Muggins, Huggins and, an expression for the personnel of a crowd. There is a theory that they are a corruption of the Dutch words *Hooge en Mogende,* high and mighty, which were used in ridicule by English writers in the seventeenth century. Butler gives them, "Hogen Mogen."

Mugwump, a word used in the United States to designate a body of Independents in politics, who in 1884 left the Republican party and supported the Democratic candidate for the Presidency. The word is of Indian origin and was used for a leader or captain; in the Indian Bible it is spelled *Mugquomp.*

Muhldenau, the minister in Knowles's drama *The Maid of Mariendorpt* (1838), who was condemned as a spy at Prague. The play is said to be from a novel by Jane Porter, *The Village of Mariendorpt.*

Mulla, The Bard of, Edmund Spenser, who gave that name to a stream near which he lived in Ireland.

Mullit, Professor, the author of some powerful pamphlets over the signature of Suturb (Brutus, reversed) in Dickens's *Martin Chuzzlewit.*

Mulvaney, one of Kipling's *Soldiers Three,* a witty and reckless private in the British army.

Mumblazen, Michael, an old man in Scott's *Kenilworth.*

Mumblecrust, Madge, a character in Udall's comedy *Ralph Roister Doister,* whose name is used also in other comedies.

Mumbo Jumbo, an African bugbear, described by Mungo Park, who says it is much used by the natives to keep the women in subjection. Disguised as the bogie, one of them comes with hideous noise, picks out the offender and proceeds to scourge her amid the jeers of the gathered crowd.

Munchausen, Baron, the fictitious author of a book of travels gathered from various sources by Rudolf Eric Raspe (London, 1786). The adventures of the Baron are taken in part from a German work, *Travels of the Finkenritter,* published 200 years earlier, and some from the "Mendacia Ridicola" in Lange's *Deliciæ Academicæ* (Heilbronn, 1665); a few also from Lucian's account of the discoveries in the moon. The name is said to have been taken from one Münchhausen (1720–1797), a German officer in the Russian service, who was notorious for his extraordinary stories of his adventures.

Mundungus, a nickname given by Sterne in his *Sentimental Journey* to one Dr. Samuel Sharp, who published a dull account of his travels on the Continent.

Murat, Joachim, King of Naples, appears in Balzac's *Colonel Chabert* and other of his novels.

Murcraft, a "projector," or "promoter," in Ben Jonson's comedy *The Devil's an Ass.*

Murdochson, Madge, known as Madge Wildfire, a pathetic character in Scott's *The Heart of Midlothian* (1818).

Murdstone, Edward, the cold, heartless stepfather of David in Dickens's *David Copperfield.*

Murray or **Moray,** James Stuart, called the "Good Regent," a natural son of James V of Scotland. He appears in Scott's novels *The Monastery* and *The Abbot.*

Muse, The Tenth: several writers have been so called: Marie Lejars de Gournay (1566–1645); Antoinette Deshoulieres, also called the "French Calliope" (1633–1694); Mademoiselle Scudéry (1607–1701), famous in connection with the "Map of the Kingdom of Tenderness"; Madame Émile de Girardin (Delphine Gay), who wrote under the name "Vicomte de Launay" (1804–1855); Juana Inés de la Cruz (1651–1695), a Mexican poet, who became a nun and lost her life caring for the victims of an epidemic, also called the "Nun of Mexico"; Anne Bradstreet (1612–1672) of Massachusetts, whose poems were issued in London in 1650, the title beginning "The Tenth Muse Lately Sprung up in America."

Musgrave, Frank, an unprincipled young man in Ouida's novel *Nancy*.

Musgrave, Hilary, and his wife, characters in *The Dolly Dialogues* by Anthony Hope.

Musidorus, a hero in Sidney's *Arcadia,* Prince of Thessalia, supposed to be intended for Fulke Greville.

Mustapha, Aladdin's father in the *Arabian Nights*.

Mustapha, Baba, a character in Meredith's *The Shaving of Shagpat*.

Myles, Stapledon, a character in *Sons of the Morning* by Eden Phillpotts.

Mylrea, Thorkell, the title character of Hall Caine's *The Deemster*.

Myriel, a character in Victor Hugo's *Les Misérables*.

Myrrha, a favorite Ionian slave of the King in Byron's tragedy *Sardanapalus*.

Mysinger. See Fenia.

Mystic, Moley, of Cimmerian Lodge, in Peacock's *Melincourt,* is intended for Coleridge.

Mytharete, Pisistratus, appears in Meredith's *One of Our Conquerors* (1891).

Nala, a legendary king of India, the subject of an episode in the *Muhâbhârata,* translated by Henry Hart Milman.

Namby, Major, a ridiculous retired officer in a sketch by Wilkie Collins, *Pray Employ Major Namby*.

Namby Pamby, the subject of a poem by Henry Carey (1663–1743) burlesquing Ambrose Philips's lines on an infant. This is said to be the origin of the term.

Nameless City, The, ancient Rome, said to have had an earlier name which it was death to pronounce.

Nana, the subject of a novel by Zola, a public singer who could not sing, but fascinated by her wonderful beauty.

Nancy, a pathetic character in Dickens's *Oliver Twist*, mistress of the brutal Bill Sykes.

Nancy, the title character of one of Ouida's best novels.

Nanon, called Nanon the Great from her height, six feet four, in Balzac's *Eugénie Grandet*.

Narcissa, in Pope's *Moral Essays*, is intended for Mrs. Oldfield, the actress.

Narcissa, in Young's *Night Thoughts*, his stepdaughter, Mrs. Temple. Philander in the same poem is her husband.

Natascha, in Gorky's drama *Nachtasyl* (The Night Refuge), is a character of mingled good and bad.

Nathan, Raoul, son of a Jewish pawnbroker, one of the best-known writers in Paris. He is a character in *Lost Illusions* and many other novels of Balzac.

Nathaniel, Sir, a grotesque curate in Shakespeare's *Love's Labor's Lost*.

Natty Bumppo. See LEATHER-STOCKING.

Navarro, Don José, an important character in Mérimée's novel *Carmen* and in the opera of that name.

Neæra, the name of a girl mentioned by Horace, Virgil, and Tibullus; it is used as a general name for a sweetheart.

Nebuchadnezzar is the subject of an opera (1842) by Verdi.

Neckett, Charlotte, called Charley, the daughter of a sheriff's officer in Dickens's *Bleak House*.

Nectabanus, a dwarf at the Hermit's Chapel in Scott's novel *The Talisman*.

Needy Knife-Grinder, The, the subject of a noted satire by Canning on the pseudo-philanthropist.

Neeld, Jenkinson, an important character in Anthony Hope's *Tristram of Blent*.

Negroni, Princess, a friend of Lucrezia and a prisoner in Donizetti's opera *Lucrezia di Borgia*.

Nekayah, a sister of the hero of Johnson's *Rasselas*.

Nehludoff, Prince, a character in Tolstoi's *Resurrection*.

Nell, Little, Nelly Trent, the heroine of Dickens's *The Old Curiosity Shop*, a lovely child, the victim of her grandfather's mania for gambling.

Nemesis, the goddess of retribution; used in the general sense of avenger—as in the title of Froude's early work *The Nemesis of Faith*. *Nemesis* is the title of a series of remarkable political satires (1831–1832) in French by Barthélemy and Méry.

Nemo, Captain, the owner and captain of the submarine boat in Jules Verne's novel *Twenty Thousand Leagues Under the Sea*.

Nerine, Doto, and **Nysê,** nereids represented in the *Lusiad* of Camoëns as guarding Vasco da Gama's ships.

Nerissa, Portia's maid in Shakespeare's *The Merchant of Venice*.

Nero, the Roman emperor from 54 to 68, is the subject of a tragedy (1675) by Lee, and of one by Stephen Phillips; also of an opera by Rubinstein (1879). He is a character in *Quo Vadis?* by Sienkiewicz, and the drama founded upon it.

Nerones, the heroine of an old morality, *The History of Clyomon and Clamydes*. She follows the knight Sir Clyomon in the guise of a page.

Neston, George, the principal character in Anthony Hope's *Mr. Witt's Widow*.

Neuvillette, Christian de, a handsome but stupid youth, loved by Roxane, in Rostand's tragedy *Cyrano de Bergerac*.

Neve, Rachel, a leading character in *The Hypocrites*, a play by Henry A. Jones.

Nevil, Oswald, Lord, a leading personage of Madame de Staël's *Corinne* (1807).

Neville, Major, in Scott's *The Antiquary*, has assumed the name Lovel, and is found to be the son of Lord Glenallan.

Neville, Miss, the friend of Kate Hardcastle in Goldsmith's *She Stoops to Conquer*.

Neville, Marmaduke, in Bulwer's *The Last of the Barons*, is the lover of Sibyl Warner.

Neville, Sir Henry, a character in Scott's *The Talisman*.

Newfangle, Nichol, the hero of an old moral play (1568) by Ulpin Fulwell, said on the title-page to be "very godly and ful of pleasant mirth."

Oberon, a pen-name used by Hawthorne in some of his contributions to periodicals. It is the name of a literary law-student in his tale *The Devil in Manuscript,* and is that of the title character in his *Journal of a Solitary Man.*

Oberthal, Count, Lord of Dordrecht, the enemy of John of Leyden, who perishes with him, in Meyerbeer's opera *Le Prophète* (1849).

Obidicut, one of the fiends in Shakespeare's *King Lear.*

O'Brallaghan, Sir Callaghan, an Irish soldier in the Prussian army in Macklin's *Love à-la-Mode* (1759).

O'Brien, Cornelius, an important character of Louis Amedée Achard's *Belle-Rose.*

Obstinate, in Bunyan's *Pilgrim's Progress,* counsels Christian not to run on a wild chase.

O'Cataract, a name applied, on account of his impetuous disposition, to John Neal (1793–1876), a versatile American writer, author of *Keep Cool* and other works. He used the sobriquet as a pen-name in some of his writings.

Ochiltree, an old bedesman in Scott's novel *The Antiquary.*

Octave de T——, hero and narrator of De Musset's novel *A Child of the Century.*

Octave or **Octavian,** a character in Molière's *The Cheats of Scapin.*

Octavia, the wife of Antony, introduced in Shakespeare's *Antony and Cleopatra* and in Dryden's *All for Love.*

Odiot, Maxime, Marquis de Champcey d'Hauterive, the title character of Feuillet's *The Romance of a Poor Young Man* and of the play founded upon it.

O'Doherty, Sir Morgan, a pen-name of William Maginn (1793–1842).

O'Donohue, a specter supposed to cross the Lake of Killarney on his white horse every May-day. The boatmen call the white waves on windy days, "O'Donohue's horses."

O'Dowd, Mrs., a character in Thackeray's *Vanity Fair,* who follows her husband, the Major, all over the world.

O'Ferrall, Trilby. See TRILBY.

Offa, a king that married a wood-nymph, the subject of a legend frequently appearing in old romances.

Ogier the Dane, a legendary hero of Charlemagne's time; he appears in Ariosto's *Orlando Furioso* and other tales and poems of romance, and in Morris's *The Earthly Paradise.*

Ogilvy, Margaret, the title character of a novel by James M. Barrie, said to be drawn from the author's mother.

Ogleby, Lord, in Garrick and Colman's play *The Clandestine Marriage,* is a benevolent old man with a weakness for affecting the graces of youth.

O'Groat, John, a traditionary character whose name appears in "John O'Groat's House," designating the most northerly point in Great Britain. The story is that John of Groat and his brothers were settlers from Holland; and that when a quarrel about precedence arose he built an octagonal house with a door in each side, and, within, an octagonal table, so that each of the eight contestants might consider himself first.

O'Hara Family, The, the subject of a work by John and Michael Banim (1825–1826), tales of Irish life.

Oldbuck, Jonathan, the title character of Scott's novel *The Antiquary,* called Monkbarns, from his estate.

Oldcastle, Sir John, a play printed in 1600, by an anonymous author, founded upon the history of Sir John Oldcastle, Lord Cobham, a follower of Wickliffe, who fell a martyr to his faith in 1417. This name was first given to Falstaff; but as the character was taken to be intended for a portrait of the real Sir John Oldcastle, Shakespeare changed the name; and, to make it clear, said in the epilogue to the second part of *King Henry IV,* "for Oldcastle died a martyr, and this is not the man."

Oldcraft, Sir Perfidious, a prominent character in the Beaumont and Fletcher play *Wit at Several Weapons* (1647).

Oldfield, Anne, a noted actress, is the heroine of a short play by Charles Reade, *Nance Oldfield,* and a character in *Richard Savage,* a play by Madeleine L. Ryley.

Old Grog: Admiral Edward Vernon (1684–1757) was so called from the grogram cloak he wore in bad weather. The word was afterward applied to the intoxicant used on his ship.

Old Man of the Mountain, The, a name sometimes given to the profile formed by the rocks on the edge of a cliff in the Franconia group of the White Mountains in New Hampshire, bearing a remarkable resemblance to the face of an old man. It suggested Hawthorne's tale *The Great Stone Face.*

Old Man of the Mountains, The, a title given to the founder of a Syrian dynasty, A.D. 1090, whose residence was in the mountains.

Old Man of the Sea, The, the monster that clung to the shoulders of Sindbad the Sailor in the *Arabian Nights.*

Olifant, the famous horn of Orlando, or Roland, the paladin.

Olifaunt, Nigel, Lord of Glenvarloch, the hero of Scott's novel *The Fortunes of Nigel.*

Oliferno, one of Godfrey's captains in Tasso's *Jerusalem Delivered.*

Oliver, one of Charlemagne's twelve peers.

Oliver, the elder son of Sir Rowland de Bois in Shakespeare's *As You Like It.*

Olivia, a wealthy countess in Shakespeare's *Twelfth Night.*

Olivia, one of the daughters of Dr. Primrose (*q.v.*).

Olivia, the title character of Knowles's play *The Rose of Aragon* (1842).

Olivia de Zuniga, the leading character in Mrs. Cowley's comedy *A Bold Stroke for a Husband* (1782). The "bold stroke" consisted in disgusting all suitors until the one of her choice appeared.

Ollapod, an apothecary in Colman's play *The Poor Gentleman,* also a cornet in the volunteers, a "jumble of physic and shooting."

Ollomand, an enchanter in Ridley's *Tales of the Genii,* destroyed in his own trap.

O'Malley, Charles, the title and hero's name of a novel by Charles Lever.

Omnium, The Duke of, a character in Anthony Trollope's parliamentary novels.

O'More, Frank, the hero of Baroness Tautphœus's *At Odds.*

O'More, Rory, the hero of a song and a novel of the same name by Samuel Lover.

Omri, in Dryden's *Absalom and Achitophel,* is the Lord Chancellor, Heneage Finch.

O'Neill, Nora, the real name of the heroine of Mrs. Croker's *Pretty Miss Neville.*

Onesta, Lady, a character in Machiavelli's novel *Belphegor.*

Only, The (*Der Einzige*), a title given to the German romancer Jean Paul Friedrich Richter.

Ophelia, the heroine of Shakespeare's *Hamlet.*

Opimian, Dr., an easy-going clergyman in Peacock's novel *Gryll Grange.*

Opium-Eater, The English, Thomas De Quincey, author of *The Confessions of an English Opium-Eater* (1822).

Ople, General Wilson, an egoistic officer, retired, in George Meredith's story *The Case of General Ople and Lady Camper.*

Orc, a devouring sea-monster in Ariosto's *Orlando Furioso.*

Ordella, in Fletcher's play *Thierry and Theodoret,* the wife of Thierry. Charles Lamb is quoted as calling her "the most perfect idea of the female heroic character, next to Ford's Calantha in *The Broken Heart,* that has been embodied in fiction."

Ordigale, the otter in *Reynard the Fox.*

Orgarita, the heroine of Stirling's drama *The Orphan of the Frozen Sea* (1856).

Orgilus, in Ford's tragedy *The Broken Heart,* was condemned to death for the murder of Ithocles, who had compelled his sister Penthea, the betrothed of Orgilus, to marry a man, Bassanes, whom she hated.

Orgoglio, a hideous giant in Spenser's poem *The Faerie Queene,* who enslaved the Red-Cross Knight and was slain by Arthur.

Orgon, the credulous dupe of Tartuffe in Molière's comedy *Tartuffe.*

Oriana, the daughter of Lisuarte, an imaginary king of England, beloved by Amadis de Gaul.

Oriana, a name applied to Queen Elizabeth in a series of madrigals, *The Triumphs of Oriana* (1601), celebrating her beauty and virtue.

Oriana, the heroine of Fletcher's play *The Wild-Goose Chase* (1652).

Oriana, the heroine of Farquhar's play *The Inconstant* (1702).

Oriande, a fay who brought up Maugis in the *Romance de Maugis d'Aygremont,* and was in love with him.

Origilla, a lady in Ariosto's *Orlando Furioso,* who deserted Gryphon for a swaggering coward, Martano.

Orillo, a magician in Ariosto's *Orlando Furioso,* vulnerable only at one hair, which Astolpho cut off and laid him dead.

Orlando or **Roland,** the nephew of Charlemagne, killed at Roncesvalles. He is the hero of many romances of chivalry, the most famous of which are Turold's *Chanson de Roland,* Boiardo's *Orlando Innamorato* and Ariosto's *Orlando Furioso.* In the last named he is driven mad by jealousy on account of Angelica's love for Medoro, but is restored to sanity by Astolpho, who brings his wits in a vial from the moon. He is always represented as a brave and beautiful character. *Roland and Farragus* is founded on the old *History of Charlemagne and Orlando.*

Orlando, the lover of Rosalind in Shakespeare's *As You Like It.*

Orleans, the lover of Agripyna in Dekker's *Old Fortunatus* (1600), described by Lamb as talking "pure Biron and Romeo" —"almost as poetical as they, quite as philosophical, only a little madder."

Orléans, The Bastard of, Count of Dunois and Longueville, one of the greatest soldiers of his time, is a character in Schiller's *The Maid of Orléans* under the name Dunois.

Orléans, Charles d'Angoulême, Duke of, a character in Shakespeare's *Henry V.* Captured at Agincourt, he was kept in the Tower twenty-five years. His son reigned as Louis XII.

Orléans, Gaston, Duke of, brother of Louis XIII, a character in Bulwer's *Richelieu* (1839). He leads an unsuccessful conspiracy to assassinate Richelieu and dethrone the King.

Orléans, Louis, Duke of, in Scott's *Quentin Durward,* is rejoiced at being released from his engagement to the Princess Joan.

Orlick, Dolge, a surly slouching workman employed by Joe Gargery in Dickens's *Great Expectations.*

Ormandine, a necromancer in *The Seven Champions of Christendom,* a noted compilation (1595), by Richard Johnson, of old Arabian romances.

Ormond, the title and hero's name of a novel by Maria Edgeworth.

Ormont, a disappointed cavalry officer married to a woman much younger, title character of Meredith's *Lord Ormont and His Aminta.*

Oronte, a personage in Molière's *The Misanthrope,* called "the man of the sonnet," in allusion to his sonnet which the misanthrope praised as "good to put into the cabinet."

Oroondates, a character noted for generosity and devotion in La Calprenède's romance *Cassandra,* in love with Statira, widow of Alexander the Great.

Oroonoko, Prince, son of the King of Angola, captured and sold as a slave in a West Indian island. Aphra Behn founded a novel on his story, and Thomas Southerne dramatized it (1696).

Orosmane, a leading character in Voltaire's tragedy *Zaïre,* carried away by unjust jealousy.

Orozembo, a brave and defiant old Peruvian in Sheridan's tragedy *Pizarro* (1799).

Orphan of the Temple, the daughter of Louis XVI, who was imprisoned in the Temple.

Orsino, Duke of Illyria, a leading character in Shakespeare's *Twelfth Night,* a suitor of Olivia.

Ortheris, a British soldier, one of Kipling's famous trio of privates in *Soldiers Three.*

Ortis, Jacopo, the supposed writer of the *Letters of Jacopo Ortis* by Ugo Foscolo, a remarkable document of Italian patriotism.

Orville, Lord, the hero of Miss Burney's *Evelina* (1778).

Osbaldistone, Frank, a leading character in Scott's *Rob Roy,* in love with Diana Vernon. His cousin Rashleigh is a treacherous villain killed by Rob Roy.

Osborne, the name of a family in Thackeray's *Vanity Fair.* Mr. Osborne is rich, avaricious, and purse-proud, and his daughters are much like him. His son George, selfish and vain, marries Amelia Sedley and is killed at Waterloo.

O'Shanter, Tam. See TAM O'SHANTER.

Osmond, Gilbert, the egoistic husband of the heroine of Henry James's novel *The Portrait of a Lady.*

Osmyn, whose real name was Alphonso, the hero of Congreve's play *The Mourning Bride* (1697), a favorite rôle of John Philip Kemble; Mrs. Siddons played Zara, the heroine.

Osric, a foppish courtier in Shakespeare's *Hamlet.*

Ossian or **Oisin,** a Celtic warrior and poet who figures in the legendary history of Ireland and the Scottish Highlands. He became known through James Macpherson (1738–1796), who issued two epics, *Fingal* and *Temora,* which he represented as translations from Ossian. They were received with great enthusiasm, but controversy soon arose over their genuineness, the weight of opinion inclining to their condemnation as forgeries. There are, however, remains of Ossian's poems in existence; an Ossianic society was formed; and the study of the ancient literature of Ireland has been promoted during the early years of the twentieth century by the work of the Gaelic League.

Oswald, Goneril's villainous steward in Shakespeare's *King Lear.*

Othello, one of the great characters of Shakespeare in *Othello: the Moor of Venice*—noble, affectionate, credulous, and inflammable, he falls an easy victim to Iago's arts. The story is from an Italian tale by Giraldo Cinthio (1565).

Otho the Great, the subject of a tragedy written by Keats in collaboration with a friend of his named Brown.

Otnit, a fabulous emperor of Lombardy; in the *Heldenbuch* (Book of Heroes) of the twelfth century he is aided by Alberich or Oberon to marry the Soldan of Syria's daughter.

O'Trigger, Sir Lucius, one of the chief characters of Sheridan's play *The Rivals,* a fortune-hunter and ready fighter.

Ottilia, a German princess with whom Harry in Meredith's novel *The Adventures of Harry Richmond* falls in love.

Otto, the victim of his brother Rollo in Beaumont and Fletcher's play *The Bloody Brother.*

Otto, Count, a character in Meredith's *The Adventures of Harry Richmond.*

Otto, Prince, the hero and title of a novel by Stevenson.

Overdo, Justice, a noted character in Ben Jonson's play *Bartholomew Fair* (1614).

Overreach, Sir Giles, a famous rascal in Massinger's play *A New Way to Pay Old Debts,* said to represent a notorious usurer of the time, Sir Giles Mompesson.

Owleglas, Tyll (*Eulenspiegel*), the hero of a popular German tale supposed to have been written by a Franciscan friar,

Thomas Murner (1475–1530). He is a droll, wandering mechanic, given to odd pranks, freaks, and practical jokes, and supposed to have been a real person. Two places claim his grave, Möllen, near Lübeck, where his tombstone has a sculptured owl and a glass upon it, and Damme in Belgium. The story has been more than once translated into English.

Oxford, Captain Harry, a character in George Meredith's novel *The Egoist.*

Oxford, John de Vere, Earl of, a character in Shakespeare's *Henry VI,* Part III, and *Richard III.* He was one of the most powerful supporters of Richmond, for whom he fought at Bosworth.

Ozymandias, a legendary king of ancient Egypt, who was said to have built the first library of which history makes mention, whose door bore the inscription "Treasury of the remedies of the soul."

Pacchiarotto, a painter of Siena, whose name is the title of a poem by Browning on theoretical reformers, a society of whom he calls Bardotti, a word meaning free horses that walk along by a load while others draw it.

Pacolet, a celebrated dwarf in the old romance *Valentine and Orson,* who had an enchanted wooden horse.

Page, Mistress, one of the merry wives in Shakespeare's *The Merry Wives of Windsor.*

Paillasse, a sort of clown of the old Italian stage, introduced into France. The word is used in French as a synonym for a "man without convictions."

Palamon. See ARCITE.

Palfrey, Prudence, the title and heroine's name of a novel by Thomas B. Aldrich.

Palinode, a shepherd in Spenser's *Eclogues,* supposed to represent the Catholic clergy.

Palinurus, in Virgil's *Æneid,* the pilot who fell asleep and tumbled into the sea.

Palliser, Plantagenet, an English statesman, an important character in *Can You Forgive Her?* and others of Anthony Trollope's parliamentary novels.

Palmerin of England, The, the hero and title of an old romance of chivalry, which, the curé in *Don Quixote* says, "shall be preserved as a relique of antiquity and placed in such a chest as Alexander found amongst the spoils of Darius and in which he kept the writings of Homer." Another book, *The Palmerin de Oliva*, he said should "be torn in pieces and burnt to the last ember."

Palmet, Lord, a character in Meredith's novel *Beauchamp's Career.*

Palomides, the hero of Maeterlinck's drama *Alladine and Palomides.*

Pamela, one of the heroines of Sidney's *Arcadia.*

Pamela, the title character of a celebrated novel (1740) by Richardson, the maid of a lady whose son marries her after trying vainly to make her his mistress—regarded as a great triumph of virtue. Goldoni, the Italian dramatist, borrowed the plot; but in deference to the class prejudices of his audiences, as he explains, he was obliged to have Pamela revealed as the daughter of an exiled nobleman disguised as a peasant.

Pamina and **Tamino,** the lovers in Mozart's opera *The Magic Flute.*

Pan, the god, in *A Musical Instrument*, by Mrs. Browning, an allegory, is represented as "making a poet out of a man"; and in *The Dead Pan* she uses the tradition that at the time of the crucifixion a sigh was heard from all the divinities of forests, streams, and mountains: "Great Pan is dead!"

Pandarus, a noted Lycian archer in the Trojan army, represented in medieval romance and in Chaucer and Spenser as a despicable go-between, giving rise to the word "pander." He appears in *Troilus and Cressida.*

Pandosto, the subject of a romance (1588) by Robert Greene, from which Shakespeare drew the story of *A Winter's Tale.*

Pandulph, the wily legate of the Pope in Shakespeare's *King John.*

Pangloss, Dr., a character in Voltaire's romance *Candide.* His name is a synonym for an absurd optimist.

Pangloss, Peter, LL.D. and A.S.S., a pompous prig in Colman's play *The Heir-at-Law* (1797).

Panjandrum, The Grand, a name used for a petty potentate, or one that assumes magisterial airs. It occurs in a nonsense paragraph written by Foote, the comic dramatist, to test the memory of an actor who had boasted that he could learn anything from one hearing.

Panscope, Mr., in Peacock's *Headlong Hall*, professes to be a universal philosopher.

Pantagruel, the subject of a satirical romance by Rabelais. He is an immense giant, able to shelter a whole army under his tongue.

Pantaloon, a foolish old man in Italian popular pantomime.

Panthea, the inane heroine of Fletcher's *King and No King.*

Panther, The, in Dryden's poem *The Hind and the Panther;* the latter is the Church of England.

Panurge, the favorite and follower of Pantagruel in the romance of the latter name by Rabelais, "a licentious, intemperate, cowardly rogue."

Panza, Sancho, the matter-of-fact, unimaginative, vulgar squire of Don Quixote.

Paolo Malatesta, a character in D'Annunzio's drama *Francesca da Rimini*, in F. Marion Crawford's drama of the same name, and in Stephen Phillips's drama *Paolo and Francesca.*

Paperstamp, Mr., in Peacock's *Melincourt*, is intended for Wordsworth, in allusion to his office.

Paracelsus, a physicist (1493–1541), the subject of a poem by Browning, in which he is represented as giving his friends a review of the significant epochs of his soul-experience.

Parbury, the hero of Haddon Chambers's comedy *The Tyranny of Tears.*

Pardiggle, Mrs., a type of philanthropist in Dickens's *Bleak House.*

Paribanou, a fairy who gives a magic tent to Prince Ahmed in the *Arabian Nights.*

Paridel, Sir, a Lothario in Spenser's *The Faerie Queene.*

Paris, cousin and suitor of Juliet in Shakespeare's *Romeo and Juliet.*

Parismus, a prince of Bohemia, subject of a once popular romance (1598) by Emanuel Foord; he fought against the Persians, loved Laurana, and went through strange adventures on the desolate island. The second part is *Parismenos.*

Parizade, the heroine of the *Arabian Nights* tale *The Two Sisters.*

Parolles, a wordy braggart and treacherous coward in Shakespeare's *All's Well that Ends Well.*

Parr, Catherine, is the heroine of Mühlbach's *King Henry the Eighth.*

Parson Runo, a Russian name for an unsophisticated clergyman, so named from the Lutheran clergymen of the Island of Runo, who are, or were supposed to be, ignorant of the ways of the world.

Parthenope, one of the sirens, and the ancient name of Naples, where she was said to be buried.

Partington, Mrs., a character created by the American humorist B. P. Shillaber, whose amusing blunders and malapropisms were once current in newspaper columns, and were published in 1854 in *The Life and Sayings of Mrs. Partington.* Shillaber probably took the name from an illustration used in a speech by Sydney Smith in 1831, where he compared the opposition of the Lords to the progress of reform to the attempt of Mrs. Partington to sweep back the Atlantic during the great storm of Sidmouth, when the tide set in upon the town in a flood.

Partridge, the attendant of the hero of Fielding's *Tom Jones,* a combination of simplicity and shrewdness.

Parsifal or **Parzival,** the hero and title of a medieval romance by Wolfram von Eschenbach, upon which Wagner based his opera *Parsifal.* Parsifal is "the guileless fool" who becomes the guardian of the Holy Grail after he has brought back from the magician Klingsor the lance that pierced the Saviour's side.

Pasquino, the remains of an ancient statue in Rome to which was given the name of a man living opposite to it, at the corner of the Orsini palace. It became a custom to hang Latin verses upon the torso; and very soon "all the literary utterances of Roman malice were gathered at his pedestal"—epigrams, sonnets, and dialogues with the name of Pasquino. These "pasquinades" began with the pontificate of Leo X.

Pastorella, a shepherdess in Spenser's *The Faerie Queene,* said to be intended for Frances Walsingham, Sir Philip Sidney's wife.

Patelin, a lawyer in an old French farce whose name has become proverbial for a crafty knave. The phrase "return to our muttons" comes from this farce. The plaintiff in a case about some stolen sheep (*moutons*), while telling his story, suddenly recognized in Patelin, the defendant's lawyer, a man who had cheated him out of six ells of cloth. He became bewildered and strayed from the sheep to the cloth, mixing up the lawyer and the sheep-thief, so as to give occasion for the judge to say repeatedly: "But, Monsieur Guillaume, let us return to our moutons."

Patrick, the patron saint of Ireland. His baptismal name was Succeath; Pope Celestine changed it to Patricius when he sent him as a missionary to Ireland. Calderon has a drama *St. Patrick's Purgatory.*

Patroclus, a Grecian general, a character in Shakespeare's *Troilus and Cressida.*

Patterne, Sir Willoughby, the title character of George Meredith's novel *The Egoist.*

Paul, the hero of Bernardin de St. Pierre's famous tale *Paul and Virginia* (1788) and of Masse's opera founded upon it.

Paul, St., is the subject of an oratorio by Mendelssohn and is a character in Sienkiewicz's novel *Quo Vadis?*

Paulina, in Shakespeare's *A Winter's Tale,* is the generous and spirited friend of Hermione.

Pauline Deschappelles, the heroine of Bulwer's play *The Lady of Lyons.*

Paulus, a character in Georg Ebers's novel *Homo Sum.*

Paulus, Herr, the title character of Besant's *Herr Paulus.*

Pau-Puk-Keewis, the "Storm Fool," whose mischiefs and transmigrations are the subject of a part of Longfellow's *Hiawatha.*

Paxarett, Sir Telegraph, a character in Peacock's *Melincourt,* "showing something of Thackeray's partiality for making a young man of fashion not quite a coxcomb."

Paynham, Mary, a character in Meredith's novel *Diana of the Crossways.*

Peace of God, The, a truce enforced by the clergy on the barons of Christendom, to prevent perpetual feuds between baron and baron.

Peredur, Sir, a knight of the Round Table, who killed monsters and oppressors and a serpent with a stone in its tail capable of conferring untold wealth on its possessor.

Pericles, the hero of Shakespeare's drama *Pericles, Prince of Tyre.* In the story on which it is founded he is Apollonius.

Pericles, Antonio Agiolopoulos, a character in Meredith's novels *Sandra Belloni* and *Vittoria.*

Perimones, Persaunt, Pertolphe, and **Peread,** four brothers that kept the passage to Castle Perilous in Arthurian romance. They were called also Night, Noon, and the Morning and Evening Stars.

Perrette, the milkmaid of Lafontaine's fable, who was so busy building air-castles that she dropped her pail and spilled the milk that was to be the foundation of her fortunes.

Peter, Lord, in Swift's *Tale of a Tub,* is the Pope.

Peterborough, Reverend Ambrose, a character in Meredith's novel *The Adventures of Harry Richmond.*

Peterloo, The Field of, a nickname given to St. Peter's Field, Manchester, where in 1819 the military attacked, by order of the authorities, a reform meeting attended by 60,000 persons, killing eight and wounding many.

Peter of Pomfret, a hermit introduced in Shakespeare's *King John.*

Peter Pan, the "boy that wouldn't grow up," in Barrie's comedy of the name.

Peter the Hermit appears in Tasso's *Jerusalem Delivered* and in Scott's *Count Robert of Paris.*

Petit André, a hangman in Scott's *Quentin Durward,* in love with his calling.

Petkoff, Raina, an accomplished liar in Shaw's play *Arms and the Man.*

Peto, Falstaff's "lieutenant," in both parts of Shakespeare's *Henry IV.*

Peto, Altiora, the title and heroine's name of a novel by Laurence Oliphant.

Petra, the title character of Björnson's novel *The Fisher-Maiden.*

Petronius, Caius, an important character in *Quo Vadis?* by Sienkiewicz.

Petruchio, the hero of Shakespeare's comedy *The Taming of the Shrew.*

Peveril, Sir Geoffrey, his wife and his son **Julian,** leading characters in Scott's *Peveril of the Peak.*

Peyral, a character in Loti's *Romance of a Spahi.*

Phebe or **Phœbe,** a shepherdess in Shakespeare's *As You Like It,* who fell in love with Rosalind.

Phellion, Felix, a professor of mathematics in Balzac's *The Middle Classes,* made famous by his works and by the discovery of a star.

Philaster, the hero of the play of the name by Beaumont and Fletcher (1622).

Philinte, a character in Molière's *Misanthrope,* whose indulgence toward the failings of others forms a contrast to the severity of Alceste.

Philip Augustus, King of France (1180–1223), appears in Shakespeare's *King John* and in Scott's *The Talisman.*

Philip II of Spain is introduced in Dumas's novel *The Page of the Duke of Savoy;* also in Tennyson's drama *Queen Mary.*

Philipson, Arthur, the hero of Scott's *Anne of Geierstein.*

Phillips, Jessie, the title and heroine of a novel (1843) by Mrs. Trollope, an attack on the poor-laws of the day.

Philoclea, in Sir Philip Sidney's *Arcadia,* is said to be intended for Lady Penelope Devereux.

Philologus, "a miserable worldlinge" in Nathaniel Woodes's moral play *The Conflict of Conscience* (1581). He is intended for one Francis Spira, an Italian who committed suicide in 1548 and whose widely known story is the subject of a poem, *Francis Spira,* by James Hain Friswell.

Philomede, in Pope's *Moral Essays,* is the Duchess of Marlborough, who married the Earl of Godolphin.

Philomène, Sœur, the title and heroine of a novel by the De Goncourts, illustrating the conflict between religious vows and natural inclination.

Philosopher, The, a title by which the Emperor Marcus Aurelius Antoninus is commonly called. It has been applied also to the Emperor of the East, Leo VI (867–911), on account of his writings, and to Porphyry, the Neo-Platonist (223–304).

Philotas, the subject of a tragedy (1607) by Samuel Daniel, supposed to be intended for the unfortunate Earl of Essex.

Philotine, in Spenser's *The Faerie Queene,* the daughter of Mammon and Queen of Hell.

Phiz, the pseudonym of Hablot K. Browne, who illustrated the works of Dickens and others.

Phœbus, Captain, a character in Hugo's *Notre Dame de Paris.*

Photine, the title character of Rostand's *La Samaritaine.*

Phroso, or **Lady Euphrosyne,** a Greek girl, the heroine of Anthony Hope's *Phroso.*

Phyllis, an important character in *The Dolly Dialogues,* by Anthony Hope.

Phyllis, in Spenser's *Colin Clout's Come Home Again,* is Elizabeth Spenser, Lady Carey.

Phyllis and **Brunetta,** rival beauties of whom *The Spectator* tells that Phyllis wore a gold brocade gown at a festival, and died of mortification because Brunetta had dressed the slave that carried her train in the same material, while she herself was all in black.

Piaveni, Laura, a prominent character in Meredith's novel *Vittoria.*

Picaro, a character of Spanish romance whose name is a synonym for "chevalier of industry."

Piccolomi, Octavio, an Austrian general in the Thirty Years' War, is a character in Schiller's two dramas *The Piccolomini* and *The Death of Wallenstein,* both translated by Coleridge.

Pickle, Peregrine, an ill-natured, ungrateful, brutal spendthrift, the hero of Smollett's novel *The Adventures of Peregrine Pickle.*

Pickwick, Samuel, the famous hero of Dickens's *Pickwick Papers,* a stout, elderly, benevolent, and unsophisticated gentleman, the founder of a club, whose members traveled through England, meeting with many amusing adventures.

Picrochole, a king in the *Gargantua* of Rabelais, noted for his vast ambitions; supposed to be a satirical suggestion of Charles V of Spain.

Pied Piper of Hamelin, The, the subject of a poem by Browning founded upon an old legend of Hamelin.

Pierre, the chief conspirator against the senators in Otway's tragedy *Venice Preserved* (1682).

Pierrot, a clown in French pantomime.

Pierson, Madame, the heroine of De Musset's novel *A Child of the Century.*

Piers Plowman, the hero of a famous poem of the fourteenth century, *The Vision of Piers Plowman,* by Robert Langlande. Piers fell asleep on the Malvern Hills, Worcestershire, and had a vision of twenty pictures, exhibiting the corruptions of the day, especially of the clergy. An imitation, called *Piers Plowman's Creed,* was written later in the century; it is a kind of allegory of human life.

Pigwiggin, an elf who is in love with Mab in Drayton's *Nymphidia.*

Pinch, a schoolmaster in Shakespeare's *The Comedy of Errors.*

Pinch, Ruth and **Tom,** brother and sister in Dickens's *Martin Chuzzlewit.* Tom, who is one of Dickens's finest characters, is the subject of a play, *Tom Pinch.*

Pinchbeck, Lady, in Byron's *Don Juan*—"olden she was—but had been very young"—"merely now was amiable and witty."

Pinchwife, Mr., in Wycherley's *The Country Wife,* is married to a raw country girl, whom he watches with constant anxiety.

Pinkerton, Miss, head of the school attended by Amelia Sedley and Becky Sharp in Thackeray's *Vanity Fair.*

Pinsent, Ora, a charming example of the irresponsible artistic temperament as developed on the stage, in Anthony Hope's *A Servant of the Public* (1905).

Piombo, Baron, a Corsican and friend of the Bonapartes. His daughter married against his will the last of the Porta family, with whom the Piombos had a feud, the subject of Balzac's *The Vendetta.*

Pip, the hero of Dickens's *Great Expectations.* Pip was his own baby attempt at his name, Philip Pirrip.

Pipchin, Mrs., a housekeeper in Dickens's *Dombey and*

Son, whose great art in managing children was to give them everything they didn't want and nothing that they did want.

Pippa, a little silk-winder of Asolo, the subject of Browning's drama *Pippa Passes*. On her one annual holiday she goes singing through the village; and her songs awaken the consciences of four persons who are on the verge of crime.

Pisani, Angela, the title and heroine of a novel (1875) by Hon. George Sydney Smythe.

Pisanio, a servant in Shakespeare's *Cymbeline*, who is ordered to kill Imogen, but befriends her instead.

Pistol, Ancient (Ensign), a swaggering bully, one of Falstaff's companions in Shakespeare's *Henry IV*, Part II, and *Henry V*.

Pizarro, a Spanish adventurer in Peru, whom Kotzebue took for the subject of a drama; this was altered and adapted for the English stage by Sheridan (1814).

Pizarro, Don, the governor of a state prison, the villain of Beethoven's only opera, *Fidelio* (1791).

Plagiary, Sir Fretful, a character in Sheridan's play *The Critic* (1779), said to be drawn for the playwright Richard Cumberland (1732–1811), noted for his vanity and irritable temper.

Planchette, an eminent professor of mechanics, a character in Balzac's *The Magic Skin*.

Plantagenet, Edith, in Scott's *The Talisman*, a kinswoman of Cœur de Lion, marries Kenneth, Prince Royal of Scotland.

Plantagenets, The, in Shakespeare's plays. See EDWARD IV and RICHARD III, also RUTLAND, CLARENCE, and RICHARD, DUKE OF YORK.

Pleiades, The, seven stars in the constellation Taurus—a name sometimes applied to seven distinguished contemporaries; the Seven Wise Men of Greece are called the philosophical pleiads; there were also the pleiads of Alexandria, poets; the pleiads of Charlemagne; and, in France, a group of poets of the sixteenth century of which Ronsard was the head, and another less noted in the seventeenth.

Pleydell, Paulus, a character in Scott's *Guy Mannering*.

Pliable, a neighbor of Christian in Bunyan's *Pilgrim's Progress*, who turned back at the Slough of Despond.

Pliant, Sir Paul and **Lady,** a henpecked husband and his second wife, handsome, silly, and deceitful, in Congreve's play *The Double Dealer* (1694).

Plume, Captain, the title character of Farquhar's *The Recruiting Officer.*

Plummer, Caleb, the toy-maker in Dickens's *The Cricket on the Hearth,* devoted to his blind daughter Bertha.

Pocket, Matthew, a "grinder," or private tutor, in Dickens's *Great Expectations,* with whom Pip studies, and whose son Herbert is a great friend of his.

Podbipienta, a simple, pious, gigantic comrade of Pan Michael in Sienkiewicz's novel *Fire and Sword.*

Podsnap, Mr. John, a well-to-do man in Dickens's *Our Mutual Friend,* who stood very high in Mr. Podsnap's opinion, believing that whatever he put behind him he put out of existence.

Poet of the Poor, The, George Crabbe (1754–1832).

Pogram, Elijah, a burlesque American patriot in Dickens's *Martin Chuzzlewit* (1844).

Poins, a companion of Prince Hal in Shakespeare's *Henry IV,* both parts.

Pole, Mr., a city merchant in Meredith's *Sandra Belloni,* with three ambitious daughters. His son Wilfrid is in love with Sandra.

Polichinelle, the French form of the Italian *Pulcinella;* in English, *Punch.*

Politian, Earl of Leinster, subject of an unfinished drama by Edgar A. Poe.

Polixenes, the King of Bohemia in Shakespeare's *A Winter's Tale,* against whom the jealousy of Leontes is directed.

Pollente, a Saracen, lord of the Perilous Bridge in Spenser's *The Faerie Queene.*

Polonius, in Shakespeare's *Hamlet,* the father of Ophelia and Laertes.

Polyeucte, the title and leading character of Corneille's tragedy (1640), a type of the martyr.

Pomander, Sir Charles, a personage of Charles Reade's novel *Peg Woffington.*

Pomfret, Barbara, the chief character of Amélie Rives's novel *The Quick or the Dead?*

Pompey the Younger appears in Shakespeare's *Antony and Cleopatra.*

Pompilia, a leading personage in Browning's *The Ring and the Book,* whose birth as a foundling, adoption by Violante, wife of the wealthy Pietro, marriage to Count Guido Franceschini and murder by him, form the tragedy of the story.

Pons, Cousin (Sylvain), the title and subject of a novel by Balzac. A drama on his life was written by Alphonse de Launay and produced in Paris about 1873.

Ponto, Major, a retired officer in Thackeray's *Book of Snobs.*

Poole, Grace, the keeper of the insane Mrs. Rochester in Charlotte Brontë's *Jane Eyre.*

Poor Richard, the name under which Benjamin Franklin issued his Almanacs, 1732 to 1757, full of homely wisdom in terse sentences. Richard Saunders was the supposed author.

Poor Robin, the name under which a series of almanacs, beginning in 1662, was published, attributed to Robert Herrick, the poet. Other books were issued under the same name.

Popinot, Jean-Jules, a lawyer in *César Birotteau* and other novels of Balzac, a judge of one of the lower courts, of benevolent impulses, which led him to seek objects of charity. Madame Popinot is one of the heroines of a play, *César Birotteau,* by Eugene Cormon.

Porte Crayon, a pseudonym of David H. Strother, an American author and illustrator (1816–1888).

Portenduère, Vicomte and **Vicomtesse,** who was Ursule Mirouët, leading characters in Balzac's novel of the latter name.

Porteous, Captain John, hanged in the Grass-market at Edinburgh by the "Porteous mob," which figures in Scott's novel *The Heart of Midlothian.*

Porthos, one of the heroes of *The Three Guardsmen,* by Dumas.

Portia, the wife of Brutus, who committed suicide after he fled from Rome, appears in Shakespeare's *Julius Cæsar.*

Portia, the heroine of Shakespeare's *The Merchant of Venice.*

Portius, an important character in Addison's *Cato.*

Portsoaken, Dr. Jabez, a villain in Hawthorne's *Septimius Felton.*

Portuguese Nun, The, the author of a series of famous letters to the Chevalier de Chamilly in the seventeenth century. Her name was Mariana Alcaforada.

Posthumus, Leonatus, the jealous husband of Imogen in Shakespeare's *Cymbeline.*

Potion, Mr., an apothecary in Smollett's *Roderick Random,* intended for a portrait of a surgeon, John Gordon, to whom Smollett was apprenticed in early life.

Potter, Sampson, the title character of Archibald Clavering Gunter's novel *Mr. Potter of Texas* and of the drama of the same name.

Pounce, Peter, a character in Fielding's *Joseph Andrews.*

Poundtext, Peter, "the indulged pastor of Milnwood's parish" in Scott's *Old Mortality.*

Pourceaugnac, subject of an amusing comedy of Molière. He is a provincial who goes to Paris to marry the pretty Julie; but her lover, Eraste, devises so many mystifications and torments and perplexities for him, that he gives up his suit.

Poyser, Mrs., a shrewd and witty farmer's wife in George Eliot's *Adam Bede,* who says that if women are foolish, "God made 'em so to match the men."

Précieuses, The, a literary society that met at Hôtel Rambouillet, Paris, in the seventeenth century. It is burlesqued in Molière's *Les Précieuses Ridicules* (1659).

Preciosa, a gipsy girl, the heroine of Longfellow's poetic drama *The Spanish Student.*

Prester John, a name applied to the kings of Abyssinia or Ethiopia—said to be a corruption of *Belul Gian,* precious stone, the first word having been translated and then corrupted into Prester. The stone was in a legendary ring given to the Queen of Sheba by Solomon.

Pretenders: James Stuart, son of James II of England, was called the Old Pretender, and his son Charles Edward the Young Pretender, whose attempts to regain the throne of their ancestors ended with the defeat of Charles Edward at Culloden in 1746. The latter appears in Scott's *Redgauntlet,* disguised at first as Father Buonaventure.

Pretintaille, Marquise de, a character created by Béranger, representing the ideas and prejudices of the *ancien régime.*

Priam, King of Troy, is a character in Shakespeare's *Troilus and Cressida.*

Price, Fanny, the heroine of Jane Austen's *Mansfield Park.*

Pridden, Martha, an "evangelist" in Meredith's *One of Our Conquerors.*

Prig, Betsey, one of the famous nurses in Dickens's *Martin Chuzzlewit,* a friend of Sarah Gamp.

Prima Donna, Lord, a character in Disraeli's *Vivian Grey.*

Primrose, Rev. Dr. Charles, his wife, **Deborah,** his sons, **George** and **Moses,** and his daughters, **Olivia** and **Sophia,** characters of Goldsmith's novel *The Vicar of Wakefield.*

Prince Prettyman and **Prince Volscius,** characters in the Duke of Buckingham's play *The Rehearsal.*

Pringle, The Rev. Dr., the residuary legatee in Galt's *The Ayrshire Legatees.*

Prinziralle, an important character in Maeterlinck's drama *Monna Vanna,* commander of the Florentine besiegers of Pisa.

Priscilla, a girl of a highly nervous and impressible temperament in Hawthorne's *Blithedale Romance,* who is in the power of a mesmerist until her love for Hollingsworth overcomes his control.

Priscilla Mullens, of the Pilgrims, married to John Alden in 1621, is the heroine of Longfellow's poem *The Courtship of Miles Standish.*

Priuli, Belvidera, daughter of a Venetian senator, heroine of Otway's play *Venice Preserved.*

Pronando, Erastus, one of the leading characters in Miss Woolson's *Anne.*

Proserpine or **Persephone,** daughter of Ceres and wife of Pluto, is the subject of a French lyric drama by Saint-Saëns and an opera by Quinault.

Prosper-le-Gai, the hero of Maurice Hewlett's novel *The Forest Lovers* and of Lancaster's dramatization of it.

Prospero, the dispossessed Duke of Milan, a leading character in Shakespeare's *The Tempest.*

Protestant Duke, The, Duke of Monmouth (1619–1685), a natural son of Charles II, whose religion was an element of his popularity with the opponents of the Duke of York, James II.

Protestant Pope, The: so Clement XIV (1705–1774) was called on account of his liberality and his bull suppressing the Jesuits.

Proteus, one of the heroes of Shakespeare's *Two Gentlemen of Verona.* The other is Valentine.

Prothero, Bailey, the principal character of *A Rogue's Comedy*, by Henry Arthur Jones.

Proudfute, Oliver, the braggart bonnet-maker in Scott's novel *The Fair Maid of Perth.*

Proudie, Mrs., the meddling and domineering wife of a bishop in Trollope's *Barchester Towers* and others of the Barsetshire series.

Prudhomme, Joseph, a celebrated character drawn by the French author Henri Monnier in his play *Grandeur and Decadence of Joseph Prudhomme* (1852), and *Mêmoires of Joseph Prudhomme* (1857). He is a type of self-satisfied and pompous banality. Among his mixed metaphors are: "This sword is the happiest day of my life"; "The chariot of State is about to capsize upon a volcano."

Pry, Paul, the title of a comedy by John Poole and its leading character, defined by the name which has become proverbial.

Prynne, Hester, the woman that wore the mark which gives the name to Hawthorne's novel *The Scarlet Letter.* She is also a character of the play founded upon the novel.

Psyche, beloved by Cupid, is the subject of a tragi-comedy (1671) by Molière.

Pucelle, La. See Joan of Arc.

Puck, or Robin Goodfellow, a sort of fairy clown, or jester, in Shakespeare's *A Midsummer Night's Dream.* In Ben Jonson's play *The Devil Is an Ass* he is a goblin and is called Pug.

Puff, a playwright and "professor of the art of puffing" in Sheridan's farce *The Critic.*

Puff, Partenopex, in Disraeli's *Vivian Grey,* gives his witticisms as quotations from his valet, his monkey, or his parrot.

Pullet, Mrs., one of Maggie Tulliver's aunts in George Eliot's *The Mill on the Floss.*

Pumblechook, an uncle of Joe Gargery in Dickens's *Great Expectations.*

Punch or **Punchinello,** a humorous character shown in puppet show, especially *Punch and Judy.* The character comes from the Italian and is said to have been named from a funny Neapolitan peasant, Puccio d'Aniello.

Pure, Simon, the name of a Pennsylvania Quaker in Mrs. Centlivre's comedy *A Bold Stroke for a Wife.* A letter introducing him to a Quaker in London, Obadiah Prim, falls into the hands of Feignwell, who wishes to marry Prim's wealthy ward, Anne Lovely. He therefore passes himself off as Simon Pure, while the real Simon is treated as an impostor. The trick is discovered just in time to prevent the marriage.

Puss in Boots, the hero of a nursery tale of the name (1697) by Perrault. The clever cat procures a rich and titled wife for a poor young miller, his master, who is called the Marquis of Carabas.

Pygmalion, who fell in love with his statue, is the subject of William S. Gilbert's comedy *Pygmalion and Galatea* (1871).

Pylades, a character in Racine's drama *Andromaque,* and as the freind of Orestes in literature founded upon the story of Orestes.

Pym, Arthur Gordon, the subject of a tale of adventure by Edgar A. Poe.

Pyncheons, The, the family whose fortunes are the subject of Hawthorne's novel *The House of the Seven Gables.*

Pyrgo Polinices, a swaggering soldier, the hero of Plautus's *Miles Gloriosus.*

Pyrrhus, a character in Racine's *Andromaque,* translated under the title *The Distressed Mother.*

Pythias, the friend of Damon (*q.v.*).

Q, the pseudonym of Arthur T. Quiller-Couch (1863).

Quasimodo, a deformed foundling devoted to Esmeralda in Victor Hugo's novel *Notre Dame de Paris.*

Quern-Biter, the sword of Haco I of Norway, with which he cut through millstones (querns).

Quex, Lord, the hero of Pinero's *The Gay Lord Quex.*

Quickly, Mistress, hostess of the Boar's Head tavern in Eastcheap, a character in the two parts of Shakespeare's *Henry*

IV and in *Henry V*. The character of the name in *The Merry Wives of Windsor*, servant to Dr. Caius, seems to be the same, but this is questioned.

Quilliam, Peter, a leading character in Hall Caine's novel *The Manxman.*

Quilp, Daniel, a dwarf in Dickens's novel *The Old Curiosity Shop.*

Quinapalus, a non-existent author to whom hypothetical quotations are referred, as in *Twelfth Night:* "What says Quinapalus?"

Quinbus Flestrin (man-mountain), a name given by the Lilliputians to Gulliver.

Quince, Peter, the carpenter who manages the play in Shakespeare's *A Midsummer Night's Dream.*

Quintessence, Queen, of Entelachie, the country of metaphysics visited by Pantagruel in the search for the "oracle of the Holy Bottle."

Quintilian, Jasper, the hero of *The Household of Bouverie* by Catherine A. Warfield.

Quinton, a personage of Anthony Hope's *Simon Dale* (1898).

Quintus Fixlein, the title and chief character of a romance (1796) by Jean Paul Richter.

Quisante, Alexander, in Anthony Hope's novel of the name, is a convincing type of the man successful without any of the moral qualities usually believed to deserve success.

Quisara, the heroine of Fletcher's play *The Island Princess.*

Quixote, Don, the knight of La Mancha, hero of the famous romance of Cervantes, a gentle and generous character, made mildly insane by reading and brooding over the romances of chivalry. In order to right wrongs and help the injured and oppressed, he goes out on his meager horse Rosinante, accompanied by a squire, Sancho Panza, a common, ignorant rustic, but shrewd in his way, and sees, as he imagines, many foes to be overcome.

Quiz, a pen-name used by Charles Dickens.

Rab, a great mastiff, true to his responsibilities, in Dr. John Brown's pathetic story *Rab and His Friends.*

Rabagas, an advocate and journalist converted from radicalism to conservatism by royal favor, the subject of a play of the name by Sardou (1872).

Rabelais: Swift and Sterne were each called the English Rabelais; William Maginn, the Modern Rabelais.

Raby, Aurora, a beautiful young English girl in Byron's *Don Juan* (1824).

Raby, The Rose of, the mother of Richard III, daughter of Nevyll de Raby.

Rackrent, Sir Condy, a character in Miss Edgeworth's novel *Castle Rackrent*, who "survived his own wake."

Radigond, the Queen of the Amazons in Spenser's *The Faerie Queene*.

Radirobanes, in Barclay's romance *Argenis*, is Philip II of Spain.

Radnor, Victor, a character in Meredith's *One of Our Conquerors*, who has deserted his elderly wife for a younger woman, Nataly Dreighton.

Ragueneau, a baker and poet in Rostand's tragedy *Cyrano de Bergerac*.

Rail-Splitter, The, a nickname given to Abraham Lincoln, who is said to have earned his living one winter by splitting rails for a farmer.

Railway King, The, George Hudson, an English railway projector and manager, whose brilliant reign came to a sudden end about 1845, when shares went down and many fortunes of investors were lost.

Raleigh, Sir Walter, is a character in Scott's *Kenilworth*, where he lays down his cloak for the Queen to step upon, and later is knighted.

Ralph, the squire of Hudibras, representing the Independents.

Ralph Roister Doister, a blustering fellow who fails in his attempt to marry a rich widow, in the play that bears his name, the first English comedy, about 1534, by Nicholas Udall.

Raltenbury, Jack, the hero of Baring-Gould's *Winifred*.

Rambaud, Monsieur, a character in Balzac's *A Page of Love*.

Rambone, a sporting parson in Blackmore's novel *The Maid of Sker*.

Raminagrobis, a character in Rabelais's *Gargantua,* whom Pantagruel and Panurge take for an arbiter. In Lafontaine it is a cat taken for a judge.

Ramona, Phail, the chief character of Helen H. Jackson's *Ramona.*

Ramorny, Sir John, a villain in Scott's novel *The Fair Maid of Perth.*

Ramsay, Adam, an upright but irascible character in Miss Ferrier's novel *The Inheritance.*

Ramsay, Margaret, the heroine of Scott's novel *The Fortunes of Nigel.*

Ramsbottom, Mrs., a pseudonym of Theodore Hook.

Ramsden, Roebuck, a character in Shaw's play *Man and Superman.*

Ramuncho, the title character of a novel by Pierre Loti.

Ranald MacEagh, chief of the Children of the Mist in Scott's *The Legend of Montrose.*

Randolph, Lord and **Lady,** leading characters in Home's tragedy *Douglas* (1757). Lady Randolph was the mother of Norval.

Random, Roderick, the title and hero of a novel by Tobias Smollett (1748).

Ranger, the chief character in Hoadley's comedy *The Suspicious Husband.*

Rank, Dr., a friend of the Helmer family in Ibsen's drama *A Doll's House,* in love with Nora. His approaching death coinciding with the impending discovery of her forgery, suggests to Nora the idea of suicide, which, however, she does not carry out.

Ranter, The Widow, subject of a comedy by Aphra Behn.

Ranthorpe, the subject of a tale by George Henry Lewes (1847).

Raoul de Nangis, the hero of Meyerbeer's opera *The Huguenots.*

Rappaccini, a doctor of Padua who brought up his daughter upon poisons, the subject of Hawthorne's noted story *Rappaccini's Daughter.*

Raquin, Thérèse, a leading character in Zola's novel of the name and in the play from it.

Rarahu, a character in Loti's novel *Le Mariage de Loti.*

Rare Ben Jonson: the story is that a gentleman gave a mason eighteenpence to cut "O Rare Ben Jonson!" on the gravestone of the poet in Westminster Abbey.

Rasni, a swaggering king of Nineveh in the play *A Looking-Glass for London and England* by Lodge and Greene. He is converted by the prophet Jonah.

Rasselas, the title and hero's name of a noted tale by Dr. Johnson. Rasselas was a "Prince of Abyssinia."

Rassendyll, Rudolf, the hero of Anthony Hope's novels *The Prisoner of Zenda* and its sequel *Rupert of Hentzau,* and of the dramatizations of them. He enters carelessly into adventure and encounters grave responsibilities and strong temptations without wavering from right and honor, is heroic and resourceful, meeting strange emergencies with the directness and simplicity of one dealing with ordinary occurrences.

Rastignac, Eugène de, an unscrupulous and successful character in many of the novels of Balzac's *Comédie Humaine.*

Rat, Doctor, a curate in the old comedy *Gammer Gurton's Needle.*

Ratti, Emilio, the title character of *The Romance of a Schoolmaster,* by Edmondo de Amicis.

Rattlin, Jack, a sailor in Smollett's *Roderick Random.*

Rautendelein, an elfish being in Hauptmann's play *The Sunken Bell,* who loves the mortal Heinrich and leads him to the heights. After being deserted by him, she becomes the mate of the hideous Nickelman who lives in the mud at the bottom of the well. She is supposed to typify the freedom and sincerity of nature without which Humanity can never reach supreme truth. See also HEINRICH.

Raven, The, plays a part in Dickens's *Barnaby Rudge;* also the subject of Poe's famous poem.

Ravenhill, Crispin, the hero of Baring-Gould's *Bladys of the Stewponey* (1897).

Ravenshoe, Charles, the hero of Henry Kingsley's novel *Ravenshoe.*

Ravenswood, Edgar, Master of, the unfortunate hero of Scott's novel *The Bride of Lammermoor,* who is lost in the quicksands of Kelpies Flow, in fulfilment of an ancient prophecy. In the opera *Lucia di Lammermoor* by Donizetti, Edgar takes his own life after the death of Lucy.

Rayland, Mrs., the lady of the manor in Charlotte Smith's *The Old Manor-House,* said by Sir Walter Scott to be a "sort of Queen Elizabeth in private life."

Raymond, Count of Toulouse, one of the leaders of the Crusades. In Tasso's *Jerusalem Delivered* he plants the standard of the cross on the tower of David.

Raynal, Commandant, a leading character in Charles Reade's novel *A Double Marriage: or, White Lies.*

Rea, Bladys, the heroine of Baring-Gould's *Bladys of the Stewponey.*

Ready-to-Halt, a pilgrim on crutches in Bunyan's *Pilgrim's Progress.*

Rebecca, a beautiful Jewess in Scott's novel *Ivanhoe,* in love with the hero; she is the actual heroine, though Ivanhoe marries Rowena. Thackeray based on the novel a satirical romance in the form of a sequel to it, *Rebecca and Rowena.*

Rebecca, a name assumed by the leader of raids upon toll-gates in Wales in 1843. The chief rioters were in women's dress. The occasion of the raids was the heavy tolls exacted; and the name, Rebeccaites, came from a grotesque perversion of a verse in Genesis where it was said to Rebecca, "Let thy seed possess the gate of those which hate them."

Red Cross Knight, The, the hero of Spenser's *The Faerie Queene,* who slays the dragon and marries Una. He represents St. George, and, allegorically, Holiness.

Redgauntlet, Sir Arthur Darsie, known at first as Darsie Latimer, the leading character of Scott's *Redgauntlet,* which is founded upon an imaginary conspiracy in favor of Charles Edward Stuart, subsequent to the defeat of Culloden. Sir Edward Hugh Redgauntlet is Darsie's uncle and is called Laird of the Lochs.

Redgill, Dr., a vulgar gourmand, a parasite of Lord Courtland, in Miss Ferrier's novel *Marriage.*

Redin, Young, the subject of an old ballad, killed by his jilted sweetheart. The ballad goes under the names also of *Earl Richard, Lord William,* and *Young Hunting.*

Red Knight of the Red Lands, The, Sir Ironside (*q.v.*).

Redlaw, the Haunted Man in Dickens's tale of that name.

Redmond, Rokeby's page in Scott's poem *Rokeby.*

Redworth, Thomas, makes a fortune in railways and marries Diana in Meredith's novel *Diana of the Crossways.*

Regan, one of the two ungrateful daughters in Shakespeare's *King Lear,* the Duchess of Cornwall.

Regulus, a Roman general captured by the Carthaginians and sent to Rome by them to treat for peace and an exchange of prisoners; but instead he advised the Senate against that course. Upon his return he was subjected to torture and death. He is the subject of tragedies in French by Dorat and Pradon, and an Italian opera by Metastasio.

Reichstadt, The Duke of, the title character in Rostand's drama *L'Aiglon,* the son of Napoleon I.

Reilly, Willy, the subject of a novel by William Carleton (1855).

Reldresal, in *Gulliver's Travels,* the Principal Secretary for Private Affairs in Lilliput.

Relling, Doctor, a man of sardonic humor but kind heart in Ibsen's play *The Wild Duck,* who reads truly the characters of the insincere Ekdal and the truth-telling Werle.

Remon, David, an important character in Henry Arthur Jones's play *The Masqueraders.*

Remus, Uncle, an old negro, fond of relating stories from negro folk-lore, in Joel Chandler Harris's *Uncle Remus: His Songs and His Sayings.*

Renault, a base conspirator in Otway's *Venice Preserved.*

Renault, Léon, the hero of *The Man with the Broken Ear* by Edmond About.

Renault, Vidal, in Scott's novel *The Betrothed,* is the name assumed by Cadwallon, the Bard of Gwenwyn.

René, the title and hero of a romance by the Viscount de Chateaubriand (1768–1848). René is "the type of minds that waste their faculties in inaction, in the vague sentiment of the infinite, in disgust for reality, who exhaust themselves with sterile desires, and complain bitterly of the obstacles they have not energy to overcome."

René or **Reignier,** Duke of Lorraine and Anjou, and titular King of Naples, Sicily, and Jerusalem, is a character in Shakespeare's *Henry VI*, Part I. Henry's Queen was his daughter. He is also a character in Scott's *Anne of Geierstein*, where the incident of his transferring his Principality to Louis XI is introduced.

René Leblanc, the notary of Grandpré in Longfellow's *Evangeline*.

Rentheim, Ella, in Ibsen's *John Gabriel Borkman*, in love with Borkman, her brother-in-law.

Renzo, the lover of Lucia in Manzoni's novel *The Betrothed.*

Republican Queen, The: so Sophia, wife of Frederick I of Prussia, was called.

Resolute, The, a title assumed by John Florio, a lexicographer, said to have suggested the two pedants in *Love's Labor's Lost*, Don Adriano and Holofernes.

Resolute Doctor, The, a title meaning one who resolves or solves philosophic problems, was given to Durandus and to Baconthorp, both medieval schoolmen. Of the latter Fuller says he "groped after more light than he saw, saw more than he durst speak of, spake of more than he was thanked for."

Restaud, Comtesse de, one of the daughters of Père Goriot in Balzac's novel of that name.

Revel, Sabine, in Hervieu's play *La Course du Flambeau*, sacrifices her mother for the sake of her daughter, and is herself in turn sacrificed.

Reynard or **Renard,** the common name for a fox, is derived from a German *Thier-Epos* (beast-epic), *Reynard the Fox*, a satire on medieval German society.

Rezio, the doctor of Barataria, who forbade Sancho Panza to eat anything he wanted and recommended a few wafers and a slice or two of quince.

Rhombus, a schoolmaster in Sidney's *Pastoral Entertainment* (1587), resembling Shakespeare's Holofernes.

Riccabocca, Dr., "a soft-hearted cynic, a simple sage, a philosopher," in Bulwer's *My Novel*.

Richard, Prince, son of Henry II, appears in Scott's novel *The Betrothed*.

Richard I, Cœur de Lion, is a character in Scott's *Ivanhoe*, where he appears as the Black Knight of the Fetterlock, coming to the help of the Disinherited at the tournament, and is called

Le Noir Faineant, the Black Do-Nothing; he is also a leading character in *The Talisman.* He is the hero of Maurice Hewlett's *Richard Yea-and-Nay.*

Richard II, of England (1366–1400), is the subject of one of Shakespeare's historic tragedies, and, for reading, the best, though it is not acted. Hartley Coleridge says: "In truth it [the play] is almost a prophecy; for Shakespeare's Richard II was the real Charles I."

Richard III (1450–1485) is in the second and third parts of Shakespeare's *Henry VI,* under the names of Plantagenet and the Duke of Gloucester.

Richelieu, Cardinal (1585–1642), minister of Louis XIII, is the subject of Bulwer's drama *Richelieu,* is a character in Dumas's *The Three Musketeers* and its various dramatizations, and the title character in Weyman's novel *Under the Red Robe* and the dramatic version by Edward Rose. He is also the subject of a novel by G. P. R. James.

Richland, Miss, the heroine of Goldsmith's comedy *The Good-Natured Man* (1768).

Richmond, Henry Tudor, Earl of (1456–1509), afterward Henry VII, is a character in Shakespeare's *Henry VI,* Part III, and in *Richard III,* where he is at the head of the Lancastrian party.

Richmond, Harry, son of Augustus Fitz-George Roy Richmond, claiming to be of royal birth, an extraordinary character and the leading interest in *The Adventures of Harry Richmond* by George Meredith.

Rickman, Savage Keith, a poetic genius, son of a bookdealer, the hero of May Sinclair's *The Divine Fire,* in love with Lucia Harden.

Ridd, John, the hero of Blackmore's *Lorna Doone.*

Riderhood, Roger, called **Rogue,** a waterside villain in Dickens's *Our Mutual Friend,* who blackmails Headstone until he drives him to desperation and both lose their lives in a fight.

Rienzi, Coladi, "the last of the tribunes," chief of a popular insurrection in Rome in 1347. He is the subject of a novel by Bulwer, a tragedy by Miss Mitford, and an opera by Wagner.

Rigaud, a *chevalier d'industrie* in Dickens's *Little Dorrit.*

Rigby, The Right Hon. Nicholas, a fawning scoundrel in Disraeli's *Coningsby.*

Rigdum Funnidos, a character in Carey's burlesque *Chrononhotonthologos,* and a nickname given by Sir Walter Scott to his friend, John Ballantyne, the publisher, a little fellow, full of fun and drollery and devoted to field sports.

Rigolette, a character in Eugène Sue's *The Mysteries of Paris,* whose name has become a synonym for *grisette.*

Rimul, Ragnhild, the heroine of *Gunnar* by H. H. Boyesen.

Rinaldo, one of the most famous of Charlemagne's paladins, a character in Boiardo's *Orlando Innamorato,* Ariosto's *Orlando Furioso,* Tasso's *Jerusalem Delivered,* Pulci's burlesque *Morgante Maggiore,* and other less famous romances. He was banished for killing the Emperor's nephew, Berthelot, with a chess-board, in a fit of anger, and afterward joined the Crusaders in the war for the Holy Land.

Rinaldo of Montalban, described in *Don Quixote* as met with in the *Mirror of Knighthood,* is said to have stolen the "golden idol of Mahomet."

Ringwood, The Earl of, a cynical nobleman in Thackeray's *The Adventures of Philip.*

Rippan, The Margravine von, a character in Meredith's *The Adventures of Harry Richmond.*

Rippenger, Julia, a friend of Harry when he was at Mr. Rippenger's school in Meredith's *The Adventures of Harry Richmond.*

Riquet, the subject of Perrault's allegory *Riquet à la Houppe* (Tuft). He was extremely ugly, but could bestow wit on the one he loved; the woman he loved was stupid and beautiful and could bestow beauty on the one she loved. So they married and he became beautiful and she intelligent.

Risler, the wronged partner in Daudet's novel *Fromont Jeune et Risler Ainé.*

Ritchie, Helena, the leading character in Mrs. Deland's novel *The Awakening of Helena Ritchie* and in the play from it.

Rivarez, Felice, the name assumed by Arthur Burton in Mrs. Voynich's *The Gadfly* when he returns from South America, and, on account of his stinging sarcasm, receives the nickname "The Gadfly."

Rivers, Anthony Woodville, Earl, a character in Shakespeare's *Henry VI*, Part III, and *Richard III*, beheaded by the order of Richard, to whom his ghost appears.

Rivière, Edouard, the lover of Rose de Beaurepaire in Charles Reade's novel *A Double Marriage : or, White Lies.*

Rizzio, David, is a character in Maurice Hewlett's novel *The Queen's Quair* (1904).

Rizzo, Bartolommeo and **Roselina,** characters in Meredith's *Vittoria.*

Robarts, Rev. Mark, and his sister **Lucy,** leading characters in Anthony Trollope's *Framley Parsonage.*

Robert Elsmere, the title and hero of a novel by Mrs. Humphry Ward.

Robert III of Scotland, in Scott's *The Fair Maid of Perth,* arranges a marriage between his son and the daughter of the Earl of March, but breaks the contract when the Earl of Douglas offers his daughter with a larger dowry.

Robert le Diable, Duke of Normandy, the subject of Meyerbeer's celebrated opera (1831), the book by Scribe. It is based on an old romance relating his crimes and his repentance.

Robert of Paris, Count, a Crusader who gives the name to one of Scott's novels.

Robert of Sicily is the subject of Justin H. McCarthy's miracle play *The Proud Prince.* Robert for his pride was degraded to be the King's Jester, while an angel took his place as King Robert; he was restored when he was brought to repent his presumption.

Robespierre is a character of Dumas's *The Countess de Charny.*

Robin Roughhead, a poor cottar who comes into a title and estate and becomes a model landlord in Allingham's *Fortune's Frolic.*

Robinson, the family whose adventures are the story of *The Swiss Family Robinson,* by Wyss.

Robinson, Galbraith, title character of John P. Kennedy's *Horseshoe Robinson.*

Robinson, Octavius, a sensitive, poetic fellow in Shaw's *Man and Superman,* in love with Ann Whitefield.

Robinson, Tom, the convict that mended in Charles Reade's novel *Never Too Late to Mend.*

Robinson, Violet, a cold-blooded, independent young woman in Shaw's *Man and Superman,* who is secretly married to Hector Malone.

Robinson Crusoe. See CRUSOE.

Rob Roy Macgregor, a noted freebooter who assumed the name Campbell because the Macgregors were outlawed, the hero of Scott's novel *Rob Roy.* Scott calls him "the Robin Hood of Scotland, the dread of the wealthy, the friend of the poor."

Robsart, Amy, secretly married to the Earl of Leicester and murdered by Varney, his retainer, a character in Scott's novel *Kenilworth* and in the play from it, *Amy Robsart.*

Rochcliffe, Lady Eleanora, the subject of Hawthorne's tale *Lady Eleanora's Mantle.*

Rochecliffe, a plotting chaplain in Scott's *Woodstock,* recognized as Joseph Albany.

Rochester, Edward Fairfax, the hero of Charlotte Brontë's novel *Jane Eyre.*

Roderick Dhu, a Highland chief and outlaw, a character in Scott's poem *The Lady of the Lake.*

Roderigo, in Shakespeare's *Othello,* is in love with Desdemona and duped by Iago.

Rodogune, the wife of Demetrius Nicator, King of Syria, the subject of a tragedy by Corneille.

Rodolphe, the poet in Murger's *Bohemian Life.*

Rodomont, a fierce Moor, King of Algiers, appears in Boiardo's *Orlando Innamorato* and Ariosto's *Orlando Furioso.* From his swaggering boastfulness is derived the word "rodomontade."

Roger Bontemps, a character taken by Beranger from an older author, and made the type of the joyous, contented man.

Roget, Marie, the girl whose murder forms the subject of Poe's tale *The Mystery of Marie Roget,* founded upon the murder of Mary Cecilia Rogers, near New York.

Rohan, Cardinal de, is a character in Dumas's novels *Joseph Balsamo, Memoirs of a Physician,* and *The Queen's Necklace;* also in Mühlbach's *Marie Antoinette.*

Roland, Jean, one of the title characters of De Maupassant's *Pierre et Jean.*

Roland or **Rowland, Childe,** the hero of an old Scottish ballad, described as telling of his perilous journey to rescue his sister, Burd Helen, from the fairies. Shakespeare gives a line in *King Lear,* "Childe Rowland to the dark tower came," quoted from this or some other old ballad.

Roland of the Army: so the Comte de Saint Hilaire (1766–1809) was called on account of his bravery and magnanimity.

Rolleston, Helen, a leading character in Charles Reade's *Foul Play.*

Romeo, the hero of Shakespeare's *Romeo and Juliet,* the tragedy of which results from the feud between the Montagues, Romeo's family, and the Capulets, to whom Juliet belonged.

Romfrey, Everard, the uncle of Nevil Beauchamp in Meredith's *Beauchamp's Career.*

Romola, the title and heroine of a novel by George Eliot, the scene of which is laid in Florence in the fifteenth century.

Rookley, Jervas, an important personage of A. E. W. Mason's novel *Lawrence Clavering.*

Ropemaker, The Beautiful. See LABÉ, LOUISE.

Roquairol, Charles, an important character in Richter's novel *Titan.*

Roque Guinart or **Rocha Guinarda,** a famous bandit of the time of Cervantes, introduced in *Don Quixote.*

Rosalba, Queen, one of the principal characters in Thackeray's juvenile story *The Rose and the Ring.*

Rosalind, the heroine of Shakespeare's *As You Like It,* daughter of the banished duke, also in Lodge's story which furnished the groundwork of the play *Rosalynde: Euphues's Golden Legacy, found after his death in his cell at Silexedra.*

Rosalind, in Spenser's *The Shepherd's Calendar,* has been identified with Rose Daniel, sister of the poet Samuel Daniel, who rejected Spenser and married John Florio.

Rosaline, one of the ladies with the Princess in Shakespeare's *Love's Labor's Lost.*

Rosaline, Romeo's first love, in Shakespeare's *Romeo and Juliet.*

Rosamond, the subject of a poetic drama by Algernon C. Swinburne.

Rose, Blanche, and Violet, the title and heroines of a novel by George Henry Lewes.

Rose and Blanche, subject of the first novel of George Sand, written in collaboration with Jules Sandeau, from whose name her pseudonym was taken.

Rose and Blanche, the heroines of Eugène Sue's novel *The Wandering Jew.* The originals are said to have been the twin daughters of Dr. Nathaniel Niles and Sue's stepmother, who married Dr. Niles after the death of his father. Dr. Niles at one time represented America in Sardinia. One of his daughters was the wife of Gen. Adam Badeau.

Rosemonde, the subject of a tragedy by Alfieri (1783).

Rosenberg, Hildegarde, the heroine of Baroness Tautphœus's novel *The Initials.*

Roses, Wars of the: Shakespeare gives the story of the origin of the emblems of York and Lancaster in the fourth scene of the second act of *Henry VI,* Part I.

Rosinante. See QUIXOTE.

Rosmer, Johannes, an idealist, dreamer, and moral coward in Ibsen's play *Rosmersholm.* Under Rebecca West's influence he breaks away from his early political and religious beliefs, but returns to them when he is undeceived as to her character. In the end they commit suicide together. See WEST.

Rosmunda, subject of a tragedy by Giovanni Rucellai, which, with Tressino's *Sophonisba,* produced earlier in the same year, 1515, were the first Italian tragedies.

Ross, a thane of Scotland in *Macbeth.*

Ross, Donald, the subject of a novel, *Donald Ross of Heimra,* by William Black.

Ross, Lord William, in Shakespeare's *Richard II,* a partizan of Bolingbroke, who made him lord treasurer.

Rossmore, Shirley, the heroine of Klein's play *The Lion and the Mouse.*

Rossville, The Earl of, the dull and pompous holder of the estates that are the subject of Miss Ferrier's novel *The Inheritance.*

Rotha, Countess of Heritzburg, the heroine of Stanley Weyman's novel *My Lady Rotha.*

Rothenfels, Graf Eugen, the real name of Eugene Courvoisier, the hero of Jessie Fothergill's novel *The First Violin.*

Rothsay, The Duke of, son of Robert III, who dies mysteriously in a dungeon, a character in Scott's *The Fair Maid of Perth.*

Roubigné, Julie de, the title and heroine of a novel by Henry Mackenzie (1783).

Rouget, Doctor, a selfish and spiteful physician in Balzac's *A Bachelor's Establishment,* who married the most beautiful girl in Issoudun, whom he made very unhappy.

Rougon-Macquart, the name of a family, portrayed in a series of twenty novels by Zola, presenting a curious theory of heredity.

Roumestan, Numa and **Rosalie,** characters of Daudet's novel *Numa Roumestan.*

Rousillon, The Countess of, a fine character in Shakespeare's *All's Well that Ends Well,* the mother of Bertram.

Rousseau, Jean Jacques, is introduced into Dumas's novels *Joseph Balsamo* and *The Memoirs of a Physician.*

Rowena, the nominal heroine of Scott's *Ivanhoe,* who marries Ivanhoe. See REBECCA.

Rowley, Old, a pseudonym of Charles II.

Rowley, Thomas, a fictitious priest of the fifteenth century, to whom Chatterton ascribed poems written by himself.

Roxana, the subject of a Latin tragedy by William Alabaster, acted at Cambridge in 1592, and founded upon Groto's Italian tragedy *La Dalida.*

Roxana and **Statira,** title characters of Nathaniel Lee's play *The Rival Queens* (1678).

Roxana, the subject of a romance (1724) by Daniel DeFoe.

Roxane, the heroine of Rostand's drama *Cyrano de Bergerac,* whom the handsome De Neuvillette courts in words spoken for him by Cyrano.

Royal Martyr, The, a title given to Charles I, beheaded January 30, 1649.

Royaume, Anne, the heroine of Stanley Weyman's novel *The Long Night.*

Ruach, an island visited by Rabelais's Pantagruel, where the people live on wind—promises, flattery, hope.

Rubek, Arnold, an artist in Ibsen's drama *When We Dead Awake*, who sacrifices love for his art, and thereby loses the source of his inspiration. After years he finds Irene, now insane, and both perish in attempting to scale the heights they had before deserted.

Rubek, Maia, in Ibsen's *When We Dead Awake*, the joyous, frivolous wife of the sculptor, who cannot fulfil his promise to lead her to the heights and show her the glories of the world.

Rubempré, Lucien de, the hero of Balzac's *Lost Illusions*, a journalist, poet, and novelist. Intoxicated with early success, he fell into a life of pleasure, which he ended in suicide.

Rudge, Barnaby, the title and hero of a novel by Dickens, a half-witted boy whose constant companion is a raven. The author said this bird was a compound of two owned by him at different times.

Rudolf, King of Puritania, an important character in Anthony Hope's novels *The Prisoner of Zenda* and *Rudolf of Hentzau* and the plays also.

Ruggiero or **Roger,** a Saracen knight in the Orlando poems, who became a Christian and married Bradamant. He became sovereign of Bulgaria.

Runningbrook, Tracy, a character in Meredith's novel *Sandra Belloni* (1864).

Runnymede, a pen-name used by Benjamin Disraeli in letters to the London *Times*, attacking Lord Melbourne's government.

Rupert of Debate, The, a title applied by Bulwer to Lord Derby (1799–1869), "the brilliant chief, irregularly great, frank, haughty, rash."

Rupert, Waldegrave, an important personage in Weyman's novel *My Lady Rotha*.

Russian Byron, The, Alexander Pushkin (1799–1837).

Rutland, the Earl of, appears in Shakespeare's *Henry VI*, Part III, where he is slain in cold blood by Clifford after the battle of Wakefield. He was a boy of seventeen.

Rutledge, the subject of a novel by Miriam Coles Harris.

Ruy Blas, the subject of a noted drama by Victor Hugo.

Ruzzani, Adele, the heroine of Barrili's novel *The Eleventh Commandment.*

Ryder, John Burkett, the chief character in Charles Klein's play *The Lion and the Mouse.*

Ryle, Peggy, the title character of Anthony Hope's *The Intrusions of Peggy.*

Sabrina. See GUENDOLEN.

Sackbut, in Peacock's *Nightmare Abbey,* is intended to caricature the poet Southey.

Sacripant, King of Circassia, a lover of Angelica in the Orlando poems.

Sadak, a general in the service of the Sultan Amurath, who seized his wife and kept her in the seraglio. But he was outwitted by Sadak, who became sultan in his stead, as told in Ridley's *Tales of the Genii.*

Saddletree, Bartoline, a learned saddler and bore in Scott's novel *The Heart of Midlothian.*

Sage of Concord, The, Ralph Waldo Emerson.

Sage of Monticello, The, Thomas Jefferson.

Sage of Samos, The, Pythagoras.

Sagramour le Desirous, a knight of the Round Table.

St. Abe, a Mormon, the subject of a satirical tale in verse by Robert Buchanan, *St. Abe and His Seven Wives.*

Ste. Aubert, the heroine of Mrs. Radcliffe's *The Mysteries of Udolpho.*

St. Barbe, a pen-name of Douglas Sladen.

St. Cecili, a Christian martyr, the subject of the *Second Nun's Tale* of Chaucer.

St. Clair, the name of the family to whom Uncle Tom, in Mrs. Stowe's *Uncle Tom's Cabin,* belonged. Evangeline St. Clair is the Little Eva of the story and the play from it.

St. Clair, Gertrude, the heroine of Miss Ferrier's novel *The Inheritance.*

St. Clare, Father, an important character in Shorthouse's novel *John Inglesant.*

Ste.-Croix, Emma, the heroine of Henry Beçque's *L'Enlevement,* a *femme savante,* who, after refusing to divorce her brutal husband, elopes at last, driven to desperation.

St. Evrémonde. See DARNAY.

St. George, Chevalier de, a name assumed by the son of James II, called "The Pretender."

Saintine, a pen-name of Joseph Xavier Boniface, author of *Picciola.*

St. John, a clergyman intending to become a missionary, whose offer of marriage is declined by the heroine of Charlotte Brontë's *Jane Eyre.*

St. Just, Eileen, the heroine of Ellen T. Fowler's novel *Place and Power.*

St. Leger, the subject of a novel by Richard B. Kimball.

St. Leon, the title and hero of a novel by William Godwin; he has discovered the philosopher's stone and the elixir of life. His wife is said to be an idealized portrait of Godwin's wife, Mary Wollstonecraft.

Saint-Maclon, Duchess of, the brilliant, indiscreet, and obstinate heroine of Anthony Hope's novel *The Indiscretion of the Duchess.*

St. Orbyn, the title character of John Oliver Hobbes's play *The Ambassador.*

St. Pierre, Adeline, a leading character in Mrs. Radcliffe's *The Romance of the Forest.*

St. Prieux, Julie's lover in Rousseau's novel *Julie: or, The New Héloïse.*

Sakuntala, the subject of a famous Indian drama by Kâlidasa, translated by Sir William Jones. She was a water-nymph married to a king, Dushyanta; their son, Bhârata, was the founder of the glorious race of the Bhâratas. Kâlidasa is said to have lived in the first century B.C. and is ranked among the great poets of the world.

Saladin, Sultan of Egypt, the Mussulman hero of the Third Crusade, is introduced in Scott's novel *The Talisman,* first in disguise as Sheerkoff, called by the Hermit, Ilderim the Lion of the Mountain, and afterward as El Hakim, a physician.

Salammbô, a daughter of Hamilcar, title character of a novel by Flaubert (1862).

Salamon, Manette, the title character of a novel by the De Goncourts, the model and mistress of the painter Coriolis, whom she ruins as an artist.

Salanio and **Salarino,** friends of Antonio in Shakespeare's *The Merchant of Venice.*

Salathiel, the subject of a romance by George Croly.

Saldar, Countess de, the sister of the hero and an important character in Meredith's novel *Evan Harrington.*

Saleh, the uncle of Beder in the *Arabian Nights,* who conquered the king of Samandal and forced him to give his daughter Giauharê to Beder in marriage.

Salisbury, Earls of, are characters in Shakespeare's *Richard II, Henry V,* and *Henry VI.* They were usually attached to the York party. Warwick, the "king-maker," was Earl of Salisbury, but is known by the title he received through his wife.

Salomy Jane, the title character of a story by Bret Harte and of the play from it by Paul Armstrong.

Salterne, Rose, burned as a heretic in Charles Kingsley's *Westward Ho!*

Saltire, Lord, a man apparently cynical and worldly in Henry Kingsley's novel *Ravenshoe.*

Salvage Knight, The, Sir Artegal.

Sam, Brother, a brother of Lord Dundreary, often spoken of by him in the play *Our American Cousin,* and the subject of a sequel, *Brother Sam,* by Oxenford.

Sambucco, Clementine, the heroine of Edmond About's novel *The Man with the Broken Ear.*

Sampson, Dominie, a noted character in Scott's *Guy Mannering.*

Sampson, Sara, the subject of a tragedy (1755) by Lessing.

Samson, the judge of Israel famous for his strength and his tragic fate. *Samson and Delilah* is an opera (1877) of Saint-Saëns, with words by Lemaire.

Sancho Panza. See PANZA.

Sand, George, the pen-name of the famous French novelist Madame Dudevant. Her first novel was written with Jules Sandeau, and the author's name was given as Jules Sand.

Sandford, Harry, one of the boys of Thomas Day's *Sandford and Merton.*

Sandus, Ruth, an important character in Henry Harland's *The Lady Paramount.*

San Giorgio, Francesco, the leading character in Mathilde Serao's novel *The Conquest of Rome.*

Sanglier, Sir, in Spenser's poem *The Faerie Queene,* cut off his wife's head and stole a squire's wife, insisting that the living woman was his own. The case was brought before Sir Artegal, who imitated the "judgment of Solomon" with like result.

Sangrado, the doctor in Lesage's *Gil Blas,* whose universal remedy was bleeding and warm water.

Saniel, Victor, the chief character of *Conscience* (1878) by Hector Malot.

Sans-Gêne, Madame, the subject of a comedy by Victorien Sardou.

Santangiolo, Beatrice, Duchess of, the heroine of Henry Harland's *The Cardinal's Snuff-Box.*

Santuzza, the heroine of Verga's play *Cavalliera Rusticana* and of Mascagni's opera from it.

Sapho or **Sappho,** the subject of a romance (1884) by Daudet and of a drama founded upon it; also of an opera by Gounod (1884).

Sapsea, Thomas, an auctioneer, afterward Mayor of Cloisterham, in Dickens's *Edwin Drood,* who wrote a notable epitaph on his wife.

Saracco, Luigi, a character in Meredith's novel *Vittoria.*

Saracinesca, Giovanni, the hero of Crawford's novel bearing his name, the son and heir of a princely Italian house, a type of the best manhood of the old nobility. He appears in several of the author's novels, as do the Prince, his father, and his sons, and a cousin, his namesake, a fine strong character, peasant-bred, whose claim to the title and estates is an incident in the romances.

Sarchedow, the subject of a novel by J. G. Whyte Melville (1871).

Sardanapalus, King of Assyria, 836–817 B.C., the last descendant of Semiramis. He is the subject of a tragedy by Byron (1820) and of an opera in French and one in English founded upon Byron's tragedy. See MYRRHA.

Sartorius, a man deriving his income from rentals of the lowest class of London tenements, a leading character in Shaw's drama *Widowers' Houses.*

Satan Montgomery, a name applied to Robert Montgomery on account of his poem (1830) *Satan: or, Intellect without God.*

Satanic School, The, a name applied, first by Southey, to a class of writers, in the early years of the nineteenth century; he named Byron as the leader, and others that have been included are Shelley, Bulwer, Moore, George Sand, Rousseau, Hugo, and Paul de Kock. In the preface to the *Vision of Judgment* (1821) Southey says: "Though their productions breathe the spirit of Belial in their lascivious parts and the spirit of Moloch in their loathsome images of atrocities and horrors which they delight to represent, they are more especially characterized by a Satanic spirit of pride and audacious impiety which still betrays the wretched feeling of hopelessness wherewith it is allied. Byron replied in a parody on *The Vision of Judgment.*

Saturninus, an emperor in Shakespeare's *Titus Andronicus,* married to Tamora, Queen of the Goths. He kills Titus and is killed by Lucius.

Satyrane, Sir, a knight in Spenser's *The Faerie Queene,* who rescues Una from the satyrs.

Saul, King of Israel, the subject of a tragedy (1773) in Italian by Alfieri and one in French (1822) by Soumet; also of an English poem in blank verse by William Sotheby (1807).

Saul, in Dryden's *Absalom and Achitophel,* is intended for Cromwell.

Sauve, Thérèse, a character in Bourget's novel *Une Cruelle Enigme.*

Savage, Captain, a naval commander in Marryat's *Peter Simple.*

Savage, Harry, the kidnaped grandson of Sir Philip in Blackmore's *The Maid of Sker.*

Savage, Richard, the title and hero of a play by Madelaine L. Ryley.

Savarus, Albert, the title and hero of one of Balzac's novels, also a character in *The Quest of the Absolute.* He was a successful lawyer, published an autobiographic novel, and was elected to the Chamber of Deputies. But, disappointed by the marriage of Madame d'Argaiölo, to whom he was attached, he became a Carthusian friar. It has been said that in *Albert*

Savarus Balzac drew a picture of the hero, which, with some modifications, might stand for his own.

Savonarola, the great Italian preacher of the fifteenth century, is introduced in George Eliot's *Romola;* and also in Mrs. Stowe's *Agnes of Sorrento.*

Savoy, Emanuel Philibert, Duke of, appears in Dumas's *The Page of the Duke of Savoy* (1846).

Sawyer, Bob, a medical practitioner of Bristol in Dickens's *Pickwick Papers,* who has a boy to rush into church with horror and dismay on his face and call his master out in great haste; and resorts to other advertising tricks.

Sawyer, Tom, the title and hero of a story of boy life in the West by Samuel L. Clemens (Mark Twain).

Say and Sele, James Fiennes, Lord, taken by Cade's men, who set his head on London Bridge, is introduced in Shakespeare's *Henry VI,* Part II.

Sbogar, Jean, the hero of a romance (1818) by Charles Nodier.

Scæva, a pen-name assumed by John Stubbes after his right hand had been cut off as a penalty for writing a book (1579) against an expected marriage of Queen Elizabeth to the Duke of Anjou. The pen-name was no doubt suggested by the surname **Scævola** (the left-handed) given to young Caius Mutius, who, being discovered in the camp of King Porsena, burned off his right hand, to show that he could bear torture.

Scanderbeg (that is, Alexander the Beg or Bey), a name given to George Castriot (1404–1467), who deserted Amurath II and fought against him for the Albanians. He is the hero of James M. Ludlow's romance *The Captain of the Janizaries.*

Scapin, a valet whose tricks are the subject of Molière's comedy *Les Fourberies de Scapin* (1671), translated by Otway with the title *The Cheats of Scapin.*

Scaramouch, a boastful soldier of popular Italian comedy, originally meant to ridicule the pompous airs of a Spanish don, and dressed in Spanish costume.

Scarlett, Hugh, the chief personage of Mary Cholmondeley's novel *Red Pottage.*

Scarlett, Will. See Hood, Robin.

Scatcherd, Miss, a cruel teacher at Lowood in Charlotte Brontë's novel *Jane Eyre,* said to be a portrait of an assistant at the school at Cowan's Bridge.

Scathelocke, one of Robin Hood's men.

Schaunard, the musician in Murger's *Bohemian Life.*

Schedoni, a criminal monk in Mrs. Radcliffe's novel *The Italian.*

Scheherazade, the Sultana supposed to tell the stories of the *Arabian Nights.*

Schemseddin Mohammed, the brother of Noureddin Ali in the *Arabian Nights* story of the latter name.

Schemselnihar, Sultana of Haroun-al-Raschid, in love with Aboulhassan Ali, Prince of Persia. They were widely separated but pined and died at the same hour and were buried in one grave. Their names form the title of their story in the *Arabian Nights.*

Schinderhannes, the title character of *The Robber of the Rhine* (1833) by Leitch Ritchie; called also Baron Wolfenstein; in history, Johann Buckler.

Schlemihl, Peter, the subject of a story by the German author, Chamisso, who sells his shadow to the devil after he has met with a disappointment.

Schönberg-Cotta Family, the subject of a novel (1862) by Elizabeth R. Charles.

Schultz, Hermann, a naturalist in *The King of the Mountains,* a novel by Edmond About.

Schwartz, Martin, the supposed relator of the story in Weyman's *My Lady Rotha.*

Scipio, the secretary of Gil Blas, a thief, but serving his master honestly.

Scotland's Scourge, Edward I of England. The title is inscribed on his tomb in Westminster Abbey.

Scourge of God, The, Attila the Hun (d. 453). The appellation seems to have been given at first to the barbarians as a body, or to the Huns; but later it was applied to Attila alone.

Scourge of Princes, The, the Italian satirist Pietro Aretino (1492–1556).

Scriblerus, Martinus, the son of Cornelius, who had given him an absurd education. Martinus, whose history is related by Pope and Arbuthnot in the *Memoirs of the Extraordinary Life, Works, and Discoveries of Martinus Scriblerus,* had a smattering of everything, but no taste or judgment.

Scrooge, Ebenezer, the partner and heir of Jacob Marley in Dickens's *A Christmas Carol,* who is transformed from a hard old skinflint to a loving philanthropist by three visions that he sees on Christmas Eve.

Scrub, a noted man-of-all-work in Farquhar's comedy *The Beaux' Stratagem* (1707).

Scudamour (shield of love), a knight in Spenser's *The Faerie Queene,* who gained the fair Amoret by winning the shield in a contest with twenty combatants.

Scythrop, Glowry, in Peacock's *Nightmare Abbey,* was intended for Shelley, who admitted the resemblance and was amused at his portrait. Scythrop was in love at the same time with Marionetta O'Carroll and Celinda Toobad.

Seaford, Lilian, the heroine of Black's novel *The Monarch of Mincing Lane.*

Searle, January, the pen-name of George Searle Phillips.

Seaton, Paul, the hero of Ellen T. Fowler's novel *Concerning Isabel Carnaley.*

Sebastian, the cruel and criminal brother of the King of Naples in Shakespeare's play *The Tempest.*

Sebastian, the brother of Viola in Shakespeare's *Twelfth Night,* who marries Olivia.

Sebastian, Don, the title and hero of a tragedy by Dryden (1690).

Sebile, in the romance *Perceforest,* was the lady of the lake, the mother of King Arthur, whose father was Alexander the Great.

Sedgett, Nicodemus, a character in Meredith's novel *Rhoda Fleming.*

Sedley, Amelia, a good but brainless girl in Thackeray's *Vanity Fair.*

Seften, Priscilla, the heroine of Robert Buchanan's novel *God and the Man.*

Seide, Mahomet's slave, the first to believe in his mission, is a character in Voltaire's drama *Mahomet.* His name has become a synonym for blind devotion.

Seidlitz, Laura, the heroine of John Moore's novel *Zeluco* (1789).

Seiglière, Mademoiselle de la, the subject of a comedy by Jules Sandeau.

Sejanus, the subject of a Roman tragedy by Ben Jonson (1603) in which Shakespeare is said to have played.

Selden, Laurence, a leading character in Edith Wharton's *The House of Mirth.*

Selima, an important character in Rowe's play *Tamerlane* (1702), who marries Axilla.

Selvaggio, the chief character in Thomson's *The Castle of Indolence.*

Selysette, in Maeterlinck's drama *Aglavaine and Selysette,* is crushed between the devoted love of her friend Aglavaine and her husband Méléandre, and seeks death.

Semiramis, a legendary queen of Assyria, the founder of Babylon with its hanging gardens. Rossini made her the subject of an opera (1823). The title **Semiramis of the North** was given to two sovereigns: Margaret (1353–1412), who received Denmark from her father, Norway from her husband, and added Sweden by conquest; and Catherine II of Russia (1729–1796), able, ambitious, and immoral.

Sempach, Countess von, a leading personage of Anthony Hope's novel *The King's Mirror* (1899).

Sempronius, a treacherous character in Addison's *Cato.*

Seraphael, Chevalier, in Elizabeth S. Sheppard's novel *Charles Auchester,* is supposed to be a portrait of Mendelssohn.

Seraphic Doctor, The, a title given to the eloquent Franciscan theologian, St. Bonaventura (1221–1274), ranked by Sixtus V as the sixth of the great doctors of the Church.

Seraphic Saint, The, St. Francis of Assisi (1182–1226).

Seraphina, the Princess in Stevenson's *Prince Otto.*

Seraphita, the subject of a novel by Balzac, dealing with mystical, supernatural phenomena.

Sergius, Lucius, a leading character in Duffield Osborne's *The Lion's Brood.*

Sergius, Prince, the hero of Anthony Hope's romance *Sophy of Kravonia.*

Sertorius, a Roman general, conqueror of Meteltus and of Pompey, subject of a tragedy by Corneille.

Servolo, Helena, Machioness of, the heroine of Anthony Hope's story *Helena's Path.*

Setebos, a deity mentioned by old travelers as worshiped by the Patagonians and said by Caliban, in Shakespeare's drama *The Tempest*, to be the god of his mother Sycorax.

Seven Champions of Christendom, The, are Saints Patrick, Andrew, David, George, Denis, Iago, and Anthony.

Seven Sages, The. See SEVEN WISE MASTERS.

Seven Sleepers, The, seven young Christians of Ephesus who, having fled to a cavern during a persecution, were found and walled in; but by a miracle they fell into a sleep that lasted 229 years; they died soon after awaking, and their bodies were taken in a stone coffin to the church of St. Victor in Marseilles. The story is told in many varying versions. In the Mohammedan version the youths were followed by a dog which remonstrated with them for trying to drive him back, saying: "I love those who love God. Sleep, masters, and I will keep guard."

Seven Wise Masters, The, the subjects of a legend told in many versions. It is of a prince who repelled the immoral advances of his stepmother, whereupon she accused him to his father, who sentenced him to death; but the seven wise men, his instructors, each in turn told a story to the father on seven successive days, causing him to waver; but the Queen counteracted their influence every night. At last the Prince himself told a story which led to the discovery of the truth and the death-sentence of the Queen.

Seven Wise Men of Greece, The, seven Greeks of the sixth century B.C., noted for their maxims, which later were inscribed in the temple at Delphi: Bias: His maxim was, "Most men are bad"; Cleobulus: "Avoid extremes"; Periander: "Nothing is impossible to industry"; Chilo: "Consider the end"; Pittacus: "Know thy opportunity"; Solon: "Know thyself"; Thales: "Suretyship is the forerunner of ruin."

Seven Wonders of the World, The: the hanging gardens of Babylon, the pyramids of Egypt, the tomb of Mausolus, Diana's temple at Ephesus, the statue of Zeus by Phidias, the pharos of

Egypt, and the colossus of Rhodes; sometimes the gold-cemented palace of Cyrus is given instead of the pharos.

Seyton, Catherine, one of Queen Mary's maids of honor, with the Queen at Lochleven. In Scott's *The Abbot* she thrust her arm as a bolt into the staples of a door to keep out Lady Lochleven, a feat attributed in history to Catherine Douglas to conceal the Pretender from his enemies.

Sforza, a prisoner for ten years at the Castle of Loches, is the subject of William W. Astor's novel *Sforza.*

Sforza, Ludovico, the title character of Massinger's play *The Duke of Milan* (1622).

Sganarelle, the title character of Molière's *The Doctor in Spite of Himself.* It is the name also of the hero of Molière's comedy *The Forced Marriage,* and is used in other plays of Molière.

Shackford, Richard, the chief character in *The Stillwater Tragedy,* a novel by Thomas Bailey Aldrich.

Shadow, one of Falstaff's recruits in Shakespeare's *Henry IV,* Part II, so thin that a man "might as well level a gun at the edge of a penknife."

Shafton, Sir Piercie, in Scott's novel *The Monastery,* an exquisite and euphuist, who is found to be the grandson of a tailor, Overstitch.

Shagpat, the merchant from whose head "the Identical" is finally taken by Shibli Bagarag in Meredith's novel *The Shaving of Shagpat.*

Shakespeare and **Spenser,** in Scott's *Kenilworth,* are greeted by Leicester with a patronizing word to "wild Will" on his way to court. "The player bowed, the Earl nodded and passed on—so that age would have told the tale—in our perhaps we might say the immortal had done homage to the mortal." Landor wrote *The Trial of Shakespeare;* and Shakespeare is a character in Black's novel *Judith Shakespeare* and the chief personage of Captain Curling's novel *William Shakespeare as He Lived.*

Shakespeare of Divines, The: so Emerson calls Jeremy Taylor.

Shallow, a feeble-minded, boastful justice in Shakespeare's *The Merry Wives of Windsor* and *Henry IV,* Part II. He is believed to be a burlesque on Sir Thomas Lucy, who prosecuted Shakespeare for deer-stealing.

Shandon, Captain, a witty, dissipated, good-humored Grub-street hack in the debtors' prison, a character in Thackeray's *Pendennis.*

Shandy, Tristram, the title character of a famous novel (1759) by Sterne, of which the hero is Captain Shandy, known as Uncle Toby, a retired half-pay officer, brave, modest, kind, and simple, one of the most admired characters in English fiction, called by Hazlitt "one of the finest compliments ever paid to human nature," and by Leigh Hunt, "divine Uncle Toby!"

Sharp, Rebecca, called Becky, a famous character in Thackeray's *Vanity Fair* (1848), small and plain, but a most attractive talker and flatterer, wholly unprincipled and unscrupulous, the finest type of adventuress. She is the leading character in the play by Langdon Mitchell, *Becky Sharp.*

Sharp, Timothy, the title character in Garrick's play *The Lying Valet* (1741).

Sharpe, Archbishop of St. Andrew's, murdered by Balfour of Burley, in Scott's *Old Mortality.*

She, a mysterious potentate in a tale by H. Rider Haggard, *She,* who has lived two thousand years, keeping herself ever young and fair by an annual bath of magic fire.

Sheba, The Queen of, a Begum in Scott's tale *The Surgeon's Daughter,* Adela de Montreville.

Shepherd of Salisbury Plain, The, the hero of a once popular sketch or tract by Hannah More, distinguished for his simple piety and homely wisdom. The original of the sketch was David Saunders, whose own service as a shepherd on Salisbury Plain, together with his father's, extended over a century.

Shepherd of the Ocean: so Spenser calls Sir Walter Raleigh in the poem *Colin Clout's Come Home Again.*

Sheppard, Jack, a noted burglar, executed at Tyburn in 1724 at the age of twenty-three. He is the hero of a romance by DeFoe (1724) and one by W. Harrison Ainsworth (1845).

Sherborne, a character in Disraeli's *Vivian Grey,* supposed to be a portrait of the author's father.

Sheridan, Richard Brinsley, is introduced in the drama *Beau Brummel* by Clyde Fitch and Richard Mansfield.

Becky Sharp (In Thackeray's Vanity Fair)

Mezzotint after a drawing by F. Barnard

Becky Sharp (In Thackeray's *Vanity Fair*)

Mezzotint after a drawing by F. Bernard

Sheva, the title character of Cumberland's play *The Jew* (1776), a philanthropist, who "ever shrank to let his left hand know what his right hand did." The Jews of England presented Cumberland with a handsome purse in acknowledgment of this tribute to their race.

Sheva, one of David's scribes. His name is used in Dryden's *Absalom and Achitophel* for Sir Roger Lestrange, censor of the press under Charles II.

Shingle, Solon, leading character in the farce *The People's Lawyer* by J. S. Jones.

Shirley, William, colonial Governor of Massachusetts, appears in Hawthorne's tale *Howe's Masquerade*, also in *Edward Randolph's Portrait.*

Shore, Jane, the wife of a London goldsmith, who became the mistress of Edward IV. She is the subject of a ballad which was reprinted from a black-letter copy in the Pepys collection, "The Woefull Lamentation of Jane Shore," which gives the old tradition that Shoreditch was so named because she died in a ditch in that suburb, though better authority says the name came from one Sir John de Soerdich of the time of Edward III. A tragedy founded on her life, by Nicholas Rowe, was produced in 1714; and William G. Wills wrote one in 1875.

Short, John, an important character in Crawford's *A Tale of a Lonely Parish.*

Shrapnel, Dr., an important character in Meredith's *Beauchamp's Career.*

Shuffleton, Hon. Tom, a character in Colman's play *John Bull*, a borrower who never pays.

Shylock, the famous Jew of Shakespeare's *The Merchant of Venice*, who hates Antonio—not altogether without provocation—and is willing to lose the payment of the borrowed money for the satisfaction of taking the pound of flesh nominated in the bond.

Sibylle, the heroine of a novel of the name by Octave Feuillet.

Sicenius Velutus, a tribune of the people in Shakespeare's *Coriolanus*, a typical politician, crafty and cowardly.

Sick Man of the East, The, a name given to the Turkish Empire, alluding to the decline of its power. The name originated with the Emperor Nicholas, who, in a conversation on European politics with a representative of Great Britain, said, alluding to Turkey: "We have on our hands a sick man, a very sick man."

Sicilian Vespers, The, the terrible massacre of French soldiers in Sicily in 1282, is the subject of a noted tragedy (1819) by Casimir Delavigne and of an opera by Verdi (1855).

Sidonia, a rich Spanish Jew in Disraeli's *Coningsby*. In an anonymous novel published in 1845, *Anti-Coningsby*, Disraeli figures under the name Ben Sidonia, is defeated in England, and goes to Syria to organize a young Palestine party. Thackeray parodied *Coningsby* in *Codlingsby*.

Sidonie, the subject of a novel by Daudet.

Sidrophel, in Butler's *Hudibras*, is intended, it is supposed, for a portrait of William Lilly, an astrologer of the seventeenth century.

Siegfried, the hero of the old German epic the *Nibelungenlied* and of various legends of the Middle Ages. The son of Siegmund and Sieglinda, he was the strongest, handsomest, and bravest young warrior of his time. He became invulnerable by bathing in the blood of a dragon he had killed, except at one spot where a leaf happened to be on his back, and at last he was killed with a lance thrust in that spot by Hagen, who was seeking the hoard of treasure which Siegfried had taken from the Nibelungen. One of Wagner's great operas is *Siegfried*, the third of the four constituting the *Nibelungen Ring*.

Sigismonda, the heroine of the tragic story of *Sigismonda and Guiscardo*, taken from Boccaccio and written in heroic verse by Dryden. She was the daughter of King Tancred of Salerno, and she secretly married her father's squire; after Tancred discovered it, she received a gold casket containing a human heart; knowing it must be Guiscardo's she took poison and died, after begging that she might be laid in his grave.

Sigismunda, the heroine of a tragedy by James Thomson, *Tancred and Sigismunda*, based on an episode in *Gil Blas*, "The Baneful Marriage."

Sigismunda, the heroine of a tale by Cervantes, the last he wrote, which he preferred to *Don Quixote*.

Sigurd, the subject of the Sigurd Saga in Scandinavian literature, the great warrior of the Volsung family. In Ibsen's drama *The Vikings of Helgeland,* Hiördis takes the part of Brunhild.

Sikes, Bill, a brutal thief in Dickens's *Oliver Twist,* the murderer of Nancy.

Silence, a justice in Shakespeare's *Henry IV,* Part II, stupid when sober and boisterous when drunk.

Silent Sister, The, Trinity College, Dublin, which is heard from comparatively seldom, though heavily endowed.

Silurist, The, the poet Henry Vaughan (1621–1695), who came from South Wales, home of the Silures.

Silver-Fork School, The, a name given to a class of writers who make much of etiquette and social forms. Bulwer is mentioned as one, also Theodore Hook, and Mrs. Trollope.

Silverman, George, a self-depreciating, self-sacrificing young clergyman, subject of a tale by Dickens.

Silvester, Anne, the heroine of *Man and Wife* (1870) by Wilkie Collins, and of the drama.

Silvia, a spirited, witty girl in Shakespeare's *Two Gentlemen of Verona,* the subject of the familiar song "Who Is Sylvia?"

Silvia, the heroine of D'Annunzio's drama *La Gioconda,* a beautiful character, slighted by her sculptor-husband Lucio for a young model, because his wife "cannot reveal to him his entire creative self."

Silvius, the long-suffering lover of Phœbe in Shakespeare's *As You Like It.*

Simonides, Don, the subject of a story (1581) by Barnabe Rich.

Simon Pure. See PURE.

Simon the Cobbler, a character in Miss Mühlbach's novel *Marie Antoinette.*

Simons, Mrs., a caricature of the Englishwoman in Edmond About's novel *The King of the Mountains.*

Simpcox, Saunder, an impostor in Shakespeare's *Henry VI,* Part II, pretending to have received his sight by a miracle.

Simple, Peter, the title and hero of a novel by Frederick Marryat.

Sindbad the Sailor, a man of many adventures in the *Arabian Nights.*

Sinfi, the heroine of Theodore Watts-Dunton's poetic drama *Aylwin.*

Singleby, Lady, a character in Meredith's *Diana of the Crossways.*

Single-Speech Hamilton, William Gerard Hamilton, whose eloquence in that one speech, November 13, 1775, "threw into the shade every orator except Pitt."

Sintram, the hero of a noted German novel by Baron La Motte Fouqué, suggested by Dürer's engraving "The Knight, Death and Satan."

Siward, Earl of Northumberland, famous in tradition, was fabled to be descended from a bear. He is the leader of the English forces in Shakespeare's *Macbeth.*

Sixteen-String Jack, a highwayman, John Rann, noted for wearing sixteen strings or tags to his breeches. This was used by Dr. Johnson as an illustration of the failure of people to distinguish between "what men in general cannot do if they would and what every man may do if he would."

Skeggs, Carolina Wilhelmina Amelia, a would-be "genteel" young lady in Goldsmith's *The Vicar of Wakefield.*

Skepsey, Daniel, a pugilist in Meredith's *One of Our Conquerors.*

Sketchley, Arthur, the pen-name of Rev. George Rose.

Skimpole, Harold, a man in Dickens's *Bleak House,* who affected to know no more about money or its equivalents than "a mere child," a sponger on his friends, bright and charming, utterly selfish. He has been identified with Leigh Hunt; but the author denied having drawn anything from Hunt but some of his mannerisms and external characteristics.

Skshetuski, Pan Yan, a model of chivalry and patriotism, the hero of Sienkiewicz's novel *Fire and Sword,* appears also in *The Deluge* and *Pan Michael.*

Skule Bardsson, Earl, the chief character in Ibsen's drama *The Pretenders,* is proclaimed king against his son-in-law, Hakon, fails, and gives himself up to the people to death, that Hakon may not have to carry out his decree against him, which would result in separating Hakon from his wife.

Slawkenbergius, Hafen, in Sterne's *Tristram Shandy,* is an author with a very long nose, and an authority on noses. A passage from his writings giving the story of a man with an extraordinarily long nose is given in the novel.

Sleary, a circus-man in Dickens's *Hard Times.*

Sleek, Aminadob, a character in Morris Barnett's comedy *The Serious Family.*

Slender, a young booby in Shakespeare's *The Merry Wives of Windsor,* a suitor of Anne Page.

Slick, Sam, a droll Yankee clockmaker and pedler, the subject of a book by Judge Thomas C. Haliburton, who was often called by his name.

Slop, Doctor, in Sterne's *Tristram Shandy,* a choleric, opinionated physician, to whom Tristram owed his broken nose.

Slope, Mr., a clergyman in Trollope's *Barchester Towers.*

Sloppy, an awkward foundling in Dickens's *Our Mutual Friend.*

Slough of Despond, a bog that Christian in *Pilgrim's Progress* had to pass through on his way to the Celestial City.

Slowboy, Tilly, Mrs. Peerybingle's nurse-girl in Dickens's tale *The Cricket on the Hearth,* very fond of the baby, but apt to carry it head downward and bang it against door-posts and furniture.

Sludge, Mr., the Medium, the imaginary speaker in a monologue by Browning, who defends the imposture in which he has been detected. It is meant for David D. Home, the Spiritualist.

Slum, Mr., a poet in the advertising line, in Dickens's *The Old Curiosity Shop.*

Sly, Christopher, the tinker who is made to believe himself a lord in the induction to Shakespeare's *The Taming of the Shrew.*

Slyme, Chevy, a dissipated vagabond in Dickens's *Martin Chuzzlewit,* whom Tigg calls "an unappreciated genius."

Smallweed, the name of a repulsive family figuring quite largely in Dickens's *Bleak House.*

Smectymnuus, a name formed from the initials of five Presbyterian ministers, Stephen Marshall, Edmund Calamy, Thomas Young, Matthew Newcomen, and William Spurstow, the authors of a celebrated attack upon Episcopacy (1641), a reply to

Bishop Hall. The following year Milton published *An Apology for Smectymnuus.*

Smelfungus, a name applied to Smollett by Sterne, on account of his *Travels through France and Italy* (1766), in which he saw nothing to praise and everything to censure. The name is occasionally used for a censorious traveler or critic.

Smike, a half-witted drudge at Dotheboys Hall, befriended by Nicholas Nickleby and found at length to be the lost son of his uncle, Ralph, in Dickens's *Nicholas Nickleby.*

Smith, Mr., the chief character of the novel of that name by Mrs. Walford.

Smith, Van Diemen, a colonist in Meredith's *The House on the Beach,* who is anxious to return to England.

Smulkin, a fiend mentioned in Shakespeare's *King Lear.*

Snagsby, a kind-hearted law-stationer in awe of his wife in Dickens's *Bleak House* (1852).

Sneak, Jerry, the type of a henpecked husband in Foote's play *The Mayor of Garratt* (1763), who was chosen mayor. The actor Samuel Russell was identified with the rôle as Jerry Sneak Russell.

Sneerwell, Lady, one of the members of Sheridan's *School for Scandal* (1777).

Snitchey and Crags, a law firm in Dickens's tale *The Battle of Life.* Snitchey always ended: "I speak for Self and Craggs"; and after his partner died, "for Self and Craggs deceased."

Snodgrass, Augustus, a poet in the Pickwick Club.

Snout and **Snug.** See QUINCE.

Snowe, Lucy, the heroine of Charlotte Brontë's *Villette,* the supposed narrator of her story.

Sobieski, Yan, the Polish King, appears in Sienkiewicz's trilogy *Fire and Sword, The Deluge,* and *Pan Michael;* also in *The Field of Glory.* Sobieski is a character in Miss Porter's *Thaddeus of Warsaw.*

Sobrino, called "The Sage," a Saracen warrior in Ariosto's *Orlando Furioso,* who became a Christian after Agramant had broken the compact he had made to trust the fate of the war to two champions in single combat, when the Christian champion won.

Sofronia, the heroine of an episode in Tasso's *Jerusalem*

Delivered. Aladine, King of Jerusalem, enraged because an image of the Virgin which he had stolen was carried away, ordered the execution of all his Christian subjects. To save the others, Sofronia declared that she had done it, and was ordered to execution; then her lover Olindo accused himself to save her, but the King sentenced both to death. They were saved through the intervention of Clorinda the Amazon, and Sofronia, who had not loved Olindo before this proof of his devotion, became his wife.

Soldan, The, in Spenser's poem *The Faerie Queene,* is interpreted as intended for Philip II of Spain.

Soliman is the hero of an old tragedy, *Soliman and Perseda,* showing "Love's Constancy, Fortune's Inconstancy, and Death's Triumphs."

Solness, Halvard, the title character of Ibsen's drama *The Master Builder.* He is "a doubter of himself cowed by the thoughts of the new generation."

Solomon of England, The, a title that was bestowed upon Henry VII, whose reign, following the Wars of the Roses, was a relief to the country; also upon James I, perhaps because he talked wisely and acted foolishly.

Solomons, Ikey, a pen-name attached by Thackeray to his novel *Catherine.*

Solveig deserts her home to join Peer Gynt, in Ibsen's drama of the latter name. He leaves her in his hut in the wood; and she waits for him there till he comes back, an old man.

Somerset, John Beaufort, Earl of, in Shakespeare's *Henry VI,* Part I, calls for allegiance to the red rose of Lancaster. His brother Edmund, the next earl, appears in *Henry VI,* Part II. He fell at St. Albans by the hand of Richard, according to the statement in the third part, where his son Edmund, Duke of Somerset, the last of the male line of the Beauforts, is introduced.

Somerset, Pembroke, the English friend of Thaddeus in Miss Porter's *Thaddeus of Warsaw.*

Somnambulus, a signature of Sir Walter Scott to *The Visionary,* political satire.

Sophonisba (235–203 B.C.), a daughter of Asdrubal, affianced to Masinissa, King of the Numidians, but married Syphax.

Afterward taken captive by Masinissa and Lelius, she married the Numidian prince, rather than live as a captive. The story is the subject of dramas in Italian by Trissino and Alfieri, in French by Mairet, Corneille, Lagrange-Chancel, and Voltaire; and in English by Marston and Thomson.

Sordello, a poet of Mantua, born near the close of the twelfth century, seen by Dante in Purgatory. He is spoken of in Dante's *De Vulgare Eloquentia* as having created the Italian language. He is the subject of a long poem by Browning, who accepts the account of his birth which makes him the son of a soldier Galinguerra, and his first wife, Retrude, of the family of the German Emperor Frederick II, but brought up as the son of an archer, Elcorte.

Sorel, Agnes, the mistress of Charles VII of France, is a character in Schiller's drama *The Maid of Orleans.*

Sorrel, Hetty, a beautiful but shallow girl in George Eliot's *Adam Bede,* engaged to Adam, but led astray by Arthur Donnithorne.

Sosia, a servant of Amphitryon in a play of the latter name by Plautus, of which adaptations have been made by Molière and Dryden. Mercury disguises himself as the double of Sosia, causing confusion and even leading Sosia to doubt his own identity. The name is a synonym for a double.

South, Dorothy, title and heroine's name of a novel (1902) by George Cary Eggleston.

South-Sea Bubble, a name given to a great stock-jobbing scheme in England, 1720, by which great numbers of investors were ruined.

Southwell, a priest and canon of St. Stephen's in Westminster, is introduced in Shakespeare's *Henry VI,* Part II. He died in the Tower before the time set for his execution.

Sowerberry, the undertaker to whom Oliver Twist is apprenticed.

Sowerby, Dudley, the son of a peer in Meredith's *One of Our Conquerors.* He jilts Nesta Radnor on learning of her birth, but later tries to renew the engagement, without success.

Spanish Brutus, The, Alfonso Perez de Guzman, who sacrificed his son rather than surrender Tarifa, of which he was governor (1293).

Spanish Fury, The, a name given to the burning of Antwerp, November 4, 1576, and the massacre of the inhabitants.

Spanish Molière, The, a name given to the dramatic poet Moratin (1760–1828), who took Molière for his model.

Spanker, Lady Gay, a popular character on the stage, in Dion Boucicault's *London Assurance* (1814).

Spartacus, a Roman gladiator, the leader of a servile insurrection, killed A.D. 71. He is the hero of Edgar Quinet's dramatic poem *Les Esclaves* ("The Slaves").

Spasmodic School, The, a name applied to a class of writers in the nineteenth century characterized by an overstrained artificial style, and satirized in Aytoun's *Firmilian: a Spasmodic Tragedy* (1854). Authors that have been named as belonging to the school are Carlyle, Philip James Bailey, Alexander Smith, and Sydney Dobell.

Spaulding, Rev. Robert, title character in Gillette's play *The Private Secretary.*

Speed, Valentine's punning servant in Shakespeare's *Two Gentlemen of Verona.*

Spendius, a Greek in Flaubert's *Salammbô,* who stirs up the mercenaries to revolt.

Spenlow, Dora, David's first wife in Dickens's *David Copperfield.*

Spens, Sir Patrick, the hero of a famous ballad, printed in the collections of old ballads. He is represented as having been drowned with his whole crew on his way home from Norway, whither he had been sent on a mission to the King.

Squeers, Wackford, the rapacious, ignorant, and brutal proprietor of Dotheboys Hall in Dickens's *Nicholas Nickleby.*

Squintum, Doctor, in Foote's farce *The Minor,* was intended to ridicule Rev. George Whitefield. Theodore Hook applied the name to the Rev. Edward Irving, who had a cast in the eyes.

Squire of Dames, the phrase, used often for a man devoted to the society of women, is taken from Spenser's *The Faerie Queene,* where the knight calling himself so was sent out by Columbell to do service unto gentle dames. His story is substantially the "Host's Tale" in Ariosto.

Staël, Madame de, the celebrated author of *Corinne,* is introduced in Balzac's *Louis Lambert,* the hero of which she discovered as a ragged urchin reading Swedenborg; she had him educated, but afterward forgot him. She appears also in *Taking the Bastile* (1853) by Dumas.

Stafford, Sir Humphrey and **William,** characters in Shakespeare's *Henry VI,* Part II, slain in Cade's rebellion. Their cousin, Lord Stafford, appears in the third part.

Stagirite, The, Aristotle, born at Stagira in Macedon.

Stäl, Ensign, supposed narrator of the Stories of Ensign Stäl, romances describing scenes of the second Finnish war, by Johan Ludwig Runeberg (1804–1877).

Stalky, the chief character of Kipling's *Stalky & Co.*, an ill-bred but clever schoolboy.

Staines, Dr. Christopher, the husband of the simpleton in Charles Reade's novel *A Simpleton.*

Stanhope, Lady Hester, famous for her career in Syria, was envied by Madame de Bargeton in Balzac's *Lost Illusions,* who called her "that blue-stocking of the desert."

Stanley, Sir John, Sir William, and **Lord Thomas,** brothers, appear in Shakespeare's *Henry VI* and *Richard III.*

Stareleigh, the justice who presided at the trial of Mrs. Bardell's suit in *The Pickwick Papers,* is said to be a caricature of Sir Stephen Gaselee, a judge of the court of common pleas.

Starvation Dundas, a nickname given to Henry Dundas, Lord Melville, who used the word "starvation" in a speech in Parliament in 1775, its first introduction into the language.

Starveling. See QUINCE.

Statira. See ROXANA.

Staunton, George, the betrayer of Effie Deans in Scott's *The Heart of Midlothian,* first appearing as Geordie Robertson. He leads the mob in the attack on the prison, disguised as Madge Wildfire.

S. T. C., the initials of the poet Coleridge, by which he is sometimes designated.

Steele, Charley, the leading character in Gilbert Parker's novel *The Right of Way.*

Steerforth, James, a school friend of the hero of Dickens's

David Copperfield, an attractive scoundrel who elopes with Little Em'ly.

Steinbock, Count Wenceslas, an important character in Balzac's *Cousin Betty.* He was a Livonian exile, became a carver and sculptor in Paris, and was encouraged and aided by Lisbeth Fischer (Cousin Betty).

Steinhoff or **Steensgaard,** a politician of low extraction who succumbs at once to the attentions of aristocrats, in Ibsen's play *The Young Men's League.*

Stella: so Sir Philip Sidney called Lady Penelope Devereux, with whom he was in love, in a series of poems, *Astrophel and Stella.* At the time of his death she was the widow of Lord Rich; she afterward married Charles Blount, created Earl of Devonshire.

Stella, a name given by Dean Swift to Esther Johnson, to whom he was privately married.

Steno, Alba, an innocent young girl in Bourget's novel *Cosmopolis* (1892), who brings about her own death on discovering the infamy of her mother.

Steno, Michel, one of the chiefs of the tribunal of Forty, whose insult to the young dogaressa and its light punishment by the Forty are the occasion of the Doge's conspiracy to abolish the tribunal—in Byron's *Marino Faliero.*

Stephano, Earl of Carnuti, an officer of the Christian army in Tasso's *Jerusalem Delivered.*

Stephano, a drunken butler with a scheme to take the island and make himself king, in Shakespeare's play *The Tempest.*

Stephen, a currish youth in Jonson's *Every Man in His Humor* (1598).

Stephen of Amboise, leader of 5,000 infantry under Godfrey in Tasso's *Jerusalem Delivered.*

Stern, Daniel, the pen-name of Marie de Flavigny, Countess of Agoult.

Steyne, The Marquis of, a character in *Vanity Fair,* whose conduct with Mrs. Rawdon Crawley (Becky Sharp) gives rise to a great scandal.

Stidman, a noted carver and sculptor of Paris, Steinbock's teacher—secretly in love with Madame Steinbock when she was neglected by Wenceslas, in Balzac's *Cousin Bette.*

Stiggins, Rev. Mr., called The Shepherd, a canting hypocrite in Dickens's *The Pickwick Papers*, a preacher at Emanuel Chapel.

Stillingfleet, Mark, the hero of Ellen Thorneycroft Fowler's *Place and Power.*

Stirling, Peter, the subject of a novel (1899) by Paul Leicester Ford, *The Honorable Peter Stirling.*

Stockmann, Dr. Thomas, a fussy fanatical enthusiast in Ibsen's *An Enemy to Society*, who is nevertheless a moral hero fighting for truth.

Storm and Stress Period, The, takes its name from a drama by Friedrich von Klinger, *Sturm und Drang;* it is applied to the closing quarter of the eighteenth century, when society and literature in Germany were in revolt against the limitations of former years.

Strafford, Thomas Wentworth, Earl of, Lord-lieutenant of Ireland under Charles I, executed for treason under a warrant of the King in 1641, is the subject of a drama by Browning in which the author represents him as actuated solely by devotion to Charles.

Straford, in Rostand's fantastic comedy *The Romancers*, is employed by Sylvette's father to disillusion her with romantic adventures.

Stralenheim, Count of, in Byron's *Werner*, intending to make way with Werner for his inheritance, is himself murdered by Ulric, Werner's son and the lover of his daughter Ida, causing the final separation of the lovers.

Stranger, The, in Hauptmann's play *Hannele*, appears to Hannele in her delirium as Christ in a glorified image of her teacher, Gottwald, the only one that has ever been kind to her.

Stranger, The, a character in Ibsen's drama *The Lady from the Sea.*

Strap, Hugh, the faithful and ill-treated servant in Smollett's *Roderick Random.*

Strephon, the shepherd in Sidney's *Arcadia*, whose name is a synonym for a sighing lover.

Stretton, Hesba, the pen-name of Miss Sarah Smith of Wellington, Salop.

Strike, Caroline, the beautiful sister of the hero of Meredith's novel *Evan Harrington,* married to an officer in the Marines.

Stromminger, Walburga, is the Geier-Wally of Wilhelmine v. Hillern's novel.

Strong, Reliance, the leading character of *Friends,* by Elizabeth Stuart Phelps Ward.

Struensee, the subject of a remarkable tragedy by Michel Beer, brother of the composer Meyerbeer; also of a tragedy by Heinrich Laube. Johan Friedrich, Count von Struensee, was a German who rose to power in Denmark and had a remarkable career. At first physician to King Christian VII, he gradually rose to supreme power and introduced many reforms whereby he gained the ill-will of the aristocrats, whose privileges and powers were affected; by his Voltairean philosophy he incurred the antagonism of the orthodox masses. A conspiracy headed by the King's stepmother, who was displeased at the prominent part of the Queen in government, brought about the imprisonment of Struensee, and he was beheaded in 1772.

Struldbrugs, in *Gulliver's Travels,* people of Luggnagg, who never die.

Stuart. See CHARLES I, CHARLES II, CHARLES EDWARD, JAMES I, JAMES V OF SCOTLAND, MARY STUART, and PRETENDERS.

Stuart Kings, The, said to have descended from Banquo, are shown in prophetic apparition to Macbeth in the tragedy.

Stuart of Italy, The Mary: so Jeanne I of Naples has been called, from the resemblance in the incidents of their lives. Jeanne's husband, André, was assassinated two years after her marriage, and she married the assassin; in 1347 she fled to Provence, and was strangled in 1382. A tragedy by La Harpe, *Jeanne de Naples,* appeared in 1765.

Stubbs, Cecilia, much admired by the youthful Waverley in Scott's novel of the latter name.

Styles, Tom or **John,** a name formerly used in legal papers as John Doe has been since.

Subtle, the title character of Ben Jonson's *The Alchemist,* who pretends to be almost in possession of the secret of transmuting metals, and dupes Sir Epicure Mammon and other believers.

Suckfist, Lord, the defendant in a suit in the *Pantagruel* of Rabelais.

Suckling, Lord, a character in Meredith's *Rhoda Fleming.*

Suffolk, Earl of, in the first two parts of Shakespeare's *Henry VI*, a friend of Queen Margaret, condemned on a charge of treason and banished; taken by pirates on the way and put to death.

Suffolk, Charles Brandon, Duke of, famous for his beauty, a favorite of the King, whose sister was his third wife, is introduced in Shakespeare's *Henry VIII*. He is a character in Charles Major's novel *When Knighthood Was in Flower.*

Sulky and **Silky,** characters in Holcroft's *The Road to Ruin* (1792). Sulky is gruff, but honest and generous. Silky is a bland hypocrite, a swindler and miser.

Sullen, Squire, in Farquhar's *The Beaux' Stratagem,* separated from Mrs. Sullen fourteen months after marriage, from incompatibility of tastes and tempers, when he was obliged to give up her dowry of twenty thousand pounds. He was sullen, she was cheerful; she wouldn't drink ale, he wouldn't drink tea; he hated ombre and picquet, she hated racing and cock-fighting; she wouldn't hunt, he wouldn't dance.

Sumfit, Mrs., a character in Meredith's *Rhoda Fleming.*

Summerson, Esther. See HAWDON, ESTHER.

Surface, Sir Oliver, and his nephews, Charles and Joseph, characters in Sheridan's play *The School for Scandal.* Charles is a scapegrace, good at heart, Joseph hypocritically correct and benevolent.

Surrey, Thomas Howard, Earl of, appears in Shakespeare's *Richard III*, a partizan of Richard. After Bosworth he was attainted, imprisoned, and deprived of his title, but restored after three years, and, having commanded at Flodden in 1513, received his father's title as Duke of Norfolk, and under that name appears in Shakespeare's *Henry VIII*, where his son is Earl of Surrey. His grandson was the famous Surrey, scholar and poet, who was executed by order of Henry VIII.

Susan, Black-eyed, the heroine of a ballad by Gay, *Sweet William's Farewell.*

Susan, Duchess of Dewlap, a character in Meredith's *Tale of Chloe.*

Sussex, Lord, in Scott's *Kenilworth,* receives the Queen at Say's Court, and attends the pageant at Kenilworth Castle.

Suteh, Lieutenant, an important character in A. E. W. Mason's novel *Four Feathers.*

Sutherland, Hugh, a leading character in George MacDonald's *David Elginbrod* (1862).

Svengali, the hypnotist and musician in Du Maurier's novel *Trilby* and in the play from it by Paul Potter. He uses Trilby's fine voice to express the music she cannot understand or execute except when under his influence.

Swan David, the subject of a "fantasy" by Hawthorne suggesting the great number of possibilities that may come within one's reach without his dreaming of them.

Swanhilda and **Falk,** in Ibsen's play *Love's Comedy,* part, that their love may remain an ideal.

Sweeting, one of the four curates in Charlotte Brontë's *Shirley.*

Sweetwinter, Bob, Mabel, and **Mark,** characters in George Meredith's novel *The Adventures of Harry Richmond.*

Swiveller, a careless, absurd, and amusing fellow in Dickens's *The Old Curiosity Shop,* always dirty, ragged, out of money, and in debt, but always light-hearted. He kept a little book to show the streets he could not pass through when the shops were open, and every purchase on credit closed up another.

Sybil, the subject of a political novel (1845) by Disraeli.

Sycorax, Caliban's mother in Shakespeare's *The Tempest.* She was a witch, and kept Ariel imprisoned in the rift of a pine-tree till Prospero released him.

Sylander. See CLARINDA.

Sylla, Cornelius, the Dictator of Rome after he had defeated his rival, Marius. He is the subject of a dialogue with Eucrates by Montesquieu (1822) and of a tragedy in French by De Juay; and Thomas Lodge produced in 1594 the *True Tragedies of Marius and Sylla.*

Sylli, Signor, a conceited Italian exquisite, a suitor to the heroine, Camiola, of Massinger's play *The Maid of Honor.*

Sylvester, Sir George, the hero of Anthony Hope's comedy *The Adventure of Lady Ursula.*

Sylvia, the heroine of Farquhar's play *The Recruiting Officer,* who, when her father opposes her marriage with Captain Plume, enlists in his company.

Sylvia, the title character of Mrs. Gaskell's *Sylvia's Lovers.*

Sylvia, the heroine of a short poetic drama, *Le Passant,* by François Coppée, and of an opera from it by Leoncavallo.

Sylvio de Rosalva, Don, the hero and title of a satirical novel by Christoph Martin Wieland.

Symkyn, Symond, the miller in Chaucer's *The Reeve's Tale.*

Syntax, Doctor, the subject of a once popular book by William Combe, *The Tour of Doctor Syntax in Search of the Picturesque* (1812).

Syphax, an old Numidian soldier in Addison's *Cato,* who deserts Cato for Cæsar.

Syphax, an Arab chief in Tasso's *Jerusalem Delivered.*

Tabor, Ariel, the heroine of Booth Tarkington's novel *The Conquest of Canaan* (1905).

Taffy, the common name for a Welshman, is a corruption of David. This name is given to Talbot Wynne by his companions in Du Maurier's *Trilby.*

Tag-Rag and Bobtail, Messrs., a pen-name used by Isaac Disraeli.

Taliesin, a legendary bard of King Arthur's time, whose story is told in *The Mabinogion.*

Tallerant, Sabine, a character in Feuillet's novel *La Morte.*

Talleyrand, the famous French diplomat (1754–1838), is introduced into Balzac's novels *The Gondreville Mystery, The Thirteen,* and others; is also a character in Conan Doyle's play *Brigadier Gerard,* and in A. R. Haven's play *Josephine, Empress of the French.*

Talus, a mythical man of brass made for Minos by Vulçan, which patroled the Island of Crete. In *The Faerie Queene* he is an attendant of Sir Artegal, is called the iron man, and uses an iron flail on law-breakers.

Tamerlane, the Tatar (1336–1405), is the subject of a play by Marlowe, *Tamburlaine the Great,* and of one by Nicholas

Rowe, *Tamerlane.* The latter was produced in 1702, and its hero is said to have been intended for William III, and Bajazet, whom Tamerlane conquered at Ancyre, for Louis XIV.

Tamino. See PAMINA.

Tamora, a treacherous Queen of the Goths in *Titus Andronicus.*

Tam o' Shanter, the subject of a famous poem by Burns, which records Tam's adventures when he was riding home one night in a somewhat unnatural state. This poem furnishes more popular quotations than any other of its length.

Tancred, one of the chief warriors of the Crusades. In Tasso's *Jerusalem Delivered* he is represented as in love with a pagan warrior-woman, Clorinda, whom he unwittingly slays. She is baptized by him before she dies. *Tancred* is the title of a tragedy by Voltaire (1760) and of an opera by Rossini (1813), also of a novel by Disraeli. Tancred, Prince of Otranto, is introduced in Scott's *Count Robert of Paris.*

Tancred and Sigismunda was the title of a play by five members of the Inner Temple, presented there before Queen Elizabeth. It is also the title of a tragedy by James Thomson (1745).

Tanner, John, the chief character in George Bernard Shaw's drama *Man and Superman* (1903), a revolutionary socialist, brilliant and fascinating, fluent and excitable, "possibly a little mad." He is determined not to marry, in spite of the attraction Ann Whitefield has for him, seeing through all her tricks and lies; but he is finally vanquished.

Tannhäuser, a famous character of German legend, subject of an ancient ballad. He deserts Lisaure to go upon the Venusberg; for Hilario the philosopher has promised that if he has the courage to go there Venus herself will meet him and he shall be her lover. After a year or more he repents, and coming down from the mountain, learns that Lisaure had died of grief. He confesses his sins to Pope Urban. But the pope tells him he can no more receive pardon than the dry wand he holds can bear leaves and blossoms. In despair Tannhäuser returns to the Venusberg; the dry wand of the pope bears leaves and blossoms, and the knight is sought for everywhere; but he never reappears. The legend is used by Tieck in his *Phantasus* and by Wagner in his opera *Tannhäuser,* in which the story varies somewhat from the legend as here given. Lisaure in the opera is Elizabeth. See also ECKHARDT.

Tanqueray, Paula, the title character of Pinero's drama *The Second Mrs. Tanqueray.* Aubrey, her husband, and Ellean, her stepdaughter, are important personages of the play.

Tapley, Mark, the servant of Dickens's *Martin Chuzzlewit;* he is always cheerful and always anxious to get into a position where it will be a credit to be cheerful; but in the most depressing circumstances he never considers that he has found such a position.

Tappertit, Simon, an apprentice in Dickens's *Barnaby Rudge,* "in years just twenty, in looks much older, and in conceit at least two hundred."

Tarlenheim, Fritz von, a character in Anthony Hope's novel *The Prisoner of Zenda,* in the drama of the same name, and in the sequel, *Rupert of Hentzau,* and the drama founded upon it.

Tarquin: the historic tale of Sextus Tarquinius and Lucretia is the basis of several tragedies: Nathaniel Lee's *Brutus* (1679), John Howard Payne's *Brutus* (1820), Arnault's *Lucrece* (1792), and Ponsard's (1843), both in French, and Alfieri's tragedy *Brutus,* in Italian.

Tartarin, of Tarascon, the title and hero of a novel by Alphonse Daudet.

Tartuffe, a famous personage created by Molière in the comedy (1667) that bears his name. He is a hypocritical priest, and has been supposed to have been suggested by Père Lachaise, confessor of Louis XIV, who was fond of truffles (*truffes*). An English adaptation of the play by Isaac Bickerstaff is called *The Hypocrite,* and the character Dr. Cartwell. Madame Delphine de Girardin wrote a comedy, *Lady Tartuffe,* which has been produced with success.

Tasso, Torquato (1544–1595), the author of the great Italian epic *Jerusalem Delivered,* is the subject of a drama by Goethe, *Torquato Tasso,* in which Leonora or Eleanore d'Este, the special object of Tasso's devotion, is a leading character.

Taverney, Andrée, afterward Countess de Charny, is a character in Dumas's novels of the names—*Andrée de Taverney* and *The Countess de Charny;* also in *Joseph Balsamo, The Memoirs of a Physician,* and *The Queen's Necklace.*

Teazle, Sir Peter and **Lady,** the leading characters in Sheridan's comedy *The School for Scandal* (1777).

Telemachus, the son of Ulysses and Penelope. After the fall of Troy he went in search of his father, who had been absent nearly twenty years. *Télémaque* by Fénelon is a romantic prose epic on this quest.

Tell, William, the legendary Swiss hero, is the subject of several stage pieces, notably Schiller's drama (1766) and Rossini's opera (1829). The story is used also in a novel (1788) by Florian, and a French tragedy by Lemierre (1766). Knowles's tragedy (1810) in English has been popular on the stage.

Telley, Maria, chief character in Galdós's story *Marianela* (1878).

Tempest, Diana, the heroine of Mary Cholmondeley's novel of the name, of which John Tempest is the hero.

Tempest, Mr., former Governor of Senegambia, and his witty daughter, Emily, are leading characters in Cumberland's play *The Wheel of Fortune* (1779), where the wheel turns up a fortune for them just in time to save Emily from a distasteful marriage.

Tempest, Sir Roger, the hero of Rhoda Broughton's novel *Nancy.*

Templar, The, Brian de Bois Guilbert, an important character in Scott's *Ivanhoe.*

Temple, Charlotte, an English girl whose misfortunes are related in Susanna Rowson's book of the name.

Temple, Gus, a character in Meredith's *The Adventures of Harry Richmond.*

Temple, Henrietta, the subject of a love-story by Disraeli.

Temple, Miss, a teacher at Lowood in Charlotte Brontë's *Jane Eyre,* who befriended Jane and the persecuted Helen Burns.

Templeton, Laurence, the name under which Scott published *Ivanhoe,* with a dedication to Rev. Dr. Dryasdust.

Terence, the title and hero's name of a novel by Mrs. B. M. Croker and of a play drawn from it. Terence is "the Desmond," tooling a public coach to support a "prodigal grandmother" in state.

Termagant, a violent ranter in old comedies. Hamlet says: "I would have such a fellow whipped for overdoing Termagant." The word was supposed by the Crusaders to be the name of a Mohammedan deity.

Terpin, Sir, a king hanged by Radigund, Queen of the Amazons, in Spenser's *The Faerie Queene,* because he refused to dress as a woman and do women's work.

Tesara, Albano, an important personage of Jean Paul Richter's novel *Titan* (1800–1803).

Tesman, George, the dense, blundering, plodding husband of Hedda Gabler in Ibsen's play of the latter name.

Tess. See DURBEYFIELD.

Tessa, the girl in love with Tito in George Eliot's *Romola.*

Tête Bottée, a name applied to Philippe de Comines from an incident described in *Quentin Durward.* The Duke required Philippe to take off his boots, and, having seen some resentment in his face, then rendered the same office to him, but took the boot and beat him brutally about the head, whereupon the Duke's jester gave Philippe the nickname.

Teufelsdroeckh, Herr, the imaginary philosopher of Carlyle's *Sartor Resartus* (*The Tailor Re-clothed*), who speculates on "the philosophy of clothes"—a satire on the illusions and pretensions that prevail in civilized society.

Thaddeus of Warsaw, the subject of a novel (1803) by Jane Porter, in recognition of which the author was elected a canoness of the Teutonic Order of St. Joachim. The Polish patriot Kosciusko figures in the book.

Thaisa, the wife of Pericles in Shakespeare's play *Pericles, Prince of Tyre.*

Thalaba, the subject of Southey's *Thalaba, the Destroyer.*

Thaumaste, an English philosopher who held a debate in pantomime with Panurge and was defeated, in Rabelais's *Pantagruel.*

Thekla, the daughter of Wallenstein, heroine of Schiller's drama *The Piccolomini,* the first part of *Wallenstein.*

Theodore, the title character of John Fletcher's *The Loyal Subject.*

Theodore, of Ravenna, the hero of Dryden's *Theodore and Honoria.*

Theodorick, the Hermit of Engaddi in Scott's novel *The Talisman,* who reveals himself as Alberick Mortimer, once of high renown in arms, but long lost to the world.

Theodorus, the physician in Rabelais's *Gargantua* who cleared that hero's brain with "Anticyrian hellebore," so that he forgot all the evil he knew.

Theodosius, the subject of a tragedy (1680) by Nathaniel Lee.

Thersites, a deformed and scurrilous reviler among the Greeks at the siege of Troy. He is introduced into *Troilus and Cressida* by Shakespeare, who gives him malicious insight into the weaknesses of the other characters.

Theseus, Duke of Athens: his marriage to Hippolyta is the occasion of the festivities in Shakespeare's *A Midsummer Night's Dream.*

Thiebault, the troubadour, who entertains Arthur in Scott's *Anne of Geierstein* on the way to Aix.

Thisbe, a beautiful girl in Babylon in love with Pyramus who lived in the next house, but was not allowed to marry him. The story is represented before Theseus by the "rude mechanicals" in Shakespeare's *A Midsummer Night's Dream.*

Thomas, the name of a family figuring in Blackmore's *The Maid of Sker.*

Thomas, Saint, the subject of a miracle play *The Incredulity of Thomas.*

Thompson, Ripton, Richard's boy-friend in Meredith's *The Ordeal of Richard Feverel.*

Thopas, Sir, an adventurer whose story, in Chaucer's *The Canterbury Tales,* is left unfinished.

Thornberry, Job, the title character of Colman's comedy *John Bull,* intended as the typical English tradesman.

Thorndyke, Sir Jasper, the chief character in *Rosemary,* a play by Louis N. Parker and Murray Carson.

Thorne, Captain, a name assumed by Louis Dumont in Gillette's play *Secret Service.*

Thorne, Doctor, the subject of a novel by Anthony Trollope.

Thornhill, Sir William, the landlord of Dr. Primrose in Goldsmith's *Vicar of Wakefield,* who assumes the name Burchell when he returns from his travels, and detects the rascalities of his nephew, Squire Thornhill.

Thornley, Christopher, whose real name is Farringdon, the hero of Ellen T. Fowler's *The Farringdons* (1900).

Thorpe, Charles, Lord Medway, the hero of Baroness Tautphœus's novel *Quits.*

Thorpe, Kampa, the pen-name of Emily W. Bellamy.

Thostrup, Otto, the title and chief character of a novel (1836) by Hans Christian Andersen.

Thoughtless, Miss Betsey, the heroine of a novel by Mrs. Heywood (1697–1758), which is supposed to have suggested Miss Burney's *Evelina.* Betsey is a good and sensible girl, but unsophisticated and regardless of conventionality.

Throssell, Phœbe and **Susan,** leading characters in Barrie's play *Quality Street.*

Thwackum, a noted character in Fielding's *Tom Jones.*

Tiburzio, in Browning's drama *Luria,* is the commander of the Pisan forces. See LURIA.

Tickler, Timothy, in the *Noctes Ambrosianæ,* is a portrait of an Edinburgh lawyer, Robert Sym.

Tigg, Montague, a swindler in Dickens's *Martin Chuzzlewit.*

Tilburina, a love-lorn damsel in Sheridan's play *The Critic.*

Tillet, Ferdinand du, a foundling and rascal introduced into many of the novels of Balzac's *Comédie Humaine.*

Tilney, Henry, the hero of Jane Austen's *Northanger Abbey.*

Timias, in Spenser's *The Faerie Queene,* is interpreted as Sir Walter Raleigh.

Timoleon (d. 337 B.C.), the Corinthian general, liberator of Syracuse, and nearly all of Sicily from the Greek tyrants, is the subject of a tragedy by Alfieri (1784), also one by Marie Joseph Chenier.

Timon, an Athenian misanthrope, the subject of Shakespeare's play *Timon of Athens.*

Tinley, Laura, a character in Meredith's *Sandra Belloni.*

Tinman, Martin, a leading personage of Meredith's story *The House on the Beach.*

Tintagiles, a child in Maeterlinck's drama *The Death of Tintagiles,* the heir to a kingdom ruled by his grandmother, who, jealous of any to come after her, has him murdered, in spite of the watchful care of his sisters.

Tinto, Dick, a poor artist in two of Scott's novels, *The Bride of Lammermoor* and *St. Ronan's Well,* whose name was taken as a pseudonym by Frank B. Goodrich, an American author.

Tippecanoe, a sobriquet given to General William H. Harrison in the canvass preceding his election as President of the United States in 1840, referring to his victory over the Indians at the battle of Tippecanoe in Indiana, November 6, 1811.

Tirante the White, the hero and title of a book of chivalry described in *Don Quixote.*

Tiraquelle, the sub-prefect in Anton Giulio Barrili's novel *The Eleventh Commandment* (1870).

Titan, The, the subject of a philosophic romance by Jean Paul Richter.

Titania, the wife of Oberon and queen of the fairies, introduced by Shakespeare into *A Midsummer Night's Dream.*

Titania: so the heroine is called in Black's novel *The Strange Adventures of a Phaeton.*

Tite Barnacle, Mr., the head of the Circumlocution Office in Dickens's *Little Dorrit.*

Titmarsh, Samuel, the chief character in Thackeray's story *The Great Hoggarty Diamond.*

Titmouse, Tittlebat, the man who inherits the fortune in Warren's novel *Ten Thousand a Year.*

Tito Melema, the husband of Romola in George Eliot's novel of the latter name.

Titurel, a pious king of Graalburg, the subject of a romance by Wolfram von Eschenbach of the thirteenth century.

Titus, the name given to the penitent thief in Longfellow's *The Golden Legend.*

Tityrus, a name by which Chaucer is called in Spenser's *The Shepheardes Calendar.*

Tizona, the sword of the Cid.

Toboso, Dulcinea del, the name given by Don Quixote to Aldonza Lorenzo, whom he chose for his lady-love.

Toby, Uncle. See SHANDY, CAPTAIN TOBY.

Todd, Lawrie, the hero of a novel founded upon the autobiography of Grant Thorburn by John Galt.

Todgers, Mrs., in Dickens's *Martin Chuzzlewit,* kept a commercial boarding-house.

Toinette, the clever servant in Molière's *Le Malade Imaginaire,* who brings about the happy dénouement.

Tolleton, Helen, the heroine of Mrs. Walford's novel *Mr. Smith.*

Tolliver, Gabriel, the title character of a novel by Joel Chandler Harris.

Tomalin, a fairy knight, whose name is sometimes used for Tom Thumb.

Tomkins, Joseph, a Parliamentarian soldier in Scott's *Woodstock,* a treacherous rascal, false to both sides.

Tonans, Marcus, a personage of Meredith's *Diana of the Crossways.*

Tonio, a young Tyrolese, the hero of Donizetti's opera *The Daughter of the Regiment.*

Topsy, a slave-child in Mrs. Stowe's *Uncle Tom's Cabin* and in the drama founded upon it, noted for her idea that she never had a father nor a mother, but just "growed."

Tord Bonde, the subject of a novel (1828) by the Swedish writer Gustaf Wilhelm Gumälius.

Torfrida, the heroine of Kingsley's *Hereward the Wake.*

Tormes, Lazarillo de, the subject of a story of the sixteenth century by Diego Hurtado de Mendoza, the first of a class of popular tales of adventure and roguery, to which *Gil Blas* belongs.

Torquil of the Oak, an old forester in Scott's novel *The Fair Maid of Perth,* supposed to be a seer.

Tosca, Floria, the heroine of Sardou's drama *La Tosca* and of an opera founded upon it by Puccini.

Touch-and-Go, Susanna, a noted character in Peacock's *Crotchet Castle.*

Touchett, Ralph, Isabel Archer's cousin in Henry James's *The Portrait of a Lady.*

Touchstone, the clown in Shakespeare's *As You Like It,* "the daintiest fool of the comedies."

Touchwood, Peregrine, an eccentric East Indian in Scott's *St. Ronan's Well.*

Toussaint, Dominique François, called **L'Ouverture**

(1743–1803), the celebrated Haytian general, is the subject of Harriet Martineau's *The Hour and the Man* (1840).

Tower of Hunger, The. See Ugolino.

Towers, Tom, the editor of *Jupiter* in Trollope's *The Warden.*

Townley, Lord, the title character of Vanbrugh and Cibber's play *The Provoked Husband* (1728). The character of Lady Townley was a favorite one with Margaret Woffington and other celebrated actresses.

Tox, Lucretia, a faded lady in Dickens's *Dombey and Son,* who flirted weakly with Major Bagstock, but had some hope of the widower Dombey.

Traddles, Thomas, in Dickens's *David Copperfield,* "the merriest and most miserable of the boys" at Creakle's school, always being caned; but he would cheer up after his suffering and draw skeletons all over his slate, the number of skeletons bearing some direct proportion to the intensity of the suffering. Dr. Mackenzie, a biographer of Dickens, says Traddles was intended for Sir Thomas Noon Talfourd.

Trailles, Count Maxime de, a witty rascal and clever politician, appears in several of the novels of Balzac's *Comédie Humaine.*

Tram, Tom, the hero of a work dating from the seventeenth century, and long very popular, *The Mad Pranks of Tom Tram.*

Tranfield, Grace, a determined young widow in George B. Shaw's drama *The Philanderer,* who refuses Charteris, though they are in love with each other.

Trapbois, a usurer in Scott's *The Fortunes of Nigel.* His daughter, Martha, makes restoration of the King's sign-manual which he has stolen.

Trecentisti, The, a name applied to the great Italian writers of the Trecento—that is, the fourteenth century—notably to Dante, Petrarch, and Boccaccio.

Trécœur, Julie de, the title and heroine's name of a novel by Octave Feuillet, a "tale of sudden, blasting passion, which recalls the most daring creations of art."

Tregarva, Paul, Squire Lavington's gamekeeper, a poet and radical, in Kingsley's *Yeast.*

Trelawney, Rose, the name part in Pinero's comedy *Trelawney of the Wells.*

Trench, Dr. Harry, in Shaw's drama *Widowers' Houses,* desires to marry Blanche Sartorius, is revolted at the source of her father's income, but yields to the temptation to make money after the Sartorius method.

Trenchard, Asa, the title character of the comedy *Our American Cousin.*

Trenchard, Sir Rowland, a character in Ainsworth's novel *Jack Sheppard* (1845).

Trenck, Baron von, noted for his autobiography, is introduced in *Berlin and Sans-Souci* by Louisa Mühlbach.

Trent, Tommy, an important character in Anthony Hope's novel *The Intrusions of Peggy* (1902).

Tresham, Katharine, the chief character in *Morton House* by Christian Reid (1871).

Tresham, Thorold, Lord, and his sister **Mildred,** leading characters in Browning's drama *A Blot in the 'Scutcheon.*

Tressady, Sir George, the subject of a novel by Mrs. Humphry Ward.

Tressilian, Edmund, in Scott's *Kenilworth,* a lover of Amy Robsart, whom she gives up to marry Leicester.

Trevalla, Trix, an important character in Anthony Hope's *The Intrusions of Peggy* (1902).

Trilby, the subject of a novel of that name by Charles Nodier (1780–1844).

Trilby O'Ferrall, the subject of George Du Maurier's novel *Trilby,* the daughter of a former clergyman ruined by drink. She has become an artist's model in Paris and is afterward a singer. See SVENGALI.

Trim, Corporal, Uncle Toby's servant, a noted character in Sterne's *Tristram Shandy.*

Trinculo, the jester in Shakespeare's *The Tempest,* is in the conspiracy to kill Prospero.

Trissotin (three kinds of fool), a vain poet in Molière's *Les Femmes Savantes,* drawn from the Abbé Cotin, a preacher and writer of poems of gallantry.

Tristram, Harry, the title character of Anthony Hope's *Tristram of Blent.* He suddenly resigns the title and estates which he believes wrongly held, on sudden impulse, not as a matter of conscience.

Tristram or **Tristan, Sir,** one of the bravest three of the knights of the Round Table.

Troil, Magnus, and his daughters, **Minna** and **Brenda,** are leading characters in Scott's novel *The Pirate.*

Troilus, a son of Priam, King of Troy; the subject of a long tale in verse by Chaucer, *Troilus and Cresseide,* and of a drama by Shakespeare, *Troilus and Cressida.*

Trotwood, Betsey, the eccentric great-aunt of David Copperfield, kind-hearted, but brusque and rude, who adopts David after his mother's death.

Troy, in Hardy's *Far from the Madding Crowd,* marries and deserts Bathsheba Everdene.

Truffaldin, a personage of popular Italian comedy, the typical tricky and lying valet.

Trunnion, Commodore Hawser, a retired naval officer in Smollett's *Peregrine Pickle,* who has his house defended by a moat and drawbridge, and obliges the servants to take turns as watch and sleep in hammocks.

Tryamour, Sir, the hero of an old English romance in verse.

Tubal, a friend of Shylock in Shakespeare's *The Merchant of Venice,* who brings to Shylock reports of his daughter's extravagance and Antonio's misfortunes.

Tuck, Friar. See HOOD, ROBIN.

Tuckham, Blackburn, the man whom Cecilia Halkett, in Meredith's *Beauchamp's Career,* marries when disappointed by Nevil's fickleness.

Tudor, Mary, a sister of Henry VIII, the heroine of *When Knighthood Was in Flower,* by Charles Major, of the drama from it, and of the comic opera *A Madcap Princess.*

Tulkinghorn, a lawyer in Dickens's *Bleak House,* wearing a ponderously mysterious air, as if holding all the family secrets of everybody. His threat to reveal Lady Dedlock's secret causes her to leave home and results in her death. He himself is a victim of his own quest for evidence of her secret.

Tulliver, Maggie and **Tom,** the chief characters of George Eliot's novel *The Mill on the Floss.*

Tupman, Tracy, a member of the Pickwick Club in Dickens's *Pickwick Papers.*

Turcaret, a dishonest parvenu, subject of a comedy (1709) of the name by Lesage. It is a typical name for an ignorant and coarse man grown rich by base methods.

Turckems, Baroness, a character in *The Adventures of Harry Richmond* (1871) by Meredith.

Turpin, Dick, a noted English highwayman, executed at York in 1739. He is introduced in Ainsworth's *Rookwood,* for which Dr. Maginn is alleged to have written the description of Turpin's ride to York on Black Bess.

Turveydrop, a false and conceited dancing-master, a model of "deportment," in Dickens's *Bleak House.*

Twedde, Leander, the chief character in Anstey's *The Tinted Venus* (1885).

Tweenways, Lord, a character in Pinero's comedy *The Amazons.*

Twickenham, The Bard of: Pope, who had a villa at Twickenham.

Twist, Oliver, the subject of Dickens's novel of the name, a child born in a workhouse, who goes through various painful adventures, but wins to good fortune at last.

Twombly, Right Honorable Sir Julian, the title character of Pinero's play *The Cabinet Minister.*

Two-Shoes, Goody, a poor child whose story is told by Goldsmith. She was so happy in the possession of a pair of shoes that she called everyone's attention to them.

Tybalt, a cousin of Juliet, in Shakespeare's *Romeo and Juliet,* who forces a quarrel with Romeo's party, kills Mercutio, and is killed by Romeo.

Tyrrel, Francis, in Scott's *St. Ronan's Well,* is the elder brother of Lord Etherington.

Uarda, the heroine and title of a novel by George Ebers.

Udeschini, Cardinal, one of the chief characters in Henry Harland's novel *The Cardinal's Snuff-Box.*

Uglyane, the daughter of Anne, Queen of Jutland, in Maeterlinck's play *Princess Maleine.*

Ulysses, the Greek hero, is a character, not only of the *Iliad* and the *Odyssey,* but also of Shakespeare's *Troilus and Cressida.*

A play founded upon his story was written by Nicholas Rome in 1706, and a poetic drama by Stephen Phillips in 1902.

Una, a lady in Spenser's *The Faerie Queene*, interpreted as a personification of Truth.

Uncas, a young Indian chief in Cooper's *Leather-Stocking Tales*. He is the last of the Mohicans.

Uncle Sam, a personification of the United States Government. It is said to have originated in this way: during the Revolutionary War, Samuel Wilson was an inspector of provisions, and was called Uncle Sam by his associates; and goods arriving for the contractor were marked with his initials E. A. followed by U. S., meaning United States. Someone read it "Elbert Anderson and Uncle Sam"; and so U. S. continued to be called Uncle Sam.

Uncle Toby. See SHANDY, CAPTAIN.

Uncle Tom, a fine character, the negro slave who is the hero of Mrs. Stowe's *Uncle Tom's Cabin*. The original of the character was Josiah Henson, born in slavery in Maryland, 1787. When a young man and a preacher he took his master's slaves to a relative in Kentucky to prevent their passing into the possession of creditors. There they were hired out to neighboring planters; and Henson worked for a Mr. St. Clair, whose little daughter used to read to him. He had saved $500 toward purchasing his freedom, when his master's son took him to New Orleans to sell, but was attacked by yellow fever. The slave nursed him through the illness and took him back to Kentucky. He escaped at last to Canada, prospered as a farmer and was pastor of a church. In 1850 he went to London, where he lectured, and was entertained by the Queen at Windsor Castle.

Undine, a water-nymph, the subject of La Motte Fouqué's famous German tale of the name.

Unknown, The Great: so the author of the Waverley novels, which were at first published anonymously, was called.

Unreason, The Abbot of, in Scott's *The Abbot*, was Adam Woodcock, disguised as Owleglasse.

Uploft, George, a character in Meredith's *Evan Harrington*.

Urban, Sylvanus, Gent., the fictitious editor of *The Gentleman's Magazine*, intimating that it was for both town and country.

Urfried, Dame, an old sibyl in Scott's *Ivanhoe;* she was Ulrica, daughter of a Thane of Torquilstone.

Urre, Sir, a knight of the Round Table, whose wounds were healed by the touch of Launcelot.

Ursa Major: this name (Great Bear) was given to Dr. Johnson by Boswell's father.

Ursel, Zedekiah, a character in Scott's *Count Robert of Paris,* who has been a rival of Alexis Comnenus for the crown of Greece.

Usher, Roderick, in Poe's tale *The Fall of the House of Usher,* is a mysterious and morbid man whose house partakes of the gloomy character of its owner.

Vadius, in Molière's *Les Femmes Savantes,* a dull pedant, embraced by Philaminte, Blise, and Armande "for love of Greek," a phrase often used in allusion.

Valancourt, the hero of Mrs. Radcliffe's *The Mysteries of Udolpho.*

Valdeschi, Susanna dei, the heroine of Henry Harland's novel *The Lady Paramount.*

Valentina, one of the two leading characters of Meyerbeer's opera *The Huguenots.*

Valentine and **Proteus,** the two chief characters in Shakespeare's *Two Gentlemen of Verona.*

Valentine, in Shaw's comedy *You Never Can Tell,* is panic-stricken when Gloria Clandon declares that she will marry him.

Valentine, in Goethe's *Faust,* a brother of Margaret.

Valentine and **Orson,** heroes of an old romance, supposed to be of the fifteenth century, sons of an emperor of Constantinople. While the mother was gone to hunt for Orson, who had been carried off by a bear, Valentine was taken away by his uncle, King Pepin.

Valentinian III, Roman Emperor, is the subject of a drama by Beaumont and Fletcher (1617).

Valirian, the husband of St. Cecilia in Chaucer's *The Second Nun's Tale.*

Valjean, Jean, the famous convict of Victor Hugo's *Les Misérables.*

Valkyrs or **Valkyrior,** choosers of the slain. They were the shield-maidens whom Odin sent out when a battle was impending, to bring in the slain warriors that were to feast in Valhalla; at the feast they served the mead or hydromel. They are also called Walkyrie. Wagner has an opera *The Walkyrie.*

Van Artevelde, Philip, the subject of a historic drama by Henry Taylor.

Vandenesse, Count Felix de, a personage of Balzac's *Comédie Humaine.*

Vane, Ernest and **Mabel,** characters in Charles Reade's novel *Peg Woffington,* and in the play *Masks and Faces* by Reade and Tom Taylor.

Vane, Sir Henry, Governor of Massachusetts (1636), appears in Hawthorne's tale *Howe's Masquerade.*

Vane, Sibyl, a leading character in Oscar Wilde's *Dorian Gray.*

Vanessa, the name given by Swift to Esther Vanhomrigh, a young woman to whom he was supposed to be attached.

Vanna, Monna, the title and heroine of Maeterlinck's drama; she is the wife of Colonna, commanding the garrison of Pisa; and to save the city she goes to spend the night in the tent of the commander of the besieging Florentine army, Prinzivalle.

Van Revel, Tom, a leading character of Booth Tarkington's *The Two Van Revels.*

Van Stone, Magdalen, the chief character of Wilkie Collins's *No Name.*

Van Winkle, Rip, in Irving's story, fell asleep on the Catskill Mountains and waked after twenty years. The tale is based on an old Dutch legend. The play from it, with Joseph Jefferson in the title rôle, has been immensely popular.

Vargas, Angelica, an important character in Mathilde Serao's novel *The Conquest of Rome.*

Varley, Lady Helen, a character in Mrs. Ward's *Robert Elsmere.*

Varney, Richard, a tool of Leicester in Scott's *Kenilworth.*

Varvilliers, Vicomte de, a character in Anthony Hope's *The King's Mirror.*

Vasa, Gustavus, King of Sweden, is the subject of a drama by Henry Brooke (1730).

Vathek, a caliph who bound himself to Eblis in order to secure the Pre-Adamite throne. He is the subject of William Beckford's famous novel.

Vaucelles, Catherine de, a character in Justin H. McCarthy's novel and play *If I Were King,* in its sequel, *Needles and Pins,* and in Charles M. Skinner's play *Villon the Vagabond.*

Vaudrey, the hero of the play *The Two Orphans.*

Vaughan, Cecilia, the heroine of Longfellow's tale *Kavanagh.*

Vautrin, the assumed name by which Jacques Collin is best known. He is a famous convict of Balzac's *Comédie Humaine.* A French play with him in the chief rôle was produced in 1840, and revived in 1868.

Vavasour, Alice, the heroine of Trollope's *Can You Forgive Her?*

Vavasour, Araminta. See TREVILIAN, MEDORA.

Veiled Lady, The. See PRISCILLA.

Velasquez, Spanish Governor of Portugal in 1640, torn to pieces by the mob in the rebellion led by Braganza; he appears in Jephson's play *Braganza* (1785).

Velvet, Rev. Morphine, a character in Warren's *Ten Thousand a Year.*

Veneerings, The, a family of parvenus in Dickens's *Our Mutual Friend.*

Venetia, the subject of a novel by Disraeli.

Venner, Elsie, the subject of a novel by Oliver Wendell Holmes, illustrating the subject of pre-natal influence.

Ventidius, one of the ungrateful friends of Timon in Shakespeare's *Timon of Athens.*

Ventidius, a general of Antony, introduced in Shakespeare's *Antony and Cleopatra* and Dryden's *All for Love.*

Vere, Isabel, the heroine of *The Black Dwarf* by Sir Walter Scott.

Verges, a stupid watchman in Shakespeare's *Much Ado about Nothing.*

Vernon, Diana, a beautiful and spirited girl with an unusual education; she is an enthusiastic partizan of the Stuarts and the heroine of Scott's *Rob Roy.*

Vesey, Georgina, a character in Bulwer's novel *Money.*

Wasp, a character in Jonson's play *The Alchemist,* supposed to have been acted by the author.

Waterproof Will, the subject of a *Lyrical Monologue* by Tennyson.

Waters, Esther, the subject of a novel by George Moore (1894).

Watson, Dr., a friend of Sherlock Holmes in Conan Doyle's stories and in Gillette's play *Sherlock Holmes.*

Wauch, Mansie, the subject of a humorous Scottish story by David M. Moir.

Waverley, Edward, the hero of Scott's novel of the name, the first of the Waverley novels.

Waynflete, Lady Cicely, the heroine of Shaw's play *Captain Brassbound's Conversion.*

Wedderburn, May, an English girl studying music in Germany, the heroine of Jessie Fothergill's *The First Violin.*

Wegg, Silas, an ignorant ballad-monger who imposes upon Mr. Boffin in Dickens's *Our Mutual Friend,* professing to be a "literary man," and is employed to read to him; he tries to blackmail his employer and is discomfited.

Weird Sisters, The, the witches in Macbeth.

Weissnichtwo (I know not where), in Carlyle's *Sartor Resartus,* is the university town in which Teufelsdroeckh is a professor.

Weisspriess, Captain, an Austrian soldier and famous duelist in Meredith's novel *Vittoria.*

Weller, Sam, a famous character in Dickens's *Pickwick Papers,* Mr. Pickwick's valet.

Weller, Tony, Sam's father, a big fat stage-driver, who was dragooned into a second marriage. His advice to his son, "Beware of vidders," has become proverbial.

Wenonah, the mother of Hiawatha in Longfellow's poem.

Wentworth, in a novel, *De Vere,* by Plumer Ward, is intended for a portrait of George Canning.

Wentworth, Austin, an important character in Meredith's novel *The Ordeal of Richard Feverel* (1859).

Wentworth, Frank, the "Perpetual Curate" of Mrs. Oliphant's *The Chronicles of Carlingford.*

Wentworth, Frederick, the heroine of Jane Austen's *Persuasion.*

Wentworth, Lady, subject of one of Longfellow's *Tales of a Wayside Inn.*

Wentworth, Rose, the heroine of Henry Ward Beecher's novel *Norwood* (1867).

Werle, Gregers, an idealist and enthusiast, and withal "a sneak and a nuisance," in Ibsen's *The Wild Duck.*

Werner, Count of Siegendorf, the subject of a drama (1821) by Byron, the story of which is from Miss Lee's *Canterbury Tales* (1797–'05).

Werner, Lars Anders, a character in Miss Bremer's *The Neighbors.*

Werther, the sentimental youth, in love with Charlotte, Albert's wife, and disgusted with the world, in Goethe's famous novel *The Sorrows of Young Werther* (1774). Thackeray wrote a humorous poem in ridicule of this novel, with the same name. *Werther* is the title of a lyrical drama by Massinet.

Wesley, Hetty, a sister of John and Charles Wesley, subject of a novel by A. P. Quiller-Couch, giving a strange picture of the Wesley family life.

West, Julian, the chief character in Edward Bellamy's *Looking Backward* (1888).

West, Rachel, the heroine of Mary Cholmondeley's *Red Pottage* (1899).

West, Rebecca, an able, daring, strong-willed woman in Ibsen's *Rosmersholm,* whose character has been undermined by corrupt influences in girlhood. She loves Rosmer and with fiendish ingenuity drives his invalid wife to suicide. When Rosmer fails to realize her ambition for him, her conscience awakens and she confesses to him, declaring that Rosmersholm has broken her will and placed a foreign yoke upon her. At his suggestion she commits suicide with him.

Western, Squire, a famous fox-hunting country gentleman in Fielding's *Tom Jones.* His daughter Sophia is the heroine.

Westervelt, a mesmerist and exhibitor of the Veiled Lady in Hawthorne's *The Blithedale Romance.* He stands in some unexplained relation to Zenobia.

Westlock, John, in Dickens's *Martin Chuzzlewit,* a friend of Martin and of Tom Pinch.

Westmoreland, Earl of, a character in Shakespeare's *Henry IV*, *Henry V*, and *Henry VI*, Part II. His son is the Westmoreland of *Henry VI*, Part III.

Wesula, Princess, in Maeterlinck's drama *The Seven Princesses,* is the only one of the seven sleeping princesses whom the Prince cannot waken, and the one he loves.

Wetter, an important character in Anthony Hope's *The King's Mirror.*

Weyburn, Matthew, in Meredith's *Lord Ormont and His Aminta,* elopes with Lady Ormont.

Wheatley, Lord, the hero of Anthony Hope's novel *Phroso* and of its dramatization.

Whiskerandos, Don Ferolo, in Sheridan's *The Critic,* the lover of Tilburina.

Whistlecraft, William and Robert, a pseudonym of John Hookham Frere (1769–1846).

Whitcomb, Joshua, the chief character of Denman Thompson's rural comedy *Our Old Homestead* and the novel founded upon it.

White, Gertrude, the heroine of William Black's novel *Macleod of Dare.*

White, Selma, an important character in Robert Grant's novel *Unleavened Bread* and the drama drawn from it.

Whitefield, Ann. See TANNER, JOHN.

White Lady of Avenel, The, an apparition in Scott's novel *The Monastery* that comes to the aid of the Avenels in emergencies.

Whitford, Vernon, in Meredith's *The Egoist,* is in love with Clara Middleton.

Whittington, Dick, the hero of a legend who made a fortune by means of his cat and became Lord Mayor of London.

Wickfield, Agnes, the second wife of David Copperfield, heroine of the story.

Wieland, a form of Völund and Wayland.

Wiggins, Flora, a typical country waitress in George Ade's comedy *The College Widow.*

Wild, Jonathan, a notorious robber executed in 1725, represented as a calculating, deliberate villain without any redeeming qualities. He is the subject of a romance by DeFoe (1725) and a famous novel by Fielding (1743). He is also introduced into Ainsworth's *Jack Sheppard* (1845).

Wildair, Sir Harry, a noted personage of Farquhar's comedy of the name, also of his *The Constant Couple.*

Wildairs, Clorinda, the chief character of Mrs. Burnett's *A Lady of Quality.*

Wilder, Molly, the heroine of Jane G. Austen's novel *A Nameless Nobleman.*

Wilderspin, in Theodore Watts-Dunton's novel *Aylwin,* is understood to be intended for Burne-Jones the Elder.

Wildfire, Madge, in Scott's *The Heart of Midlothian,* Margaret Murdockson, who has been ruined and has murdered her child and lost her reason.

Wild Huntsman, The, the ghost of a huntsman who in a wild hunt on Sunday spared neither the peasant nor his property and is doomed to fly continually before a horde of devils, by day through the caverns of the earth, by night through the air. He is the subject of a ballad by Bürger, which Sir Walter Scott and others have translated.

Wilding, Felix, the title character of Robert Hichens's novel *Felix* (1902).

Wilfer, Bella, in love with the hero of Dickens's *Our Mutual Friend.*

Wilkins, Peter, the subject of a noted tale (1750) by Robert Pultock. Peter is a sailor left alone from a wreck on a strange shore which he finds to be frequented by a winged race called glumms and gawreys. When the wings are folded they serve for dress. He marries a gawrey named Youwarkee and goes with her to a twilit land where he lives many years.

Willes, Adrian, an important personage of Henry Harland's *The Lady Paramount.*

William of Orange, a character in Dumas's novel *The Black Tulip* (1850).

Williams, Caleb, the hero of a novel by William Godwin, dramatized under the name *The Iron Chest* (1794). See FALKLAND.

Williams, Eleazer, in Mary H. Catherwood's novel *Lazarre* and the dramatization, is supposed to be the Dauphin Louis, called Louis XVII, as the Rev. Eleazer Williams claimed to be.

Williams, Flossie, a character in Robert Grant's *Unleavened Bread.*

Wilmore, Leonard, a character in Henry Arthur Jones's play *The Hypocrites.*

Wilson, David, the chief character in Mark Twain's *Pudd'nhead Wilson* and the drama from it.

Wilson, William, the subject of a singular tale of a "double" by Edgar Allan Poe.

Winchester, Bishop of, Cardinal Beaufort, an important character in Shakespeare's *Henry VI.*

Winkle, Van. See VAN WINKLE.

Winthrop, Constance, the heroine of Bronson Howard's play *Young Mrs. Winthrop.*

Winthrop, John, Governor of Massachusetts, appears in Hawthorne's *The Scarlet Letter, Howe's Masquerade,* and *Endicott and the Red Cross.*

Witch of Atlas, The, the subject of a poem by Shelley.

Witherspoon, Jane, the title character of George Ade's play *The College Widow.*

Witherington, General, in Scott's *The Surgeon's Daughter,* is known also as Middlemas and Tresham.

Withrington or **Widdrington,** a squire in the ballad *Chevy Chase,* who continued to fight after losing both legs.

Witt, Neæra, the title character of *Mr. Witt's Widow,* by Anthony Hope.

Wizard of the North, The, Sir Walter Scott.

Wodehouse, Lucy, the heroine of Mrs. Oliphant's novel *The Perpetual Curate.*

Woffington, Peg, a noted actress, the heroine of a novel by Charles Reade, of a play from it, *Masks and Faces,* by Reade and Taylor, and of *Pretty Peggy,* a play by Frances Matthews (1902).

Wogan, Charles, the hero of A. E. W. Mason's *Clementina.*

Wohlfahrt, Anton, the chief character in Freytag's *Debit and Credit.*

Wolsey, Cardinal, in Shakespeare's *Henry VIII*, one of the great characters of the historic plays. His farewell to greatness is one of the most famous passages.

Wonderful Quiz, A, a pseudonym under which Lowell published *A Fable for Critics* (1848).

Woodcourt, Dr. Allan, marries the heroine of Dickens's *Bleak House*.

Woodhouse, Emma, one of Jane Austen's best characters, the subject of *Emma*.

Woods, Charlotte, the name assumed by the fugitive slave, Camille, in Trowbridge's novel *Neighbor Jackwood*.

Woodseer, Gower, a man of genius in Meredith's *The Amazing Marriage*, understood to be a study of Robert Louis Stevenson.

Woodvill, John, the subject of a tragedy by Charles Lamb.

Woodville, Olivia, a character in Goldsmith's *The Good-Natured Man*.

Woodville, Richard, afterward Earl Rivers, who was called the handsomest man of his day in England, a character in Shakespeare's *Henry VI*, Part I. After his daughter married Edward IV he became a zealous Yorkist, was taken by Lancastrian insurgents at Edgecote, and beheaded without trial.

Woodward, Hyacinth, an important character in Haddon Chambers's comedy *The Tyranny of Tears*.

Worldly Wise-Man, Mr., in Bunyan's *Pilgrim's Progress*, tries to dissuade Christian from continuing his journey.

Wotton, Lord Henry, the evil genius of Gray in Wilde's *The Picture of Dorian Gray*.

Wrayburn, Eugene, in love with Lizzie Hexam in Dickens's *Our Mutual Friend*.

Wren, Jenny. See CLEAVER, FANNY.

Wycliffe, Wilfrid, a character in Scott's narrative poem *Rokeby*.

Wynn, Harold, the hero of Haddon Chambers's drama *John-a-Dreams*.

Wynne, Winifred, the heroine of Theodore Watts-Dunton's novel *Aylwin*.

Wyoming. See GERTRUDE OF WYOMING and BRANDT.

Wythan, Owain, in Meredith's *The Amazing Marriage*,

wooed Corinthia Jane Kirby "with dog's eyes instead of words," and with success.

Xanadu, the city in Coleridge's dream-poem *Kubla Khan,* where the "pleasure-dome" was decreed.

Xavier, a pseudonym of Joseph X. Boniface, author of *Picciola,* who used also the pen-name **X. B. Saintine.**

Xury, a Moresco boy, a servant of DeFoe's hero, Robinson Crusoe.

Yahoos, a race of brutish men in Swift's *Gulliver's Travels.* They are subject to the Houyhnhnms, horses with human reason.

Yarico. See INKLE.

Yezorkorski, Pana Barbara or **Basia,** the heroine of Sienkiewicz's novel *Pan Michael.*

Yellowley, Triptolemus, distinguished for his enthusiasm for farming, a character in Scott's novel *The Pirate.* Barbara, or Baby, is his economical sister.

Yellowplush, Jeames, the footman whose *Memoirs* were written by Thackeray.

Yendys, Sydney, a pen-name of Sydney Dobell. Yendys is Sydney reversed.

Yeo, Salvation, a profane Clovelly sailor in Kingsley's *Westward Ho!*

Yeobright, Clym, a leading character in Thomas Hardy's *The Return of the Native.*

Yeoland, Christopher, one of the heroes of *Sons of the Morning* by Eden Philpotts.

Ygerne. See IGERNE.

Ygraine, the sister of Tintagiles in Maeterlinck's drama of the latter name, who watches over him to protect him from his grandmother's ferocity.

Yniol, the father of Enid in Tennyson's *Geraint and Enid.*

Yniold, a child, son of Goland in Maeterlinck's *Pelleas and Melisande.*

Yolande, the subject of a novel by William Black.

Yorick, the King of Denmark's jester, mentioned by Hamlet in the graveyard scene.

Yorick, a lively parson in Sterne's *Tristram Shandy,* represented as a descendant of the famous jester.

York, the royal house, represented by the White Rose, whose struggles for the throne with the House of Lancaster are called the Wars of the Roses. Dukes and Duchesses of York appear in Shakespeare's historic plays from *Richard II* to *Henry VI*. The beautiful Cicely, called the White Rose of Raby, was the mother of Edward IV and Richard III.

Yorke, Hiram, a Yorkshire gentleman who, with his children, figures in Charlotte Brontë's *Shirley*.

Youma, a Creole slave-girl of Martinique, the heroine of a novel of the name by Lafcadio Hearn.

Youwarkee. See WILKINS.

Ysaie le Triste, a son of Tristram, whose adventures are related in a French romance of the name (1522).

Ysolde. See ISOLDE.

Yule, Sylvia, a character in Louisa M. Alcott's *Moods* (1881).

Ywaine, a form of Owain.

Yves, the subject of a sea-story by Pierre Loti, *My Brother Yves*.

Yvetot. See KING OF YVETOT.

Yvette, the subject of a story by Guy de Maupassant.

Zabriskie, Mina, a character in Anthony Hope's *Tristram of Blent*.

Zadig, a rich young Babylonian in a famous novel of the name by Voltaire, the purpose of which is to suggest that men are guided by influences beyond their control. The second title of the tale is *Destiny*.

Zagloba, Pan, a strangely humorous character in Sienkiewicz's trilogy *Fire and Sword*, *The Deluge*, and *Pan Michael*, old, fat, cunning, brave notwithstanding a consciousness of fear, boastful, a preposterous liar, and a most devoted friend and comrade, with a sure instinct for choosing the right side and the right man.

Zaire, the subject of a tragedy by Voltaire, translated, under the title *Zara*, by Aaron Hill. The fate of Zaire is much like Desdemona's, and the drama seems to have been inspired by Shakespeare's *Othello*.

Zampa, the subject of a noted opéra-comique by Hérold (1831).

Zaneto, the chief character of a short poetic drama by Coppée, *Le Passant*, and an opera from it by Leoncavallo.